UNCOLLECTED WRITINGS BY WILLIAM GODWIN

Engraved by Ridley from a Drawing by Lawrence in the Possession of Dr Batty.

William Godwin Esqr.

Pub by Vernor & Hood, Poultry, 31, Jan? 1805

From *The Monthly Mirror*, Vol. XIX (1805)

UNCOLLECTED WRITINGS
(1785-1822)

ARTICLES IN PERIODICALS

AND

SIX PAMPHLETS

One with Coleridge's Marginalia

BY

WILLIAM GODWIN

FACSIMILE REPRODUCTIONS

WITH INTRODUCTIONS

BY

JACK W. MARKEN

AND

BURTON R. POLLIN

GAINESVILLE, FLORIDA

SCHOLARS' FACSIMILES & REPRINTS

1968

SCHOLARS' FACSIMILES & REPRINTS
1605 N.W. 14TH AVENUE
GAINESVILLE, FLORIDA, 32601, U.S.A.

HARRY R. WARFEL, GENERAL EDITOR

L.C. CATALOG CARD NUMBER: 68-24208

MANUFACTURED IN THE U.S.A.

CONTENTS

PART I

LETTERS OF MUCIUS in *The Political Herald, and Review*:

INTRODUCTION

PART I: WRITINGS OF 1785-1795

Jack W. Marken

One result of the contemporary fame William Godwin had earned with the publication of the numerous books and pamphlets he wrote during that productive year of 1783-1784 was that he had become accepted as one of them by most of the liberals of the period. He became a regular partaker of the bi-weekly literary dinners given by Timothy Hollis of Great Ormond Street, was a frequent dinner guest of George Robinson and the elder John Murray, the important liberal printers of the time, and was recognized as a writer who could become a spokesman for the leaders of the Whig opposition in Parliament.

It was only natural that when Gilbert Stuart, the Scotland-born miscellaneous writer, gave up the task of writing the historical portion of *The New Annual Register* (the Whig competition to the more conservative *Annual Register*) for the year 1783, which had to be written, of course, in 1784, Godwin was chosen by the liberals to write the material. When Godwin's account proved to be satisfactory to the Whigs, he was installed as the writer of the historical section for future years at an annual salary of sixty guineas. He continued to write this portion of *The New Annual Register* until 1791, when he gave up this task willingly to concentrate on the harder work of writing his

ix

Enquiry Concerning Political Justice. His success with the historical section brought him to the attention of the Whig leaders as a man whose talents could be used for more important schemes.

The leaders of the Whig opposition to Prime Minister William Pitt were Charles James Fox, Richard Brinsley Sheridan, and Edmund Burke. Fox, who had been Prime Minister during most of 1783, was dismissed when his East India Bill failed to pass into law in mid-December. William Pitt became Prime Minister with the hope that he could bring stability to the government, but his gradual assumption of dictatorial power in all areas of English life alienated many people. When Fox decided to follow up the public sympathy and support that the publication of the *Rolliad* and the *Probationary Odes* had brought to the Whigs in early 1785 by establishing a journal to disseminate liberal views, he thought of Godwin as one of the principal writers for the new venture. Gilbert Stuart was selected as editor. He had an established reputation as the writer of *A Historical Dissertation of the English Constitution* and *A View of Society in Europe,* works which had gone through several editions, and he had been one of the chief writers for *The Monthly Review* and an editor of *The Edinburgh Magazine and Review.* Besides Godwin, the other chief writers were William Thomson—a writer for various reviews and author of *Travels in Europe, Asia and Africa,* the satirical novel *The Man in the Moon,* as well as a continuation of Robert Watson's *History of Philip III of Spain*—and John Logan, the poet. When Stuart fell ill in the late summer of 1785, Godwin became editor. As the journal lasted only from August 1785 to December 1786, Godwin was actually the editor for almost the whole of the journal's life. Full details on this journal are available in my article in *The Bulletin of the New York Public Library* of October 1961.

MUCIUS LETTERS

Ford K. Brown, in his *The Life of William Godwin,* 1926, is incorrect when he surmises that Godwin wrote the articles signed "Ignotus" for *The Political Herald and Review.* In a letter probably written in late 1786 to Sheridan asking that money be forthcoming to continue the journal, Godwin says that "all the letters with the signature Mucius were contributed by me." In the scarce complete sets of *The Political Herald and Review* (eighteen numbers bound in three volumes, six numbers to each volume) seven letters are signed MUCIUS. The first is addressed to William Grenville, 1759-1834, the youngest son of the George Grenville who is infamous as being responsible for stamp and other duties on the American colonies in early 1765. William Grenville was William Pitt's first cousin. This first letter appears in Number 3 of *The Political Herald,* which was issued on October 3, 1785. The second letter, addressed to Edmund Burke, appears as the first essay in Number 5, which was issued on December 1, 1785. The third letter, addressed to Pitt, appears in Number 9 for April 3, 1786. (Godwin, in his letter to Dundas, says that he wrote this letter in March, which would be right for the writing but not for the printing.) The fourth letter, again addressed to Pitt, is the first essay in Number 10 for May 1, 1786. The fifth letter, addressed to Henry Dundas, appears in Number 12 for July 4, 1786. The last two letters cannot be dated accurately because individual numbers of *The Political Herald* were not advertised in the newspapers after Number 12. The MUCIUS letter "Modern Characters" appears in Number 13, probably for August 1786. The final letter, in which Godwin addresses the People of Ireland, appears in Number 16, probably for November 1786.

The heavy sarcasm and bitter invective in the MUCIUS letters is intended to point up the wisdom and uprightness of

the Whigs, particularly Edmund Burke their passionate spokesman, in contrast to the ignorance and corruption of the Tories.
It is evident that the Whig leadership believed that if enough
ridicule were heaped upon the Prime Minister and his friends
a revulsion in public opinion would lead to a Tory downfall.

Godwin's remarks about Burke in these letters are very
flattering. I can find no record of the two having met, but it
may have happened that the famous writer and politician was
present in Beaconsfield, where he had bought an estate in 1768,
when Godwin preached there during the early months of 1783.
(In a manuscript note, Godwin enters the name Burke under
"desiderati.") Godwin praised Burke in a pamphlet of 1783
(see Burton R. Pollin, ed., *Four Early Pamphlets*, 1966) by
approving his actions in joining the coalition of the Marquis of
Rockingham, Lord North, and Fox. There he commends Burke
for his sincerity and integrity, though disapproving of his "aris-
tocratical principles." In the MUCIUS letters, Godwin's praise
of Burke is even more effusive. A reason for this, besides
Burke's close association with Fox and Sheridan, is Godwin's
approval of Burke's leadership in the investigations into the
actions of Warren Hastings, who had served as Governor-General of India and had become a favorite of the Tories.

Burke had recently succeeded in persuading the House of
Commons to vote to bring Hastings to trial for his actions in
India. Elsewhere in *The Political Herald* (III, 124), the actions
of Hastings in India are stated as containing "Instances of avarice, oppression, inhumanity, injustice, treachery, murder, and
every criminal excess, which an unprincipled mind, in the possession of an uncontrolable military authority, could perpetrate."
Even William Pitt had voted with the Whigs against Hastings,
possibly because he feared that Hastings might be too effective
as a rival if he sought political power. On the other hand,
perhaps Pitt was merely offering a sop to the Whigs. Godwin's

approval of Burke's actions in assailing Hastings is tempered
by the fear that the Irish politician will not be as diligent as he
ought to be in the prosecution, that he will withdraw in the face
of personal attacks from the Tories.

The MUCIUS letters reflect the Whig views in Godwin's
opinions about the deficiencies and reprehensibility of the Tory
leadership. At the same time, we find within these letters his
concern that the liberties of Englishmen are being subverted.
He deplores the tendency toward autocratic power, which is
always accompanied by a withering away of responsibility to
the people. His basic message to the Irish is that union with
the English would result in their giving up every independence
of any sort they now have. They would get very little economic
benefit by such a union. Godwin comes very close to advising
armed resistance for the Irish.

The only other definitely identifiable contributions Godwin
made to *The Political Herald* are the essays on the administration of George Earl Macartney in Madras. Lord Macartney,
a friend of Fox, was offered the post of Governor General in
India to succeed Hastings, but refused it, and the post went to
Lord Cornwallis. An interchange of letters between Godwin
and Lord Macartney (published in my article cited above) iden-
tifies Godwin as the writer of this series. It is logical to assume
that if the survey had been brought to its conclusion, Lord
Macartney's administration would serve as a contrast in justice
and honesty to Hastings' administration. Godwin's account appears in the final numbers of *The Political Herald,* and is one of
the longest essays in the journal. The account begins in Number 14, probably for early September 1786, continues in Numbers 17 and 18, and was never finished, as the journal expired,
ostensibly for lack of funds, in late December or early January.

Godwin next used the MUCIUS signature in a series of four
letters to *The Morning Chronicle* in February and March, 1793.

The letters were written several weeks before their publication while Godwin was making final revisions for the publication of his *Enquiry Concerning Political Justice.* The Preface, dated January 7, 1793, of the first edition of this book contains his reasons for writing the letters, as he says: "Every man, if we may believe the voice of rumour, is to be prosecuted, who shall appeal to the people by the publication of any unconstitutional paper or pamphlet; and it is added that men are to be punished for any unguarded words that may be dropped in the warmth of conversation and debate." To this sentence he adds the footnote: "The first conviction of this kind, which the author was far from imagining to be so near, was a journeyman tallow-chandler, January 8, 1793, who, being shown the regalia at the Tower, was proved to have vented a coarse expression against royalty to the person that exhibited them." As Godwin was revising his Preface as late as January 10 and did not finish it till January 29, his allusion to the trial of Crichton indicates that he thought the action so serious that he could not omit commenting on it.

In his manuscript Journal, Godwin notes that he wrote the first MUCIUS letter on Wednesday, January 16, the second and the third on the next day, and the fourth on the 18th. Letter I was published in the newspaper on February 1, 1793; Letter II on February 8; Letter III on March 26; and Letter IV on March 30.

In Letter I, written primarily to defend the freedom of speech of Crichton and all other Englishmen, Godwin says that the reign of despotism began on November 20, 1792, at the Crown and Anchor. He is implying that John Reeves, subject of Letter II, is primarily responsible for stimulating the government's persecution. Reeves (1752?-1829) on November 20 became chairman of the "Association for Preserving Liberty and Property Against Levellers and Republicans." In Godwin's mind this group had the fundamental aim of overturning the Constitution and violating the Bill of Rights of 1689. Reeves was known as the author of a two-volume *History of the English Law* (1783-1784). He was to become the subject of a prosecution for libel in May, 1796, when his pamphlet *Thoughts on the English Government* was discussed in the House of Commons. Reeves had written in his pamphlet that the government rested solely in the power of the king and that parliaments and juries are "subsidiary and occasional." Though he was found not guilty of libel, the pamphlet was adjudged improper.

In Letter III Godwin underlines the necessity for freedom of speech and the impossibility of forcing anyone to believe exactly what others believe. To try to force such conformity of opinion is to return to barbarism. In Letter IV Godwin hopes that impartial jurymen can be found who will not knuckle under to government pressure. Such jurymen would preserve society from the brutality of ministers. The foundation of society is liberty and freedom; when these are removed, the whole collapses.

CURSORY STRICTURES

In the early and mid-1790's the liberties of Englishmen were increasingly restricted by a Tory ministry which had at least a five to one majority over the Whigs in the House of Commons. The government supported an army of spies to ferret out or fabricate acts or words that would be called treasonable; the Habeas Corpus Act was suspended almost more often than it was in effect; authors and printers were prosecuted for statements and actions; and it became dangerous to express liberal sentiments anywhere, except possibly in the House of Commons. The most dramatic indication of this troubled state of society was the series of treason trials in October and November 1794.

When the Grand Jury indicted twelve men for treason on October 6, Godwin was in Warwickshire visiting Dr. Samuel Parr. Receiving a letter from Thomas Holcroft, his closest friend, now in prison as one of the accused, Godwin left Dr. Parr's house on Monday, October 13, and arrived in London that evening. In his account, printed in C. Kegan Paul's biography, I, 117-118, Godwin says: "Having fully revolved the subject, and examined the doctrines of the Lord Chief Justice's charge to the grand jury, I locked myself up on Friday and Saturday, and wrote my strictures on that composition which appeared at full length in *The Morning Chronicle* of Monday, and were transcribed from thence into other papers." Godwin's journal contains these notations:

> "Oct. 17 . . . write 8 pages
> "Oct. 18 Write 14 pages . . .
> "Oct. 19 Write 2 pages: correct . . .
> "Oct. 21 . . . Publication
> "Oct. 22 App[endix]. 6 pages . . .
> "Oct. 23 Write Defense of S."

The chronology is completed with the information that Lord Chief Justice Eyre's *Charge* was published on Thursday, October 2; the *Reply* to Godwin's *Strictures* (evidently by Sir Francis Buller, one of the judges) was published in the *Times* on October 25; and Godwin's rebuttal was published by D. I. Eaton soon after it was written. Thomas Hardy's trial began on October 25. He was acquitted on November 5. John Horne Tooke's trial took place from November 17 to 22; he too was acquitted. When John Thelwall was also acquitted, the government threw in the sponge so that Thomas Holcroft missed his desired opportunity to be tried. (We reprint the pamphlets of Eyre and Buller to which Godwin's replies make many references.)

A graphic account of the trial is given in Rosalie Glynn Grylls' *William Godwin and his World.* She begins this biography with the trial to underline its importance as showing Godwin practicing his political principles in the public arena. Godwin's incisive analysis of Eyre's attempt to change the legal definition of treason destroyed the government's case and turned public opinion in favor of the prisoners. The outcome of the trial, which established the principle that Englishmen could not be convicted of treason for what they said and wrote, is a landmark in the history of English liberty. The publication of the four pamphlets concerned directly with the trial will make it possible for scholars to study this episode with the care it deserves.

CONSIDERATIONS

Public dissatisfaction with the King and ministry in October 1795 resulted in several incidents. On the 27th of the month the London Corresponding Society held a meeting attended by 150,000 interested and curious Londoners. An address virtually declaring civil war was passed. Two days later stones were thrown at the king, breaking a window in his coach, and an airgun was discharged. When a proclamation of October 31 offering a thousand pounds for information about the miscreants produced no results, the Tory ministry decided that some measures must be taken. On November 6, William Lord Grenville introduced his Treasonable Practices Bill in the House of Lords. William Pitt introduced a companion bill in the House of Commons on November 9. Debate on the latter bill with Sheridan as the chief speaker in opposition to it, continued till

December 3, when the bill was passed. Grenville's bill had become law on November 16.

When Godwin heard about these bills, he moved with characteristic celerity. His journal entries for November include:

> "Nov. 16 (Tues.) Write Considerations, 10 pages . . .
> "Nov. 17 Write 22 pages.
> "Nov. 18 Write 16 pages; press . . .
> "Nov. 19 Write 24 pages . . . Call on Jno Robinson
> "Nov. 21 . . . Publish Cons[ns]."

Underlying his attacks on specific points in the two bills is Godwin's belief that once again the government is forcing the citizens to give up the Bill of Rights, liberty of the press, and freedom of speech.

The pamphlet was reviewed favorably for the most part in the magazines. *The Analytical Review* for November 22, 1795, summarizes the bills and says the *Considerations* are written with great ability. *The Monthly Review* for December 1795, besides giving a summary, says the pamphlet is written by "a keen, acute, and formidable pen." *The Monthly Mirror* for December 1795 disagrees with the ideas but praises the manly manner. However, the writer believes that the rapid strides toward anarchy require the government to do something. *The Monthly Magazine,* in a late review on July 4, 1796, says the "unpopular attempts to restrain the freedom of speech and writing are solidly and temperately examined."

Godwin and the Whig opposition in the House of Commons lost this battle for free enquiry and freedom of assembly when the bills passed. When England was threatened with an invasion from France in the latter part of the 1790's, the Whig opposition either rallied to support the ministry of William Pitt or withdrew from Parliament. Godwin became a creature of

abhorrence to most of the people as the conservatives strength-
ened their control. Though never silent publicly or privately,
from this period on he wrote less frequently on current political
subjects and turned increasingly to fiction and the literary essay
as vehicles for publishing his ideas.

JACK W. MARKEN

South Dakota State University
Brookings, South Dakota

PART II: WRITINGS OF 1801-1822

BURTON R. POLLIN

The words of Coleridge, inscribed in the margins of Godwin's *Thoughts Occasioned by the Perusal of Dr. Parr's Spital
Sermon* of 1801 (p. 8), are the best tribute to its superlative
quality (see the transcription of Coleridge's marginalia at the
end of this introduction). It is a matchless epitome of Godwin's
libertarian thought and faith in mankind. The occasion is
indicated by Godwin himself. He does not itemize the "scur-
rilities" and "contumelies" (p. 10) from the Anti-Jacobin press
which preceded the attack of his former friends. These are
discussed by various literary historians and biographers, such as
B. Sprague Allen, Allene Gregory, and Ford K. Brown. Pitt's
administration made every effort ruthlessly to stamp out all
traces of opposition counseling fundamental reform, and the
powers of Church and State gradually persuaded or seduced
almost all men of note to join the heresy-hunt stimulated by the
fear of Napoleon. Godwin implies the causes of these shifts
rather delicately (pp. 5-9) and evidences his own steadfast

position. Coleridge's apologetic notation (p. 8) must refer to his criticism of Godwin, expressed in *The Watchman* of 1796, and he was to remain one of Godwin's firmest friends to his death.

One should bear in mind the full background of letters and visits involving Parr and Mackintosh before Godwin published this self-defense. Mackintosh's letter to Godwin (pp. 13-15) shows no intimation of the change in opinions which would make plain James into Sir James with a lucrative post in India. Of course, Godwin and everyone knew how closely the 1799 Lectures, of which the first "Discourse" only was ever published, applied to Godwin as leader of the liberals. Lamb, Hazlitt, and others were also shocked at Mackintosh's apostasy, but at least he remained Godwin's "personal friend," who publicly praised Godwin's biographies of Milton's nephews in *The Edinburgh Review* (XXV) in 1815, when he also tried in vain to arrange to have Lord Byron donate profits from his poetry to the relief of Godwin. Mackintosh's memoirs of 1835 confess that his 1799 lectures had "approached immorality."

Godwin's pamphlet had less effect on the Rev. Samuel Parr, whom he had met in 1794 through Mackintosh. Their friendship had been welded through Parr's pupil, Joseph Gerrald, the brilliant victim of Tory hysteria, who did not survive transportation to Botany Bay. Godwin cherished Parr for his vigorous personality, his large fund of learning, and the firmness of his Whig opinions. The history of Godwin's break with Parr, told almost entirely via the letters published by C. K. Paul, has a wryly melodramatic quality, since Godwin had written on January 3, 1800, to complain of Mackintosh's apostasy and also to give Parr a copy of *St. Leon* (December, 1799). In reply came the public denunciation of the unsuspecting Godwin in the annual "Spital Sermon," delivered April 15, 1800, before the Lord Mayor. Godwin's visits had been rebuffed, and now his book was returned with a letter of total repudiation. Yet Godwin's excellent memoir of Fox (1806), given in this book, was collected in *Characters of Fox* (1809) by Philopatris Varvicensis (Samuel Parr).

Robert Thomas Malthus is handled with much delicacy in this pamphlet. Godwin's manuscript diary, in fact, records that he called on Malthus, May 22, 1801, shortly before its publication on June 12. Because he regarded as irrefutable the logic of Godwin's view of man's endless perfectibility, Malthus raised his bugaboo of the arithmetical increase of a food supply for a geometrically increasing human race. Godwin gently reproves Malthus for failing to consider that prudence regarding the sexual appetite would be part of the rational moderation generally needed for effective social improvement. Indeed Malthus ultimately adopted Godwin's check of prudence as counterbalance of the "vice and misery" that his first edition of the *Essay on the Principle of Population* proposed as inevitable. British property holders found in Malthus's phase of the "dismal science" an excuse for ruthlessly discountenancing all improvement in the condition of the working classes.

Godwin, increasingly distressed by a doctrine which owed its initial statement to his books, came to regard Malthus as the great enemy to improvement. Hence the vituperation of his voluminous answer, *Of Population* (1820). By then he was unwilling to accept the whole set of absurd ratios and wished to deny the statistical bases for Malthus's theory as well. Hence, Godwin's letter to *The Morning Chronicle* of January 11, 1822, over what he considers a betrayal by the editor. His manuscript journal shows that it was he who wrote the letter, signed "L'Ami des Hommes," which is here printed along with the editorial matter that occasioned it. The suggestion of the paper itself anent *The Examiner* is so apposite and the material itself so similar in style and content to the longer letter that we print it here as a probable piece of Godwin's composition. The intimate connection of Leigh Hunt with Godwin and with Shelley strengthens the likelihood.

I must return briefly to Godwin's answer to Parr, which he believed to be an effective work; among his papers is a memorandum, that in any future edition of *Political Justice* it "be annexed to the work . . . not so much to perpetuate the fugitive and obscure controversies which have been excited on the subject, as because it contains certain essential explanations and elucidations with respect to the work itself" (Paul, II, 71). There are many excellences to be found in this document. Notice the clever way in which he dissociates himself from the violent course of the French Revolution without disavowing his belief in its basic doctrines; the ingenious way whereby he reemphasizes his devotion to truth and sincerity; the acute reasoning about his not being named by his two principal assailants (p. 76); and the eloquence of his plea for a tolerant atmosphere of discussion (p. 79) and for faith in man's improvement (pp. 80-82).

As might be expected, *The Anti-Jacobin Review* of December, 1801, speaks chiefly of his self-contradictions and poor style; the *British Critic* of August, 1801, makes similar charges and suggests Baboeuf's fate for him. Sydney Smith, in *The Edinburgh Review* of October, 1802, commends all of Godwin's defenses and arguments except his views on infanticide. *The Monthly Magazine* allowed the pamphlet to become a "cause célèbre," first through a letter to the editor in November, 1801, claiming that he had indeed insidiously defended infanticide, then through a letter of denial from Godwin himself (given in our text), followed by a letter commenting on Godwin's, and finally through a review in the January, 1802, issue criticizing Godwin for deigning to notice Parr's remarks and presenting a weak defense. *The Monthly Mirror* of September, 1801, gives a

highly balanced account, justifying Godwin for his views and
vigor. *The Monthly Review* of March, 1802, tends to accept
Godwin's tenet as basic to Christianity but to reject his argument against Malthus. In general the reviews follow their
"party" line but pay the work the respect of serious attention.

The answer to Parr forecasts the subject of the next pamphlet
printed in our text, *Letters of Verax*, for there are two favorable
references to Napoleon (pp. 6 and 42), both of them sources
of outraged comment from Coleridge. As the menace of a
Channel crossing loomed greater and the fatigue of the war
grew more oppressive, Godwin was to receive further oppro-
brium for partiality toward the tyrant. Even in 1814 the first
issue of *The New Monthly Magazine* included a letter by
"Senex" berating Godwin for his false prophecy in the answer
to Parr concerning the future free institutions of France. There
is no need here to discuss Godwin's alarm over the renewal of
the war after Napoleon's return from Elba. In letters to *The
Morning Chronicle* Godwin pleaded for the right of the French
to institute a limited monarchy under Napoleon, with a constitution prepared by Godwin's one-time admirer Benjamin
Constant; a pamphlet containing the two letters was cancelled
because of the rapid defeat of Napoleon at Waterloo. My full
presentation of the background and my analysis of the material
can be consulted in the *Journal of the History of Ideas* of July,
1964. I am pleased that this great and rare work is now being
made available, as proof of Godwin's zeal against war and
political oppression. It also helps to answer the charge that he
shied away from political expression, in favor of security and
merely private utterance of unpopular views. The first part was
actually published on May 25, 1815, in *The Morning Chronicle*,
by a man who depended, as author and juvenile publisher, very
much upon the favor of the middle class.

The last pamphlet in our collection concerns Godwin's paramount interest—education. In *The Enquirer* (1797) he had expressed most progressive views on the scope needed for the young reader, and in his practice as conductor of the Juvenile Library he had helped to modify, even to reform, textbooks for the young, writing a number of them himself. In the second decade of the century several disciples drew his attention to an area that he had not covered, that beyond the primary level. Readers of Shelley's letters will recall a correspondence with Godwin on the role of history and the classics in a well-rounded education. On June 11, 1817, the American Gulian C. Verplanck introduced the nineteen-year old Joseph V. Bevan of Georgia to Godwin, who had long played host to visiting Americans. These had included Aaron Burr, Washington Irving, and James Ogilvie, Bevan's teacher of rhetoric at the University of South Carolina. Since Bevan visited Scotland and Ireland before returning to America almost two years later, Godwin had ample opportunity to give educational advice to Bevan. On February 12, 1818, he used this as the basis for the pamphlet which his own publishing firm issued. However, it does not appear to have been distributed at that date, to judge from the end of the letter of March 19, 1818, in *The Analectic Magazine* of Philadelphia. He printed it, he says, merely to distribute it to solicitous young men; in reality, the content was intended for the magazine of Archibald Constable, who had published Godwin's novel *Mandeville* in December, 1817. Therefore, the "reprint" of the pamphlet in *The Edinburgh Magazine*, New Series of *The Scots Magazine* in March 1818, must have preceded the official publication of the *Letter of Advice*.

This essay was to become, strangely enough, one of Godwin's most often reprinted works in an America hungry for aid in shaping its developing educational systems. First it appeared in *The Analectic Magazine*, once edited by Irving (August, 1818). Verplanck, now writing for the magazine, may have suggested it as well as the partial reprint of the *Letter* in September, 1819, together with the publication of further letters of advice sent by Godwin to Bevan. (They are included in our text, but for a fuller, more correct printing than the *Analectic's*, see Dr. Marken's article in *The Georgia Historical Quarterly* of September, 1859.) The conservative *Port Folio* of Philadelphia was chagrined to discover that the *Analectic* had anticipated its reprint and said so in September, 1818, prefacing its text with a deprecation of Godwin's stress on the imagination and the neglect of useful knowledge. On November 7, 1818, *Robinson's Magazine* of Baltimore reprinted the *Letter of Advice*. Meanwhile, Bevan was trying out his hand in journalism and was able to insert the *Letter of Advice* in the Milledgeville *Georgia Journal* of June 29, 1819. (See the biography of Bevan by E. M. Coulter.)

One might wonder about the response in England to a pamphlet of such currency in America. I have found only two reviews of the work, the first in *The Champion* of April 19, 1818, a date which indicates that Godwin did not long withhold the pamphlet from distribution after Constable's magazine had issued it. *The Champion* was laudatory, especially since it was edited by his old friend, John Thelwall, now reconciled after the breach signalized in Godwin's *Considerations*. It was said to be worth everything written on the subject since *The Enquirer*, with sound sense in the stress on the imagination rather than science and facts, on metaphysics, and on classical models of republican virtue. Even the church organ, *The Monthly Repository* of September, 1818, found the work useful and surprisingly different from his writings of the 1790's. Both reviews are correct, and Godwin's ideas will be found applicable today.

The next section concerns the interesting memoirs of celebrated, recently deceased friends of Godwin and a piece of dramatic criticism. His memoir of Joseph Ritson was published in the November, 1803, *Monthly Magazine* (reprinted in *The Monthly Mirror* of May, 1805, which text we use for its clearer type). It is an excellent portrait of a learned eccentric, who never failed to tell Godwin sharply about his shortcomings, as is amply shown in Ritson's published letters of 1833. Godwin biographers show that Godwin often drew upon Ritson's large store of knowledge. In the "Memoir of Fox," first published in *The London Chronicle* (not *The Morning Chronicle* as always stated) of November 22, 1806, Godwin expressed his veneration for the man whose speeches he followed in 1779, whose praises resound in his MUCIUS articles, and who seemed to him almost the only defense of English liberties in the perilous days of the 1790's in the administration of Pitt. Godwin's contrast of these two men in the memoir is not the only skillful device employed to hymn his approval of "the wonderful creature." Certainly all his praise is a refreshing display of devotion to a truly independent statesman. The memoir has been excerpted by Hazlitt among others, and reprinted by C. K. Paul (II, 153-157), but needs to be included with this group. The last memoir, that of John Philpot Curran, appeared in *The Morning Chronicle* of October 16, 1817, and was reprinted in the rare *Life of . . . Curran* by his son, William Henry Curran (1819), from which our text is drawn. It is not Godwin's happiest effort, being forced and formal in its praise. The last paragraph reminds one, perhaps, that despite the long-standing and firm friendship of the two, Godwin was often the butt of Curran's sallies of wit.

The last item for mention is the letter that Godwin as "Aristarchus" addressed to *The Morning Chronicle* of April 3, printed on April 5, 1809. This unsuspected piece of dramatic analysis by Godwin came to my attention through a scrap of writing in the Abinger Microfilm: "The paper on Wolsey was written, Apr. 3, 1809 & appeared in the Morning Chronicle a few days after." The journal of April 3 shows "Wolsey, pp. 8" or eight of Godwin's manuscript pages. The issue of the paper revealed an analysis of Kemble, Godwin's friend, in the role of Wolsey. Moreover, his witnessing the play *Henry VIII* "a few weeks ago" tallies with his journal entry for February 28. Godwin was an inveterate playgoer as his journal consistently shows, and he himself wrote at least three plays, two of which, *Antonio* and *Faulkener*, reached the boards with varying degrees of success. The memoirs of many theatrical persons speak of their friendship with Godwin and of his keen appreciation of their art. This letter of "Aristarchus" contributes to a largely unstudied field of Godwin criticism.

BURTON R. POLLIN

Bronx Community College
of the City University of New York

A NOTE ON THE SOURCES OF THE REPRINTS

Of the *Letter of Advice to a Young American* there are four copies of which we know, owned by the British Museum, the Carl H. Pforzheimer Library, Teachers College of Columbia University, and Jack W. Marken. Of *Letters of Verax* there is one copy in the British Museum, two copies in Harvard, and one in Yale. The other materials included in this volume are to be found only in large or specialized collections, but locations need not be specified. The following sources are gratefully acknowledged:

Letters of MUCIUS in *The Political Herald* and in *The Morning Chronicle*: British Museum, Cambridge University, and University of Pennsylvania.

Answer to Parr: British Museum.

Considerations on . . . Bills, Judge Eyre's *Charge, Cursory Strictures, Answer to Cursory Strictures,* and *Reply to an Answer to Cursory Strictures*: Yale University.

Memoirs of Curran, Ritson, and Fox and letters to *The Morning Chronicle* and *The Examiner*: Yale University.
Letter from Godwin in the *Monthly Magazine*: Columbia University.
Letter of Advice: Teachers College, Columbia University.
Further *Letters of Advice* in *The Analectic Magazine*: New York Public Library.

ACKNOWLEDGMENTS

Gratitude is expressed by B. R. Pollin to the American Philosophical Society for a grant in 1963 enabling him to examine the materials in the British Museum, Cambridge University, and Harvard and Yale; to the New York State University Research Foundation for a grant in 1967 for collecting materials and writing his part of the introduction; and to Lord Abinger and the Carl and Lily F. Pforzheimer Foundation, Inc., for the opportunity to consult the manuscript papers of Godwin. Gratitude is expressed by J. W. Marken to South Dakota State University for secretarial and other types of aid during the summer of 1967 and to Lord Abinger for the opportunity to consult Godwin's manuscript papers. The co-authors wish to express their debt to the following institutions for the opportunity to use materials included herein: British Museum and these universities: Columbia, Cambridge, Harvard, Pennsylvania, and Yale.

MARGINALIA by Samuel Taylor Coleridge
IN GODWIN'S *THOUGHTS OCCASIONED BY THE PERUSAL*
OF DR. PARR'S SPITAL SERMON

Pages 2 and 3: Had this been the fact, which the whole History of the French Revolution, in its first workings disproves a posteriori, it would have been *a priori* impossible that such a revolution could have taken place. No! it was the discord & contradictory ferment of old abuses & recent indulgences or connivances—the heat & light of Freedom let in on a half-cleared, rank soil, made twilight by the black fierce Reek which this Dawn did itself draw up. Still, however, taking the sentence dramatically, i.e., as the then notion of good men in general, it is well & just.

Pages 6 and 7: !!Let not there!! be deemed the Sneer of afterwit but see the Morning Post, then the sturdy adherent of Liberty, from the very day Buonaparte entered the seat of Legislation to the promulgation of his constitution. In these essays it was demonstrated that the reign of pure despotism (the worst of all pure despotism, military despotism), had commenced & that all the preceding victories of Humanity "all the great points embraced by the revolution" etc.") remained only to be transmuted into this most direful means or facilitations of a bloody ambition, a limitless Tyranny.

Page 7: This account is likewise erroneous—Jacobinism was then the weakest, when it excited the whole hullaballoo of alarms/& sinking from men of letters down to the labouring classes it has increased in strength & danger in exact proportion as the alarm has decreased. It is with Jacobinism as with the French Empire; we made peace just at the very time that war *first* became just and necessary.

Page 8: I remember few passages in ancient or modern authors that contain more just philosophy in appropriate, chaste & beautiful diction than the five following pages. They reflect great honour on Godwin's Head and Heart. Tho' I did it only in the Zenith of his Reputation, yet I feel remorse *ever* to have spoken unkindly of such a man. s.t.c.

Page 42: A striking instance of the danger philosophers expose themselves to, who take, tho' even suppositively, contemporary Examples, as Illustrations. The practice is beneath them. The philosopher is *always*, not *now*, except as the *now* is *always*.

Page 62: Strange, that G. should so hastily admit principles so doubtful in themselves, and so undoubtedly drea[d]ful in their consequences. There exists no proof, & none probably has been evinced by Malthus, that an excess of population arising from *physical* necessity has introduced *Immorality*, or that Morality would not, in itself have contained the true, easy, & effectual Limitation. The whole ? [question] is a business of "*which is the cause? which the effect?* God knows! it is proved, that no country yet exists, not capable under a moral government of sustaining more than its' [sic] Inhabitants—not even China, whose population is yet the effect of wicked & foolish Laws preventing Emigration.

The following pages contain sidelinings or marks of punctuation to express doubt, emotion, or emphasis: 24, 35, 36, 63, 64, 65, 66, 67, 68, 69.

PLATE XVII.

E.H. Lizars Sculpt

Edinburgh Published by A. Constable & C.º 1820.

WILLIAM GODWIN, 1816

Plate XVII in *Illustrations of Phrenology* (Edinburgh, 1820) by George Steuart Mackenzie. Engraved by William Home Lizars from the lost portrait by William Nicholson of Edinburgh.

THE

POLITICAL HERALD, AND REVIEW.

[LETTERS OF MUCIUS]

To the Right *Hon.* WILLIAM WYNDHAM GRENVILLE,
Joint Paymaster of his Majesty's Forces.

SIR,

AS you will, I doubt not, when you find yourself addressed in this public manner, be at a loss to conjecture which of your eminent qualities it is that has given
occasion to the compliment, I am willing at once to put an
end to the disagreeable sensations attendant on a state of
suspense.

fufpenfe. Your public treatment of your illuftrious predeceffor in office, Mr. Edmund Burke, is then the object of my animadverfion. You, Sir, are a member of
that fmall but memorable band of fenators who have
fingled out this man from the number of his contemporary
ftatefmen, and who, by arts the moft difingenuous, and impudence the moft perfevering, have endeavoured to deprive
the ifland of Great Britain of his abilities and his fervices.
I am willing that the world fhould underftand the merits of
your conduct. Many a beneficial project and many a
comprehenfive defign have been brought to an aufpicious
termination by a mere lucky hit; and I am willing, Sir,
that you for once fhould be informed what you have done.
For this purpofe I will acquaint you with the character and
perfonal merits of the object of your purfuit.

Mr. Burke, Sir, without being led forward to the firft
degree of eminence, as it often happens, by a long line
of titled anceftors, or by an ample fortune, has rifen
chiefly by indefatigable induftry and the energies of an uncommon underftanding. As he was not born to the inheritance of *otium cum dignitate,* or, in other words, of vacant
and fordid indolence, he feized with a mafter hand upon the
key of fcience. He made incurfions into all the regions
that had yet been tamed and cultivated by the powers of
the human mind. He poffeffed and adorned himfelf with
all the graces which nature had placed within the reach of
genius. He was not more fuccefsful in the acquifition of
the folid and fubftantial part of knowledge, than of every
thing that gives beauty and attraction and elevation. With
all the charms of a polifhed ftyle and all the infinuations of
inventive fancy, he was able to win over the heart, at the
fame time that he difpelled the clouds of ignorance and
error.

Sir, I am not to be informed that talents and knowledge by no means uniformly entitle their poffeffor to a
favourable treatment. I will confefs to you as freely as
you can defire, that a Machiavel and a Borgia are only the
more

more worthy of our enmity, the more they poffeffed of dexterity, ingenuity, and all the arts of fraud. I will grant,
in a ftyle more level to the meridian of your underftanding, that a Barrington and a Wild more deferve the animadverfion of the laws, than the petty thief, who fteals a
yard of linen, or pilfers a loaf of bread. But let me afk
you, and tell me, if you can, with the ferioufnefs and fobriety which the fubject deferves, what are the crimes,
what the mifdemeanours, that have made Mr. Burke the
object of your refentment ? I will anfwer for you. They
are his virtues : fteady, intrepid, untemporifing virtues,
that hold no council with a baftard difcretion, and that
fpare no villain, be his name ever fo exalted, and his adherents ever fo undaunted and numerous. Where is the man,
that has furveyed the events of the life of Mr. Burke, and
does not know, that they are all to be traced to the fource of
virtue ? It was this, that recommended him, at that time
humble, unknown, and unconnected with the great, to the
deliciæ humani generis, the marquis of Rockingham. It was
this, that held him true and unfhaken in his attachments to
that nobleman, when, more than any other political leader,
profcribed by the fovereign, and when ambition held out
all her trappings to tempt him to defertion. It was this,
that animated him to face the moft extenfive unpopularity,
and all the prejudices of a monarch, in his plan of œcono-
mical reform. But, Sir, I fhould find no end to my enumeration, if I fhould attempt to reckon up all his merits.
It will be fufficient to fay, that with all your ingenuity,
added to that of your illuftrious brother, the name of Grenville is not at this day loaded with a more general execration, than that of Mr. Burke is honoured by the wife, venerated by the virtuous, and efteemed, in fpite of themfelves,
by the moft relentlefs and ftupid of his enemies.

But you, Sir, who have not a heart to feel or an underftanding to comprehend the reach of his virtues, you
know him only, as the child of rhetoric, and the favourite of
the mufes. You have feen the effects of his eloquence,

Vol. I.　　　　　　　M　　　　　　　and,

and, by a kind of mifapprehenfion congenial to your talents, have miftaken an Orpheus, that civilized and difarmed the ferocity of the brute creation, for a Circe, whofe
objeĉt it was to degrade the dignity of man into the form of
the fouleft and moft difguftful of animals. If, Sir, your
apprehenfions were for yourfelf, you might have difmiffed
them with impunity. There is a man, in whom mufic
finds nothing congenial to her charaĉter and allurements,
and fuch is the man I have undertaken to addrefs. If,
with Ulyffes, you had been tempted by the fong of the
Sirens, nature had kindly endowed you with a fpecific,
more fure than the leffons of wifdom, and more invincible
than deafnefs. But no : you were incapable of fo far mif-
taking your charaĉter. You did not ftop your own ears,
but endeavoured by noife and vociferation to ftop the ears
of others. You could have trufted to yourfelf. Covered
with the invulnerable fhield of dulnefs and malignity, you
apprehended no danger. But you could not depend upon
thofe, who were not equally armed againft powers, that
were meant for the conqueft of mankind.

Sir, pofterity has to thank you for an example, without
which the charaĉter of the prefent age would never have
perfeĉtly been underftood. We have heard much of the
ofcitancy of the luxurious. We have heard of their in-
aĉtivity and inattention, their inflexible phlegm, and their
unconquerable indifference. We have been told that the
Cydnus is not fo cold as the breaft of the fribble, and
that the powers of the north do not bind the running ftream
in more indiffoluble chains. And it has been added, that,
with all this fluggifhnefs with refpeĉt to every thing
beautiful and fublime, nothing is more intolerant in its
jealoufy, more unremitting in its vengeance, and more
inimical to every fpecies of excellence. The piĉture,
though true, has long paffed for exaggerated. It is you,
Sir, that we are to thank for having filled the canvas. You
have exhibited to the world a charaĉter which was before
incredible. Qualities, that rumour and imagination had

repre-

reprefented as incompatible, you have brought into a happy combination, blended their tints, and made of them a whole worthy of the admiration of mankind.

But this is not all your merit. You have not only exhibited a conftellation of virtues in your own perfon, but you have brought into day-light qualities of your contemporaries, which, without your happy exertions, might for ever have remained unknown. However inadequate be the conceptions of the majority of mankind, the philofopher could very eafily have allowed a fufficient fhare of calloufnefs, malignity and folly to a fingle breaft. But, Sir, though bold, daring and intrepid, you have not ftood alone. You have appeared at the head of a numerous band. You have marfhalled troops of various ages, colours and denominations. Grenville, as well as Cæfar, has had " a fenate at his heels." And, however pofterity may rejeét the narrative with contempt and fcorn, it is not lefs true, that an individual, who would add new difhonour to the name of a Therfites, has been able to hold up an Ulyffes to the contempt of the world. Therfites was unfortunate. He was born a Greek, and lived in the midft of a nation who had an acute fenfe of difcipline, decorum and honour. But you, with your trufty Trojans,—

πολυς δ'ορυμαγδυς ορωρει·
Τετρηχει δ'αγρη, υπο δ'εςοναχιζετο γαια.

'Twas tumult all: at once they beat the ground,
At once with clamorous noife the roofs refound.

There is, Sir, a falfe delicacy that fometimes fuppreffes the moft important incidents in a ftory. But it would be much unbecoming of your hiftorian to give way to a miftaken impreffion of this kind. If the phrafes of " the dinner bell," and others equally ingenious, were fuppreffed; if the fcraping of the foot, the rude and unmeaning laugh, the hawking and the coughing, were left undefcribed, diftant nations and unborn ages, whom the fame

M 2   of

of Grenville has not reached, might be at a lofs to conceive by what arts the invective of a Cicero and the energy of a Demofthenes were to be refifted and difarmed.

Unwilling to leave any thing to the capricious hand of time, who might otherwife treat you and your hair-dreffer in the fame unceremonious manner, and deliver you both to a common oblivion, I will endeavour to give them fome idea of the abftracted deferts of an individual, who has fuccefsfully entered the lifts with one of the moft accomplifhed characters of the prefent age. There is a principle, Sir, to which the ceremonious gravity of a native of China is probably much attached, and which the fons of dulnefs all over the world have fought to fupport, the principle of gradation and feniority. But nature will not be bound down in the manacles of art. She ftarts away with wild diforder, and continually delights in productions that are reducible to no rules, and which no experience is adequate to predict. With this propenfity fhe has given us many a brilliant exception to the principle of feniority, and in you, Sir, and the chancellor of the exchequer, has fhewn us what a schoolboy could do in the government of the world. You have rifen upon us, not by flow and imperceptible advances, but, like the progenitor of the human race, have appeared with all your honours upon you, from the firft moment in which the world fufpected that either of you exifted. A curious obferver, who fhould have fpeculated upon the character of Mr. Grenville, previoufly to the period I am defcribing, could fcarcely have traced the fhadow of thofe virtues which were fhortly to aftonifh the world. The funfhine of political dignity had not yet reached you, and that gracious countenance, which was hereafter to be the dial of the houfe of commons, to point out to them a time to eat, and a time to be hungry, was yet unknown. To bring to light the hidden fpeck which was to unfold itfelf into fo important confequences, he might in vain have wandered through all the regions of your mind. He would have found them as vacant as they were capacious, and as dark as they were impregnable. You, Sir, have been lefs incurious, and

your

your gratitude has kept pace with your obfervation. Full
of admiration of what nature in her bounty has beftowed,
you have never been heard to regret what fhe has withheld.
    Sir, you may perhaps be furprifed at my having fingled
you out for this addrefs. Your modefty, I doubt not, will
hinder you from feeing any peculiar merit in your exertions, that fhould diftinguifh you from the gentlemen who
have fo worthily acted with you in the glorious caufe. I
will indeed confefs, though I am by no means difpofed to
rob you of one atom of your well-earned fame, that it was
not with a view to your fuperior merit that I felected you.
On the contrary, Sir, I honour you without feeling the
fmalleft diftafte to any of your illuftrious coadjutors. With
peculiar pleafure I contraft a Macnamara with a Grenville.
Impartiality obliges me to confefs, that the honours of Macnamara in one refpect furpafs your own. He, Sir, is the
countryman of the man whofe abilities he fcorns, and whofe
virtues he tramples upon. I acknowledge the profoundeft
and moft unfeigned refpect for the member of Devon, who
is not more diftinguifhed by his blind and irrational attachment to the prefent adminiftration, than by the unqualified
felfifhnefs and the favage rufticity, that could induce him
explicitly to prefer his own concerns to the claims and immunities of one of the firft cities in the kingdom. But beyond all thefe I would extol and immortalize, if my talents
were equal to the undertaking, the chancellor of the exchequer. He, Sir, began his political career under the aufpices of this forlorn and defpifed hero. While the fame
and popularity of Mr. Burke fhot forth all their branches
with exuberant fertility, Mr. Pitt was proud to repofe himfelf under the venerable fhade. But he was too wife long
to fhelter himfelf beneath a battered fortification, or to
reft under the trunk of the oak while the lightnings played
amidft its topmoft branches. Young as he was, he knew
too much of the world, to fuffer political combinations
and the ties of acquaintance and refpect to unfurl the fails
of his all-grafping ambition. At the fame time he was
too prudent to make himfelf the principal figure of the

M 3   fcene

scene that was to follow. While he was in reality the soul
of the infamous project, he did not make himself visible to
the general audience. He employed his hounds to bait the
generous animal, and sat himself in affected serenity and
indifference. It was his delight to see the feelings sported
with, and the sensibility torn to pieces, of a man, whose
virtues he had sense enough to perceive, without having
the humanity to rescue and to honour them. This, Sir,
is a merit, in comparison of which that of a Macnamara
and a Grenville is insignificant indeed. You were merely
the instruments, the pincers that tore away the flesh, and
the cinder that burnt up the nerve of the hero, while he
was the ferocious savage that directed your operations.

The reason then, Sir, for my placing your name at the
head of this address is, to deal honestly, that I may be
happy enough a little to tame the insolence of your nature,
and to plant a sting in your breast in the pride of victory.
Achilles, though early plunged in the Styx, was yet vulne-
rable in the heel; and I have adventure and confidence
enough to expect to wound you through all your native
brass. This indeed is not the only source of your fool-hardi-
ness and daring. You trusted not a little for impunity,
to your own insignificance. You knew, that the most generous blood and the most illustrious descent, had no power
to divest the foolish and the frivolous of their native obscurity. You believed, while the hurricane tore away the pine
and the alder, that the rush bending by the side of the brook
would escape unhurt. But, Sir, I would teach you, that the
poorest tool of tyranny must not trust too much to his littleness. Wickedness has a kind of prerogative that elevates
its possessor into distinction. Flagitious actions will for a
moment partake of the fate of the sublimest virtues. The
poisoner and the assassin, a Donellan and a Ravaillac, will
be hung upon a gallows as tall as the pillar of Trajan, and
will fill up the news of the day as successfully, as the vindication of a nation from slavery, or the rescue of millions
from famine and death.

MUCIUS.

POLITICAL HERALD, AND REVIEW.

NUMBER V.

POLITICAL AND HISTORICAL SPECULATIONS.

To the Right Honourable EDMUND BURKE.

S I R.

THE letter, with which I opened this correspondence, and which was addressed to the right honourable Mr. Grenville*, may have suggested to you the subject of the following epistle. Upon that occasion, however, I designed no more than, what the whole race of political writers have pretended to do before me, to expose folly, repress insolence, and hold up boastful and ungrounded pretensions to the contempt of the world. And I perceived nothing in the name of Grenville to deter me from my purpose, or make me tremble for the hardihood of my enterprise. But the task I now undertake is of a different kind. I am now undertaking to instruct consummate wisdom, and to point out to fervent and illustrious virtue the path of honour. The mediocrity of my talents might perhaps have been expected to imbue me with implicit admiration. But, like another Galileo, I have adventured to discover the spots in the sun, and to analize the defects of one of that small constellation of excellence, which, becoming gra-

---

* Vide Political Herald, No. III. p. 175.

dually vifible through fucceffive ages, has taught mankind of what their nature is capable.

Sir, there is a kind of occult quality in the effence of virtue, that in a manner banifhes every diftinction, and puts all natures upon a level. If the equality of mankind is a dogma dictated by unerring truth, it is however more fure and uncontrovertible in this limited, than it can ever be expected to be in its comprehenfive fenfe. The man who yefterday delivered a fellow-creature from impending deftruction, cannot tremble in the prefence of a Socrates or an Antonine. There is a kind of fympathy and common intereft between all thofe who partake of this *divinæ particulam auræ,* that inftructs the ignorant, and emboldens the timid, and gives the novice a fhare in the counfels of the moft finifhed hero. To be the fpectator of his fuccefs is the firft wifh of his heart; to fee his virtues univerfally acknowledged and venerated, is the confummation of his fondeft hopes. And if by any exertion of his he can prepare the generous cataftrophe, he fteps forward from his humble ftation, he forgets the inferiority of his pretenfions and the mediocrity of his talents, and for a moment becomes the hero he contemplates, and the great fublime, whofe idea he has learned to adore. This, Sir, is all the excufe I have to offer. I have no reputation and no abilities to recommend me; but I will not rank fecond to any man in an intimate feeling of your merits, a zeal for your honour, and a lively and unremitted intereft in the events of your ftory.

For a moment I will endeavour to look back upon that ftory, and to recollect fome of its principal events. It is too rich in materials and too fertile of the moft important fentiments, for me to fear, from what I have formerly faid, to be led, in the prefent inftance, into any tautology. As an author, Sir, and a man of literature, you were firft known to the world, and in this light I will firft confider you. I fhall be equally free and unreftrained in my praife as in my cenfure. I fcorn the imputation of adulation and fervility. And I have little honour and management for

the

the forms and etiquette of fociety, when I have a great and diftinguifhed purpofe that I am defirous to anfwer. Of the profe writers in the Englifh language, the moft diftinguifhed, in my opinion, are a Swift and a Hume, a Shaftefbury and a Bolingbroke. But Swift, with much purity of expreffion, and much perfpicuity and elegance of form, has a drynefs and aufterity of character, that are neceffarily repulfive to every mind. In Hume, though infinitely more courteous and amiable and attractive than Swift, we defiderate a dignity and energy of ftyle, and acknowledge neither the fternnefs nor fpirit of inflexible rectitude. With all the advantages of thefe writers, you breathe the foul of genuine freedom and untemporifing ardour, at the fame time that you lead us, by the faireft paths and through the moft enchanting profpects, to the temple of purity, devotion, and benevolence. Shaftefbury indeed is gay and amufing, but is fomething too familiar in his gaiety and too laboured in his mirth: and Bolingbroke is eloquent, energetic and ftrong, but with a complication of ftyle that diftracts our attention, and a roughnefs of manner, fomewhat allied to the freedom and irregularity of his conduct. You have rifen as much above them as might naturally have been expected from a tafte and difcernment, cultivated beyond all former example, and a fervency of imagination that knows no bounds, combined with the energies of patriotifm and the fublimity of virtue. I have often been inclined to look upon Rouffeau as the moft finifhed of the writers that have endeavoured to inftruct mankind in philofophy, or to captivate their affections with tendernefs and pathos. But you, Sir, furpafs this incomparable genius in his leading peculiarities, the fweetnefs and infinuation of his ftyle, the copious and beautiful flow of his eloquence, the vivacity and warmth of his imagination, and the loftinefs and dignity of his enthufiafm. He unfortunately diverted thefe grand and aftonifhing qualities into a thoufand channels of luxuriant defcription, or weak and melancholy delirium. But you have collected qualities fuperior to his into one focus, and

brought

brought them to act, whole and undivided, for the common benefit and happiness and honour of the universe.

Sir, as I do not propose a methodical and regular survey of your merits, I will make no longer stop in this place, than just to recollect a single incident of your life, which, though small and insignificant, when considered in reference to Mr. Burke, would alone suffice to immortalize any other hero. I mean your conduct towards and connexion with Mr. Fox. From the removal of lord Chatham from the house of commons, you engrossed the reputation of being their brightest orator. Every ear caught with eagerness the dictates of your eloquence, every tongue was ready to resound your praise, and every man ambitiously retailed those sallies of wit and flights of enthusiasm, that taught the British senate to emulate the noblest periods of Athens and Rome. In the structure of your excellence, the richest bounty of nature and the most assiduous cultivation had united their efforts. You rose from an obscure situation, and you rose by just degrees. In the very moment in which you had obtained your topmost height, the unparalleled genius of a Fox burst upon you. He did not wait for maturity of years, he did not rise by slow degrees. His earliest dawn of youth was surrounded with a meridian splendour. In that moment, had one spark of littleness harboured in the remotest corner of your breast, it must have shewn itself. But no: heaven meaned you for brothers, and you greatly vindicated the designation of nature. Generous and expansive spirits, both of you are alike strangers to the littleness of envy. Illustrious rivals in the field of fame, you have enlisted under one banner, and united your efforts in a common cause. Let it no longer be the reproach of genius, that it will not bear a brother *near its throne!*

Looking through the whole of your character and accomplishments, I am satisfied that heaven has almost in no instance blessed mankind with a genius calculated to procure them so comprehensive benefits. But with all these advantages, your fate has been rigorous and unexampled.

Sir,

Sir, I am not difpofed to qualify and fritter away any part of the truth. You have been decried in the Britifh fenate by a faction of defigning and felf-interefted men. A more numerous body, glad of the opportunity of overbearing genius, and beating down every thing that might throw a comparative meannefs and obfcurity upon themfelves, have joined in the cry, ranged in fome degree under the fame ftandard, and intitled themfelves to a fhare in the fame infamy. Circumftances have occurred, which have been eagerly feized upon by the indefatigable hand of ingenious mifreprefentation, and made the foundation of an unpopularity, which has fpread far and wide among that numerous clafs of mankind, who adopt the fentiments of others without examination, and join in the clamour of the moment, without troubling themfelves to underftand it.

It will not be difputed, that of one event there are often various caufes, and that by the energies of a fingle being a fingle effect is feldom produced. The formidablenefs of your talents, the malignity of your enemies, and the folly of mankind, have undoubtedly contributed much to the event to which I allude. But, Sir, it may ftill be permitted to enquire, whether any thing in yourfelf, any penurioufnefs of nature, any error of judgment, or impropriety of conduct, has co-operated with thefe caufes. The difcovery, if true, will not be without its value. To correct malignity, and to carry home compunction and remorfe to the hearts of the obdurate, is a tafk, though not impracticable, yet in a great degree hopelefs. Even could we fucceed in this refpect, our fuccefs would be lefs beautiful and lefs honourable than in the prefent mode. Sir, I would wifh this country to owe nothing, even to the contrition of a Macnamara and a Grenville. There is a fecret but never-failing refource, an inexhauftible elafticity in genius and virtue, that render them all fufficient to themfelves. They may be degraded, but they never can be broken; they may be trampled upon, but they can never be difhonoured. It is the contention between the fun and the cloud. For a moment a condenfation of empty and

tumid

tumid vapours may withdraw from mankind the cheering light of day, and fpread defolation and deformity over the plains. But the fervor of the fun and the brightnefs of his beams cannot fail fpeedily to regain the afcendancy, and to relume the world with unwonted ferenity and luftre. If, Sir, it were a trifling purpofe that I had to anfwer, I might indulge to the leffons of decorum and the impreffions of inferiority. But convinced as I am of the critical and dolorous ftate of my country, perceiving as I do that fhe bleeds at every pore, and perfuaded that almoft no abilities and no integrity but your own are equal to her melioration and recovery, I feel an anxiety for the revival of your popularity and influence, which I am unable to defcribe. Even were the crifis a common one, I fhould ftill conceive, that the reftoration of capabilities, like thofe which I believe to exift in your breaft, to their natural order and funétions, was of more confequence to our common nature and to the lateft pofterity, than the refcue of hundreds from misfortune, or the turning afide the calamities of war from a quarter of the world.

There are perhaps two circumftances originating in yourfelf that have contributed to the fuccefs of your enemies, and by an attention to which that fuccefs may yet be rendered ignominious and futile. One of the characteriftics which accompany uncommon genius, efpecially when it is more converfant in imagination than in abftraét fcience, and has more to do with morals and fentiment than with pure fpeculation, is a refined and exquifite fenfibility. This is the quality to which we are bound to afcribe that weaknefs and imbecility of the charaéter of Rouffeau, which we have already ftated. Tremblingly alive to the malice of his enemies and the negligence of his friends, he became the fport of defigning vice. He created to himfelf a new world, which impreffed him on every occafion, inftead of that which really exifted, and afcribed to men a variety of motives, extremely different from thofe by which they were aétuated. Your good fenfe and intelleétual fuperiority have defended you from the
visionary

vifionary valetudinarjanifm of Rouffeau. But, Sir, may
it not have happened, that through a fimilar ftructure of
conftitution, you have fallen into a fimilar, though lefs
apparent error? Sir, it would be as reafonable for me to
fuffer an ant or fly to difturb the current of my happinefs,
as that you fhould permit the progrefs of your comprehenfive plans, and the career of your public virtues, to be interrupted by the furlinefs of a Rolle, or the arrogance of
a Grenville. You are a being of a fuperior order. You
dwell in a fphere of your own. Would you fuffer the
threats of a mob, or the violence of a tyrant, the imaginary fears of fuperftition, or the formidable tempefts of
the ocean, to fhake the fettled purpofe of your foul? No,
Sir, you would not. How much lefs then ought this to
be the effect of impertinence or vulgarity! The unaffected contempt of a dignified underftanding, or the occafional farcafm of an unruffled eloquence, is, of all the
modes that can be adopted, the beft calculated to awe them
into filence. But at any rate fuch empty pretenders as
thofe to whom I allude, will never long detain the attention
of the public, if they are found to produce no effect upon
a fuperior mind.

Another circumftance which has contributed to this in-
dignity has been pretended to be, the frequency and cheap-
nefs of your public orations. There is a *facra fames*, an
accurfed thirft of novelty incident to mankind, which
would not fuffer them to attend for a confiderable perpetuity to the leffons of angelic wifdom, delivered with all
the attractions of celeftial eloquence. Permit this confideration to dwell for a moment in your memory. Collect
and concentrate all the energies and the potency of your
talents for important occafions. Exercife a noble and beneficent avarice of thofe powers which God and nature
have put into your hands, for the lafting welfare of mankind. Referved and exalted, as it were, to an infinite
diftance from vulgar mortals upon every common and trivial
deliberation, defcend upon us with ten-fold luftre and
aftonifhment when the occafion is worthy of your powers.

Never

Never lavish upon us the golden stores of your soul with a generous but unreflecting prodigality. Suffer us not to listen to you without expecting those unrivalled bursts of eloquence, at which Cicero would sicken and Demosthenes turn pale, nor without having our expectations completely gratified. With a plan like this, you would arrest the attention and captivate all the powers of the soul.

> ————*Such a sacred and home-felt delight,*
> *Such sober certainty of waking bliss,*

would teach the malicious and the abandoned to sit in involuntary attention, and barbarians and idiots to murmur applause.

Sir, in a situation like yours, all inferior considerations and petty decorums are to be forgotten and trampled upon. A refined selfishness is in this case the noblest and most extensive benevolence. Talk, Sir, of your services and your merits. Vindicate with energy and indignation your injured honour and your eternal fame. Teach your adversaries to perceive at once their nothingness and their folly. Drag forth into the light of day their secret, but their real commander. Strike him with the duplicity of his conduct, and the hardness of your cruelty. Celebrate with all its genuine lustre the merit which could borrow the patronage, and fight under the banners of a hero, in order to rise upon his ruins, and, in some unguarded and unsuspecting moment, pierce him to the heart.

I know, Sir, that it has been affirmed, that your want of a magnificent ancestry and a splendid patrimony, has formed one principal cause of the clamour with which you have been decried, and will prove an everlasting bar to your complete success. But no, Sir. It is not in man to resist the efforts of which you are capable, when conducted with equal penuriousness and enterprise. I am willing to confess, that this may have contributed something to swell the tumult of vociferation. But it can never constitute an invincible obstacle. Mankind are not yet so degenerate and so

stupid

ftupid as not to liften to the dictates of wifdom, till it has produced the rent-roll of its eftate and the heraldry of its name. Were this true, no wealth could have been created by public fervice; and no foundation could be laid in the prefent day for the honour and ennoblement of a pofterity. Confider then, Sir, what it is that is incumbent upon you. You are not called upon merely to vindicate your own name, to build up your own honour, and to hand down your renown clear and unfullied to future ages. This would be a great and indifpenfible duty. Self-prefervation is the firft law of nature. Self-defertion is the difgrace and difhonour of the moft confummate talents. But, Sir, upon the event which I could wifh to haften, and to which I look forward with the moft fanguine hopes, depend a thoufand bleffings, which otherwife muft be for ever loft. All the fchemes which wifdom can dictate, all the projects that an active and unwearied benevolence can infpire, thefe, Sir, muft be executed or forgotten, according as you are honoured or unpopular. How much knowledge and ge-nerofity and improvement are you capable of communi-cating to the men who now exift! How many evils of ignorance and flavery may you avert, how many advan-tages of peace and good government and immortal heaven-defcended truth, are you capable of procuring for genera-tions yet unborn! As much as millions exceed an indivi-dual in importance, fo much does this view of the fubject fwallow up the regards of your own reputation and hap-pinefs, though you fhould be the foremoft of the human fpecies. As much as the foul is more excellent than this material frame, fo much is the independance you are cal-culated to create, and the truth you are enabled to diffufe, more excellent than the political clemency of an Auguftus and the humane and enlightened defpotifm of a Trajan.

MUCIUS.

To the Right Honourable WILLIAM PITT.

SIR,

THE events of your adminiſtration have been many
and various. The ſituations in which you have been
placed, have afforded every thing that the moſt ardent ambition could deſire for the exhibition of virtue; and, if
any thing narrow, contemptible, and diſhonourable, had by
chance ſkulked in any corner of your ſoul, theſe alſo would
have been brought forward to the obſervation of your
countrymen. It has fallen to your lot, Sir, to new-model
the conſtitution, to give to privilege and prerogative limits
unknown before, and to open new channels for the exertions of aſpiring ambition. You, Sir, have received this
country under your auſpicious patronage, when exhauſted
by a ruinous war; and to you we have committed all our
hopes

18

hopes for the melioration of our revenue, and the liquidation of our debts. It has been yours to frame treaties of alliance and treaties of commerce; and the plains of Germany and the court of Versailles exhibit the monuments of your glory. It was you, from whom we expected that reform in our reprefentation, upon which the continuance of our expiring liberty depends; and that new fyftem of government, for the moft important of our remaining dependencies, which was to give happinefs and fecurity to thirty millions of men. Your merit, Sir, under all thefe departments, is palpable and unqueftioned.

The eager eye of the thinking individual, that looks back upon the bright volume of your fame, would be ready to doubt the poffibility of any frefh acquifitions. He would lift up his hands with wonder, and exclaim, " This of all " miracles is the greateft ! This man, as yet unefcaped " from the anxious guardianfhip of his preceptor, may boaft " with more truth than Cæfar, *I have lived enough for nature,* " *and enough for glory !"* But happily, Sir, the narrow limits of human imagination are not permitted to fix the termination of your drama. You have an invifible divinity, an aufpicious genius, that watches the progrefs of your ftory, and produces, not merely what the ear has not heard, but what the heart of man was inadequate to conceive. After having wielded empires and conftituted the fate of millions, after having exercifed every executive and every legiflative function, you appear at laft in that character, which, as Montefquieu has informed us, fills up the circle of political power, the character of a judge. You conceive of yourfelf, and juftly, as being in reality, though not in name, the Lord High Steward for the King of Great Britain, upon a trial of which the univerfe are fpectators.

There are various circumftances, Sir, that this beneficent agent has collected to illuftrate your fituation. Whether we look to the culprit, the accufer, or the caufe, we are equally overwhelmed with the magnitude of our object. The culprit, Sir, is a man, who, of vulgar birth and humble education, has emulated the characters of a Warwick and

and a Richlieu. Seated, in a manner, upon the throne of the East, he has descended from his eminence, and stands a solitary individual at your bar. The accuser is a person, whose unrivalled abilities Europe has compelled his countrymen to acknowledge. We hear at length from his bitterest enemies the late, the ungracious, but the irresistible confession *, that he is not more " ingenious" than " good," and that " his imagination, his learning, and his taste" find their counterpart in " his benevolence and his virtue." The patriotic life of this man has been filled up with a thousand examples of comprehensive policy and indefatigable zeal. Having exerted every faculty and every excellence within the circle of the human mind, he closes this long and splendid career with a great public prosecution, the example of which may wash away the stains of Britain, and ensure security and peace to generations yet unborn. Such, Sir, is the cause now brought forward for trial, that the innumerable nations of the East look up to it, with one consent, as that which is to decide their political sentiments and feelings for ever; and our ancient rivals are wild enough to expect, from the imaginary hebetude of your understanding, or depravity of your heart, a sentence, which is finally to give the last of our remaining dependencies into their hands. Your impartiality in this great cause, the accurate balance you were to hold between the two parties concerned in this memorable transaction, must irrevocably fix your reputation and your fame.

Upon this transaction, Sir, you have looked down with your wonted composure. You ruffled not a muscle of your visage. Placid, gentle, and serene, you were prepared to contemplate with the same feelings every part of the universal spectacle, the melting of a bubble and the destruction of a world. Measuring the unbounded varieties of human nature by your own narrow standard, you believed every man, incapable of this apathy and unconcern, to be an in-

---

* Vide English Review for February 1786.

competent leader in political transactions. You have
learned the admirable lesson, at once to sport with the miseries and the feelings of mankind. By the first of these dif-
ciplines you prepared yourself to meet every untoward event,
and by the second, to ward off every formidable attack upon
your administration. In the prosecution of this momentous suit, you saw a man, however superior to you in capacity, whom you believed you could easily baffle by mean
and inglorious arts. You imagined, that the lion was to be
daunted by the braying of the ass.

At the moment, Sir, in which I have the honour to address you, you have felt, and severely felt, the disappoint-
ment of this fond expectation. The man, whom you
looked to find warm, unguarded, and irritable, you have
found the reverse of all these. Persons of your nature and
depth have but one character. Whatever it is that belongs
to them appears upon the surface. Even their hypocrisy is
no better than the wiles of the ostrich: they hide their
heads in the sand, but their refuge is to be discovered by
the most common observer. But genius, Sir, though it
abhor the very shadow of hypocrisy, includes in its structure a thousand resources. Human sagacity and human
invention cannot prescribe limits to it. It is never overwhelmed; and its powers seem to be created by the events
that befal it. When it appears exhausted, unobservant,
and lethargic, at that very moment it is collecting its energies and concentring its fire. And though you should
imagine you have destroyed and annihilated it, it rises unhurt, and revives like a phoenix from its ashes.

Such, Sir, has been the simplicity, the mildness, and the
composure of Mr. Burke upon this great occasion. You
have seen him sudden and impetuous as the forked lightnings. He is now undisturbed as the western sky, when
the summer sun sinks beneath the horizon. He has baffled
your efforts: he has vindicated that superiority, which to
have deserted, were to belie the bounties of the munificent
creator. You had yet another reserve. If you could not
disturb a temper, which you represented to yourself a mere
train

train to be let off at your pleafure, you could, however, deny him the materials upon which it was neceffary for him to found his accufation. To the ignominy of this proceeding you were callous. You knew the man you had undertaken to protect, and you were affured he would thank you for a kindnefs, which he dared not demand at your hands. "What a precious farce," exclaimed Mr. Fox, "is daily acting within thefe walls! We fee the friends of Mr. Haftings affecting to be eager that every document fhould be produced. We fee the king's minifters rifing to declare, that nothing, confiftent with prudence, and requi-fite to juftice, fhall be refufed. We fee other gentlemen, calling themfelves independent and impartial, exclaiming, ' By all means let the houfe know the whole, and be put in poffeffion of every fpecies of information.' And yet we fee all of thefe men dividing together, to enforce a negative to a motion for fuch information; and helping each other with hints and whifpers during the debate, juft as I and my honourable friend would affift each other, when we are maintaining the fame point, and arguing for the fame purpofe!"

One kind of ingenuity I am willing to afcribe to you. You knew that the tafk of an accufer was undefirable and ungrateful. You believed that few men would venture to incur the indignation and the enmity of a powerful indivi-dual, for the fake of a good, to be divided among thoufands, and the gratitude for which was little likely to prove the advantage of its author. And a certain gentlenefs and de-licacy in your own nature, upon which I do not chufe to beftow its proper denomination, induced you to conceive, that a defpotic and imperious veteran, juft defcended upon us from among the children of the fun, was a man, to have been attacked perhaps at a diftance, but not to have been met, fearlefs and intrepid, in the way of a criminal charge. If the profecutor, as you fagacioufly prefaged, had wifhed to fhrink from the moment of conflict, you were amicably difpofed to extend to him the broad fhield of pretext and

palliation.

palliation. Unfortunately, Mr. Burke loved the cause of mankind more than his own ease, and feared to do what was base and inglorious, but was not afraid of the open enmity or secret malice of any man.

But your power was plenipotentiary and ample. If you could not awe him into flight, or bribe him into surrender, you still believed, you could traverse him so completely, and deny him so much, as to make it impracticable for him to proceed. Here however, that fatal superficiality, that boyish ignorance and imposture, which have defeated all your preceding schemes, disgraced you in one instance more. You undertook much, but you understood nothing. You conceived that something was to be conceded for the sake of appearance. Uninformed of the transactions and the story you had determined to varnish, you were not aware, that, in granting one body of information, you granted every thing. If Cicero, instead of six, had produced only one of his orations against Verres, Verres must nevertheless have been condemned. And Mr. Hastings's government is too rich of the most glaring colours in every page, to leave us at a loss for matter of accusation. Your antagonist was conscious of this. He followed you inch by inch, and told you, with a confidence that astonished and confounded you, that, counterwork him as much as you would, and raise as many obstacles as you pleased, he was nevertheless determined to proceed; and though he should have been deserted, as you insinuated and eagerly hoped, by his friends and mankind, the great cause in which he was engaged should never be abandoned.

We are not, Sir, better acquainted with the nature of the conduct you have held, than with the principles from which it was derived. The master-key to the whole was put into the hands of a discerning public, by that characteristic measure of your administration, the confirming and lending the name and authority of Britain to the debts of the nabob of Arcot. We easily see through the extensive and stupendous chain of connexion, from a Dundas to an Atkinson,

ſon, and from an Atkinſon to a Benfield *. We perceive, at a ſingle glance, the whole memorable band of Eaſt Indian culprits united in a league of mutual defence. You they have worthily ſelected as the preſident of this league. There might have been crimes and enormities in India before the period of your political exiſtence. But it was the money, that was deſtined to buy the ſixteenth parliament of Great Britain, that firſt gave to theſe abuſes ſubſtance and perpetuity. You have been preceded in the honourable buſineſs of corruption by a Danby and a Walpole, the profligates of our earlier and our later ſtory. The career of theſe men was opened by proſecution, impriſonment, and fine. They ſold themſelves, from their earlieſt initiation, to perform all the menial ſervices of an unprincipled party. Branded with infamy in the firſt inſtance, perfected by the moſt aſſiduous proſecution of wickedneſs in the ſecond, and dead to virtue and to ſhame, they ſtand conſpicuous the diſgrace of hiſtory. It was reſerved to us, to ſee a young man of noble birth, and crowned with paternal laurels, in the firſt ſtep of his progreſs ſurpaſs theſe great maſters of contamination and depravity. You, Sir, have happily connected vices, that before ſtood moſt aloof from each other, ſubornation and extortion : with one hand you have drawn away the reſources and perpetuated the oppreſſions of a ruined world; and with the other you have ſcattered laviſhly that baleful infection, which is to root away the laſt remains of Britiſh honour and Britiſh virtue.

But, whatever be the motives and whatever the deſcription of your conduct, it is now ſufficiently evident, that the impeachment of Mr. Haſtings will be crowned with the moſt entire ſucceſs. Your folly, Sir, is greater than your hypocriſy; and at the moment in which your effrontery would have blaſted, your ignorance has re-

---

* Vide Political Herald, No. III. p. 222, &c.

deemed, the name of Britain. The firft document you
granted, the firft paper that was laid upon the table of the houfe of commons, was the record of Mr.
Haftings's condemnation. While you imagine that you
fit fecure among your creatures, the honour of a Britifh parliament revolts againft your profligacy. You believed, Sir, as I have hinted, that you had paid the purchafe
money of a fenate; but you were miftaken. Though you
fhould have fucceeded in fome inftances with the electors,
you did not with the elected. The veil you once fo fuccefsfully drew before their eyes, has long fince vanifhed.
Some minifters have been followed in all the meafures
they thought proper to fuggeft. But, Sir, there are men,
whom the fincereft well-wifhers, and perfons the moft defirous to fupport, are obliged to defert. There are meafures
fo unplaufible and barefaced, that innocence itfelf cannot be
deceived refpecting them, and folly cannot be induced to
patronife and efpoufe them. The vote of the prefent
feffion, in regard to the duke of Richmond's fortifications,
is the harbinger of your fuccefs in the acquital of Mr.
Haftings. A moderate acquaintance with hiftory told you,
that one unguarded vote might fometimes be obtained in the
face of truth and juftice. And this was the point to which
you wifhed to have reduced us. But in the prefent inftance, virtue and ingenuoufnefs and rectitude have been
more than a match for treachery and deceit. The body of
men is yet to be found, that can go on to vote acquital after
acquital in the face of the blackeft crimes and the moft undoubted evidence. I can imagine, then, that I fee, in the
fpirit of forefight, one honour referved for you, that may
confummate your character. I can conceive a charge,
hardly fought, and carried againft the whole weight of adminiftration in the houfe of commons, defeated, by means
that I need not name, in the houfe of lords.

One word I will beg leave to addrefs to you, upon an
excufe you are fond of urging in behalf of Mr. Haftings,
and from which you expect the greateft effects. Sir
George

George Rodney was charged before the house of commons in the affair of St. Euſtatius; but the victory of the 12th of April arrived opportunely, and put an end to the proſecution. Thus you tell us, whatever guilt Mr. Haſtings might have contracted in the earlier part of his adminiſtration, and whatever charges your virtuous friend Mr. Dundas may have thought fit to bring againſt him, the peace with the Mahrattas effaces all. And what was the benefit that accrued from the peace with the Mahrattas ? Why, it put an end to a confederate war, which was lighted up by the arbitrary and unrelenting ambition of Mr. Haſtings. True, it was concluded in the midſt of duplicity and treachery. We excited factitious diſcord among our enemies; we deſerted and put up to auction our allies and our friends. Still however, the peace was concluded. Still, in the midſt of profligacy and crimes, tranquillity was reſtored to the Britiſh ſettlements.

But no, Sir, craft, duplicity and vice, were never yet the parents of ſubſtantial benefit. The peace with the Mahrattas was not left to be a ſolitary exception to an eternal maxim. By a ſingular courſe of negociation they indeed were detached from the alliance of Tippoo, and, in a moment favourable to this country, the ſultan ſheathed the ſword of deſtruction. But the diſſimulation and falſehood of Britain have at length been brought to light. The peace with the Mahrattas appears to the natives of Indoſtan in all its odious and glaring colours. Tippoo and the Mahrattas, thoſe hereditary enemies, that long divided the peninſula of India, are once more united againſt the common foe. Scarcely a nation or a tribe, however inſignificant, has failed to enrol its name in the patriot confederacy. All meaner quarrels are forgotten in a common oppoſition to the enemy of India and mankind. A league, ſo formidable and ſo determined, cannot fail to complete our extirpation, unleſs their juſt reſentment is expiated by one memorable victim to the injured rights of humanity.

MUCIUS.

M 4

POLITICAL HERALD, AND REVIEW.

NUMBER X.

POLITICAL AND HISTORICAL SPECULATIONS.

To the Right Honourable WILLIAM PITT.

SIR,

I MAY perhaps ftand in need of an apology for this fecond addrefs. It may be fuppofed, that you are already fallen into hands adequate to the diffection of your political character in the writer of the Critique of your Adminiftration. I am not at all defirous of encroaching upon the defign of this gentleman. But the occafion I have had to look into one feature of your ftory, in the affair of Mr. Haftings, I am ready to confefs, has excited my appetite for a farther correfpondence. When we fit down to the perufal of the great poets of ancient or modern date, we may perhaps intend only a relaxation. But we are not always able to overcome the fafcination and refift the enthufiafm of our author, at the moment in which prudence demands it. I am thus, Sir, the victim of your attractions; and whatever credit fo humble an example may add to your character, I am chearfully and unrefervedly willing to pay. It may happen indeed, that my tafk will not fo far interfere with that of my predeceffor as may at firft fight be imagined. He has undertaken to follow you in chronological order; and it is probable fo illuftrious a ftory will feldom be unprolific of the moft ufeful inftruction. But it is my defign to felect your

beauties, and bring together fingle and unconnected parts to
illuftrate each other. The flood of brightnefs, that diftin-
guifhes the galaxy, does not hinder its including orbs of a
different magnitude. I have at this moment only a fingle
object in my view, and fhall confequently obtain a degree
of wholenefs and unity, which cannot be expected from
the regular hiftorian.

It happens in the fubject of politics, as in that of religion,
that fome perfons of a catholic, or a fceptical, turn of
mind, have confidered all fyftems as alike indifferent. This
however can fcarcely happen to the venerable teacher of
the one, or the active difciple of the other. I, Sir, am
an Englifhman; and, notwithftanding all the declama-
tions I have heard, I am fecretly inclined to prefer liberty
to defpotifm, and privilege to prerogative. You fet out in
public life under the imputation of the fame prejudice.
Your celebrated father, whether from conviction or policy,
had generally acted on that fide, and your public career
was begun with the warmeft profeffions for purity and
renovation. I, Sir, was one of your converts. I was
unable to afcribe to you fo practifed an hypocrify, as I
muft have done, had I regarded you as a concealed tory.
I knew that youth was the period of ingenuoufnefs and
humanity. I believed that the fame ardour that brought
you forward fo early in political difcuffions, would render
you a whig of no common diftinction. And fo ftrongly
was I impreffed with this perfuafion, that it was not a few
unconnected inftances that could induce me to retract it.

The creed of a whig, Sir, neceffarily taught me to imagine the houfe of commons the firft power in the conftitution. All the checks it was permitted to exert upon the
ariftocracy, but efpecially upon the monarchical branch,
were to me in the utmoft degree precious. The exclufive
grant of the public money, the right of difmiffing his
majefty's minifters, and the claim to have their confidence
confidered as an indifpenfable requifite in the nomination
of a cabinet, appeared the palladiums of liberty and the
bulwarks of the conftitution. With thefe prepoffeffions, I
                                                        could

could not regard, but with an unfavourable eye, the conduct you held at the commencement of your adminiftration. I was not fo blind as not to perceive, that the fteps
you purfued were thofe of a tory. But, whether from
impartiality, from candour, or from folly, I believed they
were the dictates of your ambition, and not of your underftanding; and I ftill gave you credit for a clandeftine
attachment to the caufe of the people.

The fond illufion is now diffolved. Sir, from the moment I faw you feated quietly at the helm, I of courfe employed myfelf to watch your conduct. I did not watch it,
however, with an eye of jealoufy and diftruft; I was not
difpofed to mifreprefent and mifconceive your actions. But
I beheld it with the attention of a philofopher and the
anxiety of a Briton. I ardently looked for the favourable
moment when the cloud, which your ambition had fpread
around you, fhould vanifh, and when you fhould fhew
yourfelf, if not adventuroufly, at leaft unequivocally, the
friend of freedom. I did not indeed exaggerate either your
abilities or your virtues. I did not look up to you as the
faviour of your country, nor expect from you a model of
unblemifhed integrity. But I believed, that thofe honeft
prejudices, which your education, your youth and your
fobriety might be expected to have created, would occa-
fionally fhew themfelves. If I had reprefented you to myfelf as an hero or a demi-god, I might have deferved what
followed. But my mind was ferene, and my expectations
were reafonable; and I did not look to be difappointed. I
have, however late, been at length undeceived, and I am
willing the public fhould reap the fruit of my difcoveries.

One of the firft meafures in which you defired to be
thought to take an active part, was in the bill appointing
commiffioners to inquire into the fees, emoluments, and
perquifites received in the feveral public offices; a bill
which you firft fuggefted in the year 1783, but which was
not paffed into a law till the year 1785. In this bill, Sir,
you kindly put into our hands the clue which might conduct us into the remoteft receffes of your character. To

reform

reform the public offices, to ſupprefs the exorbitant fees which had been taken, particularly under your auſpices in the Lanſdown adminiſtration, was undoubtedly a ſpecious pretence. But let us inquire, under the fair face of œconomy and reform, of what ſort was the poiſon you really concealed. There muſt ever, Sir, be a certain harmony and proportion between the end we propoſe to accompliſh, and the means that are employed to carry it into effect. To aboliſh, or, more properly, to diminiſh, the perquiſites of office, was undoubtedly to relieve individuals. But what benefit did it add to the national welfare ? Did any wholſome ſtreams of revenue and redemption flow from this ſource into the public coffers ? Are theſe the materials out of which your boaſted ſinking fund is to originate ? Or has that idol alike of Rome and Britain, general and individual liberty, received any freſh acceſſion from this wonderful bill ? You will not pretend it. And yet, what were the means that were here employed ? Sir, they were interrogatory upon oath. They were a kind of general warrant, dragging individuals from their peaceful roofs, calling without appeal for books, papers, and records, at the diſcretion of your creatures. In a word, the means employed to effect a trifling and ſlender advantage, an advantage that might have been gained without a moment's delay, by one grain of honeſt reſolution and diligence in a chancellor of the exchequer or a ſecretary of ſtate, did not fall ſhort of the moſt celebrated refinements of Dionyſius of Syracuſe, or the inquiſition of Madrid. If, Sir, nature, forgetful of her uſual bounty and ſuperintending providence, had deprived us of your ineſtimable ſervices at the time that you produced this firſt child of your invention, the hiſtorian might perhaps have been puzzled to account for the ſtrange diſproportion and abſurdity. But we are now informed beyond the ſhadow of a queſtion, that in this bill you intended to feel the pulſe, and make an experiment upon the temper, of the people of England. Your ſuccefs ſurpaſſed your expectations, and your ſubſequent ſteps have been worthy of ſo auſpicious a commencement.

Your

Your India bill of the ſame year afforded us a more memorable diſplay of your true character. With one daſh of
your pen, with one ſweeping effort of your all-graſping
ambition, you took from us the trial by jury, and you extended ſtill farther your favourite inquiſitorial proceedings.
Wiſely you apprehended, that ſo ſpirited a meaſure muſt
both be well timed and nicely calculated in point of geo-
graphy, in order to be tolerated for a moment. But though
you exerciſed ſome preſcience upon both theſe heads, in
both you were entirely deceived. Whatever of ſpirit remained in Engliſhmen, revolted at the picture of Hindoo
ſlavery. Whatever of humanity remained to us, ſtarted
with horror from the caprices of tyranny and the oppreſſions of avarice in that quarter of the world. But the madneſs of a Haſtings, and the upſtart inſolence of a Benfield,
though not ill underſtood in this country, were not ſufficient
to colour the violence of your meaſures. And though you
might imagine the Europeans of India callous from vice,
and callous from the ſpirit of our government there, yet
the ſlavery you introduced was ſomething too much even
for the education they had received. How eaſy were it to
enlarge the powers of a jury, and yet preſerve its eſſential
features! How abſurd to imagine, that oaths could bind
thoſe whom honour and conſcience, and all that is ſacred
among men, could not reſtrain! But no, Sir. You ſought
deſpotiſm, and you did not find melioration. Arbitrary
power was the god of your idolatry; and the auſpicious
union in which you found it with villainy and corruption,
could not daſh the ardour of your devotion.

From your earlier parliamentary proceedings, to give ſome
relief to the ſcene, I turn to the kingdom of Ireland. There had
been miniſters, Sir, your predeceſſors in office, who ſaw with a
jealous eye the volunteering, the aſſociations, and the con-
greſſes of Ireland. They wanted not the inclination to beat
down the generous efforts of liberty and renovation, and to
reduce all the ſubjects of the Britiſh crown to one ſervile, abject, unmanly level. But they trembled on the brink of
action, and let " I dare not, wait upon I would." You,

Q 3   Sir,

Sir, trampled upon the object of their honeſt terrors, and employed the bold and deciſive proceedings of accompliſhed tyranny. You ſilenced their newſpapers, you impriſoned the printers; you ſerved their ſheriffs and the chairmen of their counties with writs of attachment. By what pretence did you ſeek to diſguiſe theſe proceedings? Even your unbluſhing effrontery could employ none. With whatever colours you varniſhed your bill of officereform, your bill of Indian judicature, and other meaſures of the ſame kind, it was here naked, honeſt, unplauſible deſpotiſm. Will any man believe that you can be the friend of liberty in Britain, and its foe in Ireland? Will you any longer dare to aſſume that worn-out lie of parliamentary reform, when the whole ſpirit of your meaſures in Dublin has been the ſuppreſſion of every ſhadow of reform?

Sir, it were endleſs to trace the whole tenor of your meaſures in that devoted country. I pretend to ſelection, and not to detail. Were it not that it would draw out this addreſs into an unreaſonable length, I would bring forward thoſe parts of your celebrated propoſitions, which, if they had paſſed into a law, might have made the Iriſh parliament envy the more liberal prerogatives of the Turkiſh divan. And I would deſcribe with all the epithets of honeſt indignation, your maſter-blow, your legiſlative attack upon the liberties of the Hibernian preſs. To ſtrike at the liberty of the preſs, is the laſt effort of political profligacy, the concluding refinement of acknowledged deſpotiſm. But, Sir, you ſet indignation at defiance. You have diſcovered an invaluable ſecret to diſtract the reſentments and confound the memory of mankind. The bold and unprincipled meaſures of your adminiſtration are ſo numerous, that they drive one another from our recollection, and will not, as you fondly perſuade yourſelf, be felt by a ſupine and credulous people, till they ſhall riſe up at once in dreadful array, and overwhelm us with the aſtoniſhment and deſperation of our ſituation.

I turn, Sir, to the more recent and glaring examples of the preſent ſeſſion, which have in reality been my incitements

ments to the prefent addrefs. If there be a man in this country more attached to the true and unadulterated principles of monarchy than another, it is your coadjutor and bofom friend, Mr. Henry Dundas. The favourite fcheme of this man, in the wildeft excurfions of his defpotic propenfity, was that of a viceroy for the Britifh Eaft Indies. By a fcheme like this he would be able to train up a numerous race of men, the natural fubjects of the Britifh realm, in the principles of paffive obedience. He would teach us to look on fupine at the eftablifhment of unlimited tyranny in one province of the Englifh monarchy. And we are not now to learn, how fubtle and dextrous is this gentleman at arguing from precedent to precedent, and wrefting from us, piecemeal, the fhadow of freedom that yet remains to us. It is not, however, to the fingle bleffing of tyranny that the operation of this fcheme confines itfelf. Rich is the harveft that you and your friend expect to derive from Indian delinquency. The crimes of Englifhmen in that country were already arrived to a pitch that would have fatisfied the views of an ordinary ftatefman. But the brilliancy of your imagination figured to itfelf a degree of profligacy at which they were not yet arrived. An abfolute government, you well knew, was the prolific mother of every fpecies of depravity. And the more arbitrary and inquifitorial is the mode of inveftigation that was prepared for criminals of this fort, the dearer you were aware they would be willing to purchafe impunity. Such were the views that induced you to patronife a propofition which no other firft minifter of this country would at any time have dared to efpoufe.

But the mortal and unconquerable antipathy to which you were confcious againft the trial by jury, was not fatiated with the efforts you had already made. One more precedent you were refolute to add to the ineftimable collection. This, Sir, you prefented to us in your new model of the mutiny bill. I am fomewhat inclined to fufpect, that you intended in this inftance to do us good by ftealth, and that your claufe fhould be quietly palmed upon the

Q 4

public

public without notice and obſervation. We thank you, Sir, for the refinement of your benevolence, and we thank you for your unbluſhing defence of your manœuvre after it was detected. To try a free-born Engliſhman, unverſed in camps, unbenefited by military emolument, by the mode of a court-martial, merely becauſe he had at ſome for-gotten period been a member of the army, was a project worthy of the extenſive reputation and popularity you en-joyed. To hold out by this means a threat *in terrorem* over multitudes of men, whether lords or commoners, who ſhould dare to oppoſe your meaſures, was a piece of treachery and inſidious cowardice that cannot eaſily be paralleled, but the effects of which may endure long after your body is pe-riſhed, and your memory execrated through ſucceſſive ge-nerations.

But I am willing to cloſe the reproachful catalogue. The inſtance that remains to me is that of Mr. Marſham's bill for the better ſecuring the freedom of election. Upon this occaſion, Sir, I know not how to do juſtice to the intrepidity of your ſpirit, and the gratuitouſneſs of your exertions. That you ſhould have ſpoken ſtrenuouſly, openly, am-bitiouſly, againſt a meaſure ſo dear to every whig, ſo anxiouſly deſired by every friend to freedom or to virtue, is an example of ſhameleſs impudence unequalled in hiſtory, and incredible to fiction. Could you not have truſted to the well-known and well-marſhalled bands of courtly de-pendants? Could you not have truſted to the imperiouſneſs, the dictatorial arrogance of lord Thurlow? Could you not have hugged yourſelf in the reflection, that the warmth of liberal enthuſiaſm was now ſubſided? and that in the houſe of lords ſuch bills had ever been rejected by a conſiderable majority? In this inſtance, Sir, your exertions were un-neceſſary and uncalled for. You ſtood forth a glorious and ever-honoured volunteer in the cauſe of ſlavery. This ſa-crifice you were eager to make at the ſhrine of royal pre-judice. We doubt not, Sir, that you have found the way to the heart of your gracious maſter. And we ſhall ſcarcely

waſte

wafte ourfelves in one expreffion of wonder, if you fhould become a more notorious minion than lord Bute himfelf.

Thus, Sir, I have reviewed a few meafures of your adminiftration, fcattered in point of time, but perhaps not unconnected in the mind of their author. I am ambitious to recommend myfelf to your good opinion and your favour. I will therefore beg leave, before I difmifs you, to contraft the bleffings you have accomplifhed with the immaturity of your years. Henceforth, I truft, we fhall hear no more of your modefty and your innocence, your inexperience and your fincerity. The man muft be blind and incredulous indeed, who, reviewing the inftances I have related, will not allow that you prefent us with a finifhed character. If heaven had made you a contemporary of a *Louis the Eleventh* of France, your deftiny would have been more fortunate, and your conduct more memorable, than that of the model after which you fo humbly copy, the cardinal Richlieu's, could poffibly be under fo poor and paffive a mafter as Louis XIII. In our prefent fovereign, indeed, we have a fecurity againft the baleful contagion of your vices; and in the fpirit and underftanding of the people of England we have the moft undoubted affurance of your final mifcarriage. The tranfient and ephemeron popularity that attended you has long fince been declining. Inftead of it, Sir, there is now growing in the people of England a deteftation of your fervility and your hypocrify, equal to the contempt in which they hold your abilities. You fit at prefent in a falfe fecurity; but the cloud will fhortly overwhelm your fortune and annihilate your courage, and you will be eftimated by all men at your true value. The confequences of the difcovery I had rather leave to your reflections, than take upon myfelf the thanklefs office of painting them in their native terror.

M U C I U S.

To the *Right Honourable* HENRY DUNDAS, *Treasurer of the Navy.*

SIR,

THE accusation of Mr. Haftings continues to appear to me not inferior in importance to any bufinefs that was ever brought before a Britifh parliament. The fcribblers of the newf-papers, and the ingenious and indefatigable reporters of parliamentary debates, are it feems of a different opinion. But, with all the deference I entertain for thefe gentlemen, I cannot depart from fo ferious and deliberate a fentiment. Earneftly do I deprecate the moment when the houfe of commons itfelf, made up of men of various defcriptions, merchants, place-hunters and fine gentlemen, fhall become weary of the length into which the bufinefs muft inevitably run, and lofe in its continual recurrence the honefty of inquiry and the value of the fubject. It fhall be my bufinefs, in my humble fphere, to endeavour to keep alive the attention of the public by fuch hints, animadverfions and reflections, as a bufinefs fo various in its tenour, and comprehenfive in its fubject, cannot fail to fuggeft. In the purfuit of this idea, Sir, in the equitable diftribution of commendation and blame, it would be ftrange indeed if the name of Dundas were not among the firft that fuggefted itfelf to my recollection. I have to entreat your indulgence, for having, in my letter of March*, ceded the priority in this refpect to Mr. Pitt. But you are not to be informed, that place and precedence give a title to refpect, and that whoever fits upon the treafury bench will receive the incenfe of a thoufand adorers, even though he were a mere tool in the hands of you or Mr. Jenkinfon.

---

* Vide No. IX. p. 175.

It

It will be neceſſary for me, before I conclude this addreſs, to treat your reſpectable name with ſome degree of freedom. But, that I may convince you that I do this, not from any perſonal pique or private reſentment, I am willing to accoſt you with a peace-offering. The practice is regular; and it would appear to you ſingular indeed, if a ſtranger came to addreſs you upon a ſubject of Eaſt Indian tranſaction without bearing a preſent in his hand. To a man of your learning, and you know, Sir, that " in Scotland every man has a mouthful," an hiſtorical parallel muſt be particularly amuſing. It ſhall not be far fetched, or violent in its application. I will ſimply go for it to a ſtory well known, and that has been quoted more than once in the affair of Mr. Haſtings.

When Cicero undertook the accuſation of Verres—Do not be terrified, Sir: I am not going to lay myſelf out in the eulogium of Mr. Burke, or to affront you with the praiſes of a rival, who ſimply took up the buſineſs of the governor general of Bengal where you laid it down. I leave him to his own noble ſentiments, and to the conſcious worth and integrity of his conduct, convinced that my applauſes could add little to his happineſs or his laurels—When Cicero undertook the accuſation of Verres, the poſture of affairs at Rome, ſo far as related to the proſecution of the peculators and oppreſſors of the diſtant provinces, was to the laſt degree miſerable and degenerate. Repeated efforts had been made to bring the moſt notorious criminals to juſtice, and they had always eſcaped with impunity. They ſeem in various caſes rather to have received the thanks of their country, for the addition to the revenues that occaſionally reſulted from their barbarity and impoſition, than to have ſuffered the juſt reward of their demerits. It was Cicero who firſt openly and fearleſsly ſtated to the public the cauſe of this miſcarriage. The proſecutions had been undertaken upon juſt grounds, but by inſufficient advocates. And he fairly told the court before which he conteſted the right of proſecuting the Roman prætor, that, in " the paſs to which things were arrived, amidſt the profli-
" gate corruption of the governors, the ruin of the moſt valuable
" dependencies, and the diſcredit into which even the ſenatorial
" order had ſunk, in conſequence of theſe repeated acquitals, no

D d 2   " remedy

" remedy could be found to fo numerous inconveniencies, but
" that the bufinefs of accufation fhould be transferred to men
" like himfelf, men of firmnefs and integrity, whofe reputation
" and character were the refult of a courfe of public conduct,
" who had fomething at ftake, and fomething to lofe."

The affairs of Sicily had been particularly the fubject of in-
quiries of this fort. The granary of Italy, the province which
furnifhed Rome with its moft valuable fupplies, it had been
marked out as the devoted fubject of the rapacity and plunder
of thofe who were invefted with delegated power. There were
two kinds of men, as Cicero has told us, that had been fucceffively the profecutors of the provincial defaulters, and whofe
attacks were conceived to lofe their terror with the defaulters
themfelves, as including a kind of unfuitablenefs for the undertaking of fo momentous a meafure. They are defcribed by the
orator with the appellations of *pueri nobiles, quos adhuc eluferunt ;
feu quadruplatores, quos non fine caufa femper contempferunt, ac pro
nihilo putârunt.*

The defeat, Sir, of the profecutions which have been commenced againft men, who, fince the acceffion of our prefent gracious fovereign, have difgraced the name of Britain in India, is
not lefs aftonifhing than the examples I have cited from ancient
hiftory. But the utility of hiftory is to enable us to difcover
from former examples, the clue that may guide us through the
intricacies of thofe which are prefent. It may happen that caufes,
not very diffimilar to thofe which defeated the earlier profecutions in Rome, have contributed to the efcape of criminals
in our own day. Afconius and the ancient commentators
have told us, that one of the profecutions alluded to by Cicero,
as carried on by the noble and generous youth of Rome, was
that of Dolabella, a governor-general of Sicily, in which the
profecutor had been no lefs a man than the illuftrious Julius
Cæfar ; but who was yet very young, and was defirous of
emerging into fame, from the obfcurity of pupilage, by an action of this fort. His meafures however, though well intended, were rafh, injudicious and undigefted ; and were defeated
by the wealth of Dolabella, his political connexions, and the
practiced fubtlety of Hortenfius. The example of Dolabella will
not

not appear to the political obferver very difcordant to that of lord Clive. Like Dolabella, lord Clive had committed crimes that deferved the fevereft animadverfions of the law. Like Dolabella, he was profecuted by one of the moft accomplifhed men of his age, a man diftinguifhed equally in the field of Mars, and by the elegance and beauty of his literary compofitions. General Burgoyne, if we confider him in himfelf, was every way equal to the tafk he had undertaken; but the meafures he adopted were hafty, unconnected and ill advifed. The evidence upon which he meant to cenfure lord Clive was chiefly his own. The felect committee in which general Burgoyne prefided, had been appointed with the view of digefting meafures for the future melioration of the company's affairs, and not with a retrofpect to the paft. Under this impreffion, lord Clive gave in an evidence of an unguarded kind. Add to this, that the evidence, whatever it was, had not been delivered in the houfe; and that no power on earth ought to affume the privilege of delegating their rights in a judicial proceeding. But perhaps the fundamental miftake in the whole bufinefs was, that the plan of general Burgoyne, which went to the proper extent of reprehending the criminal, and confifcating his ill-gotten wealth, terminated as well as commenced in the houfe of commons. The *ex parte* evidence that came before that houfe, furnifhed a good ground for their finding a bill againft lord Clive as a grand jury, but a very infufficient one for their proceeding againft him in the laft refort. Influenced by thefe confiderations, perhaps the houfe of commons did right in their public capacity, in fuperfeding the proceedings of general Burgoyne. In whatever light we confider them, they however went certainly much too far in voting their applaufes and their thanks to fo notorious an impoftor and extortioner.

If, Sir, in the ftory of our Indian tranfactions we can find a model for Cicero's *juvenes nobiliffimi*, we can fcarcely be at a lofs in difcovering the counterpart of his other clafs of infufficient profecutors of public delinquents, the *quadruplatores*. I will defcribe to you, Sir, with all the accuracy with which it is handed down to us, the character and objects of thefe men; and I believe I may then fafely leave it to yourfelf and the world

to make the application of my ſtory. They were, Sir, in general, men obſcure in their beginning, verſed in all the chicanery
and tricks of the law, and whoſe views were mean, perſonal and
pecuniary. The other proſecutors of Rome, whether they
were the *juvenes nobiliſſimi* or the *viri fortes ſpeſtatique*, acted
upon public and honourable motives. Neither their Cæſar
nor their Cicero deſcended to the acceptance of a fee. The
proſecution of delinquents was with them only a generous and
manly way of recommending themſelves to popularity, promotion and public favour. But the purſuits of the *quadruplatores*
were of a different kind. In Rome, as well as in Britain, it was
found neceſſary to hold out to informers and pettifoggers, and
the loweſt claſs of the people, a pecuniary prize as the ſtimulus
of their ſervices. By the laws of Rome, every proſecutor in a
public cauſe, upon the conviction of the offender, was entitled
to a fourth part of the confiſcated eſtate. This was the glorious
object that was continually in the ſight of the *quadruplatores*.
This glittering prize haunted their dreams, animated their
labours, and ſtimulated them to the ſevereſt and moſt unremitting attacks upon delinquents. From this glorious circum-
ſtance they derived their appellation, and the name by which
they were called was the badge of their character. Greatly
were it to be wiſhed, that in modern times, and in recent tranſactions, a ſimilar and no leſs indelible ſtigma were to be fixed
upon the mercenary proſtitute! We are not told whether theſe
honourable gentlemen were known to quit their proſecution in
the height of its progreſs, for the ſake of a conſiderable bribe.
But the information was unneceſſary. Some of us, Sir, have
only to aſk our own hearts, and argue from the *poſtulata* of congenial meanneſs. " Was it not," ſuch a man may inquire,
" the remembrance of the proffered confiſcation that actuated
" their purſuits? And what is there that ſharpens the ſenſe,
" and enlightens the underſtanding, ſo effectually as money?
" Would not therefore an adequate bribe have its mechanical
" and proportioned effect upon them? The event of a proſe-
" cution is future, precarious and uncertain. Fifty thouſand
" pounds in poſſeſſion is worth a plum in reverſion." Such,
Sir, have been the reaſonings of ſome among ourſelves ; and if
the

the world does not belie you, a character formed upon this principle is not totally a stranger to Mr. Dundas.

From lord Clive, and any other person who may have been accused before a British parliament, I turn to Mr. Hastings. I have told you, Sir, that I would not insult you with the eulogium of Mr. Burke, and I will endeavour to keep to my engagement. Let us not talk then of Britain, but of Rome. Let us forget the redeemer of England, and talk of the avenger of Sicily. It is well known how venal and profligate the whole character of the Roman people was become at the time of which I am speaking. The memorable reflection of Jugurtha will not soon be forgotten. When this base and contemptible tyrant had repaired to Rome in order to gain his acquital of the most ungrateful and unprincipled murders, upon his return to the kingdom they had bestowed, he exclaimed, looking back to the city, " O Rome, thou wouldst sell even thyself, if thou couldst but meet with a purchaser!" The character of Rome did not improve from the times of Jugurtha to the times of Verres. Repeated accusations had been brought against the most atrocious delinquents, and they had as often been overborne and defeated. Already Dolabella had been acquitted ; already Terentius Varro had come off with impunity. Already men despaired of the character of the republic and the health of the provinces. Profligate men perpetrated the worst of crimes with gaiety and confidence. They appeared with an erect countenance, and defied the assailant and the prosecutor. The sober, the accurate and the reasoning had long since despaired of the republic. Such as were engaged in the pursuit of fortune or of fame, were so far from undertaking an affair of this kind, that even the youth of Rome gave it up as puritanical and obsolete, and the *quadruplator* was silent. No common integrity, no common zeal in behalf of the republic, no common energy, resolution and firmness would have led a man to encounter so principal a delinquent as Verres. But Cicero burned with the love of his country. He could not bear that the Roman name, of which from his infancy he had learned to make his boast, should cover him with blushes and confusion. His humanity was aroused by the sufferings of the defenceless dependents of the state. He

D d 4

felt

felt that the conftitution of his country was expofed to the moft imminent danger, from fuch pernicious examples and fuch unhallowed fountains of wealth. He undertook the caufe of the whole of the people of Sicily, and in theirs he informs us that he undertook the caufe of every province of the empire, and the character of Rome. And what is moft important of all, his fuccefs was adequate to the generofity of his exertions. Thofe very judges, irrefolute, indecifive or corrupt, who had acquitted a Dolabella and a Varro, could not refift the eloquence of a Cicero and the accumulated guilt of a Verres. From this moment the government of the provinces was moderated; the guilty became timid, cautious and filent. It is perhaps from the fentence againft Verres that we are to account for the protracted duration of the Roman empire.

But I have done, Sir, with retrofpect and parallel, and I come to that which was my immediate incitement to the prefent addrefs. The character of the accufers of a Clive, a Rumbold and an Haftings, has long fince been underftood. The precife merits of the profecution againft the two former have been decided upon. We can readily and familiarly affign, where they were rightly taken and ftrongly put, and what were the immediate caufes of their failure. But the conduct you have held, Sir, within a few weeks paft, is a recent fubject, and I fhould be forry to be foreftalled in fo rich a harveft. The refolutions that you moved in the month of May 1782, are ftill frefh in the memory of every man. We remember in how ftrong and unqualified terms you cenfured the wantonnefs, the impolicy and the cruelty of the Rohilla war. We remember how you endeavoured to move the compaffion of the houfe for the injured rajah of Benares. We recollect how decifively you brought thefe crimes home to Mr. Haftings. We admire and approve the language in which you induced parliament to cenfure him, as having " acted in a manner repugnant to the honour and policy of Britain," as having " brought great calamities on India, and enormous expences on the Eaft India company."

It was naturally to be expected, after having exhibited fo ftrong charges, after having openly profeffed to build your reputation and character on the labours you employed in the reform
of

of India, that you fhould have ftood forward to accufe a man guilty of fo atrocious crimes. But it feems you thought it impolitic : you thought that fubfequent merits, which no other eye but yours could trace, ought to exempt this prefiding conqueror over a mercantile fettlement from the punifhment due to his delinquencies. All this, Sir, is poffible. There have been cafes where fuch a principle ought to prevail. If you faw the peace with the Marattas in an oblique and unnatural point of view, other good men have had their obliquities and paradoxes before Mr. Dundas was born. But, Sir, though you refufed to impeach, it was impoffible you could retract a fentiment the refult of mature examination. Though you did not chufe to drag Mr. Haftings into public, it was impoffible you could ceafe conftantly to affign to him his true character. You might even refufe a general vote of impeachment. But that you fhould vote that the Rohilla war was innocent and unimpeachable in its tenour, is a fact of fo extraordinary a nature, that, if it ftood alone in your character, the hiftorian muft have weight and authority indeed that could prevail upon pofterity to believe it.

Your vote however refpecting the Rohilla war, though fubverfive of every idea of manlinefs and honour, was not unexpected. by a difcerning public. But of all the periods in your hiftory this is the climax. You may live long, you may do much. But human nature can exhibit nothing at once fo incredible and inftructive as your vote refpecting the rajah of Benares. Hitherto you had preferved a ftrange kind of placid and plaufible inconfiftency through the whole tenor of your conduct. The public knew it well, under whatever pretences you thought fit to conceal it, that your fentiments of 1782 were completely different from your fentiments of 1786. A different circle of fociety gradually and infenfibly warped your fentiments. Perfonal views and immediate intereft had actually made you behold the whole continent of India in a point of light quite different from that which had preceded. To the difgrace and blot of creation it muft be acknowledged, that the character of Mr. Dundas had not hitherto been without its fellow.

But

But though, on the fecond of June, the Rohilla war had been fpotlefs, innocent and pure, in contradiction to all your former fentiments, yet, on the ever memorable thirteenth of June, the confifcation and expulfion of the rajah of Benares conftituted, as Mr. Pitt exprefled it, "a crime, a high crime, a high mifdemeanor, a fit fubject for impeachment." What, Sir, is an object of exactly the fame tenour, connected with the fame man, accompanied with the fame *fet-offs*, defcribed by yourfelf with the fame aggravations, an innocent, a fair and a venial action on Friday, and a juft ground for impeachment on the Wednefday night following! This, Sir, is a fpecies of inconfiftency of which the practiced ftatefman and the hackneyed courtier cannot form an idea. From this moment effrontery, arrogance and impudence have loft their name. All that before was moft diffolute and abandoned, is to be regarded as coy referve and virgin purity. For heavens fake, Mr. Dundas, furnifh us with fome excufe, fome plea, fome palliation! Remove from us a burthen which bears down the honeft and ingenuous advocate of human naturein the duft! Permit us not to believe that fuch a caitiff, fuch a wretch, fuch a profligate exifts, as he, who, without a reafon, in dumb mockery of honour and confcience, in a legiflative affembly, and on a fubject involving the fate of millions, can deliver an opinion on Friday, and retract it on Wednefday.

But I quit, Sir, a fubject with horror, which nothing but the interefts of my country and the magnitude of the bufinefs could have prevailed with me to have touched on for a moment, I turn to a character lefs deteftable and abhorrent to every genuine feeling of humanity. The conduct of Mr. Pitt, though lefs pledged and implicated in a thoufand ways than yourfelf, has not failed to excite the aftonifhment of his country. The generous, the philanthropical and the candid are willing to overlook the inferences that might be made from his paft conduct, and to derive his recent vote from an honourable fource. I will not, Sir, invidioufly enter into the reafonings that might be employed on the other fide. I will not with a cold and untimely hand blaft that triumph, which, if it be fhort, he will always regret, but will never regain. I will only tell him with the difinterefted honefty that might grace a counfellor or a friend,

what

what will be the confequences if he does not realife the hopes and promifes he has created in the people of England.   If, Sir, he prove an hypocrite in this great bufinefs, your character may be more ridiculoufly abfurd and more outrageoufly contemptible, but he will be confidered as having arrived at a depth, a deliberation and a fobriety of vice that can never be furpafled. To cheat the fuffering Indian, to cheat the caufe of mercy and humanity of its laft remaining hope, by fo refined a ftrain of policy, as that of voting for one of the charges, in order the more fuccefsfully to traverfe and difarm the whole ! Let him not for a moment flatter himfelf, that the world will be duped into the idea that he ferioufly believed Mr. Haftings to be guilty in the affair of the rajah of Benares, and that he committed no crime in making treaties clafh with treaties, in deferting ally after ally, in imprifoning and plundering the princeffes of Oude, in infulting their confidential fervants, and ftarving their innocent and numerous retinue of either fex.   This would be to fkin over the wound indeed.   No, Sir, all the world knows, no man can refufe to acknowledge, that the tranfactions of the Rohilla war were more inhuman, the counter treaties with Ragoba and Moodagi Boofla more ruinous, and the long perfecution of the princeffes of Oude more truly flagitious and infamous, than the expulfion of the rajah of Benares.   The affair of the Rohillas had fome extenuations.   It had paffed thirteen years before.   It had been neglected and overlooked when it ought to have been profecuted.   But let Mr. Pitt beware.   This is the crifis of his fame.   The affair of Mr. Haftings will rank him among the honeft men or the villains that by turns have conducted the affairs of Britain.   It cannot be difguifed, that in former inftances he has been guilty of hypocrify, difingenuity and prefumption.   But it is not yet too late to redeem his character.   An indulgent public is prepared to afcribe his having wandered into crooked and difhonourable paths, to the inexperience of youth, to the baleful counfels of a Dundas, a Prettyman and a Jenkinfon.

M U C I U S.

Modern Characters, by the Right Honourable WILLIAM PITT, *as they were exhibited in* Saint Stephen's *Chapel, during the Debate respecting the Raja of* Benares.

MORNING CHRONICLE.

Die Martis, 13 *Junii,* 1786.

MR. FOX.

" HE said he should take care to avoid entering into the business with that sort of temper and spirit which some gentlemen manifested; and should particularly guard against any *impression, similar* to that which the right honourable mover had been so desirous of making on the house, in a manner which he thought of all others the most unfair and most inconsistent with every principle of law and justice. He should neither suffer such means to bias him in voting a censure, where he did not think censure was merited: nor, on the other hand, would he permit his *indignation* at such *unjustifiable* conduct so far to get the better of him, as to make him refuse such a vote, where he thought he was in conscience bound to give it."

MR. BURKE.

" The second part of the charge, Mr: Pitt said, was intitled, " Designs of Mr. Hastings to ruin the raja of Benares," and it stated that " Mr. Hastings seemed early to have resolved, " when opportunity should occur, on a severe revenge; and " that having obtained in his casting vote a majority in coun- " cil, on the death of Sir John Clavering and Mr. Monson, " he did suddenly make an extraordinary demand on the raja." Mr. Pitt desired the house to *pause* for a moment, to consider the full force of the insinuation contained in these words. Could there, he asked, be a more *malignant* charge brought against any man, than that which he had just stated ? In the mean time, all that would be necessary for him to state to the committee, as a complete antidote to every unfavourable impression which might have been created by the *unwarrantable acrimony* of the charge, was, that two days before the resolution for exacting the five

lacks

lacks of rupees from Cheit Sing had been propofed in council, Mr. Haftings had received the account of the breaking out of the French war. To have paffed over fuch a circumftance as this, fo ftriking and fo obvious, and to difcover a motive fo bafe and diabolical as was here imputed, could be accounted for only on principles *extremely injurious to the candour and integrity* of the right honourable gentleman ; or by fuppofing that the laborious and pertinacious attention, which diftinguifhed his conduct in every other part of this proceeding, had thrown him in the prefent inftance, *more unfortunately for himfelf* than Mr. Haftings, fomewhat off his guard."

MR. FRANCIS.

" Mr. Pitt was through his whole fpeech *uncommonly fevere* upon Mr. Francis, making feveral pointed allufions to certain publications of that gentleman, and contrafting, comparing and combining many apt quotations from them and from his *fpeeches,* that feemed to have a ftriking effect upon the houfe ; but, *not being in poffeffion of the papers to which he referred,* we are unable to give a fketch of thefe paffages to our readers."

The above paffages naturally fuggeft to the mind of the reader a crowd of reflections. But that the fenfation they excite may not lead us to be guilty of any impropriety, we will firft examine the juftice of the kind of reafoning upon which one of thefe characters is built. That of Mr. Burke is the moft confpicuous and animated, and fhall therefore be felected for our difcuffion.

The controverfy refpecting Mr. Haftings's conduct towards the raja of Benares, 9 July 1778, lies in the choice we are to make between two motives to which it may be imputed. Did Mr. Haftings demand of the raja of Benares £.50,000 in addition to his annual rent of £.240,000, becaufe he entertained fome fecret difpleafure againft the raja? Did Mr Haftings make

this

this demand, becaufe a war had taken place, or was likely to take place, between Great Britain and France? The latter of thefe queftions muft undoubtedly, unhefitatingly, be anfwered in the affirmative. But there are two confiderations to be taken into our view, in deciding upon any action : the one the occafion, the other the principle ; the one the pretence, the other the motive. The breaking out of a war between Great Britain and France, was certainly the occafion and pretence of Mr. Haftings's extraordinary demand. Let us take Mr. Haftings's character as low as you pleafe. In his fituation, and with his high office, fome plea, fome palliation, fome colouring was abfolutely neceffary. Did Dionyfius of Syracufe, or any of the tyrants of antiquity, ever impofe a fine upon a man, without at the fame time imputing a crime to him ? Imputations of this fort are the cheapeft things in the world. Impofe filence on the accufed, and you may tell what ftory you pleafe. The point is only to make a Cheit Sing a fugitive, and to hang a Nuncomar. The abfent and the dead tell no tales. If the war with France had not opportunely occurred, Mr. Haftings muft have been a fhallow fellow indeed, if he could have found no other pretence for extorting money. The art of calumny is not a whit more refined than the art of fwindling.

But more than we have here granted may be true. It might not only be the occafion and pretence of Mr. Haftings's action, it may have been a real motive of his conduct, to provide againft the contingencies of war. Mr. Haftings had already fent a body of troops acrofs the peninfula, to place the fceptre of the Marattas in the hands of Ragoba. He had already opened a negociation with Moodagi Boofla, the profeffed object of which was to difpofe of the fame fovereignty to him. This was fcattering the feeds of a moft extenfive war. Mr. Haftings might forefee that neither Hyder Ali, nor Nana Furnavefe, nor Madagi Scindia, nor Nizam Ali, would be the tame fpectators of fuch unprecedented tranfactions. It is fair then to fuppofe, that to maintain the war, which he had thus wantonly accumulated, was one object in the view of Mr. Haftings. But does it therefore follow, that he had no other object ? It is poffible ;

but

but muft we conclude every thing that is poffible to be true?
Did Mr. Pitt never hear of the affociation of ideas? Has he
never learned that one action might have, not two, but two
hundred caufes, concurring in its production? Did he never
read Hartley, or Locke, or any of the great philofophers who
have treated of this fubject? Did he never find in Pope, the
moft fuperficial of all the pretenders to philofophy, that

> " One fingle action fhall its end produce,
> " Yet ferves to fecond too fome other ufe."

It appears then, which Mr. Pitt does not feem to imagine,
that the motive affigned by Mr. Burke might be a leading motive in Mr. Haftings's conduct. And if it might be fo, then
it may be alfo, that Mr. Burke very fincerely and very honeftly
believed that it was fo. But let us confider Mr. Haftings's fubfequent treatment of the raja of Benares; let us reflect upon
the immenfe fine of £.500,000, which Mr. Haftings had refolved
to impofe upon the raja, without in reality the fhadow of a
crime. Let us recollect, that he refufed Cheit Sing fo much as
a hearing; that he conftrued his humble and abject fubmiffions
into fo many marks of contumacy; that he arrefted this prince
in his own palace, in the midft of his fubjects; that, without
compunction, and without remorfe, he drove him out to wander
as a fugitive through the nations of India. Was all this done
only to maintain the war of Great Britain againft France? Or
is it not natural to imagine, that a conduct fo connected, fo
regular, and fo unrelenting, did, from its beginning to its termination, proceed from the fame motive, and originate in the
fame refentments? The motive that Mr. Pitt affigns for the firft
demand, for the conduct he approves, will not apply to the
concluding proceedings, and the conduct he condemns. Let
Mr. Pitt then tell us what was the motive in the laft inftance,
and we will tell him what was the motive in the firft. But this
will lead us to the fame conclufion with Mr. Burke; to the fame
" bafe and diabolical" influence, the fuggeftion of which has
already excited Mr. Pitt's warmeft indignation. And this is
what

what he has treated as an example of "malignity," as an idea
not to be accounted for but from a want of "candour," and a
want of "integrity!" And this is what he has defcribed, by a
phrafe he fo well underftands, by the watch-word of a daftardly
cabal*, as an imputation made by Mr. Burke " unfortunately
for himfelf."

It is impoffible that the imputation of want of candour and
integrity can ever be unfuccefsfully made, without its rebound-
ing with ten-fold force upon the head of the calumniator. What
principles, we are naturally led to afk, could induce Mr. Pitt to
fcatter about thefe infamous afperfions upon all the moft diftinguifhed characters in oppofition to him? If a man fees every
object difcoloured, the defect is not in the object itfelf, but in
his diftempered optics. If a man thinks every one around him
a knave and a fcoundrel, the impartial fpectator will not afcribe
the obliquity to thefe characters, but to the man that mifrepre-
fents them.

And is this conduct any thing new in Mr. Pitt? Let us look
through the ftory of this angry boy, this impertinent Kaftril,
from the commencement of his political career. It was thus he
treated lord North in the American war. It was thus he treated
Mr. Sheridan and Mr. Burke. It is with this language he has
conftantly oppofed Mr. Fox. It was in the fame fpirit that he
formerly treated the difinterefted interference of Mr. Powys, as
the duplicity and the treachery of a SPY! Is it fhallownefs of
intellect that reduces this man, for want of argument, continually to have recourfe to mean perfonalities? Is it any fingular
ftructure of mind that leads him continually to behold every
thing under thefe dark, infidious and unmanly colours? Let
us afcribe to him, individually, as much fincerity as you pleafe;
that foul is narrow to a proverb, that can never think well of
thofe who differ from him. Mr. Pitt, when we examine him
in this light, is to be confidered as the Political Methodift. The
latter is liberal of damnation in the other world; the former is
equally liberal of profligacy, and want of principle, in this.

It is natural, upon this occafion, to compare the conduct of
Mr. Pitt towards his opponents, with the conduct of his op-

* Vid. Pol. Herald, Vol. I· p. 179.

ponents towards Mr. Pitt. Never, we will venture to fay, in the annals of mankind, has any man been treated with fo unexampled liberality. How prodigal were the compliments he received from lord North, at the fame time that he purfued that nobleman like a pirate and a murderer! With what generofity, with what lenity and mildnefs has he not been treated upon every occafion by Mr. Fox! While the world imputes to him a fhare in the nefarious proceedings of Mr. Dundas, his adverfaries will not fuffer a whifper of this kind to efcape them. While the whole kingdom laughs at the fhallownefs of his plans and the puerility of his experiments, they continue to fpeak of his abilities with management and refpect. At the very moment that we write, a friend whom we truft with the firft fight of our literary effufions, hints to us, that we are in danger of being too fevere, and that the public will not give us credit for our impartiality. Good God! what is the meaning of impartiality? Does it mean a cold and phlegmatic balance between virtue and vice, that would not for the world give the one a preference to the other? Does it mean a poor, unenterprifing timidity, that trembles to defcribe things as they are? Oh, that we could once fhake off this lethargic and ill-judged moderation! Mr. Pitt would no longer dare to throw about his wanton afperfions and his unmanly calumnies. We may fay to him, as an injured man once did to a daftardly clergyman: " It is your gown protects you! Your cloth gives you the pitiful courage to employ language that no gentleman would utter, and no gentleman fhould hear! If the world would but once fhake off the idle and ridiculous prejudice in favour of your profeffion; would eftimate you by your real merits, and try you by the fame laws which govern all other men, we fhould no longer fee virtue trampled upon, honour infulted, and all the decencies of fociety violated with impunity."

M U C I U S.

To the People of Ireland.

LETTER I.

Freemen and Citizens,

THERE are two nations in the prefent day, that have entered the career of heroifm and liberty, and have boldly fought to inrol their names with the moft illuftrious periods of Athens and Rome. Thefe two nations are America and Ireland. The honours of America, the diftinguifhed names of their heroes, a Franklin and a Paine, a Wafhington and a Montgomery, and the generous efforts of every private citizen, were dearly earned and perfeveringly exerted, and will wear well. Believe me, the reflections that are now fought to be caft upon their rifing polity, will be as evanefcent, as the more honeft and bold faced illiberality that treated them with the epithets of robbers, rebels and traitors. Miftakes may have been made by the individual ftates of particular provinces; but the conduct of the general reprefentative body has been uniform and unimpeachable. Men, as yet unexperienced in the conduct of nations, may be induced into error; but their errors will not be leading, and their misfortunes will not laft. After a few impotent aud injudicious efforts, they will affume the firmnefs of manhood and the adroitnefs of experience. They have fet out too well, to fell their honours at a bafe and ignoble market.

I have not endeavoured to make my voice be heard acrofs the ftraits that feparate Great Britain from Ireland, in order to addrefs you with the voice of mifreprefentation and flattery.

flattery. This it would difgrace me to utter, and it would
difhonour you to hear. I do not therefore hefitate to tell
you, that America holds the firft place in the honourable field,
and that you are only entitled to the fecond rank. She
began earlier and has done more. Ireland, however noble
have been her beginnings, has not yet proceeded to the termination which fhe marked out for herfelf. If fhe ceafe at the
prefent moment, fhe will yet be remembered with honour.
Thofe names, which may now be blackened by envy, or
wrought into miftaken hoftility againft each other, a Charle-
mont, a Grattan, a Sharman and a Flood, will be inrolled
by pofterity in the brighteft pages of hiftoric fame. But
after all, their memory will be accompanied with a deep
regret, that fo great abilities fhould have exifted, and fo gene•
rous efforts been employed, with fo little fuccefs.

You have too objects to purfue, which, if it be defirable
to unite, it is ftill requifite not to confound. Your objects
are commerce and conftitution. Much, very much you have
obtained, under the firft of thefe heads. It may be doubted
whether any thing can be added to your exifting acquifitions.
The diftreffes of your manufacturers, and the cry for protecting duties, appear indeed, at firft fight, to demonftrate
that fomething yet remains to be done. But this fort of
proof is queftionable and indecifive. The advantages of
an extended commerce are not obtained in a moment. The
harveft cannot be reaped on the fame day in which the feed
is committed to the earth. The moft falutary revolutions of
commerce are productive of temporary and partial diftrefs.
The views and the purfuits of numerous bodies of men
cannot quietly be turned from their old channels. Thus
when the foldier and the failor are difbanded, and returned
again to the arts of peace, a momentary confufion is created ;
our roads are infefted by daring plunderers, and our houfes
broken through by the pilferer and the profligate.

It muft be granted indeed that commerce never ftands
on fo noble and fair a bafis, as when it is made free as the
air we breathe, and every fpecies of manufacture and exchange
is committed whole and unmutilated to the hands of induftry.

It

It muft be granted that the majority of nations, that have ultimately become fuccefsful in the arts of wealth, have fet out with protecting their infant commodities. But perhaps neither of thefe are effential to your welfare. At any rate, be affured, that neither of them are worth the being purchafed at the expence of your independence. Protecting duties muft never be expected to be tolerated by the government of Britain. If you are determined on thefe, you muft bid farewel to her friendfhip, her patronage and her alliance. You muft caft yourfelves into the arms of France, and you muft be contented to incur thofe expenfive eftablifhments, that are neceffary to enable a nation that ftands alone to make itfelf refpected in the eyes of Europe. That freedom of commerce, which fhall open to you the ports and the markets of Great Britain, is not fo utterly incompatible with your fituation. But after all I doubt, though I do not mean to decide, whether it be not more for your intereft, to run with Great Britain the generous race of foreign markets, than to interfere with a proud, a wealthy and a jealous nation in the articles of her home confumption.

Such is the balance of the account on the fide of commerce. The article of conftitution requires a nicer fcrutiny and a more " dragon watch." It would be impertinent in a private inhabitant of Great Britain, to point out to you the dangers that were included in the fyftem of commercial intercourfe, propofed to you eighteen months ago by Mr. Pitt. It was impoffible that fo intelligent and quick fighted a nation fhould be blind to the confequences of the important conceffion of the whole prerogative of their external legiflation. You difcovered the treacherous hook, and you expofed it with an indignation that will do you honour to the lateft pofterity. Your caution and your vigilance need not to be awakened to a fubject like this. Let the commercial propofitions come to you at what time and under what transformation they may, you will proudly vindicate your original decifion.

But it is unqueftionably certain that adminiftration have at this moment fome grand and confiderable meafure *in petto* refpecting the politics of your fide of the water. The boon

they

they fo generoufly offered has been rejected by you; and they retained for twelve months a childifh and unmanly refentment and fullennefs. They have now however recovered their good humour. All the fympathetic chords of their foul are in motion, and fpontaneoufly vibrate to the name of Ireland. Whatever they deny to India or to Britain, whatever they refufe to the cry of oppreffed millions, or however they may cheat us upon the darling topic of our national debt, all their bounty is collected to be beftowed in one illuftrious gift upon the fons of Hibernia. Here they mean to confecrate their benevolence and to immortalize their names.

There is a fenfe in which your happy country has nothing to do with the character of fucceffive adminiftrations. You are bound to purfue your interefts and your claims, unbiaffed by the whiftling of a name, and undiverted by the character and the virtues of thofe who may fit at the helm of Britain. But though you fhould never be led away by the popularity or manlinefs of individuals in power, yet it is impoffible your jealoufies fhould not be more indignantly awakened againft the infidious, the defpotic and the profligate. The character of the perfons who now direct the affairs of this country can never be mufic to your ear. The men, to whom in reality the knee of every Briton bows, a Thurlow, a Hawkefbury and a Dundas, are a triumvirate of the greateft tories, the moft determined adventurers in the caufe of arbitrary power, that this country ever boafted. In regard of the docility and the improvement of their pupil, the oftenfible firft minifter of England, if he had partially withheld all marks of it from his native foil, Ireland however would be a fufficient witnefs of his rapid progrefs, and his fpeedy promife of confummate perfection. The bill againft the liberty of the prefs, the proceedings by attachment, the promotion of the moft obnoxious and unpopular characters in Ireland, the eftablifhment of an arbitrary police, are a part only of a catalogue of depotifm, always repeated, and never to be forgotten.

The prefent that is intended you by thefe men, will come to you no doubt under fpecious names and impofing appearances. But truft them not. All that they will ever offer

you,

you, will infallibly either be the odious propositions under a different form, or a political and legislative union. The first of these it surpasses their skill to disguise even from the most shallow penetration; and the last is by much the most probable. Leaving therefore for the present the discussion of those measures by which they are conceived to have been willing to pave the way for their decisive effort, and which may afford ample subject for future discussion, I will merely suggest some of those considerations that ought most to awaken your fears, respecting the consequences of a political union.

The principal circumstance that is calculated to imprefs the mind of him, who reflects upon this idea, is the very different situation of the two countries proposed to be united. England has run her career of glory, has suffered the gradual exchange of sturdy heroifm for effeminate weaknefs and political profligacy, and it remains as a problem for the fpeculative politician, whether, under these circumstances, she can preferve her greatnefs, her liberties and her independence. But granting, which appears to be the idea that incefantly gains ground as the fubject is more examined, that she will be able to preferve her place in the balance of foreign nations, it will however still be true, that her greatnefs will not be such as to form an object of envy to the moralift and the philofopher. The virtues of public fpirit, of a generous oblivion of interefts, and a kind of union of hearts and exertions, those virtues, which can alone render a people venerable and illuftrious, will at any rate be claimed by few among her fons. The eftablifhed and the general character will be the oppofite of all this. Frivolity and falfe refinement will have an univerfal fpread, and the honour of the duelift and the courtier be every where fubftituted for the magnanimity of the citizen.

From Great Britain, the center of empire, I turn my attention to Ireland. This country, though long recorded in the annals of the world, may be affirmed not to have begun her career through the various ftages from barbarifm to refinement. She has been borne down by the remorfelefs hand of fictitious patronage and real defpotifm. She has been

nipped

nipped by the untimely blights of neglect. An arbitrary power, that centered in her own bofom, could never have been productive of fo fatal effects. The interefts of a court, however uncontroulable, will for the moft part coincide with the interefts of the country. The means, which are to make that rich and profperous, are the only means to make the prefiding power great and refpectable. But the policy of England with regard to your country has been widely different. She has affiduoufly deprived you of the means of vigour. She has crufhed all your efforts in behalf of liberty and commerce. She has defired to make your ifland a fource of penfion and emolument to her creatures, and a free port to her merchants and manufacturers. In every other refpect her object was your political annihilation. But you have rifen fuperior to the influence of this miferable fyftem. You feized the aufpicious moment, and you made your voice be heard with energy and effect. The depreffion in which you had fo long been held, feemed only to give you vigour and fternnefs. You fpurned the yoke, and the elafticity you difcovered, upon the removal of the weight that oppreffed you, was equal to the moft arduous objects.

Perhaps there could appear to the eye of the philofopher few objects more calamitous or more unnatural, than the union of two countries circumftanced as I have defcribed. It is like that refined piece of cruelty, fcarcely to be named by the tongue, or indured by the recollection of humanity, of tying a living body to a dead one, and caufing them to putrify and perifh together. All your efforts and your conceptions are to be crufhed in the bud. You are to be hurried at once from the feeblenefs of infancy to the inanition of old age. The bloom of manhood, the firmnefs of maturity, all that is worthy of a rational being or of a great nation, is to be profcribed you. You are to be ftretched in the bed of Procruftes, and from the vigour and nerve of an Hercules, to be brought down to the unwholefome lanknefs of one expiring under a gradual decline. Is this an idea to be endured for a moment ? Is there any thing from which the mind recoils fo inftinctively and fo irrefiftibly?

The generous sons of Hibernia have for some time been infpired with the glowing conceptions of privilege and freedom. If you have not gained any thing permanent for yourfelves, that will weigh in the fcale againft the acquifitions of America, in another point of view you have excelled her. The chara&er of her refiftance was rather fullennefs and inflexibility than adventure. The pulfe of her financial operations uniformly ran low. Her armies were muftered flowly, reluĉtantly and for the emergence of the moment. Your condu&t was meafured by another fcale. To you was referved the wonderful exhibition of an army of eighty thoufand men, colle&ed by no motives of intereft, and kept together by the abftra&, but liberal principles of independence and conftitution. What might we not promife from beginnings like thefe? What was the excellence and value of the things you a&tually purfued? A legiflature independent of every other power, and a legiflature that fhould be the adequate and incorruptible reprefentative of the nation. By a political union, every thing you have gained and every thing you looked for are to be given up together. From the independence you have earned you are to recede. The intire and unfi&titious liberty, the conception of which you formed, you are to abjure for ever. And what is it you are to gain by all this? The privilege of yielding a new fphere of patronage to the minifter, of corrupting and poifoning the conftitution of Britain, after you have bafely yielded up your own.

I have mentioned thefe confiderations firft, becaufe they are of a thoufand times the greateft importance, and becaufe they are what no fophiftry can difpute with you. There are other matters worthy of your matureft confideration. You are to examine what will, upon the proje&ted meafure, be the ftate of your taxation. In Scotland, the land-tax only is lower than that of England, and almoft all the other revenues are colle&ed by the fame meafure on both fides the Tweed. Thus it was obferved by Mr. Dempfter, that the horfe-tax, which bears lightly upon the farmer of England, has in many places completely ruined the cultivator of Scotland. Other cafes

in

in point might be eafily be adduced. "But what you lofe in "revenue, you will gain in commerce." And is this likely to be the cafe? I will not now urge you with the remark, that commerce would be an ill exchange for conftitution; but I will afk you how reafonable is this plan for the acquifition of commercial profperity? You are to reduce yourfelves to a petty province of the empire of Great Britain. Your court, your capital, every thing that yet retains among you any part of the noble and the opulent is to be deftroyed. You are to part with liberty, with conftitution, with independence. And thefe are the lures by which you are to invite merchants to feitle among you; thefe are the means of creating capital and attracting commerce. Is it by fuch pretenfions that you are to be deceived? Are you clear-fighted and intelligent to a proverb, merely that at laft you may be taken in by affertions, hollow and deftitute of the flighteft plaufibility?

M U C I U S.

POLITICAL HERALD, and REVIEW.

N U M B E R   XIV.

POLITICAL AND HISTORICAL SPECULATIONS.

Memoirs of the Administration of the Government of Madras *during the Presidency of Lord* MACARTNEY.

THE affairs of India have become every day more important and interesting. The distance of the country, the intricacy of its government, the uncouth names by which men and things have usually been described to us, and perhaps we may add, the obscurity that has sedulously been thrown upon the subject, deterred for a considerable time, the bulk of the inhabitants of this country from affording it that curiosity and attention which its importance deserved. But this sort of prejudice is fast wearing away. The magnitude of the object has increased by the loss of America; and the transactions of India have engrossed so much of the discussions of parliament, that the natural bias of Englishmen can no longer be indulged, consistently with an ignorance of this subject. The public do not now reject information respecting the affairs of the East; on the contrary, they desire information, provided it be conveyed to them in a manner, easy, methodical, intelligent and perspicuous. We know not whether it is foreign to this consideration to add, that perspicuity has been rendered more attainable by the circumstance of the sudden changes of power, which once took place in that country, having been for some time suspended. With the exception of the dominions of Hyder, there is fcarcely one of the great princes of India who has not filled the throne for twenty years.

The curiofity of the public can fcarcely take a more ufeful direction ; and we are defirous both to indulge and to affift it. The character and the profperity of this country are both of them infeparably involved in the bufinefs of India. It is impoffible that every man of benevolence and philanthropy fhould not be anxious for the firft of thefe. That cruelty, tyranny, ufurpation and avarice fhould be confidered as conftituting the character of Britain in any part of the world, he will fincerely lament. Perhaps he will lament it more for the fake of human nature, than for the fake of England; more from his regret for the calamities it may produce than for the temporary difhonour and obloquy it may involve. To defire to afcertain the truth of fuch imputations is a laudable propenfity. It is particularly fo at this moment, when the French are forming a new Eaft India company, when that country feems to be the favourite object of their politics, and when it is well known and openly avowed, that their next ftruggle for fuperiority with Britain will be made in Afia.

In felecting a portion of Indian tranfaction for our difcuffion, we could fcarcely avoid giving a preference to the adminiftration of lord Macartney. Popular prejudice and the general and loofe ideas that are entertained upon the fubject, have been the guide of our choice. The government of this nobleman has been fuppofed to be equally guided by integrity and capacity. He has been ftated under the afpect of a reformer, at the fame time that he avoided the vifionary errors and the premature misfortunes too often attendant upon that character. We are more willing to hold up an example to attract than an example to deter.

But this has not been the thing that has ftruck us principally in the fituation of lord Macartney. His reception in this country has been too fingular not to excite attention. He has been hailed with general praife, not with enlightened and difcriminating approbation. An extreme mifunderftanding has arifen between him and fome of thofe perfons who were the principal objects of his government ; and the accufed and the accufing

have

have been treated with fimilar applaufe. Nothing has been inquired into, nothing illuftrated ; but a general veil of encomium has been extended, where the probe of juftice and the torch of truth would have been much more properly employed. In the official papers of the board of controul lord Macartney has been blamed for employing " too little of addrefs, civility and conciliation" towards thofe very perfons, who inveighed againft him in the grofleft terms, and accufed him of every crime that could have difgraced the governor or the man. There feems to be a fpirit too general in this country, of confounding the virtue and the vice, the right and the wrong of the perfons who have been concerned in the direction of our affairs in India. But the example is of the moft fatal tendency. We muft never expect to fee rectitude and honour fpringing up in that foil, if we do not diftribute to its different characters, the different degrees of honour and reproach to which they are juftly entitled.

Before we enter upon that which it is the immediate object of this paper to illuftrate, we fhall allow ourfelves in fome meafure in an hiftorical retrofpect of the fituation and ftate of the countries to be governed. It will appear in the progrefs of our narrative, that the fubject of lord Macartney's adminiftration could fcarcely be underftood, and that its merits could in no fort be eftimated without fome previous information of this kind. Ever fince the Eaft India company has been eftablifhed in its territorial acquifitions, two countries, of confiderable magnitude, have been fubject to their regulation. The provinces of Bengal, Bahar and Oriffa, which conftitute the largeft portion of their dominions, have been fubject to the prefidency and government general of Calcutta. The region of the Carnatic on the coaft of Coromandel is under the direction of the council of Madras. The fubject of the former of thefe two governments is by much the moft uncomplicated and intelligible. Though the family of the nabob was fuffered to exift, the prince was deprived of all fhadow of power, and his diftinction confifted merely in the externals of a court and an honourable kind of imprifonment. The power of the company is as abfolute

and

and uncontroulable over the dependencies of Calcutta, as that of the pefhwa in the empire of the Marattas, or of Hyder, under the appellation of dayva, in the kingdom of Myfore. On the contrary, in the dependencies of the prefidency of Madras, the nabob of Arcot has not merely retained the fhow and eftablifhment of a prince, he has alfo preferved in his hands the collection of the revenue and the maintenance of a confiderable number of troops. In this country therefore there exifted a double government of no very pleafant and dignified nature. The company were here, as in Bengal, the natural fovereigns. Their troops were fcarcely lefs numerous, and were a thoufand times better difciplined than thofe of their dependant and ally. Their will could not fail to conftitute the ultimate law; and whatever thing it was upon which the fervants in India, or their mafters at home were unalterably refolved, muft infallibly be carried into execution. The fituation of the nabob, was neceffarily unpleafant and exafperating. To poffefs all the trappings of monarchy, the revenue, the army, the mint, and at the fame time to be unable to chufe a fingle meafure, or fuccefsfully to counteract a fingle oppreffion, was a fituation new in a manner in the hiftory of the world.

The perfonal character of Mahomet Ali did not difpofe him quietly to acquiefce in this fupine and inefficient fituation. His difpofitions might for a time be enigmatical to the inhabitants of this country; but our experience upon the fubject has been fo ample, that it cannot at this late period be eafy for us to miftake them. We fhall not greatly expofe ourfelves to the hazard of contradiction, if we defcribe the nabob of Arcot as a man of mean talents and fordid inclinations. Oppreffive and inhuman, imbecil and abject, his ambition kept pace with his weaknefs. The more he was formed to excite the contempt and derifion of mankind, the more eager was his paffion for extenfive empire and irrefiftible fway. The mode in which only this paffion could be gratified, was, fince he could not openly oppofe, to apply himfelf fecretly to undermine the meafures of the company. If he could not browbeat the government of Madras in the cabinet, or vanquifh them in the field, it was ftill poffible for him to enter into an invidious fort of
collufion

collufion with them. If his troops were an undifciplined rabble, money however has an eftablifhed currency in every country, and among the fubjects of every nation.

There were two objections to this being employed in the open and eftablifhed methods of corurption and bribery. The fervants of the company were ftrictly forbidden the acceptance of prefents; and, however their inclinations might prompt them to receive them, their timidity in many cafes would be as ftrong as their avarice. Befide this, the revenues of the nabob of Arcot were limited. They were eftimated in their moft flourifhing ftate, at £1,200,000 per annum, and the furplus of this fum was infufficient to fatisfy the cravings of European rapacity. A method was difcovered that fuperfeded each of thefe difficulties. By granting to the fervants of the company pecuniary bonds and affignments of territory, under the denomination of repaying a loan, the prohibition againft prefents was evaded. The bonds of the nabob bore an enormous intereft, and were therefore infinitely more profitable than prefents to a fimilar amount, in the firft inftance, could poffibly be. It is of the very nature of avarice to be incapable of fatiety; a benefit therefore, which was unlimited in its ultimate amount, was perhaps, of all others, the beft calculated to fatisfy the refinements of this paffion.

We cannot readily trace the period in which this fort of commerce originally commenced. From the year 1749, in which Anaverdi Khan, the father of Mahomet Ali, died, to the conclufion of the peace of Paris in 1763, both the nabob and the prefidency were too deeply involved with their common enemies, to be at liberty to watch with accuracy the proportion of power that was engroffed by either. Accordingly, at the termination of the adminiftration of governor Pigot, who returned to Europe at this latter period, the pecuniary commerce of the nabob of Arcot with the fervants of the company does not appear to have been in a flourifhing ftate. Soon after, its progrefs was confiderable; and previoufly to the year 1766, the debt of the nabob was faid to amount to £960,000. In order to carry on thefe tranfactions with greater fuccefs, and to a wider extent, the nabob quitted his

his capital of Arcot, and took up his refidence in a mean houfe in the fuburbs of Madras. He perhaps obtained the double advantage of reducing the expences of the durbar*, and of having the government of the company immediately under his eye, and within reach of his controul.

It was about this period that a plan was formed by Mahomet Ali, on one part, and his creditors and affignees on the other, of the moft extraordinary nature that is perhaps recorded in the annals of hiftory. Undifmayed by the lofs of power and fovereignty which he had fo recently incurred, he confpired to extend the limits of his empire beyond the bounds of the Carnatic, and to reduce all the fouthern part of the peninfula, comprehended under the general name of the Decan, into his fubjection. For this purpofe, he propofed to enter into an offenfive alliance, and a treaty of partition with the nation of the Marattas. Hyder Ali on the weft, and Nizam Ali Khan to the north of the Carnatic, were to be the facrifices of this comprehenfive defign. The company, influenced by the gratitude and admiration of his acquifitions, were to render him perfectly independent, and his independence was to be guaranteed to him by the French. From this moment the Englifh were to be extinguifhed as a fovereign power in that part of India, and were to appear in no other light than as contractors for the provifion of armies, and the hire of mercenaries. They accordingly withdrew the company's garrifons out of the forts and ftrong holds of the Carnatic; and they affected to decline the receiving the ambaffadors from foreign courts, and to refer them to the nabob of Arcot.

It was probably in connexion with this project, that a war was undertaken by the nabob and the prefidency, fo early as the year 1765, againft Nizam Ali. The titles of this prince are, fuba of the Decan and king of Golconda; and his original pretenfions amounted to a feudal fovereignty over Myfore, the Carnatic, and the contiguous principalities of the

---

* A Perfian term for the ceremonial eftablifhment of a public character.

peninfula. They have however, almoſt all of them, obtained by degrees an entire independency. The operations of the preſent war terminated in the obtaining for the Engliſh a tract of land, commonly called the Northern Circars, connecting the Carnatic with the Bengal provinces, and calculated to put into our hands the entire command of the whole coaſt bordering upon the bay. It was to be held by them as a fief of the fuba of the Decan, and they engaged to pay a certain annual tribute. The concluſion of peace was almoſt immediately fucceeded by a general confederacy of Mahomet Ali, Nizam Ali Khan and the Marattas, to conquer and divide among them the territories of Hyder. But that able ſtateſman and illuſtrious warrior foon found means to fow diſſention among the allies; and the Engliſh and the nabob found themſelves in a few months left alone to oppoſe the power, and contend with the juſt reſentment of the monarch of Myſore. The reſult of theſe proceedings was the invaſion of the Carnatic by Hyder, who ſpread ravage, calamity and deſolation over the face of that once flouriſhing province, and at length dictated a peace to the ſervants of the company, at the gates of Madras.

This ſeries of mortifications might naturally have been expected to have infuſed a degree of ſobriety and moderation into the councils of the nabob of Arcot and his European confederates. It ſo far fucceeded as to induce them to turn their efforts againſt princes of a lower rank, and enemies leſs incapable of being brought under ſubjection. The firſt ſovereign that felt the effects of this change in their deſigns, was the raja of Tanjore, a country to the ſouth of Madras, and furrounded on every ſide by the dominions of the nabob. The ſecret motive that influenced the Engliſh creditors, and tended to increaſe the harmony between them and their royal debtor, was the deſire of enlarging the extent of a prey, with whoſe agreeable nature they were ſo well acquainted. In undertaking a war againſt the fuba of the Decan, and the prince of Myſore, they had readily conceived that the vaſt acquiſition of territory which would have been the reſult of fucceſs, would have enabled the nabob to indulge his gratitude, in be-

ſtowing

ſtowing the moſt unbounded rewards upon the founders of his fortune. But ſuppoſing him diſappointed, and this perhaps did not appear to them altogether improbable, they perceived the greateſt preſent advantage in the contracts of his army, the jobs that attend upon a war, and the plunder that they ſuppoſed muſt infallibly attend ſo promiſing a deſign. The ſame motives doubtleſs had their ſhare in exciting them to declare againſt the raja of Tanjore. They had already exhauſted the treaſury, and already obtained aſſignments on the moſt fertile and beſt cultivated territories of the nabob of Arcot. The raja of Tanjore was ſuppoſed to have accumulated the greateſt riches of almoſt any of the princes of India. His country had been ſtiled the paradiſe of the Carnatic, and it had yet been untouched by thoſe devouring locuſts, the Engliſh ſoucars.* In this ſituation, it is not wonderful that the creditors of the nabob ſhould have diſcovered in the raja a diſpoſition to rebel. Mahomet Ali applied to the preſidency of Madras, to aſſiſt him in ſubduing that diſaffected chief, on the eighteenth of September 1771. Accordingly, an expedition was ordered for that purpoſe, by governor Dupré, under the command of general Richard Smith. When the town of Tanjore was upon the point of being ſtormed, the raja was ſo happy as to find means of obtaining a compromiſe from Omdat ul Omra, the eldeſt ſon of the nabob, who ſuperintended the incurſion, on the twenty-fourth day of October.

An expedition formed upon the ſame motives with that againſt Tanjore, was undertaken in the year 1772, againſt the polygars or renters of land, in the diſtricts of Nalcooti and Marawa. The polygars had already been a fruitful ſource of rebellion and military tranſaction to the nabob of Arcot, in every part of the province of the Carnatic; and this ſpecies of miſunderſtanding, is a demonſtrative proof of the miſgovernment and decline of this plentiful country. The deſign of the nabob appears not ſo much the reduction of the polygars of Marawa to any particular mode of ſubmiſſion, as

---

* A Perſian word nearly ſynonimous with that of banker.

totally

totally to deprive them of their zemidaries, and root them out of the country. When general Smith marched upon his deftination, he found the bulk of the inhabitants, far from being prepared for refiftance, employed in all the purfuits of agriculture. But his power did not extend to the opening any fort of negotiation with them. Reprefentations were made to the nabob and the prefidency, that the objeĉt prefcribed to the army, under thefe circumftances, muft neceffarily require extremities of the moft fhocking nature. But the reprefen-tations were unattended to, and the orders of the military were peremptorily repeated.

The year 1773 was diftinguifhed by an incurfion, more decifive and peremptory than thofe which had preceded, againft the raja of Tanjore. The European friends of Ma-homet Ali had warmly expreffed their diffatisfaction with the inadequate conclufion of the war of 1771. They were defirous, not of mulĉting the raja, and permitting him to retain his territory, but of placing the region of Tanjore immediately under the government of the nabob. Their confederate was not averfe to the views of his creditors; and to a prince determined to deftroy his inferior, it is not perhaps difficult to difcover pretences of quarrel. It was in illuf-trating the detail of thefe, that the celebrated name of Mr. Benfield was firft brought under public difcuffion. Mr. Ben-field early poffeffed the moft valuable fhare in the affignments of the nabob; and his character and his hiftory are too memorable to fuffer us to pafs over any opportunity of throw-ing light upon them. The ftory to which we allude, was perfonally confirmed to lord Pigot by the raja of Tanjore, in the year 1776.

A perfon who has confiderable dealings in the negotiation of money, muft of courfe be obliged to employ the inter-vention of agents. The principal agent, or dubafh, of Mr. Benfield, was a black interpreter of the name of Comroo. This man happened to be at Tanjore at the time when the raja was moft apprehenfive of the difpofition to cavil that was breaking out in Mahomet Ali. The raja, in order to buy off the the invafion of 1771, had engaged to pay to the nabob

and

and others, the fum of £520,000; and of this fum £120,000 was ftill due. Alarmed at the idea of a fecond expedition againft him, and defirous to avoid the enmity of his powerful neighbour, the raja applied to Comroo, to grant him bills upon Madras for the fum in queftion. The bills of Comroo were drawn upon Mr. Benfield, and the adjuft-ment was notified by the raja to his refident with the nabob. It appeared however in the fequel, that the nabob denied having received the money, and Comroo denied having granted the bills. Mr. Benfield, when it was too late, pro-feffed to have protefted the bills as of no authority, and the tranfaction was doubly calamitous and ruinous to the raja of Tanjore.

The expedition of 1773 was conducted with more refolu-tion and perfeverance than the expedition of 1771. The raja, in the mean time, was not attacked unprepared, · and he found means to mufter in his caufe an army of twenty thou-fand men. But the generous refiftance of the vaffal could hope for little fuccefs againft the lord paramount and his Englifh ally. The war againft Tanjore was refolved by governor Wynch and his council, on the twenty fecond of June 1773. The progrefs of the war was diftinguifhed by few events that can give relief to the narration of fo unequal a conteft. The fuccefs was decifive ; the raja and his family were made prifoners ; and the plunder of the country is faid to have amounted to five millions fterling.

The government of the Eaft India company were not equal partakers with their fervants abroad, of thofe fruits of thefe military manœuvres, the profpect of which had ori-ginally brought them into act; and they were more immedi-ately under the infpection and reftraint of their countrymen at home. In this cafe they made a decifive and manly effort, to vindicate the Fnglifh name from the difhonourable imputa-tion in which it was ready to be involved. They refolved, on the twelfth of April 1775, the complete reftoration of the the raja of Tanjore. They entered not into the pretences and complaints of the nabob of Arcot, which were numerous and complicated. It was enough for them that the motives of

the

the Englifh prefidency were evidently fuch as could not bear the light. The anceftors of the raja had come into poffeffion of the country, according to the account of his enemies, in 1680; and now in a day he was ftripped of his inheritance and his dominions, to gratify the peculation and avarice of a few obfcure individuals.

But the Eaft India company would have done nothing, if, at the fame time that they refcinded the meafures, they had not changed the adminiftration of Madras. It was fcarcely to be fuppofed, that the government which had already contravened the fpirit of their general orders, could not now traverfe and defeat their moft pofitive refolutions. Accordingly governor Wynch was fufpended, and lord Pigot was fixed upon to execute the reftoration of the raja. He was recommended to them, not lefs by the circumftance of his having been the perfon to conclude the treaty of Tanjore in 1762, under which the raja claimed all his privileges; than by his eminent fervices during the period of the general war, which were fuppofed to have been the inftrument of preferving the nabob of Arcot and the kingdom of the Carnatic.

Lord Pigot arrived at his government in the beginning of December 1775. But the tafk he had undertaken, was in the laft degree arduous and critical; and all the reputation, the intrepidity and integrity of this nobleman, were fcarcely fufficient to bear him out in the execution. The whole region of Tanjore was already mortgaged to the Englifh counfellors of Mahomet Ali. A prey fo rich as this, the cultivation of which had even been improved under the nabob, it was not to be fuppofed they would quietly relinquifh. Accordingly lord Pigot, when he opened the object of his commiffion to Mahomet Ali, on the thirtieth of December, found in him the moft determined and inflexible refolution and obftinacy. He was fixed, not to fuffer his new acquifition to efcape him but in the laft extremity: and it was not till early in February 1776, that he could even be prevailed upon, to admit into Tanjore a neutral garrifon of Englifh troops. So large were his offers, and fo eager his inclination, that it appeared in the fubfequent difcuffion of the bufinefs,

that

that a gift of £600,000 was propofed to lord Pigot, merely to fufpend the reftoration of the raja till application could be made, on the part of the nabob, to the company at home. An offer of £40,000 was made to Mr. Dawfon, a gentleman who acted with lord Pigot in the council of Madras, merely to abfent himfelf upon one important difcuffion. But thefe fteps were not taken till the unalterable refolution of the prefident became an object of confiderable notoriety; and in the earlier part of the bufinefs, he was fupported by his council with confiderable unanimity.

Lord Pigot was not unacquainted with the peril of his fituation. He knew the importance that belonged to Mr. Benfield in this bufinefs, and he appears to have been willing to conciliate him, by every reafonable conceffion. The affignments on Tanjore, avowedly amounted to £800,000; and befide his proportion of thefe, Mr. Benfield advanced a private claim, to the amount of £80,000. To the reprefentations of the dictator of the Carnatic, lord Pigot lent a favourable ear. It was better that he fhould be permitted to draw from the country by inftalments a definite fum of money, than that this rich and populous region fhould be for ever expofed to thofe oppreffions and arbitrary proceedings on the part of Mr. Benfield, of which the inhabitants complained. Impreffed with this idea, when lord Pigot was appointed to go in perfon to Tanjore, to effect the reftoration of the raja, in the clofe of the month of March, he permitted Mr. Benfield and Comroo to travel in his fuite.

The return the prefident experienced for this indulgence, was for Comroo to intrude himfelf into the prefence of the raja, when retired to fleep, on the very night of their arrival, in order to guard him againft the duplicity of the prefident. He told him lord Pigot would recommend to him to put his country under the protection of the company, and require an Englifh garrifon to be kept in the fort. He advifed the raja to be firm in refufing thefe propofitions, and to reply, that he would govern the country as his father had done, and protect it with his own troops. In the mean time he offered to fupply him with any fum of money he might want; and

added,

added, that he was supported in what he did by seven members of the council of Madras. The raja reprefented this intrufion and thefe advices to lord Pigot, and the prefident ordered Comroo to be whipped upon the public parade.

After a ftep of this fort no meafures could be held between lord Pigot and the Englifh minifter of Mahomet Ali. Exafperated at fo marked a contempt for himfelf and his fervant, Mr. Benfield broke all meafures, and openly declared himfelf the enemy of the prefident. At the fame time he endeavoured to commence a negotiation with the council of Madras in lord Pigot's abfence; and colonel James Stuart was commonly confidered as the agent of Mr. Benfield on this occafion. But the fuccefs of his machinations was progreffive and gradual. The public ceremony of the reftoration of the raja took place on the eleventh of April, and on the fifth of May following lord Pigot returned to Madras. He immediately fubmitted an account of his proceedings to the gentlemen of the council, and they were unanimoufly approved.

On the twenty-ninth of May, the claims of Mr. Benfield on the country of Tanjore were regularly brought under confideration. Whatever indulgence lord Pigot might imagine it was politic to extend to this gentleman, while he preferved any fort of moderation, he conceived, in the prefent circumftances, would be in the laft degree fuperfluous and abfurd. Accordingly the claims of Mr. Benfield were rejected, and the affignments of the nabob declared inadmiffible, by a majority of one. The difaffection and coldnefs of feveral members of the council had already difplayed themfelves in feveral fymptoms; and it was upon this queftion that it firft appeared on which fide the conteft between the oftenfible, and the fecret governor, would finally terminate. On the third of June, Mr. Henry Brooke, who had voted with lord Pigot againft Mr. Benfield, moved that the proceedings of the twenty-ninth of May fhould be reconfidered. They were accordingly put a fecond time to the vote on the fourteenth of June, and were carried in the negative by a fimilar majority.

It

It is the duty of every friend to rectitude and integrity, to record the names of Mr. George Dawson, Mr. Claude Ruffel, Mr. Alexander Dalrymple and Mr. Maxwell Stone, who supported the prefident in this arduous conteft. It was impoffible they could be animated by any other motives than fuch as did honour to their character; while againft thofe that conftituted the new majority, there exifted fomething more than the fufpicion of undue influence. The queftion that brought the bufinefs to its crifis, was that refpecting the refidency, and the command of the Englifh troops, in the country of Tanjore. Mr. Ruffel was appointed to the former, early in June, and colonel Stuart to the latter, in the month of July. The counfellors in the intereft of Mr. Benfield, were determined that Mr. Ruffel fhould not proceed upon his deftination; and lord Pigot was equally peremptory, that colonel Stuart fhould not go to Tanjore, till the fame liberty had previoufly been granted to Mr. Ruffel. The queftion was now, whether the governor could in any cafe fuperfede the voice of his council, or whether he was, in all cafes, bound to abide by the decifion of the majority; and precedents were anxioufly fought, and eagerly produced on both fides. But the queftion was to be decided by force, and not by argument. Lord Pigot could neither fee his meafures in Tanjore reverfed, nor facrifice a prerogative that he deemed inherent in his office. The majority, on the other hand, were unalterably attached to their principles, and bore no common friendfhip for the new caufe in which they were engaged.

On the twenty-fecond of Auguft, when the inftructions for colonel Stuart in his new appointment, were intended to be ultimately decided on, lord Pigot gave notice, that he had a charge to move againft Mr. Stratton and Mr. Brooke, the two eldeft counfellors in the party of the oppofition; and he brought forward a ftanding order of the company, that no member fhould fit in council when a charge was delivered againft him. The two gentlemen were accordingly obliged to retire; and a refolution, that they be now fufpended from the company's fervice, being moved, it was carried in the affirmative by the cafting voice of the prefident.

The

The next day, lord Pigot proceeded to order the commander in chief, fir Robert Fletcher, to be put under arreft; and the command of the army, of courfe, devolved upon colonel James Stuart. The fituation appears to have been lefs embarraffing to this gentleman, than it would have been to almoft any other perfon. Colonel Stuart fpent the evening of the twenty-third, and the morning of the twenty-fourth of Auguft, in the houfe of the prefident; and lord Pigot, notwithftanding his vehement fufpicions, was induced to believe that he accepted of his new employment under the nomination of the prefident. But evidence was produced by Mr. Stratton and his friends, " that colonel Stuart was never heard to come to a direct acceptance of the command; and that his converfation was fo exceedingly evafive, and his addrefs fo fingular, as to reflect honour on his conduct as a foldier executing his orders, and to extricate the adminiftration from the moft imminent danger." Colonel Stuart invited himfelf to dine with lord Pigot, and afterwards to fup at the prefident's houfe without the fort. It was here only, that lord Pigot could be arrefted, without expofing the perfons employed to the accufation of mutiny. Accordingly the chaife with colonel Stuart and lord Pigot, was ftopped upon the road, and by the affiftance of the colonel, his perfon was fecured. He was immediately conveyed into cuftody at Saint Thomas's Mount, in a poft-chaife, the property of Mr. Benfield. It was boafted by Amir ul Omra, the nabob's fecond fon, who, in the difgrace of his elder brother, was the minifter of his father, that the violence committed on lord Pigot, was the contrivance of himfelf, colonel Stuart, and Mr. Benfield, and that he was now able to do whatever he pleafed in the council of Madras.

One of the firft proceedings of the Englifh minifter of the nabob, in this fituation, was to repair to Tanjore, where he arrived on the fifteenth of September. He immediately waited on the raja, with letters from Mr. Stratton, the new governor. He demanded from him an account of the prefents that had been made to lord Pigot, as well as the inftant payment

payment of the affignments which Mr. Benfield had obtained from the nabob. He infifted that the raja fhould only
write fuch letters to Madras as Mr. Benfield fhould approve,
and offered to prepare draughts for that purpofe, to be figned
by the prince. To all this the raja replied, that he did not acknowledge the validity of the demands of the nabob, and that
he had no concern with his affignments; that he had never
given any prefents to lord Pigot, though he owed every thing
to that nobleman; and that as to his correfpondence with the
Madras government, he would not trouble Mr. Benfield, but
would write his letters himfelf. The next day, however, Mr.
Benfield produced the draught of fuch a letter as he defired;
but the raja finding that it infinuated an accufation of lord
Pigot, declined having any concern with it. He, however,
communicated to Mr. Benfield the anfwer he intended to
write, which Mr. Benfield treated as improper, and returned
by his interpreter Comroo. In returning it, Comroo did not
deliver it into the raja's hands, but threw it contemptuoufly
upon the ground; adding to the raja, " Mark what will hap-
" pen after our departure from hence. You will repent of
" your conduct when it is too late. I fhall fee the time when
" you will be in the fame fituation with your late patron; and
" then fee what will befall you."

It was during Mr. Benfield's refidence at Tanjore, that he
wrote a letter to the prefidency of Madras, to the following effect.
" That having never given caufe to lord Pigot to draw his re-
" fentment on him, he had been at a lofs to find out the rea-
" fon, why his lordfhip had been induced to take meafures
" againft him fo injurious to his credit and fortune. That
" he had fince however difcovered, that his lordfhip's views
" in this conduct were interefted; and that it was his own
" good, not that of the company, that he purfued during
" his late adminiftration. That as a fervant to the company,
" and wifhing to bring to light the true motives of lord Pigot,
" as well as in juftice to himfelf, he took occafion to inform
" them, that he had arrived at the knowledge of certain
" tranfactions of that nobleman, fuch as his obtaining very
" large fums of money, and jewels and plate to a great amount,
" from

" from Indian princes, contrary to covenant and to the re-
" peated orders of the company, which conftituted him guil-
" ty under the penalties of the late act of parliament. That
" as he was refolved to take every legal method by profecution
" or otherwife, here and in England, to eftablifh fuch delin-
" quency and breach of public truft in his lordfhip ; and as he
" fhould have occafion to apply for the affiftance of the prefi-
" dency in procuring certain evidences exifting in the diftrict of
" Tanjore, or in places belonging to his highnefs the nabob of
" Arcot, he trufted he fhould meet with their countenance and
" fupport."

Such were the proceedings that were held immediately under the eye of the nabob of Arcot. But the confequence of thefe meafures, when they came to be difcuffed in
Great Britain, was ftill more extraordinary and memorable.
Before we proceed to mention them it may be proper to obferve,
that one of the firft meafures of the new government of Madras
was, to fufpend from their feat in council Mr. Ruffel and the
other gentlemen who fupported the adminiftration of lord
Pigot. If this event prove any thing, its only tendency is to
fhow that the fituation was fuch as to require exertions of extraordinary power ; that lord Pigot had not acted rafhly and
unadvifedly in the fteps he had taken, and that that meafure could
not be very capricious or very abfurd, which thofe who cenfured it were obliged to adopt the moment he was removed
from the government. Lord Pigot died in confinement on the
eleventh of May 1777.

While the double government of Madras were thus active
in thofe proceedings which the occafion demanded, they did not
forget what was indifpenfible to their interefts and their fafety
in their native country. The fpectacle exhibited in the year
1777, was new, extraordinary and inftructive. The Englifh
prefs was deluged with an infinity of Letters from the nabob
of Arcot, and collections of Papers relative to the Bufinefs of
Tanjore, replete with the moft pointed invectives againft the
raja and unmeafured abufe of lord Pigot, and appealing to the
people of England to do juftice to the caufe of Mahomet Ali.
It would feem to have required an extraordinary degree of
firmnefs and ferenity in fuch men as Mr. Benfield, to have

been thus forward to bring their caufe before the bar of a difcerning public.

The tranfactions relative to the depofition of lord Pigot
were brought under the confideration of the proprietors of the
Eaft India company at their general court on the 26th of March
1777. A refolution was carried in this meeting, ordering the
court of directors to take effectual meafures for the reftoration
of lord Pigot to the full exercife of the powers vefted in him
by the company, and for inftituting an inquiry into the conduct of the principal actors in his depofition and imprifonment. The numbers in the ballot upon this queftion were
382 to 140. But the refolutions of the court of proprietors
were not deftined to have greater duration than thofe of their
prefidency abroad. The queftion was again brought under the
confideration of the proprietors on the 9th of May. The annual election of directors had taken place in the interval. The
intrigues of a petty prince, the dependent of a trading company, defpifed by the neighbouring powers both for perfonal
and political imbecility ; and thofe of Mr. Benfield, a man,
with whom no perfon of rank and character in this country
would have entered into open alliance, were crowned with the
moft entire fuccefs. It was carried by a majority of 414 to
317 that lord Pigot fhould be reftored to his government ; that
he fhould be called upon immediately after to refign ; and that
himfelf together with the whole council of Madras, whether
friends or enemies, fhould be immediately recalled to Europe.

[*To be continued.*]

Memoirs of the Adminiftration of the Government of Madras, *during the Prefidency of Lord* MACARTNEY.

[*Continued from No.* XIV. P. 98.]

DURING the tranfactions relative to lord Pigot, Mr. Haftings enjoyed the appointment of prefident of Bengal, to which he had been nominated in the year 1772. A diftinction however is to be made, before we can properly decide refpecting the interference of that celebrated ftatefman in the affairs of the Carnatic. He had not indeed at this moment any caufe, like that of Tanjore, interefting to the fentiments of juftice and the feelings of humanity, that called for his interference; but in other refpects his fituation was not altogether diffimilar from the nobleman in queftion. He was
rather

rather a nominal than a real governor. General Clavering, colonel Monfon and Mr. Francis, who had been fent out under the regulations of lord North, received a prejudice againft the governor immediately upon their arrival in Bengal, and formed a decifive oppofition againft him. They conftituted the majority of the council; and, if the emergence had been equal, it would not have been equally practicable to Mr. Haftings toget rid of counfellors, appointed under the authority of an act of parliament.

Thus circumftanced, it would perhaps be natural to prefage, that Mr. Haftings would have felt a kind of fympathy with the fituation of lord Pigot. His fenfe of dignity, his pride of authority, his difdain of counteraction, were at leaft equal to the injured feelings of the fubordinate governor. It is well known, and Mr. Haftings has taken much pains to inform the public, that his opinion is decidedly in favour of an uncontroulable delegation of power for the adminiftration of a diftant province. In the prefent inftance however he was not biafled either by his private feelings, or by that fort of abftract judgment, which will not always apply to the practice of life; and he accordingly entered into a private correfpondence with Mr. Stratton and his confederates. The public fanction which their meafures afterwards received from the majority of the Bengal council, is not altogether of a fimilar nature. It might partly be dictated by the neceffity of the cafe, and the danger of an unqualified condemnation of the proceedings of the victorious party; and it is not underftood to have flowed from an entire and cordial approbation of the meafures, that were adopted in oppofition to lord Pigot.

If the knowledge of a bufinefs fo celebrated, as that of the reftoration of the raja of Tanjore, were a neceffary preface to the illuftration of the meafures of lord Macartney, the delineation of the principal features of the war, which lately overfpread India, is not lefs fo. In the former inftance, we are introduced to the acquaintance of thofe perfons, with whom lord Macartney had moft to do in his government of Madras. We fee their conduct in a bufinefs, which, in the lapfe of ten years, and the total removal of every perfon who oftenfibly conducted

ducted it, it is to be hoped, has furvived the violence of prejudice and the mifreprefentation of party. Such as were Mahomet Ali, Mr. Benfield and colonel Stuart, in the affair of Tanjore; fuch they will probably be found through the fteps of their contention with lord Macartney. The kind of prejudgment that we form of a man, from the conduct of the former half of his life, does not deferve the name of a prejudice. Converfions are a fort of rare incident in the human drama; and he, who, though now a good man, was long a bad one, muft be contented to labour under that fort of difinclination that we feel to a character of depravity. Acquainted however with the actors upon the fcene, we are now to trace the firft fteps of the plot. It was when the rage of the war was at its utmoft height, that lord Macartney took upon himfelf the government; and the propriety of his meafures muft be determined from the real fituation of the Carnatic and the neighbouring powers.

The firft Maratta war, of which the fubfequent ones were only a fort of continuation, was commenced by the government of Bombay, fo early as the year 1774. The object of it was to place Ragoba, an affaffin and a fugitive from the family of the pefhwa, upon the throne of Poona. The enterprize was ftrongly condemned by the new council of Bengal, and a peace, negociated under their aufpices, was concluded on the firft of March 1776. This peace, diftinguifhed by the appellation of the Poorunder, has generally been confidered as a good one. Though the fuccefs of the Bombay expedition had not been uniform, and though its operations had been concluded with the gain of a battle on the part of the Marattas, yet the conquefts of the Englifh, the ifland of Salfette and the territory of Broach, were confirmed to them. But if the peace had no other defects, it had at leaft the difadvantage of being concluded in defiance of the pertinacious oppofition of Mr. Haftings. Accordingly, the fucceffive deaths of Mr. Monfon and Mr. Clavering, and the confequent revolution in the council of Bengal, were immediately followed by a project for an amendment of the treaty of Poorunder by the governor general. The new conditions were offered in rather a peremptory manner, and the confequence of their rejection

was

was to be an immediate war. While Mr. Haftings was thus active, the original friends of Ragoba were not idle. A new expedition was concerted nearly in the fame moment on the fide of Bombay; and thus the queftion refpecting the origination of the fecond Maratta war, to which both the Englifh prefidencies were equally difpofed, has been given up to doubt, litigation and controverfy. Thefe were the tranfactions of 1777.

The confequence of the rejection of Mr. Haftings's terms by the court of Poona, was not a little extraordinary. While our armies in America were not able to march fifty miles from the coaft, without being confequently reduced into a ftate of captivity, an inland march of eleven hundred miles, acrofs the whole continent of India, was projected by the government of Bengal. But Mr. Haftings well knew the character of the nations through which they had to pafs. They were not the hardy fons of nature contending for their liberties, but the weak and effeminate children of the fun, formed to flavery, and at this time weakened and disjointed by political faction. The government of the Marattas was full of diffention, and the inferior powers were inert, impotent and imbecil. The principal obftacles to the expedition were the oppofition of the elements, and the danger of making every power, through whofe territories we paffed, the inexorable enemies of the Englifh name. Through the firft of thefe circumftances, the army was expofed to the utmoft diftrefs for want of water; and in one day three or four hundred men are faid to have died raving mad, oppreffed by intolerable thirft and exceffive heat. How the matter ftood under the latter head, we fhall prefently have occafion to obferve.

Colonel Leflie and his detachment did not march from Bombay for Surat in order to place the Maratta crown upon the head of Ragoba. The character of this man was probably underftood by the governor general. A deteftation fo rooted and fo general, feems almoft never to have prevailed againft any individual of the human fpecies. It was of fome confequence to his European allies, as well as to the fubjects they deftined for his government, to confider whether his character was truly exhibited by Nizam Ali, when he ftyled him

" an

" an invincible villain, incapable of faith." The plan of the
governmentgeneral was to open a negociation with Moodagi
Boofla, the raja of Berar, and fovereign of the largeft of the
Maratta provinces. He was nearly related to the family of
the raja of the Maratta ftate, and from that circumftance had
fome pretenfions to the imperial crown. The royal family
had long been held in a kind of eaftern imprifonment, and the
actual adminiftration had vefted in the family of the pefhwa
or viceroy. It was the plan of Mr. Haftings to reftore the
diadem to its primæval luftre, and thus to give concert and
energy to the various members of this great empire. He conceived, and as it fhould feem with perfect juftice, that the
friendfhip of Moodagi to the Englifh nation was entire and
unalterable. Of confequence, fuch a monarch, placed upon the
throne of Poona, would be able, together with his Englifh
confederates, to hold with firmnefs and efficiency the balance
of Indoftan.

Still further to work upon the ambition and the paffions of
Moodagi, Mr. Haftings propofed a joint effort in the affertion
of certain claims, which Moodagi had long fruitlefsly advanced againft the fuba of the Decan. But he feems to have
miftaken the prefent character and difpofitions of his ally.
Moodagi had felt the fentiments of ambition, and he appears
formerly to have dwelt with fome pleafure upon his pretenfions of confanguinity. But he was now old, tranquil and
indolent. He profeffed the utmoft friendfhip for the Englifh
government, and he evinced it by concealing, fo far as depended upon him, the fecret of the negociation. But he
would give no ear to the projects of war. The active genius,
the enterprifing fpirit and the refined policy of Mr. Haftings
could neither find, nor create a fympathy, in the hoary monarch of Berar.

The expectations of the prefidency of Bombay, appear to
have been at firft confiderably raifed refpecting the numbers
and power of the friends of Ragoba through the Maratta dominions. Whether they had difcovered the fallacy of thefe
profpects, or by whatever motive their conduct was directed,
they fpent the whole of the year 1778 in tranquillity and inaction.

action. In the month of December however their spirit of enterprise returned. They resolved not to wait the arrival of the detachment of Bengal, nor divide with them the splendor and profits of their success, but immediately, in conjunction with the malcontents, to conduct Ragoba to the capital of the empire. Their operations however were not conducted with that boldness and rapidity, which seemed essential to their design. A whole month was engrossed in the fortifying a difficult pass; and in all that time, no motion appeared on the part of those who had been expected to croud in multitudes to the British standard. In the beginning of the subsequent year, they marched into the country, were surrounded by the enemy, and reduced to surrender. A treaty was dictated to them by the victorious party, by which the conquests which had been guaranteed to them by the peace of Poorunder were to be given up, the protection of the company withdrawn from Ragoba, and two of the most considerable persons in the camp delivered as hostages for the execution of the treaty. Ragoba died in the month of December 1783.

The treaty of January 1779, usually denominated the treaty of Worgaum, was disavowed by the presidency of Bombay, by the council of Bengal, and even by that very body, who in the moment of their calamity had conceded to its stipulations. A pacific spirit however was in some degree produced by the miscarriage of the expedition, in both the English presidencies, who had been concerned in the commencement of the war. During the course of the summer several ineffectual attempts were made to open a negociation with the court of Poona. These proceedings however did not prevent the governor general from continuing to press with the greatest urgency, but without the smallest shadow of success, upon Moodagi Boosla, the system of confederacy and conquest which had been opened in the preceding year. Such were the measures pursued in the northern division of the peninsula, and such the motives, by which the nation of the Marattas was prevailed upon to yield its consent to the general confederacy, which was now formed for the extirpation of the English name. The concern

cern of Hyder, the moft formidable Afiatic chieftain of the prefent age, was more intimate with the prefidency of Madras. He had long been involved in a fort of inexpiable war with the Maratta nation, which had been fufpended by truces, never by a treaty of peace; and he appears, after the clofe of the Carnatic irruption in 1769, to have been very defirous to have made a common caufe with the Englifh nation againft the great enemy of his dominions. But this it fhould feem was not the harveft which principally engaged the affections of the Englifh minifters of Mahomet Ali; and accordingly, that prince fhowed himfelf conftantly averfe to the very hearing of the project. Meanwhile, as a counterbalance to the fuggeftions of Hyder, the nabob was warm in his recommendation of a confederacy with the Marattas.

It may be a queftion of fome curiofity to determine what in this fituation was the line of conduct, which it would have been moft wife and judicious in the Coromandel prefidency to have purfued. War, it feems generally to be admitted, was not a bufinefs in which they fhould have been defirous to engage; but it will fometimes happen, that in avoiding it with too great eagernefs, and holding ourfelves too feparate and unconnected with neighbouring powers, we fhall be found to have incurred the moft imminent rifk of deftruction. It has not feldom been found practicable to maintain a good underftanding and to confer acceptable favours on a neighbouring court, without engaging in meafures of offence. Since then it was our bufinefs, to maintain a kind of balance, not to make conquefts upon the princes of India, it would appear moft natural and precedented, to unite ourfelves with a ftate at a moderate diftance, rather than with our immediate neighbour; and thus to hold in awe any turbulent leader that might arife, by the mutual good underftanding of the two oppofite countries by which his dominions were confined. There is perhaps yet another argument in favour of this preference of the Marattas over Hyder. By both of thefe powers our alliance was courted; but the fultan of Myfore appears to have expected at our hands an actual reinforcement of troops; and this probably would not have been demanded by the Marattas.

But

But the government and council of Madras appear to have been little difpofed to adopt either of thefe plans. Their con-duct was even lefs defenfible than it would have been, if they had held themfelves wholly neutral, and confined their pro-ceedings within the limits of their territory. Though they had not the art of conciliating friends, they do not feem to have been to feek in the bufinefs of exciting to themfelves enemies. Without making advances, or entering into corre-fpondence with the Marrattas, they certainly treated Hyder with a degree of neglect and fupercilioufnefs bordering on contempt. This fpecies of conduct could be little brooked by the haughty and ferocious fultan. His attachments were pof-fibly ftrong and fincere; but we are fufficiently convinced that his averfions were deep, gloomy and inextinguifhable. In this difpofition, every event that occurred fupplied fuel to his re-fentment. The capture of the French fettlements, and par-ticularly thofe in his own dominions, was regarded by him as a perfonal infult. It was generally fuppofed, that had he been difengaged from the hoftilities at that time carried on againft him by the Marattas, he would have marched to the fuccour of Pondicherry in the autumn of 1778. But his complaints againft the meditated attack upon Mahie were explicit and vehement. He warned the Madras government againft under-taking it in the firft inftance, and when it was actually befieged in April 1779, the Englifh troops, which were employed in that fervice, were in a manner furrounded and hemmed in by the military of Hyder.

But it was now fufficiently evident that a war in the Car-natic was inevitable. The fteps taken by Hyder at this period, are to be regarded as the opening to the calamitous and tragical invafion by which they were fpeedily fucceeded. He reduced about this time under his fubjection the zemidars and petty princes of Cuddepa and Canoul, which immediately bordered upon the Carnatic. The Englifh indeed could not be induced to regard the war as a matter of complete certainty. They depended in fome meafure upon the continuance of the hoftili-ties of the Marattas. And though not deceived by any want of fincerity on the part of the fultan, they egregioufly mifconftrued the line of diftinction he made between the different prefidencies, and the civilities and favours he was difpofed to extend to the government of Bombay.

The prefidency were encouraged by thefe fentiments, in the moft entire and improvident neglect of preparation to refift an irruption into the heart of their dominions. They however took fome fteps in the northern divifion of the Carnatic, and engaged deeply in a train of conferences and negociation, for which the Englifh are particularly eminent in that part of the world. We have mentioned in the firft fection of thefe Memoirs,* that the government of Madras had poffeffed itfelf in the year 1765, of a tract of land commonly called the Northern Circars, connecting the Carnatic with the Bengal provinces, and calculated to put into our hands the entire command of the whole coaft bordering upon the bay. This however is true only with a certain reftriction. Of the Circars, which are five in number, four were put into our hands, with the refervation of a fmall annual tribute to the fuba of the Decan. The fifth, denominated the Guntoor, was conferred as an appanage or provifion for life, with a reverfion to the Englifh fettlers, upon Bazalet Sing, the younger brother of Nizam Ali Khan, and nabob of Adoni. The new acquired provinces of Hyder, Cuddepa and Canoul, formed a direct line of interfection between the principality of Adoni and the appanage of the Guntoor.

The Englifh, it fhould feem, had repeatedly caft a wifhful eye upon the territory of Bazalet. As they were exprefsly reftrained by the treaty with the fuba, under which they held the other Circars, from entering into any negociation with the zemidar upon this fubject, their overtures had hitherto been made immediately to the lord paramount, Nizam Ali Khan. But the motive which infpired their eagernefs, the defire of poffeffing the port of Mootapilli and excluding the fuba from the communication with the fea, was not likely to fmooth the difficulties which might arife on the part of that monarch. Befide the circumftance we have mentioned, the
Guntoor

---

* No. XIV. p. 87.

Guntoor would have afforded another advantage to the prefidency of Madras, fince one of the diftricts of the Arcot dominions was cut off from the reft by the intervention of this territory.

Repulfed as they had been by Nizam Ali, they in this emergency applied immediately to Bazalet Sing, the tenant for life, and were by fome means enabled to purfuade him to put the Guntoor, and as it fhould feem, the principality of Adoni, under the protection of the Englifh. A fpecific annual revenue was to be paid out of them for life to Bazalet Sing, and the treaty was concluded in April 1779. This and the preceding meafures are to be afcribed to fir Thomas Rumbold, who entered upon the government of Madras on the eighth of February in the preceding year. It fhould feem that the fpirit of the Englifh government may eafily be traced, from a proceeding which belongs to the prefent period. The Guntoor was no fooner put in poffeffion of the Englifh, than it was immediately farmed to the nabob of Arcot.

The offence that fprung to the fuba of the Decan from this and other contemporary circumftances, were multiplied and various. To treat with the vaffal for the ceffion of a territory, that had been granted him, was a proceeding contrary to all the ideas of government that had hitherto prevailed in India. The irritation and the infult were increafed by the circumftance of the land being immediately put into the hands of the nabob. Nizam Ali remembered, with the ftrongeft fentiments of refentment, the attack which had been made upon his dominions and his prerogatives in the year 1765, by Mahomet Ali Khan, and he was not likely to be foothed by fo unwifhed for a neighbourhood. To complete the affront that was offered, the Englifh, who had for fome time fuffered their annual tribute to run into arrears, took this opportuntity to propofe to the fuba its total abolition, or at leaft its reduction to a fmaller amount.

But the concern of Hyder was fcarcely lefs intimate in the affair of the Guntoor, than that of the fuba of the Decan. The nabob was by this meafure equally introduced into the neighbourhood of this prince, and his refentment was of a ftill

deeper

deeper and more lafting dye than that of Nizam Ali. The provinces of Hyder, which confined upon the Guntoor, were recent conquefts, and his authority can fcarcely be fuppofed to have yet attained among them the neceffary degree of weight and tranquility. But the prefidency of Madras were not contented with this indirect attack. They marched their troops immediately into the diftrict of Cuddepa, under orders, as it was faid, for the Guntoor, but, as would feem more probable from an infpection of the map, with a view to fortify and fecure the principality of Adoni. They were however immediately acquainted by Hyder's officers, that their march would not be permitted. Accordingly, after having paffed fome days in the fultan's dominions, they were obliged, in confequence of the cbftructions that were feduloufly oppofed to them, to fall back upon the Carnatic, and to purfue that direction, which, if their object was truly declared, would in the firft inftance have been the moft natural and obvious.

Thus we are prefented with the fteps, which, whether they fhould appear adequate or inadequate to their purpofe, led to that general oppofition and hoftility to the Britifh, which foon after broke out in the utmoft violence. In judging of the proceedings refpecting the Circar of Bazalet Sing, it is certainly fair that we fhould take into our confideration the extreme animofity with which Hyder was impreffed previoufly to this tranfaction. It fhould feem fufficiently natural for a power, reduced to the alternative of going to war, to feize as much as poffible upon the advantages of country, and fuch other benefits as opportunity and policy may place within its reach. But the conduct of the Englifh prefidency was not fufficiently confiftent and fyftematical. Either a war with Hyder was inevitable, or it was to be regarded in the light of a contingency. In the latter cafe it certainly was not the wifdom of our government, to adopt the moft unqueftionable means of working upon the haughtinefs, the fpirit and the ferocity of the fultan. In the former cafe the meafure they employed was partial, inadequate and ufelefs. They ought to have ftrengthened the vital parts of the Carnatic, and then to have thought of improving the condition of its extremities.

In

In this bufinefs too Hyder was not the only perfon to be confidered. When they were about to eucounter with one great
and formidable enemy, it was not prudent in them to provoke
the refentment of another. The whole bufinefs was rendered
the more fatal, by the want of all kind of fympathy and concert between the fouthern and the northern prefidencies.
While the government of Madras was engaged in no friendly
conteft with the fuba of the Decan and the fultan of Myfore,
the Marattas encountered a regular feries of provocations from
the unprovoked attacks of the Englifh, and from their repeated
difavowal of different treaties. The year clofed, in conformity
with the preparatory fteps, with a peace between thofe inveterate enemies, Hyder and the Marattas, and a general confederacy againft the Englifh, to which the contracting parties
were the courts of Syringpatnam and Poona, of Naigpore
and Hyderabad.

The proceedings we have related, though in a confiderable
degree complicated, have been rendered more notorious, than
ufually happens to tranfactions of a fimilar nature, in confequence of the long and laborious inveftigation to which the
bufinefs was expofed, both in parliament and elfewhere. The
fubfequent events are ftill more public and more univerfally underftood. The unexampled want of preparation on the part
of the prefidency, the imbecil and contemptible conduct of
the nabob of Arcot, the inactivity and treafon of his officers
and fubjects, and the univerfal defertion of his troops, are matters generally known. Hyder did not enter the Carnatic till
month of July 1780. His invafion was carried on with that
fiercenefs and feverity which might be expected from the rigour and keennefs of his refentment. Having met with no
oppofition in the pafs of the mountains that feparated his dominions from the Carnatic, and finding no enemy to face him
upon his arrival, he fwept the whole country with his un-
refifted cavalry. Though his appearance had been expected
for feveral months, and though he had made no fecret of his
intention, the different battalions of the Britifh forces were
difperfed among the moft diftant parts of the coaft of Coromandel. The council of Madras, as ufually happens in cafes

Y 3   of

of notorious mifconduct and negligence, were torn by inteſ-
tine factions. Mr. Sadlier, one of its members, for having
ſtrongly expreſſed his difapprobation of the proceedings of the
government, was on the firſt of Auguſt ordered to be ſufpended.
The ſelect committee, by which the affairs of the province
were actually conducted, confiſted at this time of four perſons, and two of theſe, Mr. Charles Smith and Mr. Samuel
Johnſon, were in violent hoſtility to the meaſures that were
adopted. Mr, Whitehil, who had ſucceeded to the government upon the departure of ſir Thomas Rumbold for England,
early in the month of April, of confequence carried every
queſtion by his caſting vote. He was affiſted and feconded in
his proceedings by ſir Hector Monro, the commander in chief.
The original plan of this officer had been immediately to aſſemble an army in the neighbourhood of Conjeveram ; and
the execution of this meaſure was committed to lord Mac-
leod, ſon to the earl of Cromarty, who had lately arrived from
Europe with a new raiſed regiment of troops. This proceeding was adopted in confequence of an opinion, that the coun-
ſel of the commander in chief rendered his prefence more neceſſary at Madras, than at the head of the army. Lord Mac-
leod in the mean time declared his difapprobation of the plan
of ſir Hector Monro, and propoſed certain variations ; at the
fame time adding, that he could not " aſſume a refponfibility
in the execution of meaſures that did not coincide with his
own judgment." This difference of opinion occaſioned ſir
Hector Monro finally to quit Madras on the twenty-fifth of
Auguſt, and to command the army in perſon. Previouſly to
his departure it was refolved that Mr. Alexander Davidfon
ſhould be appointed a member of the ſelect committee in his
abſence. And though this were an infringement upon the
letter of their conſtitution, it was declared to be neceſſary, in
order " that the reputation of the commander in chief might
have a fair chance, which was little to be expected from the
conſtruction that would probably be put upon his actions by·
Mr. Smith and Mr. Johnſon."

The preparations on the part of the nabob of Arcot were
ſtill

ftill more remifs, and attended with more fatal confequences than thofe of the prefidency of Madras. Upon the arrival of fir Hector Monro at the army, which was encamped at a fmall diftance from the fort, the fingle regiment of cavalry belonging to Mahomet Ali declared their refolution to ferve no longer, unlefs the arrears of their pay were immediately difcharged. The principal officer of the nabob, who was prefent, refufed to comply with their demand ; and they were of confequence ftripped of their arms and their horfes, and ordered to be fent under guard prifoners to Madras. The Mahometan officer however took his opportunity, and enlifted the whole of them the next morning into his body guard. In the mean time a detachment under the command of colonel Cofby, which was expedited with a view of cutting off the provifions of the enemy, appears to have failed, merely through the difaffection of the inhabitants and the treachery of the fervants of the nabob. In repeated inftances, reinforcements of Britifh troops were refufed to be admitted into the fortreffes of the Carnatic. While Hyder was able to boaft that he was acquainted with every movement on the part of the Englifh, the commander in chief applied in vain for the affiftance of the agent of the nabob, refiding in his camp, for fuch purpofes as were neceffary to his army. The anfwer of this perfon was, that he had the nabob's orders for attending upon fir Hector Monro, but that he had no authority to procure either provifions or intelligence. The advances in the mean time of the fultan, were rapid and extenfive. He proceeded at once againft Trichinopoli, the Circars and the capital of the Carnatic. He appeared in the vicinity of Madras fo early as the tenth of Auguft, and he formed the fiege of Arcot on the twenty-firft day of that month.

Though the Englifh forces were confiderably difperfed, it would feem to have been practicable, if the orders for that purpofe had been immediate, to have effected an entire junction, in fpite of the oppofition of Hyder. But the fickleness and indecifion that difplayed themfelves in the prefidency, were here attended with the moft fatal confequences. Colo-

Y 4 nel

nel Baillie, the commander of the devoted force that had been originally marched for the protection of the Guntoor, encountered the feverest obstacles in his endeavour to reach the rendezvous of Conjeveram. For a confiderable time however they yielded to his fuperior perfeverance and skill. It was not till he arrived within a few miles of the principal army that he found himself unable to proceed any farther. The whole force of the invader, amounting to more than fifty thoufand men, was between him and fir Hector Monro. He was totally unfupplied with provifions, and in this fituation he communicated to the general, the circumftances in which he was placed. Accordingly a ftrong detachment, confifting of the flower of the army, under the command of colonel Fletcher, was difpatched to his relief; and though the guides that had been furnifhed acted in concert with the enemy, colonel Fletcher was enabled, by a fagacious precaution, and by fuddenly changing his route, to form a junction with the forces of Baillie. Previoufly to this junction, the leader of the Guntoor army had defeated two feveral detachments under the command of the brother-in-law, and Tippoo Saib, the fon of the fultan of Myfore. Upon the prefent occafion, on the tenth of September, after a long and fevere conteft, victory declared on the fide of the Englifh. But at this moment the waggons which contained the ammunition of the army, and were placed in the center of the Britifh line, by fome accident blew up. The whole army was immediately thrown into the utmoft confternation and diforder; and Tippoo, who upon all occafions had difplayed an equal readinefs of perception and rapidity of execution, feizing upon the incident with eagernefs and skill, decided the fate of the day. Nearly the whole army, to the amount of four thoufand fepoys and fix hundred Europeans, were put to the fword. Colonel Baillie only, with about two hundred Europeans, was made prifoner of war. This decifive action in a manner put a termination to the conteft. Sir Hector Monro immediately broke up his camp; and the capital of Arcot furrendered to the conqueror on the thirty-firft of October.

Such

Such was the campaign of 1780 in the southern division of India. Our contest was not equally unfortunate with the other members of the grand confederacy. Moodagi Boosla, who appears still to have retained a considerable friendship for the British, and who had been in a manner forced into the union against us, and Nizam Ali, from principles of indolence, supiness and imbecility, took no steps that could greatly tend to entangle or prejudice any of our settlements. The detachment which had been marched for Bombay and Surat, had already conquered their principal difficulty, and though they remained in inaction during almost ten months from their arrival, they however opened the campaign with a considerable degree of military splendour, in the year 1780. Amedabad, the capital of the Guzzerat, yielded to their efforts: Madagi Sindia, the most warlike of the Maratta chiefs, was forced into action by them, and defeated: and a detachment of twenty thousand men, under the same commander, was repulsed by a foraging party of the English. Equal success attended our arms in the more centrical parts of the empire. The fortress of Gualior in particular, which had been deemed impregnable, and which appears to have been furnished with the most extraordinary defences by the gift of nature, yielded to an enterprise, almost romantic in its conception, but which was crowned with success by the hands of fortune. Though these victories were attended with some instances of a policy so refined as to border upon perfidy, yet they served to humble the spirit of enterprise in the Maratta state, and give a kind of veneration and terror to the name of Britain. After some actions of unequal moment, in the year 1781, and a third victory obtained over Madagi Sindia in the month of April, this general, not less subtle in council than active in the field, made secret overtures of peace. A separate treaty was concluded on the thirteenth of October, and this event was almost immediately succeeded by a general cessation of hostilities between the English and the Marattas.

Such was the situation of India in the close of the preceding year, as to call for the greatest exertions on the part of the gover-

nor

nor general of Bengal, whether he afcribed the prefent crifis to his own meafures, or whether he were animated merely by the confpicuoufnefs of his fituation, and his defire of promoting the common caufe.   The news of the defeat of colonel Baillie was no fooner received, than the moft vigorous meafures of relief were adopted.   A confiderable reinforcement of Europeans, together with a fum of money to the amount of 150,000l. was prepared to fail for Calcutta, and fir Eyre Coote, the commander in chief of the forces in India, was requefted to take upon him the conduct of the expedition.   The fuperftitious averfion, entertained by the native troops, for committing themfelves in any cafe to this element, rendered it unfafe to attempt to include the fepoys in the detachment by fea.   Accordingly, a negociation was opened with Moodagi Boofla, and a treaty concluded, by which he was detached from the confederacy, and induced to permit a fecond reinforcement to march through his dominions.   Thefe advantages were purchafed by a douceur to this prince of the fum of 160,000l.   To thefe fteps, for the relief of the Carnatic, was added a refolution for the fufpenfion of Mr. Whitehil from the government of Madras. Though the feafon of the year was unfavourable, the paffage of fir Eyre Coote was unufually calm and fpeedy.   He arrived on the fifth of November; and the refolution againft Mr. Whitehil being carried into execution in two days, Mr. Charles Smith fucceeded to the government.

[*To be continued.*]

POLITICAL HERALD, AND REVIEW.

N U M B E R XVIII.

POLITICAL AND HISTORICAL SPECULATIONS:

Memoirs of the Administration of the Government of Madras,
during the Presidency of Lord MACARTNEY.

[*Continued from No.* XVII. *P.* 346.]

THE actions of fir Eyre Coote fill too confpicuous a
place in the fubfequent hiftory of the coaft of Coromandel, not to make it defirable that we fhould derive as much
light as poffible upon his character and conduct, at leaft during
the period of his laft refidence in India. He arrived in Bengal, with the appointment of commander in chief of the forces,
on the twenty-feventh of March 1779; and foon after propofed in council the making a progrefs through the different
ftations of the Indian army. It had long been the practice of
that government, to canton a certain proportion of their troops
in the dominions of our ally and dependent, the nabob of
Oude. The country of the nabob was therefore included in
the circuit of the general; and he croffed the Caramnaffa in his
return from this progrefs in the month of Auguft 1780, a
fhort time previous to his failing for the relief of the Carnatic.

The falary of fir Eyre Coote, as a member of the fupreme
council, was fixed by the exifting conftitution of the Eaft
India company at £10,000 per annum. In addition to this
fum £6,000 per annum was annexed to his office in lieu of
travelling charges, and of all other emoluments and allowances
whatfoever. But it had long been the practice of the fervants
of the Britifh government in this quarter of the world to grafp
at the largeft fums; and as the climate was extremely unfa-

vourable to European conftitutions, to endeavour to counter-balance this circumftance by a rapid acquifition of wealth. Examples of this fort are in a high degree contagious, and few men will be found, who will be firm enough to pride themfelves in an honeft poverty, in the midft of the luft of accumulation and the arrogance of fudden profperity. It was probably from a principle of this fort, that the emoluments of brigadier general Stibbert were continued to him after he had been fuperfeded in the Bengal command by fir Eyre Coote, and that a field eftablifhment, to the amount of upwards of £18,000 per annum was at the fame time provided for the new commander in chief. This fum was ordered by the governor general and council to be carried over to the account of the nabob of Oude, from the time that fir Eyre Coote entered his dominions. The new eftablifhment was condemned by the court of directors, and declared by them to appear in a light " fo very extraordinary and fo repugnant to the fpirit of their conftitution, as to induce them pofitively to direct its immediate difcontinuance." The order of the directors was received at Bengal in the month of April 1781. But though it was formally directed by the council to be put in execution, and though fir Eyre Coote had recroffed the Caramnaffa ten months before its arrival, yet the amount, by a fecret agreement between Mr. Haftings and the general, continued to be paid to him by the nabob till the time of his death.

But however we may decide upon the propriety of the conduct of fir Eyre Coote in this inftance, the fuccefles obtained by him, and the favourable change that took place in the Britifh government and army immediately upon his arrival at Madras, are too palpable to admit of controverfy. Harmony once more appeared in the government, and thofe diffentions in the felect committee, which had long fince introduced the moft fatal fymptoms of anarchy and confufion, were immediately removed. The name of this fuccefsful commander feemed to infpire new hopes into the Britifh, and to ftrike their fierce and tremendous adverfary with veneration and terror. The whole force of the Englifh did not exceed feven thoufand men, and of thofe only one thoufand feven hundred were Europeans.

This

This force however was fo fkilfully managed by the commander in chief as to effect the immediate relief of Vandivafh, Vellore and feveral other places clofely befieged by the enemy. Hyder, immediately upon the appearance of the Britifh army, retired before them with precipitation, on the feventeenth of January 1781. Pondicherry, which, though dependent upon the Englifh government, appears to have difplayed feveral marks of difaffection, was at the fame time difarmed, and this, fortunately for the Englifh, almoft immediately previous to the arrival of the French fquadron under the command of M. d'Orves from the Mauritius. He was accordingly obliged to return to the place from which he had failed ; at the fame time that fir Edward Hughes, the Englifh admiral, employed himfelf in the deftruction of the infant navy of Hyder on the coaft of Malabar.

But thefe partial fucceffes were only introductory to the fplendid victories obtained by fir Eyre Coote at Porto Novo, at Perimbacan, the fpot which had been rendered memorable by the fatal defeat of colonel Baillie, and at Sholingur. Thefe advantages were of courfe accompanied with the recovery of feveral important towns and fortreffes ; and the campaign was clofed with the capture of Negapatnam and Trincomale, by fir Edward Hughes and fir Hector Monro. The confequences of our gaining the firft of thefe were the immediate return of the inhabitants of Tanjore and Marawa to the Britifh ftandard ; and of the laft, the poffeffion of a moft advantageous fituation for fheltering and refitting the Britifh fleets.

It was in the midft of this fuccefsful campaign, and on the twenty-fecond of June 1781, that lord Macartney arrived in India, and took upon himfelf the government of Madras. By felecting this nobleman for fo important an office, the perfons concerned in the government of the Eaft India company thought, that they fhould at leaft avoid the perpetuating a crime, which had been loudly charged upon their fervants, of exhibiting the moft unbounded rapacity, together with the moft confummate indifference to the maintenance of a character in this fituation, which they had not before acquired in another. This charge had been too fuccefsfully urged againft lord Ma-

cartney's

cartney's immediate predeceffor, fir Thomas Rumbold, and the
defolation occafioned by former rapacity, as well as the injuries
inflicted by a deftructive war, required the moft determined
forbearance and the moft lenient management, in order to reftore
the country to vigour, fertility and happinefs.

Lord Macartney was himfelf of a refpectable anceftry in
Ireland, and by marrying a daughter of the earl of Bute had
become connected with fome of the firft families in this kingdom. Early in life he had gone ambaffador to the court of
Ruffia, where he diftinguifhed himfelf with honour, and concluded a beneficial commercial treaty with the prefent emprefs.
He was afterwards, for four years, fecretary to lord vifcount
Townfhend in the office of lord lieutenant of the kingdom of
Ireland. The adminiftration of lord Townfhend was the
æra of the abolition of the ariftocratical cabal, which had long
fwayed the government of that country, and the introduction
of the act for octennial parliaments. Under lord Townfhend
Mr. Macartney diftinguifhed himfelf by a liberality and difin-
tereftednefs, which, though the emoluments of his office were
confiderable, rendered it impoffible for him to improve his
fortune. The lieutenancy of lord Townfhend terminated in
1772; and in 1775, Mr., now fir George Macartney, was appointed to the government of Grenada in the Weft Indies,
together with Dominica, St. Vincent and Tobago, which
he held till the capture of Grenada by the French in 1779.
A nobleman, who had thus paffed through a variety of ftations
of honour and refponfibility, and who had acquitted himfelf
with credit in them all, was not likely to facrifice his reputation in an ignoble manner ; and his paft actions were conceived by many to afford the moft perfect fecurity for the rectitude of his future conduct.

At the commencement of the campaign of 1781, the Britifh
fettlement on the coaft of Coromandel could fcarcely be faid
to afford fcope for the exercife of the talents of the legiflator
and the ftatefman. It was a field for the difplay of warlike
atchievements ; and it was neceffary that the country fhould
be wrefted from the hands of an all deftroying enemy before
it could be made the object of civil government. The mili-

tary

tary fuccefs of fir Eyre Coote had now opened a field for the political virtue or fkill of the new prefident. Palnaud, Ongole and Nellore, the northern diftricts of the Carnatic, and which had not yet been laid wafte by the fword of Hyder, feemed now to be at liberty to promife themfelves in fome degree a period of calmnefs and tranquility. Tinevelli, Madura, Ramnadaporum and Trichinopoli, the fouthern provinces, which had been fpoiled either by the forces of the fultan, or the devaftations of the difaffected polygars, were, by the capture of Negapatnam and the general effect of the campaign, delivered from the more immediate calamities of war.

If the fituation of the Carnatic afforded an opportunity for the introduction of order and good government, the prefent ftate of the war did not feem lefs urgently to demand it at the hands of the prefident. Notwithftanding the victories that had been obtained, the invader of the Britifh dependencies was far from being fubdued. The Indian armies under the command of this confummate warrior, were not, as in former inftances, fcattered and difperfed by a fingle defeat. It was referved for Hyder, to fhow the example of a multitude of troops formed under his management, who fhould be kept together in fpite of mifcarriage, and fhould be able almoft immediately to refume a regular appearance in the face of a victorious adverfary. He accordingly ftill retained poffeffion of the metropolis of the Carnatic, together with a great number of ftrong pofts and important fortreffes. But what made the profpect of the enfuing campaign efpecially critical, was the expectation, almoft approaching to certainty, in which we were of reinforcements from France. The land forces of that country might well be expected to throw a confiderable weight into the fcale of our opponent; and the navy might poffibly become fo fuperior to ours, as to deter fir Edward Hughes from undertaking any thing of importance, or as totally to deftroy our entire fleet. Amidft the multitude of Hyder's forces, and the alienation and difaffection of the inhabitants, it had already been found impracticable for the Englifh army to march to any confiderable diftance, without the immediate affiftance and co-operation of the navy. Notwithftanding

therefore

therefore the brilliancy of the campaign of 1781, it did not feem very romantic or improbable, to expect on the part of the enemy, that the campaign of 1782 might fee our fleets and armies in this quarter of the world, fwept away to entire deftruction.

The principal refources for the maintenance of the war in the Carnatic, were undoubtedly to be expected from the fupreme government of Bengal. But lord Macartney was not willing that the province under his direction fhould fit down in fupine dependence upon the fuperior prefidency, without endeavouring at any exertion of her own. Even if revenue and the fupport of military undertakings were not to be looked for, yet the introduction of fome fort of order and good government in the country, that was, as it were, the feat of war, might be expected to be productive of the moft falutary effects. But what was the fituation of thofe dominions, into which regularity and policy was to be endeavoured to be introduced? The reader has already had reafon to fee in our narrative of the events that refpected lord Pigot, what fort of government was that of the Carnatic in a time of profound tranquility. Every where involved in the tranfactions of foucars and money lenders, torn as it were piece-meal by affignments to a thoufand individuals, its revenue had funk one third of the original value, before an individual of Hyder's army made his appearance in the Carnatic.

The devaftation that followed upon the appearance of this celebrated invader, was of the wideft and moft unlimited defcription. Full of indignation againft the Englifh, full of the implacable hatred he bore to the nabob, he vented his fury upon the innocent inhabitants. Every fpot that came within the march of his army was laid wafte with fire and fword. As that army was made up in a great degree of cavalry, they fpread rapidly over the country in every direction. We find a party of his horfe ravaging in the neighbourhood of Madras, a few days after his army had been led through the paffes of the mountains. In the mean time the towns and villages were burnt to the ground. The inhabitants, male and female, young and old, were driven before him. The whole of the diftricts
of

of Arcot and Trichinopoli in particular, were reduced to one fcene of favagenefs and defolation ; and, as we are informed by the committee foon after appointed by the government of Madras for the examination of this bufinefs, through thefe whole provinces " fcarcely a veftige remained, either of population or agriculture." To add to the calamity of this fituation, the fertility of the Carnatic was not maintained, like that of European countries, by the benign infiuence of rains and the favourable operation of the feafons, but by the collection of waters, which fell at periodical returns, and which being preferved in artificial refervoirs, were from thence diftributed over the country. Thefe refervoirs, which amounted probably through the Carnatic to ten thoufand, were, fo far at leaft as the forces of Hyder had penetrated, either deftroyed or cut through, fo as to render them for the prefent totally ufelefs.

In relating thefe circumftances, we would not be underftood to intend to reprefent Hyder as a monfter of barbarity, unparalleled in hiftory. It is a refpect we owe to ourfelves, to do juftice to the character of our enemy; and this fhould feem ftill more ftrongly incumbent upon us, when his capacity and his atchievements have rendered his character doubly confpicuous. The genius of Hyder will fcarcely be difputed. In the midft of a people, paffive, indolent and fubmiffive, furrounded by princes, emafculated, nervelefs and imbecil, he had a mind to conceive the greateft defigns, and a perfeverance and intrepidity to carry them into execution. He created an army fuch as India never faw; and he was employed, though checked and counteracted by the fortune of war, in the creation of a navy, a thing wholly unparalleled in the hiftory of that country. His defign was great, and, relatively at leaft to the nations among which he lived, generous and noble. He was determined to root out of India the political fettlements of Britain, the only European power that had been able to make any confiderable progrefs in the fubjugation of the country. Succeeding in this, he would probably have fought to revive in his own perfon the empire of Tamerlane and Aurungzebe, and perhaps with more fplendour than it had ever been found to exift among their fucceffors.

In

In addition to thefe features of his public conduct, many things may be added in honour of his private character. He was not naturally remorfelefs and cruel. To his dependents he was mild, equitable and humane; to his relations and family, affectionate, indulgent and kind. He was a ftranger equally to hypocrify in his own conduct, and to the fufpicion of it in others; and his temper was always cool, placid and equable. With regard to his conduct in the invafion of the Carnatic, he cannot certainly be defended; but if his proceedings were marked with defolation and calamity, we are however to remember, that thefe things are far from being unprecedented in the hiftory of the moft civilized nations of Europe. Hyder's treatment of the dominions of Arcot may be paralleled with the devaftations of the refined and accomplifhed Turenne in the province of Alface. And Hyder had at leaft an extenuation to plead, which cannot be advanced in the fimilar inftance. The provocations he had received from the nabob were continued and extreme; and the conduct of the Englifh, refpecting their poffeffions in India, had certainly been marked with repeated inftances of duplicity, treachery and ill faith. We do not however mean to apologize for proceedings fimilar to thofe we have recited. They are fuch as no provocation can juftify; and whether dictated by a native ferocity, or improper example, equally deferve to be marked with our fevereft execration.

But to return to the fituation of the Carnatic. The inefficiency of its government, the diforder of its adminiftration and the difaffection of its inhabitants had been placed in a ftriking light, by the events that fucceeded upon the irruption of Hyder; and it was probable, that, as long as its affairs continued in the fame hands, thefe fymptoms of degeneracy and decay would rather be increafed than diminifhed. Thus circumftanced, the plan that lord Macartney conceived, was bold, daring, adventurous. To this moment it had been the practice of the Englifh government to throw all power, and particularly all the bufinefs of executive detail, into the hands, whether oftenfible or fecret, of the minifters of the nabob. To this prince, as the wife legiflator, the confummate ftatef-

man

man and the benign father of his natural subjects, we difpofed of the management of every fpecies of territory that came into our hands. Did we obtain a jaghire or province round the capital of Madras? It was farmed to the nabob of Arcot. Did we wreft certain diftricts or circars by force of arms from the fuba of the Decan? They were farmed to the nabob of Arcot. Did we fecure to ourfelves, by a fubdolous treaty with Bazalet Sing, the brother of the fuba, the remaining diftrict or the Guntoor? This alfo was farmed to the nabob of Arcot.

It might perhaps be fuppofed, that lord Macartney did not fee all the rifque which he incurred to his perfon or authority by this tranfaction. The example of lord Pigot was a fufficient proof how dangerous it was, to counteract the views of the court of the nabob; and the fyftem laid down in the prefent inftance was ftill more inimical to the defigns, and fatal to the hopes of this court, than the reftoration of Tanjore. But the public expediency of the meafure, and not any private views of intereft, appear to have determined lord Macartney to encounter every oppofition that might be created to him. He was further extremely fortunate in the period that was deftined for the execution of this meafure. The bankers and creditors of the na-bob had hitherto been too watchful, for the prefervation of his power and of the materials of their rapacity, to fuffer any en-croachment to be made upon their prerogatives. But even thefe men had been confounded and alarmed by the invafion of Hyder. Not the ears of avarice could be completely fhut againft the cries of the miferable, nor the heart of rapine fuf-ficiently fteeled againft the execrations of a people. For years they had made their harveft of the rich and noble provinces of this fertile foil. Adverfity and deftruction had at length over-taken them. They had no armour, with which to oppofe themfelves to the all conquering force of Hyder. With hope-lefs reluctance they gave up a country they were no longer com-petent to hold; and in the month of December 1781 an af-fignment was voluntarily executed by the nabob, to lord Ma-cartney on the part of the company, of the revenues of the Carnatic. The conditions of this affignment were, that the revenues fhould remain in the hands of the prefidency during

the

the continuance of the war; that they fhould be at liberty to grant leafes of the provinces to different renters for three or five years; and that they fhould pay a certain monthly allowance to Mahomet Ali for the maintenance of the durbar.

But though the governor of Madras was defirous of taking out of the hands of the affignees of the nabob the collection of the revenue, and the profperity of the people, he did not mean that they fhould ultimately center in himfelf. He conftantly applied the maxim, honourable to his own character and falutary in its confequences, of delegating every important truft, whether of finance or regulation, to perfons whofe whole attention fhould be turned to this fingle point, and who fhould be directly and notoriously refponfible for the meafures they recommended. Accordingly, a committee of affigned revenue was appointed under the authority of the prefident and council, confifting of five perfons, Mr. Charles Oakley, Mr. Eyles Irwin, Mr. Hall Plumer, Mr. David Haliburton and Mr. George Moubray. Thefe gentlemen delivered in an exact report of the ftate of the Carnatic, and of the conduct they had adopted in the difcharge of their truft, on the twenty-feventh of May 1782; and they accompanied it with a comparative ftatement of the revenues and expences of the feveral diftricts, exclufive of that of Arcot, which was ftill in the hands of the enemy. From this paper it appears, that, though the rent they obtained under the new leafes, granted for one, three and five years refpectively, was fcarcely equal to the rent which the nabob profeffed to have made in the years immediately preceding the war, yet, that by a reduction of the expences, the prefent net revenue fomething more than doubled that which had been made in the former inftance. The net revenue upon the fix diftricts they made to amount to £493,350. Their fyftem was to take place on the twelfth of the following July.

We have already obferved, that Hyder was far from being fubdued by the victories of 1781, and that he entertained expectations, neither unjuft nor irrational, of the moft decifive fuccefs in the enfuing campaign. Exertions were accordingly demanded, and ftrenuoufly made by the Britifh governors in
every

every part of India. It may not be a little amufing and inftructive, to contraft the meafure of lord Macartney, which
we have attempted to defcribe, with the tranfactions which
were at that moment carrying on under the prefidency of Bengal. Mr. Haftings was employed in the autumn of 1781, in
making his celebrated progrefs to Lucknow, the capital of
Oude. One of the events of this progrefs was, the fine, the
arreft and the expulfion of the raja of Benares. The principal pretence to this expulfion was the meditated rebellion of
the raja. Upon the folidity of this charge we are immediately
enabled to judge, when we find Mr. Haftings ftating, that, " if
Cheit Sing's people, after they had effected his refcue, inftead
of crouding after him in a tumultuous manner, in his paffage
over the river, had proceeded to the quarters of the governor
general, they would probably have fealed their fuccefs in his
blood, as he could not have affembled more than fifty fepoys
for his whole defence." In this charge of rebellion however
were involved the mother and the grandmother of the nabob
of Oude; and they were accordingly imprifoned, and, together with their numerous families and fuite, fubjected to the
moft cruel treatment, and expofed to the extremities of hunger,
for more than twelve months. If we fhould fuppofe Mr.
Haftings to have been compelled, by the urgency of the cafe,
to adopt thefe methods of feeding the war, it muft at leaft be
granted, that the meafures in which lord Macartney was engaged, were more worthy of the ftatefman and more congenial
to the man of humanity.

The firft event of the campaign was fufficiently favourable to the expectations of Hyder. After the capture of
Negapatnam and the recovery of the circumjacent countries, colonel Braithwaite was ftationed in the dominions of
Tanjore, with a body of about two thoufand men for its
defence. One of thofe mifunderftandings, fo frequently the
precurfors of the moft fatal events in war, had recently broken
out between him and fir Eyre Coote. The darknefs which
hangs over many fimilar tranfactions in India does not permit us to underftand the nature of their difpute. It is ftated by the latter, that he " waited the refult of his reference

rence to the governor general, as that which fhould reftore him to his authority over the fouthern troops." It is not perfectly intelligible, what new powers the commander in chief of the forces in India could in this inftance have obtained, or how the fouthern detachment could have gone beyond the reach of his authority. Be this as it will, Tippoo, the warlike fon of Hyder, prefently perceived the danger to which colonel Braithwaite was expofed by being cantoned in a flat and open country, and he advanced upon him with the utmoft celerity, at the head of twenty thoufand men. With this force he was enabled to furround the detachment, and though they defended themfelves with the moft obftinate bravery, they were completely cut to pieces or made prifoners, on the fixteenth of February. On this occafion M. Lally, the French officer who accompanied Tippoo, diftinguifhed himfelf by an effort of generofity, in faving at the imminent rifk of his life, the wretched remains of the Britifh from the blind and indifcriminate fury of the Indian cavalry.

In the following month M. Duchemin, with the long expected fuccours from France, to the amount of three thoufand five hundred men, debarked in the neighbourhood of Pondicherry. With this reinforcement Hyder was enabled to feize upon the important fortrefs of Cuddalore, on the eighth of April, and foon after he alfo made himfelf mafter of Permacoli. From hence he marched againft Vandivafh; and for this important object fir Eyre Coote expected to be able to force the fultan to the alternative of a battle. Hyder in the mean time had learned caution from the events of the preceding year, and immediately broke up the fiege. In purfuance of the fame object, the general now marched againft Arni, the great arfenal and depot of provifions for the Myfore army. For the prefervation of this place Hyder was induced to hazard another battle, on the fecond of June; but the conflict was of no long duration, and it terminated in nothing decifive. In the meanwhile, by continually hovering over us and referving his force, he was foon after enabled fo far to deceive the vigilance of fir Eyre Coote, as to cut off a fmall divifion of
the

the Britifh army called the grand guard. This was the laft important event of the campaign, as the Britifh commander was rendered unable, through ill health, to continue any longer in the field, and accordingly embraced this opportunity of failing for Bengal.

But the naval campaign of 1782 was of ftill more confequence, and more hardly contefted than that which was carried on in the fields of the Carnatic. Admiral Suffren, who had fought with commodore Johnftone, and relieved the cape of Good Hope during his paffage, had efcorted the fuccours of M. Duchemin. M. d'Orves having died at the Mauritius, Suffren fucceeded to the command, and failing with the commencement of the year for Madras, he expected with one blow to annihilate the weak and unequal fquadron of fir Edward Hughes. Fortunately however, captain Alms, who had been detached by commodore Johnftone with three fhips of the line, arrived a few days previous to Suffren, and difappointed his hopes. A battle however was prefently fought between the two fleets, and this was fucceeded by three others in the courfe of the year, more ftrongly contefted, and accompanied with greater bloodfhed, than had ever been known in an equal portion of time in any naval war. Undoubtedly both commanders had great profeffional merit in the bufinefs, and fir Edward Hughes had the fuperior advantage of being well feconded upon all occafions by the officers of his fleet. Upon the whole however, the ability of M. Suffren appeared to predominate, as he gained in various ftruggles the wind of the enemy, and as, by a mafter-piece of generalfhip, he was enabled in the clofe of the month of Auguft, to wreft from us the important poffeffion of Trincomale. The autumn of this year was marked by a dreadful hurricane, which was equally injurious to the Englifh fleet, and to the crops of rice which were the fubfiftence of the inhabitants. From this event, together with the devaftations of the year, enfued a dreadful famine. It affords an inftructive, though melancholy illuftration of the human character, to reflect on the unfortunate Gentoos, who in this emergency perfifted in their refufal of animal food, and fubmitted to the moft deplorable

plorable of human calamities, rather than violate a miftaken principle of rectitude. The victims of the famine in
the capital of Madras, were computed to amount, for fome
time, to fourteen hundred perfons every week.

The refult of the campaign of 1782, could not be expected
to decide the war. But operations were at this time commenced on the other fide of the peninfula, which feemed to
promife a more favourable iffue. The kingdoms of Myfore
and Canara had long been unviolated by the unhallowed touch
of war. They were full of riches and affluence, and if a paffage could once be fecured beyond the mountains that fkirted
the fea fhore, there was nothing that could refift the violence
of an enemy. The troops of the fultan might therefore by
this means be recalled to the defence of his native dominions,
and the French being left alone to oppofe our armies, we
might form a rational expectation of ultimate fuccefs.

The principal fettlement of the Englifh on the Malabar
coaft confifted in the town and fortrefs of Telicherry; and
this had been preffed by the forces of Hyder from the commencement of the war. So early as December 1781, a detachment had failed to its relief under the command of major
Abingdon. This officer obtained fome fuccefs beyond the
limits of the garrifon, and a farther reinforcement having arrived in Auguft, they penetrated to a confiderable depth in
the fouthern divifion of Myfore. Tippoo however croffed
the peninfula with his ufual celerity, and drove them with
fome rifk back to the coaft. He was repulfed in an attempt to
force their lines, in the month of November, and was foon after
recalled, probably by the death of Hyder, to the army in the
Carnatic.

The prefidency of Bombay, which had been enabled to
make thefe efforts, now fent out an armament of two thoufand men under the command of general Matthews, to the
relief of the little army in Myfore. This officer learned upon
his paffage the favourable change in the condition of the original force, and immediately refolved to land in Canara, which
was more diftant from the fcene of action in the Carnatic,
more penetrable, and, as it fhould feem, more rich than the
kingdom

kingdom of Myfore. He arrived here in December 1782, and foon after captured by ftorm the fea port of Onore. Here he received orders from the Bombay prefidency, who were inftigated to this enterprize by the death of Hyder, to march immediately againft the capital of Hydernagur. For fome time he hefitated in his compliance, but at length yielded to the inftances of the government. In the execution of his project he met with little refiftance, and entered into poffeffion of the metropolis, the feat of government, and the treafures of the fultan, early in the month of February 1783. The difgraceful events that followed are well known. Never was a fcene of greater confufion, cruelty, anarchy and plunder. We are unwilling to ftain our page with the animofities that enfued, or the barbarities that were practifed. The refolution that feems to have been formed upon all occafions, to yield no quarter to the inhabitants, the difgraceful tergiverfation that was employed refpecting the treafures that were found, and the beautiful women that were offered up a bloody facrifice at the capture of Annanpore, complete a picture difhonourable and fhocking to humanity. But the plunderers of Canara were not fuffered long to enjoy their booty. Tippoo, inftigated by the tale of horror that reached him from all fides, immediately repaffed his army through the ftraits of the mountains, and made himfelf once more mafter of his capital, on the twentyeighth day of April.

We have brought together in this place the moft confiderable of thofe events that decided upon the fortune of the war. But it was long before the time of which we are fpeaking, that the nabob of Arcot and his minifters began to repent of the affignment of the Carnatic, which had been made to lord Macartney. It was, as we obferved, a ftep that would never have been conceded to in the firft inftance, but from the operation of terror and defpair. Whatever had been the principles upon which the nabob's government had been conducted for many preceding years, whatever had been the emoluments and perquifites of his minifters, whether Englifh or Muffulman, thefe obvioufly received a fatal check, by the immediate
management

management of the country being taken out of their hands. It was not long before they recovered their prudence and their reafon.   Perhaps they had expected to find it eafy, as undoubtedly they had found it in fome preceding inftances, to enter into collufion with the government of the company, and thus to carry on their practices under a higher fanction, and with the advantage of diverting from themfelves the general odium. But lord Macartney had no fooner obtained the delegation, than he placed the detail of it out of his own power.   Every thing appears to have been carried on upon principles of opennefs and notoriety.   The diftricts of the Carnatic were leafed to the different renters, in conformity to propofals received upon public advertifement; and the whole was placed in the hands of the perfons, who offered the beft terms, and who bore the moft refponfible character.   Irritated therefore perhaps by the firmnefs of lord Macartney, and of his committee of revenue, the old cabals were fpeedily revived in the court of the nabob, and they were directed in the moft pointed manner againft the governor of Madras.   We have feen the language that was employed by Mr. Benfield and his affociates againft lord Pigot; but their charges were made with ftill greater effrontery, and in a ftyle of more virulent invective,   againft lord Macartney.

[*To be continued.*]

[FREEDOM OF SPEECH]

To the EDITOR of the MORNING CHRONICLE.

LETTER I.

SIR,

I was taught from my earliest youth to regard the English Constitution as a model of excellence. I was told " that other countries in other ages of the world might have more of the pageantry and exterior of liberty ; but that we had the substance. The ancient Republics were capable of extraordinary public exertions ; but their individual members were trenched upon by sumptuary laws, and agrarian laws, and tormented with ostracisms and tumults. They might have more political liberty, more equal voice in the transactions of the State, than we have ; but we have more of civil and personal liberty, the end to which political liberty is valuable only as a means. An Englishman is equally secure from monarchical and popular tyranny ; his house is his castle ; he cannot be arbitrarily imprisoned ; he may discuss the measures of government, and utter his sentiments of politics and religion without fear of molestation. In England there are neither spies nor informers ; the press is open to men of all opinions, provided they deliver their opinions with any degree of decency in the manner ; nor need any inhabitant of this country, as under the Republic of Venice, or the despotism of Spain, stand in awe of criminal animadversion for every hasty or unadvised expression that may drop from his lips." Such was the Constitution which my progenitors instructed me to cherish ; and they added, " that, if Englishmen should ever be imprudent enough to desire to change it for a Constitution apparently more free, they would be obliged to part with some portion of that personal independence which is the most valuable of all our possessions."

At prefent that a zeal for the Conftitution is echoed from all parts of the ifland, it would be ftrange if an argument in its favour, which was formerly dwelt upon with rapture, fhould be treated as unfafhionable. You will obferve, Mr. Editor, that this argument is altogether independent of the queftion of reform, or no reform. Whatever may be my fentiments on that fubject, I am not egotift enough to trouble you with them on the prefent occafion. I plead only for principles " delivered down by our renowned forefathers."

I agree, Mr. Editor, with my neighbours on every fide, who with full-mouthed, unthinking cry, proclaim, that the Conftitution is in danger. I admit with them, that there is a confpiracy in exiftence for the deftruction of the moft valuable part of our inheritance. I allow that we muft not truft to profeffions; and that we fhall find fecret enemies among thofe who tell the moft plaufible tale. It fhall be the bufinefs of this letter, and a few fubfequent ones, which, with your approbation, I mean to communicate to the public, to unmafk thefe confpirators.

What is the true meaning of this cry in favour of the Conftitution ? What part of the Conftitution is it about which the attention of thefe new affociators is engaged ? It is the old, boafted privilege of Englifhmen ; liberty of fpeech ; but their attention is not engaged to confirm, but to deftroy it. The Conftitution is left at this moment almoft without a defender; and thofe who fanctify their proceedings with its name, are taking the direct road to erect defpotifm upon its ruins. Is there one principle of the Conftitution that is held in efteem by them? I acquit the majority of my countrymen. They are led heedlefsly on by the magic of a name. But there are men at the bottom of the project, who are eager to make ufe of the prefent occafion to deprive us of our moft invaluable privileges.

The immediate motive of my prefent addrefs is the trial of Daniel Crichton, upon the eighth of this month, at the Quarter Seffions, at Clerkenwell, for feditious and treafonable words. This man, it feems, a tallow chandler by trade, had come from Scotland to London in purfuit of that trade, and the day after his arrival had got intoxicated with his friends. In this condition he went to fee the Tower of London ; and, while obferving the armoury, and other things there exhibited, faid, " Damn the King ; we have no King in Scotland, and we will foon have no King in England." The ftory of his intoxication is told, not by his friends, but by the witneffes for the crown. For this offence he was thrown into prifon, thruft among felons, loaded with irons, and after having thus fuffered for feveral weeks, he is convicted by a Britifh jury, and fentenced by his judges, in their clemency, and in confideration of thefe previous hardfhips, to imprifonment for three months, and to give fecurity for his peaceable behaviour for one year, himfelf in one hundred pounds, and two furetics in fifty pounds each.

Mr. Editor, the trial of Crichton muft form an epocha in the hiftory of this country. Englifhmen, though they are afleep, are not dead. They will become fenfible to this wound to the deareft part of their birthrights. The late King of Pruffia, that model of defpots, yet permitted his fubjects to talk of his government as they pleafed. The moft barbarous mafter, while he lafhes his miferable flave, yet allows him to groan. But our fituation is worfe than this; if we will not allow men to enquire whether they are well, and to utter the fentiments they conceive.

The attack upon Crichton has every poffible aggravation. He is an induftrious, inoffenfive man, quietly purfuing the duties of his calling. I grant, that, according to the practice of the Englifh Conftitution, words of a certain fort are the proper fubject of criminal proceeding. I may utter words that fhew me to be privy to a formidable confpiracy. But the words of Crichton were uttered in intoxication, are not the words of a cool and deliberate traitor, but of fudden and intemperate paffion.

What is the meaning of our boafted liberty ? It is the liberty of a Portuguefe, to be unmolefted, as long as he attends folely to his private affairs, and refrains from thinking or fpeaking refpecting the government of his country.

Englifhmen fhould recollect, why it is that this privilege has been fo highly valued. It is better not to live at all, than to live in perpetual fear. The moft crying evil of a defpotic Government, is fpies and informers. How miferable is the ftate of thofe men,

114

who are surrounded with smiling, fawning enemies; who dare trust to no appearances; from whose intercourse confidence and kindness are for ever banished; who must set a guard upon the door of their lips; who must look round, and anxiously watch every countenance, before they begin to speak!

Mr. Editor, till lately we heard of such things from a distance, and some of us lent an incredulous ear to their possibility. They are now brought home to us. Englishmen were lately free. The reign of despotism began on the 20th of November, 1792. On that day, an Association at the Crown and Anchor Tavern, in the Strand, under pretence of protecting liberty and property, formed a plan for overturning the Constitution. They did not begin with its out-posts; they attacked it at once in its vitals. From that day we have been surrounded with spies; spies of the worst sort; not merely the spies of Government, who might be marked, but every timid observer, and every rancorous disputant we may happen to encounter.

It will be a singular story in the British Annals, if it shall be found, that in the beginning of the present reign, an universal alarm for our liberties was conceived from the affair of general warrants; and that no apprehension is now entertained from a danger a thousand times more extensive. Few men comparatively write upon the subject of Government; but every man is instigated to speak upon it. The alarm was then against a bad precedent, which might at some future period be made a subject of imitation. We should do great injustice to the prosecution of Crichton, if we regarded it merely as a precedent. The Associators are hungry for blood. They have subscribed sums of money to prosecute every man that utters a syllable they do not approve; and they are ever on the watch to find opportunities to spend these sums. Scarcely a day passes that does not bring me news of some fresh information; and no man can tell whose turn will be next. The Attorney General's Office is loaded with them. These men are no underminers. They do not think of taking our liberties by sap. They have commenced a general storm; and it is instantly necessary that Englishmen should display their indignation, if they do not wish that six months hence the Constitution should be an empty name.

MERCIUS.

For the MORNING CHRONICLE.

LETTER II.

To Mr. REEVES, Chairman of the Society for protecting
Liberty and Property against Republicans and Levellers.

SIR,

You have conceived or profeſſed an alarm for the
ſafety of your country. Some of the grounds of that
alarm are as follows : Aſſociations have been entered
into in various parts of the kingdom, for the purpoſe
of diffuſing opinions and concentring exertions among
the middling and lower orders of the community.
Pamphlets, tending to produce rancour and diſſenſion,
have been both ſold at a trivial price, and diſtributed
gratis. Hand-bills have been paſted upon the walls
and diſperſed in the ſtreets. Abſurd and barbarous
inſcriptions have been ſcribbled on the outſide of
churches and other buildings.

Sir, I agree with you that theſe things are unſeemly
and injurious. I am no friend to force either on the
part of the Populace or of Government : but, if you
had employed none but the regular and moderate interference of coercion to ſuppreſs them, you would
certainly never have heard from me upon the preſent
occaſion. Your exertions have been indefatigable.—
The Aſſociations are ſilent ; the pamphlets are no
longer ſold ; the walls have ceaſed to be made the inſtruments of diſloyalty. If you had ſtopped here, you
might have paſſed for an honeſt man. But your next
ſtep brands you and your party (except thoſe who
blindly follow your inſidious guidance) for the moſt
ignominious of cowards.

You deprive the intemperate advocates of Reform
of the inſtruments they were ſo forward to employ.
You tell them, and you tell them true, that ſuch inſtruments are diſgraceful to a civiliſed community.—
And what is the next thing you do? Will any one,
not a witneſs to the tranſaction, believe me when I affirm, that a man of liberal education, a writer of re-
pute upon the Hiſtory of Engliſh Law, could forget
himſelf ſo far as, having wreſted theſe weapons from
his antagoniſts, inſtead of daſhing them indignantly to
the earth, to employ them himſelf for the purpoſe of
wounding thoſe he had already diſarmed ?

116

Sir, you may boldly challenge all the annals of despotism and injustice to match this iniquity. You have all the honours of originality. Dionysius and Nero would have scorned so base a proceeding. You must have the credit of adding a new phenomena to the philosophy of the human mind. There is no instance upon record of a man, avowedly and in the face of a great nation, silencing his antagonist that he only might be heard ; and coming forward gravely with this maxim, " Hear one side only, that you may be able to judge."

Good God ! what species of monster is this Thomas Paine, that all the rules of equity cease to be rules the moment he is the subject of animadversion ? I was myself present at the trial of this man. We all know by what means a verdict was procured : by repeated proclamations, by all the force, and all the fears of the kingdom being artfully turned against one man. As I came out of court, I saw hand-bills, in the most vulgar and illiberal style distributed, entitled, The Confession of Thomas Paine. I had not walked three streets, before I was encountered by ballad singers, roaring in cadence rude, a miserable set of scurrilous stanzas upon his private life. You know best, Sir, what concern you had in these things. But the people of England will need very strong evidence to convince them of your innocence. Other parts of the transaction you openly boast. No sooner were the cheap pamphlets of Mr. Paine, and the hand-bills of his partisans suppressed, than pamphlets, printed sheets, and hand-bills without number issued from the press in answer to his reasonings.

You may imagine, Sir, that you shall escape the detestation annexed to such proceedings : but you are mistaken. An infatuated people may, for the present, even applaud them. But you shall be recorded to the latest posterity for shameless injustice and effrontery unparalleled. If it were possible that such machinations should be crowned with success, you should be inscribed, not perhaps on your tomb, but on the deathless page of history—" Reeves, the assassin of the Liberties of Englishmen."

What is there in these instruments of hand-bills, ballads, and pamphlets, that should render them, though before profane, sacred the moment they come into your hands? If Mr. Paine may not inflame the vulgar against the House of Brunswick, by what right do you excite them; for that is the direct tendency of your proceedings, to pull down the houses and destroy the property of Dissenters? Sir, a liberal, a manly, and an honest mind, would not point the animosities of the populace against any man, as little against the obscurest individual, as against the Princes upon the throne. What is more clear than that you ought, in the outset of this business, to have chosen your alternative; either to have met those Republicans at their own weapons, or to have proscribed all such irregular and ungenerous warfare? But you resolved to engross to yourself all the advantages of both plans; and, having power on your side, to make that serve you instead of argument, decency, and truth.

I said, in my former letter, that I was educated in a respect for the English Constitution. You have done more, Sir, to annihilate that respect in the breasts of your countrymen, than any Englishman in this inglorious reign. Is it possible for me to value any thing that I do not deem consonant to truth? Is it possible for me to be the champion of a system that will not stand the test of argument? What sort of Constitution is it that you pretend to recommend to our reverence? A Constitution that can be defended only by your declarations, while your antagonists are silenced—a Constitution that must always be applauded, and never examined: a Constitution that can only be supported by hand-bills, ballads, and misrepresentation, that exists by the shouts of a mob, and the burning of an effigy. Sir, you are the most virulent of all libellers. One column of your hand-bills is as effectual to excite serious doubts in the dispassionate mind against the English Constitution, as all Mr. Paine's pamphlets. I impeach you at the bar of my country as a conspirator against its liberties.

But you, Sir, are an insignificant individual; it is only your vices and your impudence that exalt you into notice. I turn therefore from you to the Public at large. I call upon my countrymen to consider whether this character, which your proceedings have fixed upon the English Constitution, be that to which it is truly entitled; if it be, for God's sake let it be fairly known, that every man of honour may set his face against the Constitution. It is the worst feature of the worst governments that they may not be written or spoken against. What should Englishmen fear? If our Constitution be truly good, it will pass every ordeal, and come out the purer for the scrutiny to which it shall have been subjected. Every sincere advocate for the Constitution will wish for no better than a fair and tranquil field of debate, and an honourable surrender on both sides of all the means of inflammation. He would think that he betrayed his sentiments and blasted his cause, the moment he had recourse to one illiberal and insidious weapon.

Sir, I affirm, without the shadow of hesitation, that you are not a sincere adherent of the English Constitution. I appeal to your own evidence to prove my assertion. Every disputant that breaks out into rage, scurrility, and violence, proves that he has no confidence in the strength of his arguments. If you believed what you pretend to believe, you would scorn to take advantages; you would not fear for the event of the contest. I affirm more than this, that you have formed a plan for the destruction of the Constitution. Can you be a friend to the Revolution in 1688? Can you be a friend to the Bill of Rights? I appeal to every article of your proceedings. You employ the vulgar artifice of raising a cry against Democrats and Levellers, and then hope, under favour of this cry, to strip us of every one of our privileges. But you shall be disappointed. A very few months only shall elapse, before multitudes of your present followers will be astonished at the first success of your deception, and will execrate the deceiver. It is not in the nature of Englishmen to be juggled by so paltry and palpable a device out of every thing that is dear to them.

MUCIUS.

For the MORNING CHRONICLE.

The following Letter was sent to us before the late Law changes took place. Although Sir ARCHIBALD MACDONALD be no longer Attorney General, the matter of the letter is neither less important, nor less applicable.

LETTER III.

TO SIR ARCHIBALD MACDONALD, ATTORNEY GENERAL.

SIR,

In addressing myself to you, it is my intention to return to my original subject, the trial of Crichton. In the account of that trial, printed in the public newspapers, I read your declared resolution to prosecute all persons who shall incur the charge of intemperate language on the subject of the English Constitution, and to bring them to condign punishment. It is the design of this letter to remonstrate with you upon that resolution, and to lead you to re-consider the the reasons upon which it is founded.

I do not despair of making some impression upon you. I have heard you applauded for liberality and candour. If you have one particle of their reality, and will read this letter with attention, I am well assured, so sound and unanswerable is the cause I have to plead, that I shall bring you over to my party. Sir, you ought not to shrink from the truth, though it come from an anonymous writer in a newspaper. I am not your enemy, but your friend ; I am the friend of every thing that bears the name of man. But, remember, the expostulation I make, if admitted, will demand some fortitude at your hands. It will not perhaps require that you should part with your present dignity and emoluments. But it will require a spectacle seldom seen at St. James's, that you should announce your determination, rather to part with them, than violate your conscience, or proceed in the dishonourable task in which you have unwarily been engaged. Such a declaration from you would perhaps recal the least hackneyed part of the Cabinet to their senses, and prevent a catastrophe, which none would deplore, more than myself, and none is at this moment more anxious to prevent the people from being irritated into a resolution to do justice to themselves against those Magistrates who were created to defend, but who are too much disposed to violate their rights.

Your situation is singularly important. It is probably in your power, either inextricably to plunge your country into those evils which you so loudly deprecate, or by an easy, yet honourable exertion of fortitude, to acquire to yourself immortal renown, and be hailed the Saviour of Britain.

Were I even to suppose you a friend to absolute power, it would make little difference in the argument. The present scene can have but one issue, the confirmation or increase of our liberties, and can only be varied in the mode in which that issue shall be produced. The last hope of tyrants is, that they shall be able to bring back ages of ignorance; but this hope is in the highest degree visionary and absurd.

I confess myself at a loss to state the grounds of your late declaration, so as to give it a moment's plausibility. You are determined that no one shall say any thing but what you say. It is easy no doubt to work one's self up into a temper of resentment and rage, and to feel angry with every one that think differently from ourselves. But have you considered the consequences of endeavouring to give effect to this sentiment?

Such was the temper of the barbarous ages respecting the only subject which at that time engaged the curiosity of mind, religion. But experience at length taught the world the absurdity of persecution. You, it seems, are willing to revive the experiment with a small variety in the application. Sir, this is not an age for the experiments of despotism to be tried with impunity.

Let us suppose it to be tried by you even in your own family. Educate your son with as much care as you please; you will not find at twenty that his creed altogether coincides with your own. That which you cannot effect upon one individual, always under your eye, do you expect to effect it upon a nation?

Precipitation and vanity may prompt me to resent the insolence of any man who dares to differ from me in opinion. But the smallest attention to the nature of mind will show me that the difference is unavoidable, and that resentment, instead of healing the injury, makes it more obstinate and incurable.

There is another light in which the subject may be considered. Let us suppose that you were a Planter in the West India Islands; would you punish your negroes every time they dropped a difrespectful word concerning you, every time that, in the gaiety of their hearts, or when you had given them some agreeable beverage to relieve the severity of their labours, they forgot the distance that in your opinion ought to be maintained? Surely your boasted liberality would shrink from this tyranny. Surely you would shrink from a barbarity that a negro-driver would contemplate with horror. Is the English nation to be worse treated than the negroes in the West India plantations?

But you will say, "that this intemperate speaking, pardonable enough in itself considered, is pregnant with danger." In the West Indies there are twenty blacks to a white. This disparity is surely full of danger. Are there here, as there are there, twenty persons to one, who might reasonably expect to be benefited by the overthrow of the existing government?

"Intemperate speaking is pregnant with danger," What danger? What evil can we fear, worse than that which you declare your resolution to impose upon us? You tell us, that we must watch every word that we speak, lest we should in your opinion incur political guilt. You tell us, that in every coffee-house and place of public resort we must look round to see whether we have not one of your runners at our elbow. We must not only take care that no such perversity of intellect should ever befal us, as should tempt us to think ill of the English Constitution: we must never suffer our hearts to be exhilarated with social intercourse or with wine, lest in any unguarded moment we should utter a word that our sober thoughts disapproved. We may be irritated with debate; our enemy may have formed the plan of provoking us; he may first intoxicate us with liquor that he may afterwards ensnare us into the topic of a criminal prosecution. My very footman from behind my chair may be enticed by the ten guineas, so liberally proffered by the new Associations, to betray me, and thus procure to himself the accursed wages of despotism. It may be that it may argue some imperfection on my part to be the victim of any of these mischiefs: but is it a crime for which a man ought to be torn from his family, from his trade and his prospects, and endeavoured to be rendered infamous to the world? I repeat it; what can we fear from Republicans and Levellers worse, than this revival of all the principles of the inquisition with which you have recently threatened us?

Let us consider the objection above stated in one light more. "Intemperate speaking is pregnant with danger." You have yourself furnished the strongest argument to convince us that it is impotent in this respect. Sir, it is your conduct that is pregnant with danger—danger to the cause you pretend to espouse, and not the words of an intoxicated Tallow-chandler. There is no method that leads so surely and so suddenly to the diffolution of power, as an endeavour to stretch it beyond its ability. It was thus that the treacherous Sunderland ruined his too easy master, King James the Second. Without the penetration of Sunderland to discern remote consequences, you have fallen upon the very same plan. You are trying at this moment how much the patience of Englishmen will endure. For God's sake, open your eyes, before you have irritated them past reconciliaton. Do not madly hurry forward a cataltrophe, which we may all of us rue when it is too late. Do not rouse a sleeping lion— do not imagine that because we are now patient, we are incapable of refentment.

Sir, I am the advocate of peace. I do not know what the ingenuity of a lawyer can make of this letter. But I know that no man can be more indefatigable in his exertions for the maintenance of tranquillity than I am and will continue to be. It is you that are hurling the firebrands of war. Willingly would I arreft your arm, before you have involved the whole fabric of the English Government in conflagration.

I have chosen, Sir, to address you in the style of amicable expoltulation. I have restrained the indignation which tyrannical principles are too apt to excite in the mind, and the invective which your unreflecting precipitation in an affair of so great moment richly deferved. I was willing at least to make one experiment with you of the benevolent kind. It is to be hoped your conduct in future will render any experiment of another sort unneceffary.

MUCIUS.

For the MORNING CHRONICLE.

LETTER IV.

TO SUCH PERSONS AS MAY BE APPOINTED TO SERVE
UPON JURIES FOR THE TRIAL OF SEDITIOUS AND
TREASONABLE WORDS.

GENTLEMEN,

The importance of your fituation is fo great as to imprefs me with confiderable awe when I undertake to addrefs you. It is out of all comparifon fuperior to that which you would be called on to fill, if you were individually Members of the Britifh Houfe of Commons. There, with the beft intentions and the moft conftant refolution, you might be overpowered by influence or by numbers. In your fituation as jurymen this is impoffible. You have to expoftulate with a fmall number of your countrymen, untramelled in the myfteries of political corruption, and who from education are more open than their more learned and felf-fatisfied countrymen to the voice of conviction. The very circumftance of the unanimity which the law requires from them, renders them tractable. It is impoffible that one juryman, fully poffeffed of the reafon of the cafe, and endowed with moderation, intrepidity, and benevolence, fhould not bring over the whole pannel to his fide.

Thus extenfive is the truft that your country repofes in you. I call not upon you for gratitude, I appeal to a higher principle. Be deeply impreffed with the magnitude of the concern in which you are engaged. Be duly anxious to difcharge the duty it demands of you. Refolutely determine to give no quarter to favour, partiality or refentment. Withdraw yourfelves from the current of popular and temporary paffions. Act as you fhall wifh to have done, when the fentiments of the hour are no more. Elevate your minds, that you may view the fubject in the fame light as it will be feen by your pofterity, and that you may do what that pofterity expects at your hands.

Great God, what honours might not a just and intrepid juryman deserve in times of clamour and alarm like these! How I envy you the patriotism of which your situation is capable! One upright and intelligent juryman might put a close to that scene of persecution which is the disgrace of Britain. Let us figure this man to ourselves, contending with the prejudices and passions of his colleagues. Let us figure his mildness and equanimity in the midst of their impatience, and perhaps their scurrility. Let us figure to ourselves that clear, simple, unornamented understanding, which furnishes him with a plain and undeniable answer to all their objections. Let us suppose truth by his instrumentality victorious, not merely over the passions, but over the understanding of united numbers. Let us follow him from the apartment in which the jury was inclosed, back to the presence of the judge. Let us suppose it possible that a judge should be found, the slave of a court, the unrelenting adversary of the prosecuted party, who shall undertake to brow beat, to insult, and to compel the jury into a desertion of their duty. Let us figure to ourselves this juryman defeating by plain good sense and determined honesty, the practised wiles of a hoary lawyer invested with the symbols of authority. Let us farther conceive him attacked by the venal pens of prostituted writers as turbulent and factious ; and let him show by a frank and simple tale, that he is the true friend of order and peace, and that his pannel by their verdict have redeemed their country.

Is there no such man? Oh, for a man like this, to suspend the torrent of absolute power, and prove that I am not fallen upon an age of savage barbarism and ignorance! Oh, for a man like this, to inscribe his name upon the page of history, and eclipse with its lustre the renown of Hampden and Russel!

Integrity never appears more divine in human form, than when it bursts forth from obscurity : than when it appears, unornamented by rank, unassisted by learning, invincible, though alone ; than when it disdains circumlocution, tells a plain and artless tale, and shows that all the powers of sophistry and intimidation are impotent, when set in opposition to it.

While we are surveying this portrait, do none of your hearts pant to resemble it? Have you no generous feelings that sympathize with the description?

Are none of you willing to acquire renown at so cheap a price ? Is there not a man that will put forth a finger to save his country?

Your duty is so plain in the present case, that nothing can be more astonishing than the universal consent with which all late juries in such questions have neglected it ? I know that narrow-minded and bigotted persons, though honest, have a strong propensity to quarrel and hate where they find difference of opinion ; but this is so palpable a folly, that common sense cannot be made its dupe for any length of time. I know that the persons who are concerned in the selection of juries are anxious to avoid all obnoxious and disaffected characters. But the character required in the present case, is so simple and moderate, that the most shameless government would scarcely venture to proscribe it.

He need not be the enemy, but on the contrary, may be the warmest friend of the English Constitution. He has only to bear in mind one plain principle, and to say, " This man, though he differs from me, may yet be honest." Liberty does not consist in giving a favourable verdict when we think the accused party has delivered the exact truth. It consists in allowing every man, in the way of enquiry and argument, to speak what he thinks. It consists in delivering us from the empire of spies and informers, in not subjecting us to perpetual watchfulness and reserve, in not putting an instrument of vengeance into the hands of every man who may think proper to quarrel with us.

Good God! what had this poor tallow-chandler, this Crichton done, that ought to have rendered him amenable to the justice of his country ? Was he to overturn the government of his country? Was he engaged in any conspiracy for that purpose ? Nothing of the kind is alledged against him. He merely got drunk, and then talked idly, as men when they are drunk usually do. Is the fabric of our law in danger from the ramblings of an intoxicated journeyman ? No, he has not overturned the constitution of his country ; but the constitution of his country is to be overturned by prosecuting him. Do you know how much injury this man may sustain from his sentence ? Do you know what miserable wretches the people of England will become, if they live in hourly fear of such prosecutions? There is not one of us, however sober and loyal, that is not obnoxious to them. Where is the man that was never intoxicated ? Who will answer for himself, that, when intoxicated, he may not be played upon by some spy, some treasury runner, some mercenary informer, some malignant enemy, and provoked to say, "Damn the King?" Would to Heaven it were practicable for this cause to be tried over again, and that the laws of my country would permit me, who am no lawyer, to plead it. It would be impossible for any jury to resist the clear justice and the strong reason with which it might be pleaded. It might be brought home to every one of them. They might be shown that such a prosecution could lead only to slavery in its most atrocious form, and that none but the foulest traitors (had the reason of the case been fully and powerfully exhibited to them) could bring in a verdict of guilty.

Is it possible that I should, at this day, be pleading in England such a principle as this? I no longer know my country. England was once the land of liberty and good sense. We understood the principles of toleration, civil and religious. Our liberties were purchased by our ancestors, by the struggle of a century. Our Constitution has been cemented with the blood of patriots and martyrs. Shall it be destroyed in a day by the insidious arts of unblushing courtiers; shall it be destroyed by an hypocrisy unparalleled in the annals of history; an hypocrisy that pretends reverence for the Constitution, at the very moment that the daggers of these hypocrites revel in its vitals?

Countrymen and Britons, I ask not for the confidence of my readers, I desire to find you incredulous. The less easily you are satisfied and the more you enquire, the more will evidence accumulate upon you. Is the language I use the mere hackneyed language of declamation? Is the constitution in no danger from these trials *ex officio*? What constitution shall we have left, when the trial of Crichton has passed into a precedent, and been confirmed by two hundred other verdicts obtained upon the same principle? Are you in love with the mere form of King, Lords and Commons, and careless about the personal independence and security, for the sake of which only that form was cherished by your ancestors?

I will fuppofe that you are envious about nothing but your mercantile wealth. Are you fo ftupid as not to perceive that, when liberty of fpeech and liberty of the prefs are gone, your mercantile wealth will not be worth the having? It is by liberty of fpeech and liberty of the prefs alone, that abfolute power is kept at bay. If you would know what mercantile wealth is worth in an arbitrary country, tranfport yourfelves to Ruffia, where no man may fell his commodities but under permiffion of the Emprefs. Tranfport yourfelves to Morocco, where the Emperor regularly makes the progrefs of his dominions, and demands of every man a little more opulent than his neighbour, juft fuch a gift as he in his good pleafure fhall think proper to require. This is the ftate of fociety, when liberty of fpeech and liberty of the prefs are no more. If you be infenfible to the love of independence, if you be willing to part with all that adorns fociety and elevates the human mind, can you yet be fo ignorant as to imagine, that to part with thefe privileges is the way to fecure to yourfelves that wealth by which your very fouls are engroffed?

It was but laft year that thefe privileges were placed on fuch a footing as not to be at the mercy of the officers of the Crown*. Have you taken them into your own hands only, that you may refign them with the more indelible bafenefs? No country ever furrendered to fo broad a fhame. No country ever dated in the fame year, an improvement of its freedom, and the epocha of its flavery. What has been the caufe of fo dreadful a reverfe? Has the Emprefs of Ruffia overwhelmed us with her Coffacks, or the Houfe of Auftria with its Pandours? This would be difgrace enough, if freemen could fubmit to be put in chains by a band of licentious favages. But we ftrip our own fhoulders, prepare the fcourge with our own hands, and invoke the approach of defpotifm, when it is yet at a diftance.

LUCIUS.

* By Mr. Fox's Libel Act.

THE CHARGE

DELIVERED BY

The Right Honourable Sir JAMES EYRE,

Lord Chief Juſtice of His Majeſty's Court of Common Plea

And One of the COMMISSIONERS

Named in a Special Commiſſion of Oyer and Terminer, iſſued
under the Great Seal of *Great Britain,*

TO ENQUIRE OF CERTAIN

HIGH TREASONS,

AND

MISPRISONS OF TREASON,

Within the County of MIDDLESEX,

To the GRAND JURY,

At the SESSION HOUSE on *Clerkenwell Green,* on *Thurſday* the 2d
Day of October, 1794.

———————

Publiſhed at the Requeſt of the GRAND JURY;

And printed and ſold by DANIEL ISAAC EATON, at the COCK
AND SWINE, Newgate-ſtreet.

1794.

GENTLEMEN of the Grand Inqueft,

YOU are affembled under the Authority of the King's Commiffion, which has been iffued for the hearing and determining of the Offences of High Treafon and Mifprifions of Treafon, againft the Perfon and Authority of the King.

That which hath given Occafion for this Commiffion is that which is declared by a late Statute, namely, " *That a traiterous and deteftable* " *Confpiracy has been formed for fubverting the exifting Laws and Con-* " *ftitution, and for introducing the Syftem of Anarchy and Confufion which* " *has fo lately prevailed in France ;*" A CRIME OF THAT DEEP MA-LIGNITY which loudly calls upon the Juftice of the Nation to inter-pofe, " *for the better Prefervation of His Majefty's facred Perfon, and for* " *fecuring the Peace, and the Laws and Liberties of this Kingdom.*"

The firft and effective Step in this, as in the ordinary criminal Pro-ceedings, is, that a Grand Jury of the Country fhould make public In-quifition for the King, fhould diligently enquire, difcover, and bring forward to the View of the criminal Magiftrate, thofe Offences which it is the Object of this fpecial Commiffion to hear and to determine.

You

You are Jurors for our Sovereign Lord the King; you are fo ftiled in every Indictment which is prefented; but let the true Nature of this Service be underftood. The King commands you to enter upon this Enquiry; but the Royal Authority in this, as in all its other Functions, is exerted, and operates ultimately for the Benefit of His People. It is the King's Object, His Duty, to vindicate His Peace, His Crown and Dignity, becaufe HIS PEACE, HIS CROWN AND DIGNITY, are the SUBJECTS PROTECTION, THEIR SECURITY, AND THEIR HAPPINESS.

It is ultimately for them that the Laws have thrown extraordinary Fences around the Perfon and Authority of the King, and all that Attempts againft the one or the other are confidered as the higheft Crimes which can be committed, and are punifhed with a Severity which nothing but the *Salus populi* can juftify.

The Bufinefs of this Day calls upon me (in order that you may the better underftand the Subject which is to come before you) to open to you the Nature of that Offence, which I have before fpoken of in general.

An ancient Statute, 25 Edward III, has declared and defined it. I fhall ftate to you fo much of that Declaration and Definition as appears to me to have any probable Relation to the Bufinefs of this Day.

By that Statute it is declared to be HIGH TREASON *to compafs or imagine the Death of the King,* provided fuch Compaffing and Imagination be manifefted by fome Act or Acts proved (by Two Witneffes) to have been done by the Party accufed in Profecution of that Compaffing and Imagination; that is, from the Moment that this wicked Imagination of the Heart is acted upon, that any Steps are taken in any Manner conducing to the bringing about and effecting the Defign, the Intention becomes the Crime, and the Meafure of it is full.

Thefe Acts or Steps are technically denominated *Overt Acts*; and the Forms of Proceeding in Cafes of this Nature require that thefe Overt Acts fhould be particularly fet forth in every Indictment of Treafon; and, from the Nature of them, they muft conftitute the principal Head of Enquiry for the Grand Jury.

Thefe

Thefe Overt Acts involve in them Two diftinct Confiderations; 1ft. The Matter of Fact of which they confift; in the next Place, the Relation of that Fact to the Defign.

With refpect to the mere Matter of Fact, it will be for the Grand Jury to enquire into the true State of it; and I can have very little to offer to your Confideration refpecting it: And with refpect to the Queftion, whether the Fact has Relation to the Defign fo as to conftitute an Overt Act of this Species of Treafon, which involves Confiderations both of Fact and of Law, it is impoffible that any certain Rule fhould be laid down for your Government; Overt Acts being in their Nature all the poffible Means which may be ufed in the Profecution of the End propofed; they can be no otherwife defined, and muft remain for ever infinitely various.

Thus far I can inform you: that Occafions have unhappily, but too frequently, brought Overt Acts of this Species of Treafon under Confideration; in confequence of which we are furnifhed with judicial Opinions upon many of them; and we are alfo furnifhed with Opinions (drawn from thefe Sources) of Text Writers—fome of the wifeft and moft enlightened Men of their Time, whofe Integrity has been always confidered as the moft prominent Feature of their Character, and whofe Doctrines do now form great Landmarks, by which Pofterity will be enabled to trace, with a great Degree of Certainty, the boundary Lines between High Treafon, and Offences of a lower Order and Degree.

It is a fortunate Circumftance that we are thus affifted; for it is not to be diffembled that, though the Crime of High Treafon is " *the* " *greateft Crime againft Faith, Duty, and Human Society,*" and though " *the Public is deeply interefted in every Profecution of this Kind well* " *founded,*" there hath been, in the beft Times, a confiderable Degree of Jealoufy on the Subject of Profecutions for High Treafon; they are State Profecutions, and the Confequences to the Party accufed are Penal in the Extreme.

Jurors and Judges ought to feel an extraordinary Anxiety that Profecutions of this Nature fhould proceed upon folid Grounds. I can
eafily

eafily conceive, therefore, that it muft be a great Relief to Jurors placed in the refponfible Situation in which you now ftand, bound to do Juftice to their Country and to the Perfons accufed, and anxious to difcharge this truft faithfully; fure I am that it is Confolation and Comfort to us, who have upon us the Refponfibility of declaring what the Law is in Cafes in which the Public and the Individual are fo deeply interefted; to have fuch Men as the great Sir Matthew Hale, and an eminent Judge of our own Times who, with the Experience of a Century, concurs with him in Opinion, Sir Michael Fofter, for our Guides.

To proceed by Steps : From thefe Writers upon the Law of Treafon (who fpeak, as I have before obferved, upon the Authority of adjudged Cafes) we learn, that not only Acts of *immediate* and *direct* Attempts againft the King's Life are Overt Acts of compaffing his Death, but that all the *remoter Steps* taken with a View to affift to bring about the actual Attempt, are equally Overt Acts of this Species of Treafon; even the Meeting and the confulting what Steps fhould be taken in order to bring about the End propofed, has been always deemed to be an Act done in Profecution of the Defign, and as fuch an Overt Act of this Treafon—This is our Firft Step in the prefent Enquiry. I proceed to obferve, that the Overt Acts I have been now fpeaking of have Reference, nearer or more remote, to a *direct* and *immediate* Attempt upon the Life of the King ; but that the fame Authority informs us, that they who aim directly at the Life of the King (fuch, for Inftance, as the Perfons who were concerned in the Affaffination Plot in the Reign of King William) are not the only Perfons who can be faid to compafs or imagin the Death of the King. *The entering into Meafures which, in the Nature of Things, or in the common Experience of Mankind, do obvioufly tend to bring the Life of the King into Danger, is alfo compaffing and imagining the Death of the King ;* and the Meafures which are taken will be at once Evidence of the compaffing, and Overt Acts of it.

The Inftances which are put by Sir Matthew Hale and Sir Michael Fofter (and upon which there have been adjudged Cafes) are of Confpiracies to *depofe* the King; to *imprifon* Him; to *get His Perfon into the Power of the Confpirators* ; to *procure an Invafion of the Kingdom*. The Firft of thefe, apparently the ftrongeft Cafe, and coming the neareft to the direct Attempt againft the Life of the King ; the laft, the fartheft
removed

removed from that direct Attempt, but being a Measure tending to deftroy the public Peace of the Country, to introduce Hoftilities, and the
Neceffity of refifting Force by Force, and where it is obvious that the
Conflict has an ultimate Tendency to bring the Perfon and Life of the
King into Jeopardy; it is taken to be a found Conftruction of the Statute 25 Edward III. and the clear Law of the Land, that this alfo is
compaffing and imagining the Death of the King.

If a Confpiracy to depofe or to imprifon the King, to get His Per-
fon into the Power of the Confpirators, or to procure an Invafion of
the Kingdom, involves in it the compaffing and imagining of His
Death, and if Steps taken in Profecution of fuch a Confpiracy are
rightly deemed Overt Acts of the Treafon, of imagining and compaf-
fing the King's Death; need I add, that if it fhould appear that IT
HAS ENTERED INTO THE HEART OF ANY MAN, WHO IS A SUB-
JECT OF THIS COUNTRY, TO DESIGN TO OVERTHROW THE
WHOLE GOVERNMENT OF THE COUNTRY, TO PULL DOWN
AND TO SUBVERT FROM ITS VERY FOUNDATIONS THE BRI-
TISH MONARCHY, THAT GLORIOUS FABRIC WHICH IT HAS
BEEN THE WORK OF AGES TO ERECT, MAINTAIN, AND SUP-
PORT, WHICH HAS BEEN CEMENTED WITH THE BEST BLOOD OF
OUR ANCESTORS; TO DESIGN SUCH A HORRIBLE RUIN AND
DEVASTATION WHICH NO KING COULD SURVIVE, A CRIME OF
SUCH A MAGNITUDE THAT NO LAWGIVER IN THIS COUNTRY
HATH EVER VENTURED TO CONTEMPLATE IT IN ITS WHOLE
EXTENT; need I add, I fay, that the Complication, and the enormous
Extent of fuch a Defign, will not prevent its being diftinctly feen,
that *the compaffing and imagining the Death of the King is involved in it,
is in in Truth of its very Effence.*

This is too plain a Cafe to require farther Illuftration from me. If
any Man of plain fenfe, but not converfant with Subjects of this Nature, fhould feel himfelf difpofed to afk whether a Confpiracy of this
Nature is to be reached by this Medium only; whether it is a *fpecific*
Treafon to compafs and imagine the Death of the King, and *not a
fpecific* Treafon to confpire to fubvert the Monarchy itfelf; I anfwer,
that the Statute of Edward III, by which we are governed, hath not
declared

declared this (which in all juſt Theory of Treaſon is the greateſt of all Treaſons) to be High Treaſon.

I ſay no Lawgiver had ever ventured to contemplate it in its whole Extent; the *Seditio Regni*, ſpoken of by ſome of our ancient Writers, comes the neareſt to it, but falls far ſhort of it : Perhaps if it were now a Queſtion whether ſuch a Conſpiracy ſhould be made a ſpecific Treaſon, it might be argued to be unneceſſary : That in ſecuring the Perſon and Authority of the King from all Danger, the Monarchy, the Religion and Laws of our Country are incidentally ſecured ; that the Conſtitution of our Government is ſo framed, that the Imperial Crown of the Realm is the common Centre of the Whole ; that all traiterous Attempts upon any Part of it are inſtantly communicated to that Centre, and felt there ; and that, as upon every Principle of public Policy and Juſtice they are puniſhable as traiterous Attempts againſt the King's Perſon or Authority, and will, according to the particular Nature of the traiterous Attempt, fall within One or other of the ſpecific Treaſons againſt the King, declared by the Statute of 25 Edward III; this greateſt of all Treaſons is ſufficiently provided againſt by Law.

Gentlemen, I preſume I hardly need give you this Caution, that though it has been expreſsly declared, by the higheſt Authority, that there do exiſt in this Country Men capable of meditating the Deſtruction of the Conſtitution under which we live ; that Declaration, being extrajudicial, is not a Ground upon which you ought to proceed.

In conſequence of that Declaration it became a public and indiſpenſable Duty of His Majeſty to inſtitute this ſolemn Proceeding, and to impoſe upon you the painful Taſk of examining the Accuſations, which ſhall be brought before you ; but it will be your Duty to examine them in a regular judicial Courſe, that is, by hearing the Evidence, and forming your own Judgement upon it.

And here, as I do not think it neceſſary to trouble you with Obſervations upon the other Branches of the Statute 25 Edward III. the Charge to the Grand Inqueſt might conclude ; had not the particular Nature of the Conſpiracy, alledged to have been formed againſt the

State

State, been difclofed, and made Matter of public Notority by the Reports of the Two Houfes of Parliament, now in every ones Hands: But that being the Cafe, I am apprehenfive that I fhall not be thought to have fulfilled the Duty, which the Judge owes to the Grand Jury, when Queftions in the criminal Law arife on new and extraordinary Cafes of Fact; if I did not plainly and diftinctly ftate what I conceive the Law to be, or what Doubts I conceive may arife in Law, upon the Facts which are likely to be laid before you, according to the different Points of View in which thofe Facts may appear to you.

It is Matter of public Notority that there have been Affociations formed in this Country, and in other Parts of the Kingdom, the profeffed Purpofe of which has been a Change in the Conftitution of the Commons Houfe of Parliament, and the obtaining of Annual Parliaments; and that to fome of thefe Affociations other Purpofes, hidden under this Veil, Purpofes the moft traiterous, have been imputed; and that fome of thefe Affociations have been fuppofed to have actually adopted Meafures of fuch a Nature, and to have gone into fuch Exceffes, as will amount to the Crime of High Treafon.

If there be Ground to confider the profeffed Purpofe of any of thefe Affociations, a *Reform in Parliament*, as mere Colour, and as a Pretext held out in order to cover deeper Defigns—Defigns againft the whole Conftitution, and Government of the Country; the Cafe of thofe embarked in fuch Defigns is that, which I have already confidered. Whether this be fo, or not, is mere Matter of Fact; as to which I fhall only remind you, that an Enquiry into a Charge of this Nature, which undertakes to make out that the oftenfible Purpofe is a mere Veil, under which is concealed a traiterous Confpiracy, requires cool and deliberate Examination, and the moft attentive Confideration; and that the Refult fhould be perfectly clear and fatisfactory. In the Affairs of common Life, no Man is juftified in imputing to another a Meaning contrary to what he himfelf expreffes, but upon the fulleft Evidence. On the other Hand, where the Charge can be made out, it is adding to the Crime meditated the deepeft Diffimulation and Treachery, with refpect to thofe Individuals, who may be drawn in to embark in the oftenfible Purpofe, as well as to the Public, againft which this dark Myftery of Wickednefs is fabricated.

B   But

But if we suppose these Associations to adhere to the professed Purpose, and to have no other primary Object; it may be asked, is it possible, and (if it be possible) by what Process is it, THAT AN ASSOCI-ATION FOR THE REFORM OF PARLIAMENT CAN WORK ITSELF UP TO THE CRIME OF HIGH TREASON? All Men may, nay, all Men must, if they possess the Faculty of thinking, reason upon every Thing which sufficiently interests them to become Objects of their Attention; and among the Objects of the Attention of free Men, the Principles of Government, the Constitution of particular Governments, and, above all, the Constitution of the Government under which they live, will naturally engage Attention, and provoke Speculation. The Power of Communication of Thoughts and Opinions is the Gift of God, and the Freedom of it is the Source of all Science, the First Fruits and the ultimate Happiness of Society; and therefore it seems to follow, that human Laws ought not to interpose, nay, cannot interpose, to prevent the Communication of Sentiments and Opinions in voluntary Assemblies of Men; all which is true, with this single Reservation, that THOSE ASSEMBLIES ARE TO BE SO COMPOSED, AND SO CONDUCTED, AS NOT TO ENDANGER THE PUBLIC PEACE AND GOOD ORDER OF THE GOVERNMENT UNDER WHICH THEY LIVE; and I shall not state to you that Associations and Assemblies of Men, for the Purpose of obtaining a Reform in the interior Constitution of the British Parliament, are simply unlawful; but, on the other Hand, I must state to you, that they may but two easily degenerate, and become unlawful, in the highest Degree, even to the enormous Extent of the Crime of High Treason.

The Process is very simple: Let us imagine to ourselves this Case. A few well meaning Men conceive that they and their Fellow Subjects labour under some Grievance; they assemble peaceably to deliberate on the Means of obtaining Redress; the Numbers increase; the Discussion grows animated, eager, and violent; a rash Measure is proposed, adopted, and acted upon; who can say where this shall stop, and that these Men, who originally assembled peaceably, shall not finally and suddenly too, involve themselves in the Crime of High Treason. It is apparent how easily an impetuous Man may precipitate such Assemblies into Crimes of unforeseen Magnitude, and Danger to the State: But, let it be considered, that bad Men may also find their Way into such Assemblies,

blies, and use the innocent Purposes of their Affociation as the Stalk-ing Horfe to *their* Purpofes of a very different Complexion. How eafy for fuch Men to practife upon the Credulity and the Enthufiafm of ho-neft Men, Lovers of their Country, loyal to their Prince, but eagerly bent upon fome fpeculative Improvements in the Frame, and internal Mechanifm of the Government? If we fuppofe bad Men to have once gained an Afcendancy in an Affembly of this Defcription, popular in its Conftitution, and having popular Objects; how eafy is it for fuch Men to plunge fuch an Affembly into the moft criminal Exceffes? Thus far I am fpeaking in general, merely to illuftrate the Propofition, that Men who affemble in order to procure a Reform of Parliament may involve themfelves in the Guilt of High Treafon.

The Notoriety to which I have alluded leads me to fuppofe, that the *Project of a Convention* of the People, to be affembled under the Advice and Direction of fome of thefe Societies, or of Delegations from them, will be the leading Fact, which will be laid before you in Evidence, refpecting the Conduct and Meafures of thefe Affociations; a Project, which perhaps, in better Times, would have been hardly thought wor-thy of grave Confideration; but, in thefe our Days, having been at-tempted to be put in Execution in a diftant Part of the United King-doms, and, with the Example of a neighbouring Country before our Eyes, is defervedly become an Object of the Jealoufy of our Laws: It will be your Duty to examine the Evidence on this Head very carefully, and to fift it to the Bottom; to confider every Part of it in itfelf, and as it ftands connected with other Parts of it, and to draw the Conclu-fion of Fact, as to the Exiftence, the Nature, and the Object of this Project of a Convention, from the Whole.

In the Courfe of the Evidence you will probably hear of *Bodies of Men having been collected together, of violent Refolutions voted at thefe and at other Meetings, of fome Preparation of offenfive Weapons, and of the Adoption of the Language, and Manner of proceeding of thofe Conventions in France, which have poffeffed themfelves of the Government of that Coun-try:* I dwell not on thefe Particulars, becaufe I confider them, not as fubftantive Treafons, but as Circumftances of Evidence, tending to afcertain the true Nature of the Object, which thefe Perfons had in

B 2   View,

View, and alfo the true Nature of this Project of a Convention, and to be confidered by you in the Mafs of that Evidence ; which Evidence it does not fall within the Province of the Charge to confider in Detail ; my prefent Duty is, to inform you what the Law is upon the Matter of Fact, which in your Judgment fhall be the Refult of the Evidence.

I prefume that I have fufficiently explained to you that A PROJECT TO BRING THE PEOPLE TOGETHER IN CONVENTION IN IMITATION OF THOSE NATIONAL CONVENTIONS WHICH WE HAVE HEARD OF IN FRANCE IN ORDER TO USURP THE GOVERNMENT OF THE COUNTRY, and ANY ONE STEP TAKEN TOWARDS BRINGING IT ABOUT, fuch as for Inftance, *Confultations, forming of Committees to confider of the Means, acting in thofe Committees,* would be a Cafe of no Difficulty that it would be the CLEAREST HIGH TREASON ; it would be compaffing and imagining the King's Death, and not only His Death, but the Death and Deftruction of all Order, Religion, Laws, all Property, all Security for the Lives and Liberties of the King's Subjects.

That which remains to be confidered is, *the Project of a Convention having for its fole Object the effecting a Change in the Mode of Reprefentation of the People in Parliament, and the obtaining that Parliaments fhould be held annually ;* and here there is Room to diftinguifh. Such a Project of a Convention, taking it to be criminal, may be criminal in different Degrees, according to the Cafe in evidence, from whence you are to collect the true Nature and Extent of the Plan, and the Manner in which it is intended to operate ; and it will become a Queftion of great Importance, under what Clafs of Crimes it ought to be ranged.

In determining upon the Complexion and Quality of this Project of a Convention, you will lay down to yourfelves One Principle which is never to be departed from ; THAT ALTERATIONS IN THE REPRESENTATION OF THE PEOPLE IN PARLIAMENT, OR IN THE LAW FOR HOLDING PARLIAMENTS, CAN ONLY BE EFFECTED BY THE AUTHORITY OF THE KING, LORDS, AND COMMONS, IN PARLIAMENT ASSEMBLED. This being taken as a Foundation ; it feems to
follow

follow as a necessary Consequence, that *a Project of a Convention, which should have for its Object the obtaining a Parliamentary Reform without the Authority of Parliament, and Steps taken upon it, would be* HIGH TREASON *in all the Actors in it;* for this is a Conspiracy to overturn the Government. The Government cannot be said to exist, if the Functions of Legiflation are usurped for a Moment; and it then becomes of little Confequence indeed, that the original Confpirators, perhaps, had only meditated a Plan of moderate Reform: It is, in the Nature of Things, that the Power fhould go out of their Hands, and be beyond the Reach of their Controul. A Confpiracy of this Nature is therefore, at beft, a Confpiracy to overturn the Government, in order to new model it, which is, in Effect, to introduce Anarchy, and that which Anarchy may chance to fettle down into; after the King may have been brought to the Scaffold, and after the Country may have fuffered all the Miferies, which Difcord, and Civil War fhall have produced.

Whether *the Project of a Convention, having for its Object the collecting together a Power, which should overawe the Legislative Body, and extort a Parliamentary Reform from it,* if acted upon, will alfo amount to HIGH TREASON, and to the fpecific Treafon of compaffing and imagining the King's Death, is a more doubtful Queftion. Thus far is clear; a Force upon the Parliament muft be immediately directed againft the King, who is an integral Part of it; it muft reach the King, or it can have no Effect at all. Laws are enacted in Parliament by the King's Majefty, by and with the Advice and Confent of the Lords and Commons, in Parliament affembled. A Force meditated againft the Parliament, is therefore a Force meditated againft the King, and feems to fall within the Cafe of a Force meditated againft the King, to compel Him to alter the Meafures of His Government: But, in that Cafe, it does not appear to me that I am warranted by the Authorities to ftate to you, as clear Law, that the mere Confpiracy to raife fuch a Force, and the entering into Confultations refpecting it, will alone, and without actually raifing the Force, conftitute the Crime of High Treafon. What the Law is in that Cafe, and what will be the Effect of the Circumftance of the Force being meditated againft the King IN PARLIAMENT, againft the King in the Exercife of the Royal Function in a Point, which is of the very Effence of his Monarchy, will be fit to be folemnly confidered, and determined when the Cafe fhall arife.

It

It may be stated to you as clear, That *the Project of a Convention, having for its sole Object a dutiful and peaceable Application to the Wisdom of Parliament on the Subject of a wished-for Reform, which Application should be entitled to weight and Credit from the Universality of it, but should still leave to the Parliament the freest Exercise of its Discretion to grant or to refuse the Prayer of the Petition* (great as the Responsibility will be on the Persons concerned in it, in respect of the many probable, and all the possible, bad Consequences of collecting a great Number of People together; with no specific legal Powers to be exercised, and under no Government but that of their own Discretion), *cannot in itself merit to be ranked among that Class of Offences* which we are now assembled to hear and determine.

Upon this last Statement of the Fact of the Case, I am not called upon, and therefore it would not be proper for me to say more.

Gentlemen, You will now proceed upon the several Articles of Enquiry, which have been given you in Charge : If you find that the Parties, who shall be accused before you, have been pursuing lawful Ends by lawful Means, or have been only indiscreet, or, at the worst, if criminal, that they have not been criminal to the Extent of those Treasons, to which our Enquiries are confined, then say, that the Bills which shall be presented to you ARE NOT TRUE BILLS: But, if any of the accused Persons shall appear to you to have been engaged in that traiterous and detestable Conspiracy described in the Preamble of the late Statute; or, if without any formed Design to go the whole Length of that Conspiracy, they have yet acted upon the desperate Imagination of bringing about Alterations in the Constitution of the Commons House of Parliament, or in the Manner of holding Parliaments, without the Authority of Parliament, and, in Defiance of it, by an usurped Power, which should, in that Instance, suspend the lawful Authority of the King, Lords, and Commons, in Parliament assembled, and take upon itself the Function of Legislation; (which Imagination amounts to a Conspiracy to subvert the existing Laws and Constitution, differing from the former only in the Extent of its Object); YOU WILL THEN DO THAT WHICH BELONGS TO YOUR OFFICE TO DO.

In the Third View of the Case of the accused Persons; that is, if you find them involved in, and proceeding upon, a Design to collect the

the People together againſt the Legiſlative Authority of the Country, for the Purpoſe, not of uſurping the Funſtions of the Legiſlature, but of overawing the Parliament, and ſo compelling the King, Lords, and Commons, in Parliament aſſembled, to enaſt a Law for new modelling the Commons Houſe of Parliament, or for holding Annual Parliaments; and that Charges of High Treaſon are offered to be maintained againſt them upon this Ground only; perhaps it may be fitting that, IN RESPECT OF THE EXTRAORDINARY NATURE AND DANGEROUS EXTENT AND VERY CRIMINAL COMPLEXION OF SUCH A CONSPIRACY, that Caſe, which I ſtate to you as a new and a doubtful Caſe, ſhould be put into a judicial Courſe of Enquiry, that it may receive *a ſolemn Adjudication, whether it will, or will not, amount to* HIGH TREASON, in order to which the Bills muſt be found to be true Bills.

Gentlemen, I have not opened to you the Law of *Miſpriſion of Treaſon*, becauſe I am not aware that there are any Commitments for that Offence; and therefore I have no Reaſon to ſuppoſe that there will be any Proſecution for that Offence. It conſiſts of *the Concealment of Treaſon committed by others*, (which undoubtedly it is every Man's Duty to diſcloſe), and the Puniſhment is extremely ſevere; but the Humanity of modern Times hath uſually interpoſed, and I truſt that the Neceſſities of the preſent Hour will not demand, that the Law of Miſpriſion of Treaſon ſhould now be carried into Execution.

Gentlemen, I diſmiſs you with confident Expectation that your Judgment will be directed to thoſe Concluſions, which MAY CLEAR INNOCENT MEN FROM ALL SUSPICION OF GUILT, BRING THE GUILTY TO CONDIGN PUNISHMENT, PRESERVE THE LIFE OF OUR GRACIOUS SOVEREIGN, SECURE THE STABILITY OF OUR GOVERNMENT, AND MAINTAIN THE PUBLIC PEACE, IN WHICH COMPREHENSIVE TERM IS INCLUDED THE WELFARE AND HAPPINESS OF THE PEOPLE UNDER THE PROTECTION OF THE LAWS AND LIBERTIES OF THE KINGDOM.

CURSORY STRICTURES

ON THE

CHARGE

DELIVERED BY

LORD CHIEF JUSTICE EYRE

TO THE

GRAND JURY,

OCTOBER 2, 1794.

FIRST PUBLISHED IN THE MORNING CHRONICLE OCTOBER 21.

LONDON:

Printed for, and Sold by D. I. EATON, at the COCK AND SWINE, No. 74, Newgate-ftreet.

1794.

*** The following Work was originally publifhed by
Mr. KEARSLEY, who, on receiving a menace from the
Treafury, difcontinued its fale:—DANIEL ISAAC EATON,
who does not, perhaps, confider a menace from that place
in the fame way as Mr. Kearfley,—but believes that a
TREASURY MANDATE is not yet generally adopted
as the law of the land, was *thereby* induced upon application made to him, not only to fell what remained of
the firft edition, but alfo to offer to the public, at half price,
a work, which as its only crime is, perhaps, the containing more law than the Charge on which it animadverts,
cannot but be very acceptable to thofe who would rather
expend fix-pence than a fhilling. And as pofterity
may need every proof that a charge, fo fraught with labour and invention, was ever given, the Charge itfelf is
annexed at the fame reduced price.

CURSORY STRICTURES, &c.

A SPECIAL Commiffion was opened on the Second day of October for the trial of certain perfons apprehended upon fufpicion of High Treafon, the greateft part of whom were taken into cuftody in the month of May 1794. Upon this occafion a charge was delivered to the Grand Jury, by Sir James Eyre, Lord Chief Juftice of the Court of Common Pleas.

It is one of the firft privileges of an Englifhman, one of the firft duties of a rational being, to difcufs with perfect freedom, all principles propofed to be enforced upon general obfervance, when thofe principles are firft difclofed, and before they have, by any folemn and final proceeding, been made part of a regular eftablifhed fyftem. The Chief Juftice, in his Charge to the Jury, has delivered many new and extraordinary doctrines upon the fubject of Treafon. Thefe doctrines, now when they have been for the firft time ftated, it is fit we fhould examine. In that examination, I fhall deliver my opinions in a manner perfectly frank and explicit. No man fhould feek to offend high authorities and elevated magiftracy; but the object before us is of an importance paramount to thefe confiderations. Decorum is an excellent thing; but we ought not to facrifice to the faftidious refinements of decorum, all that is moft firm in fecurity, or moft eftimable in focial inftitution.

The Chief Juftice has promifed a publication of his Charge, and I fhould have been glad to have waited for the opportunity of an authentic copy. But there are only a few days remaining, previous to the commencement of trials, of the higheft expectation, and moft unlimited importance. He who thinks as I think, that the beft principles of

civil

civil government, and all that our anceftors moft affectionately loved, are ftruck at in the moft flagrant manner in this Charge, will feel that there is not an hour to be loft. While I animadvert upon its enormities, it is with fome pleafure that I fhall reflect upon the poffibility of the enormities being aggravated or created by the imperfect and irregular form of the publication before me. Every friend of his country will participate the higheft fatisfaction, at finding them anfwered, by a regular publication of the Charge to the Grand Jury, ftripped of the illegal and deftructive doctrines that now appear to pollute it.

Among the various branches of the Englifh Conftitution that have for centuries been a topic of unbounded praife, there is none, that has been more, or more defervedly, applauded, than that which relates to the law of Treafon. " The crime of High Treafon," fays Chief Juftice Eyre, * " though the greateft crime againft faith, duty, and " and human fociety, and though the public is deeply interefted in " every well founded profecution of this kind, has yet, at the beft " times, been the object of confiderable jealoufy, in refpect of the pro- " fecutions inftituted againft it : they are State profecutions." It is therefore of the utmoft confequence, that the crime of High Treafon fhould be clearly defined, and the exquifite jealoufy allayed, which muft otherwife arife in every benevolent mind. This has been done by the act 25 Edward III. one of the great palladiums of the Englifh conftitution. This law has been fanctioned by the experience of more than four centuries; and, though it has been repeatedly attacked by the encroachments of tyrannical princes, and the decifions of profligate judges, Englifhmen have always found it neceffary in the fequel to ftrip it of mifchievous appendages and artificial gloffes, and reftore it to its original fimplicity and luftre. By this law all treafon, exclufively of a few articles of little general concern, is confined to the " levying war againft the King within the realm, and the compaffing " or imagining the death of the King." Nay, the wife framers of the law were not contented to ftop here : they not only fhut out the mifchief of arbitrary and conftructive treafon for themfelves, but inferted a particular claufe, provided that " if in any future time it " might be neceffary to declare any new treafons, that fhould only be

---

* P. 4, He adds, " it is not to be diffembled."—Will any one venture to fay, that the Judges of England would diffemble, if they could, in matters of the utmoft value to the fubject ; and that it is with reluctance they confefs any thing, that tends moft to general fecurity, equity, and welfare ?

" done

" done by a direct proceeding of parliament for that special purpose."

It is obvious upon the face of this wife and moderate law, that it made it extremely difficult for a bad king, or an unprincipled admini-ftration, to gratify their refentment againft a pertinacious opponent by inftituting againft him a charge of treafon. Such kings and minifters would not fail to complain, that the law of Edward III. fhut up the crime within too narrow bounds; that a fubtle adverfary of the pub-lic peace would eafily evade thefe grofs and palpable definitions; and that crimes of the higheft magnitude, and moft dangerous tendency, might be committed, which could never be brought under thefe dry, fhort, and inflexible claufes. It is not to be denied, that fome mifchief might arife from fo careful, lenient, and unbloody a provifion. No doubt offences might be conceived, not lefs dangerous to the public wel-fare, than thofe defcribed in the act under confideration. But our an-ceftors expofed themfelves to this inconvenience, and found it by no means fuch as was hard to be borne. They experienced a fubftantial benefit, a proud and liberal fecurity, arifing out of this ftatute, which amply compenfated for the mifchief of fuch fubterfuges as might occa-fionally be employed by a few infignificant criminals. If we part with their wifdom and policy, let us beware that we do not fubftitute a mortal venom in its ftead.

The Chief Juftice has thought proper to confine himfelf to that ar-ticle of the ftatute of King Edward III. which treats of " compaffing and imagining the death of the King." This compaffing and imagin-ing, he very properly obferves, " requires that it fhould be manifefted " by overt acts; * and he adds, " that they who aim directly at the " life of the King, are not the only perfons who may be faid to com-" pafs or imagine his death. The entering into meafures, which in " the nature of things do obvioufly tend to bring the life of the King " into danger, is alfo compaffing and imagining the death of the King; " and the meafures which are taken, will be at once evidence of the " compaffing and overt acts of it. The inftances which are put under " this head by Sir Michael Fofter and Sir Matthew Hale, and upon " which there have been adjudged cafes, are [principally four, viz.] " of a confpiracy to depofe the King, to imprifon him, to get his " perfon into the power of the confpirators, and to procure an invafion " of the kingdom." † He farther ftates, " that occafions have unhap-

* P. 2.   † P. 5.
" pily

" pily but too frequently brought overt acts of this species of treafon
" under confideration, in confequence of which we are furnished with
" judicial opinions upon many of them. We are alfo furnished with
" opinions drawn from thefe fources of text writers, fome of the wifeft
" and moft enlightened men of their time, whofe integrity has always
" been confidered as the moft prominent feature of their character, and
" whofe doctrines do now form great land marks, by which pofterity
" will be enabled to trace with confiderable certainty the boundary
" line between High Treafon, and offences of a lower order and de-
" gree. It is a fortunate circumftance," continues the Chief Juftice,
" that we are thus affifted. I can eafily conceive that it muft be a
" great relief to Jurors, placed in the refponfihle fituation in which
" you now ftand; and fure I am that it is a confolation and comfort to
" us, who have upon us the refponfibility of declaring what the law
" is, in cafes in which the public and the individual are fo deeply in-
" terefted." *

In all this peramble of the Chief Juftice, there is certainly fomething
extremely humane and confiderate. I trace in it the language of a conftitutional lawyer, a found logician, and a temperate, difcreet, and honeft man. I fee rifing to my view by juft degrees a judge, refting
upon the law as it is, and determinedly fetting his face againft new,
unprecedented, and temporizing conftructions. I fee a judge, that
fcorns to bend his neck to the yoke of any party, or any adminiftration ; who expounds the unalterable principles of juftice, and is prepared to try by them, and them only, the perfons that are brought before him. I fee him taking to himfelf, and holding out to the Jury
the manly confolation, that they are to make no new law, and force
no new interpretations ; that they are to confult only the ftatutes of
the realm, and the decifions of thofe writers who have been the lumi-
naries of England.

Meanwhile what would be faid by our contemporaries and by our
pofterity, if this picture were to be reverfed; if thefe promifes were
made, only to render our difappointment more bitter; if thefe high
profeffions ferved merely as an introduction to an unparalleled mafs of
arbitrary conftructions, of new fangled treafons, and doctrines equally
inconfiftent with hiftory and themfelves ? I hope thefe appearances
will not be found in the authentic charge. But whoever be the un-

* P. 4.

principled

principled impoftor, that thus audacioufly faps the vitals of human liberty and human happinefs, be he printer, or be he judge, it is
the duty of every friend to mankind to detect and expofe his fo-
phiftries.

Chief Juftice Eyre, after having ftated the treafons which are moft
ftrictly within the act of Edward III. as well as thofe which are fanctioned by high law authorities, and upon which there have been adjudged cafes, proceeds to reafon in the following manner.

" If a confpiracy to depofe or imprifon the King, to get his perfon
" into the power of the confpirators, or procure an invafion of the
" kingdom, involves in it the compaffing and imagining his death,
" and if fteps taken in profecution of fuch a confpiracy, are rightly
" deemed overt acts of the treafon of compaffing the King's death,"
what ought to be our judgment, " if it fhould appear that it had
" entered into the heart of any man, who is a fubject of this country,
" to defign to overthrow the whole government of the country, to pull
" down and to fubvert from its very foundations the Britifh Mo-
" narchy, that glorious fabric, which it has been the work of ages to
" erect, maintain, and fupport; which has been cemented with the
" beft blood of our anceftors; to defign fuch a horrible ruin and de-
" vaftation, which no king could furvive * ?"

Here we are prefented with the queftion which is no doubt of the
utmoft magnitude and importance. Is the proceeding thus defcribed
matter of High Treafon, or is it not? It confeffedly does not come within the letter of 25 Edward III. It does not come within the remoter
inftances " upon which there have been adjudged cafes." Chief
Juftice Eyre has already enumerated thefe, and, having finifhed that
part of his fubject, gone on to fomething confeffedly different.

Are we reafoning refpecting law, or refpecting a ftate of fociety,
which, having no fixed rules of law, is obliged to confult the dictates
of its own difcretion? Plainly the former. It follows therefore, that
the aggravations collected by the Chief Juftice, are totally foreign to
the queftion he had to confider. Let it be granted, that the crime, in the
eye of reafon and difcretion, is the moft enormous, that it can enter into
the heart of man to conceive, ftill I fhall have a right to afk, Is it a crime
againft law? Show me the ftatute that defcribes it; refer me to the

* Page 6.

precedent

precedent by which it is defined; quote me the adjudge cafe in which a matter of fuch unparalleled magnitude is fettled.

Let us know the ground upon which we ftand. Are we to underftand that, under Chief Juftice Eyre, and the other Judges of the Special Commiffion, reafonings are to be adduced from the axioms and dictums of moralifts and metaphyficians, and that men are to be convicted, fentenced, and executed, upon thefe? Are we to underftand that henceforth the man moft deeply read in the laws of his country, and moft affiduoufly conforming his actions to them, fhall be liable to be arraigned and capitally punifhed for a crime, that no law defcribes, that no precedent or adjudged cafe afcertains, at the arbitrary pleafure of the adminiftration for the time being? Such a miferable mifcellany of law and metaphyfical maxims; would be ten thoufand times worfe, than if we had no law to direct our actions. The law in that cafe would be a mere trap to delude us to our ruin, creating a fancied fecurity, an apparent clearnefs and definition, the better to cover the concealed pitfalls with which we are on every fide furrounded.

The Chief Juftice is by no means unaware of the tremendous confequences that would refult from fuch an adminiftration of criminal law. He fpeaks refpecting it, when the fubject is firft ftarted, with great temperance and caution. He fays, " That the crime of confpiring to " overthrow the monarchy, is fuch an one, as *no lawgiver in this* " *country has ever ventured to contemplate in its whole extent.* If any " man of plain fenfe, but not converfant with fubjects of this nature, " fhould feel himfelf difpofed to afk, whether a confpiracy of this ex- " traordinary nature is to be reached by the ftatute of treafons? whe- " ther it is a fpecific treafon to compafs and imagine the death of the " King, and not a fpecific treafon to confpire to fubvert the Monarchy " itfelf? I anfwer, that *the ftatute of Edward III. by which we are* " *bound, has not declared this,* which undoubtedly in all juft theory of " treafon is the greateft of all treafons, *to be a fpecific high treafon.* I " faid, NO LAWGIVER HAD EVER VENTURED TO CONTEMPLATE IT " IN ITS WHOLE EXTENT *."

The language here employed is no doubt ftrong and decifive. From hence it follows, with the moft irrefiftible evidence, that that " which " the ftatute by which we are bound, has not declared to be treafon," that " which no lawgiver has ever ventured to contemplate," can never

* Page 6.

be

be conftrued into treafon, till all law is annihilated, and all maxims of jurifprudence trampled under foot and defpifed.

No author has reafoned with greater accuracy, and in a more fatif-factory manner upon this important branch of the Englifh confti-tution than the celebrated David Hume, in his Hiftory of England. This author is well known to have been fufficiently favourable to the prerogative, yet his reafoning upon this fubject, in the cafe of Lord Strafford, are as minutely applicable to the cafe before us, as if he had written them with the proceedings of the Special Commiffion of October 1794, lying before him upon his table.

" Of all fpecies of guilt, the law of England has, with the moft " fcrupulous exactnefs, defined that of treafon ; becaufe on that fide it " was found moft neceffary to protect the fubject againft the violence of " the King and of his Minifters. In the famous ftatute of Edward III. " all the kinds of treafons are enumerated, and every other crime, be- " fide fuch as are there exprefsly mentioned, is carefully excluded " from that appellation. But with regard to this guilt, *An endeavour* " *to fubvert the fundamental laws,* the ftatute of treafon is totally filent ; " and arbitrarily to introduce it into the fatal catalogue, is itfelf a " fubverfion of all law ; and, under colour of defending liberty, re- " verfes a ftatute the beft calculated for the fecurity of liberty, that " was ever enacted by an Englifh Parliament *."

The following are a few fentences from the defence of Lord Strafford, as quoted by Mr. Hume, a nobleman, whom the republicans of that time fo vehemently hated, and were fo fixed to deftroy, as to render them little fcrupulous of overftepping the fimple and unbending provi-fions of the law.

" Where has this fpecies of guilt lain fo long concealed ? Where has " this fire been fo long buried, during fo many centuries, that no " fmoke fhould appear till it burft out at once to confume me and my " children ? Better it were to live under no law at all, and, by the " maxims of cautious prudence, to conform ourfelves the beft we can " to the arbitrary will of a mafter, than fancy we have a law on which " we can rely, and find at laft, that this law fhall inflict a punifhment " precedent to the promulgation, and try us by maxims unheard of till " the very moment of the profecution. Where is the mark fet upon " this crime ? Where the token by which I fhould difcover it ? It has

* Vol. vi. chap. liv. p. 403.

           " lain

" lain concealed; and no human prudence, no human innocence,
" could fave me from the deftruction with which I am at prefent
" threatened.

" It is now full two hundred and forty years fince treafons were
" defined. Let us be content with what our fathers left us; let not
" our ambition carry us to be more learned than they were, in thefe
" killing and deftructive arts! To all my afflictions add not this, my
" Lords, the moft fevere of any, that I, for my other fins, not for my
" treafons, be the means of introducing a precedent fo pernicious to
" the laws and liberties of my native country * !"

Chief Juftice Eyre's charge confifts of three parts. The firft five
pages contain principally a found and conftitutienal expofition of the law
of treafon, as exhibited in the books. In the two following pages we
are prefented with this portentous fpeculation, this new treafon of
" confpiring to fubvert the Monarchy;" though the Chief Juftice, as
has already appeared, has qualified his fpeculation, with expreffions,
proving, by accumulated evidence, and in the moft precife terms, that
this new imaginary treafon is no treafon by the laws of England.

Here, as the Chief Juftice obferves, the charge might have concluded. Here, if a proper regard had been paid to the effential principles of criminal juftice, it would have concluded; if not in reality
a little fooner. The remainder of the charge is made up of hypothefis,
prefumption, prejudication, and conjecture. There is fcarcely a fingle
line that is not deformed with fuch phrafes as " public notoriety,"
" things likely," " purpofes imputed," " meafures fuppofed," and
" imaginary cafes."

The plain reafon of all this is, that the Chief Juftice fufpected, that the
treafon defcribed in the ftatute 25 Edward III. and thofe founded upon
precedent, or deducible from adjudged cafes, even with the addition of
the Chief Juftice's new conftructive treafon, founded, as he confeffes,
upon no law, precedent, or cafe, and which therefore is in reality no
treafon, did not afford fufficient ground of crimination againft the prifoners. He is therefore obliged to leave the plain road, and travel out
of the record. No law, no deduction, or conftruction of law, that could
be forced or drawn out of a mere view of the ftatute, would anfwer
the purpofes of the Special Commiffion. He is therefore obliged to
indulge himfelf in conjecture, as to what the prifoners may have done,

* Vol. vi. chap. liv. p. 403.

and

and what are " the facts likely to be laid before the jury *." Two flagrant iniquities are included in this mode of proceeding. *First*, the
Chief Juftice implicitly confeffes himfelf unable, by direct deductions of
law, to fhow us what it is we ought to avoid, and is reduced to the neceffity of reafoning, not forward from general rules of action to the
guilt or innocence of particular men, but backward from actions
already performed to the queftion, whether or no they fhall fall under
fuch or fuch provifions of law. *Secondly*, by this perverted mode of
proceeding, he completely prejudges the cafe of the prifoners. He
does not proceed, as a judge ought to proceed, by explaining the law,
and leaving the Grand Jury to fix its application upon individuals; but
leads them to the felection of the individuals themfelves, and centres
in his own perfon the provinces of judge and accufer. It may be
doubted whether, in the whole records of the legal proceedings of
England, another inftance is to be found, of fuch wild conjecture, fuch
premature prefumption, imaginations fo licentious, and dreams fo full
of fanguinary and tremendous prophecy.

The conjectures of the Chief Juftice refpecting the probable guilt of
the accufed fall under two heads. Firft, " affociations, the profeffed pur-
" pofe of which has been a change in the Conftitution of the Commons
" Houfe of Parliament, and the obtaining of annual parliaments †." Secondly, " the project of a Convention to be affembled under the ad-
" vice and direction of fome of thefe affociations." ‡

The Treafons which the Chief Juftice imagines himfelf capable of
fixing upon fome of thefe affociations for a Parliamentary Reform, are
of two kinds.

Before we enter upon thefe, let us paufe a moment, and confider the
unexplored country before us. Every paragraph now prefents us with
a new treafon, real or imaginary, pretendedly direct, or avowedly conftructive. Divifion and fubdivifion rife upon us, and almoft every one
is concluded with the awful denunciation of Treafon. The Chief
Juftice is no longer contented with the plain treafons of 25 Edward
III. or the remoter treafons of Fofter and Hale. His whole difcourfe
hangs by one flender thread. He perpetually refers to the new and
portentuous treafon of his own mere creation, " a confpiracy to fub-
" vert the Monarchy;" a treafon, which he ingenuoufly avows " no
" lawgiver in this country has ever ventured to contemplate," and

* P. 8.   † P. 8.   ‡ P. 10.

B 2   " the

" the ftatute of Edward III. by which we are bound, has not declared."
Upon this felf-conftituted treafon he hangs his other conjectures and
novelties as well as he is able, by the help of forced conftructions, of
ambiguous and deceitful words, and all the delufions of a practifed fo-
phifter. Was it neceffary for the deftruction of twelve private and un-
titled men, to create all this confufion, to produce all this ruin, to overturn every thing that is valuable in Englifh liberty, and place us for
time coming under the moft atrocious and inexplicable defpotifm that
the world ever faw ?

Let us attend to the opinion of Judge Blackftone upon this fubject.

" By the ancient common law, there was a great latitude left in the
" breaft of the judges, to determine what was treafon or not fo ; where-
" by the creatures of tyrannical princes had opportunity to create
" abundance of conftructive treafons; that is, to raife, by forced and
" arbitrary conftructions, offences into the crime and punifhment of
" treafon, which were never fufpected to be fuch. To prevent thefe
" inconveniences, the ftatute 25 Edward III. chapter 2, was made. *
" —This is a great fecurity to the public, and leaves a weighty *me-*
" *mento* to judges to be careful, and not overhafty in letting in treafons
" by conftruction or interpretation, efpecially in new cafes that have
" not been refolved and fettled.—The Legiflature was extremely li-
" beral in declaring new treafons in the unfortunate reign of King
" Richard the Second ; but, in the firft year of his fucceffor's reign, an
" act was paffed, which at once fwept away this whole load of extra-
" vagant treafons. Afterwards, particularly in the bloody reign of
" Henry VIII. the fpirit of inventing new and ftrange treafons was
" revived ; all which new-fangled crimes were totally abrogated by the
" ftatute 1 Mary, chap. 1 ; fince which time the Legiflature has be-
" come more cautious upon this fubject." †

The firft mode in which, according to Chief Juftice Eyre, an affociation for Parliamentary Reform, may incur the penalties of High Treafon, is, when " other purpofes, befides thofe of Parliamentary Reform,
" and of the moft traiterous nature, are hidden under this veil †." The
purpofes he may be fuppofed to mean, are thofe of his new-fangled
treafon, of " confpiring to fubvert the Monarchy." Thus, in the firft
place, we have an innocent purpofe conftituting the profeffed object of
this fuppofed affociation; and behind that the Grand Jury are to dif-

* Book iv. chap. 6, p. 75.   † P. 85, 86.   ‡ P. 8.

cover,

cover, if they can, a fecret purpofe, totally unlike that which the affociators profefs; and this purpofe Chief Juftice Eyre declares to be
treafon, contrary, as he avowedly confeffes, to all law, precedent, and
adjudicated cafes.

The fecond mode, in which the Chief Juftice is willing to pre-fup-
pofe High Treafon in an affociation for Parliamentary Reform is by
fuch an affociation, not in its own nature, as he fays, " fimply unlawful,
" too eafily degenerating, and becoming unlawful in the higheft degree *."

It is difficult to comment upon this article with the gravity, that may
feem due to a magiftrate, delivering his opinions from a bench of juftice. An Affociation for Parliamentary Reform may " degenerate,
" and become unlawful in the higheft degree, even to the enormous
" extent of the crime of High Treafon." Who knows not that ? Was
it neceffary that Chief Juftice Eyre fhould come in 1794, folemnly to
announce to us fo irreftible a propofition ? An affociation for Parliamentary Reform may defert its object, and be guilty of High Treafon. True : fo may a card club, a bench of juftices, or even a cabinet
council. Does Chief Juftice Eyre mean to infinuate, that there is
fomething in the purpofe of a Parliamentary Reform, fo unhallowed,
ambiguous and unjuft, as to render its well wifhers objects of fufpicion, rather than their brethren and fellow fubjects ? What can be
more wanton, cruel, and inhuman, than thus gratuitioufly to fingle out
the purpofes of Parliamentary Reform, as if it were of all others, moft
efpecially connected with degeneracy and treafon ?

But what is principally worthy of obfervation in both thefe cafes, is,
the eafy and artful manner in which the idea of treafon is introduced
into them. Firft, there is a " concealed purpofe," or an infenfible
" degeneracy" *fuppofed* to take place in thefe affociations. Next, that
" concealed purpofe," or infenfible " degeneracy," is *fuppofed* to tend
directly to this end, the " fubverfion of the Monarchy." Laftly, a
" confpiracy to fubvert the Monarchy," is a treafon, firft difcovered
by Chief Juftice Eyre in 1794, never contemplated by any lawgiver,
or included in any ftatute. Deny the Chief Juftice any one of his three
affumptions, and his whole deduction falls to the ground. Challenge
him, or any man living, to prove any of them ; and you require of him
an impoffibility. And it is by this fort of logic, which would be

* P. 9.

fcouted

scouted in the rawest graduate in either of our Universities, that Englishmen are to be brought under the penalties of treason!

Of these assumptions, the most flagrant perhaps, if in reality there can be any gradation in such groundless assertions, is that which imputes to the associations a " conspiracy to subvert the Monarchy." The Chief Justice knows, for no man is ignorant, that there is not the shadow of evidence of such a conspiracy. If any man in England wishes the subversion of the Monarchy, is there a man in England that does not feel, that such subversion, if effected at all, can only be effected by an insensible revolution of opinion ? Did these associations plan the murder of the King, and the assassination of the royal family ? Where are the proofs of it ? But the authors of the present prosecution probably hope, that the mere names of Jacobin and Republican will answer their purposes; and that a Jury of Englishmen can be found who will send every man to the gallows without examination, to whom these appellations shall once have been attributed!

If Chief Justice Eyre, or his Majesty's servants, have any charge of High Treason to advance, let them advance it. The purpose of Parliamentary Reform, as the Chief Justice confesses, so far from being treasonable, is not " simply unlawful." If the persons now under confinement have been guilty of High Treason, that is the point to which our attention is to be called. Their treason is neither greater nor less, for their being engaged in a lawful object, the associating for a Parliamentary Reform. Tell us what they have done that is criminal, and do not seek to excite extrajudicial prejudices against them for what is innocent.

Having dismissed the immediate purpose of a Parliamentary Reform, the Chief Justice goes on in the last place to consider " the project of " a Convention, to be assembled under the advice and direction of " some of these associations." *

And here it was impossible not to recollect, that Conventions and meetings of delegates are by no means foreign to the English history ; and that twelve or fourteen years ago, many of his Majesty's present Ministers were deeply engaged in a project of this nature. Accordingly, the Chief Justice makes a very memorable distinction. He calls it " a project, which in better times would have been hardly thought " worthy of grave consideration; but in these, our days, when it has

* P. 10.

" been

" been attempted to be put in execution in a diftant part of the united
" kingdom, and with the example of a neighbouring country before
" our eyes, is defervedly become an objeât of jealoufy to the law." *

This remark conftitutes one of the moft flagrant violations of the
principles of executive juftice, that was ever heard of or imagined. If
the times require different meafures of juftice, we are already inftruâted
by the aât 25 Edward III. as to the proceeding fitting to be employed.
" The Judge," fays the aât, " fhall tarry, without going to judgment
" of the treafon, till the caufe be fhown and declared before the King
" and his Parliament, whether it ought to be judged treafon or other
" felony." Parliament, the legiflative authority of the realm, may
make new provifions of law in accommodation to circumftances; but
the Judges, the bare expounders of the law, are bound to maintain
themfelves in an atmofphere unaffeâted by the variations of popular
clamour, minifterial vengeance, or the ever changing nature of circumftances. They are to be feverely and unalterably the fame. The
meaning they found in the ftatute yefterday, that meaning, and no
other, they are to find to day. An interpretation, fhifting with every
gale of accident, may produce undefiable terrors in its miferable victims, may devote its authors to eternal execration, but can have none
of the venerable features either of law or juftice.

Some of the dreadful confequences involved in this loofe and fluâtuat-
ing interpretation, fhow themfelves in the very next fentence.

" It will be your duty," fays the Chief Juftice to the Jury, " to ex-
" amine the evidence on this head very carefully, and to fift it to the
" bottom to confider every part of it in itfclf, and as it ftands conneâted
" with other parts of it; and to draw the conclufion of faât, as to the
" exiftence, the nature and objeât of this propofed Convention, from
" the whole.

" In the courfe of the evidence *you will probably hear* of bodies of
" men having been colleâted together, of violent refolutions voted at
" this and other meetings, of fome preparation of offenfive weapons,
" and of. the adoption of the language and manners of thofe Conven-
" tions in France, which have poffcffed themfelves of the government
" of that country. I dwell not on thefe particulars, becaufe I confider
" them not as fubftantive treafons, but as circumftances of evidence,

* P. 10.

" tending

" tending to afcertain the true nature of the object which thefe perfons " had in view *."

Here we have fet before us in the moft unblufhing and undifguifed manner, that principle of Conftructive Treafon, which has upon all occafions formed an object of execration in Englifh hiftory. Let us hear what Hume fays upon the fubject in the farther progrefs of that very paffage which has been already quoted.

" As this fpecies of treafon, difcovered by the Commons," in the cafe of Lord Strafford, " is entirely new and unknown to the laws; fo " is the fpecies of proof by which they pretend to fix that guilt upon " the prifoner. They have invented a kind of *accumulative* or *conftructive* " evidence, by which many actions, either totally innocent in them- " felves, or criminal in a much inferior degree, fhall, when united, " amount to treafon, and fubject the perfon to the higheft penalties " inflicted by the law. A hafty and unguarded word, a rafh and paf- " fionate action, affifted by the malevolent fancy of the accufer, and " tortured by doubtful conftructions, is tranfmuted into the deepeft " guilt, and the lives and fortunes of the whole nation, no longer pro- " tected by juftice, are fubjected to arbitrary will and pleafure †."

It is not eafy to conceive of two paffages more parallel to each other, than the doctrines here delivered by Chief Juftice Eyre, and the condemnation pronounced upon them by way of anticipation by the illuftrious Hume. Thus, " a hafty and unguarded word,"—" Adoption of " the *language* of the Convention in France."—" A rafh and paffion- " ate action,"—" Violent refolutions voted at this and other meet- " ings—fome preparation of offenfive weapons."—" Actions either " totally innocent in themfelves, or criminal in a much inferior de- " gree,"—" I confider not thefe particulars as fubftantive treafons."

Can any thing be more atrocious, than the undertaking to meafure the guilt of an individual, and the interpretation of a plain and permanent law, by the tranfitory example that may happen to exift " be- " fore our eyes in a neighbouring country ?"

The Chief Juftice fpeaks of two forts of Convention. The firft, " a Convention, in imitation of thofe which we have heard of in " France, in order to ufurp the government of the country ‡."

There lurks a memorable ambiguity under this word *Convention. A Convention* was held no long time ago, of delegates from the different

* P. 11. † P. 403. ‡ P. 11.

in

counties in Scotland, to confider of a reform in the reprefentation of
thofe counties. Of this Convention, the prefent Lord Advocate of
Scotland, among others was a member. A *Convention* was propofed in
1780, of delegates from the different county meetings in England held
at that period. Both thefe Conventions were confiderably more formidable in their ftructure than that which is the fubject of prefent
animadverfion. The royal burghs, and the meetings of freeholders in
the feveral counties, confift of bodies more or lefs recognized by the
conftitution, and poffeffing a degree of inherent authority. The *Convention* propofed in the prefent inftance, was fimply of delegates from
the different focieties, voluntarily affociated for the purpofe of Parliamentary Reform. They could poffefs no inherent authority. The
perfons who conftituted them, muft have been actuated by the moft perfect infanity, before they could have dreamed of ufurping the government of the country. No delufion therefore can be more grofs, than
an attempt to ftyle, as Chief Juftice Eyre ftyles, fuch a Convention *"A
" Convention of the People."**

In defcribing his firft fort of Convention the Chief Juftice roundly
affirms, " that the project of fuch a Convention, and any one ftep taken
" towards bringing it about, fuch as, for inftance, confultations, form-
" ing committes to confider of the means, or acting in thofe commit-
" tees, would be a cafe of no difficulty ; it would be the cleareft High
" Treafon ; it would be compaffing and imagining the King's death ; and
" not only his death, but the death and deftruction of all order, reli-
" gion, and laws, of all property, and fecurity for the lives and liber-
" ties of the King's fubjects." †

There is a figure in fpeech, of the higheft ufe to a defigning and
treacherous orator, which has not yet perhaps received a name in the
labours of Ariftotle, Quintilian, or Farnaby. I would call this figure
incroachment. It is a proceeding, by which an affirmation is modeftly
infinuated at firft, accompanied with confiderable doubt and qualification; repeated afterwards, and accompanied with thefe qualifications ;
and at laft afferted in the moft peremptory and arrogant terms. It is
thus that Chief Juftice Eyre expreffes himfelf, refpecting a " confpiracy
" to overturn the Monarchy." It is firft a Treafon, " not declared
" by the ftatute 25 Edward III." a Treafon, " which no lawgiver in
" this country has ever ventured to contemplate;" a Treafon, " not

* P. 10. † P. 11.

C

" resting for its authority upon any law, precedent, or adjudged case."
It is not this thing, nor it is not that; " the *seditio regni* spoken of by
" some of our ancient writers," but *which is no part of our law*, " seems
" to come the nearest to it,"* but will not apply. " The particular
" nature of the traiterous attempt, will fall within *one or other* of the
" specific treasons of the statute of Edward III."† A strange crime,
which the judge knows is provided against by the first or the second
principal clause, but is unable to determine whether it is by the former
or the latter! Afterwards the Chief Justice speaks of it with less
hesitation; and at last, as we have seen, affirms it to be " a case of no
" difficulty, and the clearest High Treason."
Can any play upon words be more contemptible, than that by which
the Chief Justice, finding the King's death the subject of one of the clauses,
and determined to trace at least some remote analogy between that and
the subversion of the monarchy, describes the latter by the appellation
of " the *death* and destruction of all order, religion, &c. &c. ?"
The second sort of Convention in Chief Justice Eyre's arrangement
is a Convention, which, not intending to usurp the government of the
country, " has for its sole object the effecting a change in the mode of
" representation of the people in Parliament, and the obtaining that
" Parliaments should be held annually. And here," says the Chief
Justice, " there is room to distinguish. Such a project of a Conven-
" tion, taking it to be criminal,"——‡
" *Taking it to be criminal!*" Was ever postulate, more extraordinary, or more intolerable? Did ever Judge, sitting upon the bench,
previously to this instance, assume the whole question; affirm at his
case, and without the shadow of an authority, scriptural or nuncupa-
tory, statute or report, the whole criminality; and then proceed at
his leisure to distribute the assumed criminality into all its different
degrees? Meanwhile, after this loud and peremptory preamble, the
Chief Justice is obliged to grant, that one sort of Convention, one
" degree of criminality," " a Convention, having for its sole object
" a dutiful and peaceable application to Parliament by petition, cannot
" of itself be ranked among this class of offences."§ He dares not affirm
that it is to be ranked among any class of offences whatever.——But
to proceed to the distinctions he undertakes to enumerate.
The first sort of " Convention, which has for its object the obtain-

* P. 6.   † P. 7.   ‡ P. 12.   § P. 14.
                                                            " ing

" ing a Parliamentary Reform, and that object only, is a Convention,
" propofing to obtain it without the authority of Parliament," and for
that purpofe " ufurping, at leaft in this inftance, the functions of le-
" giflation." * This the Chief Juftice determines, upon juft the fame
grounds as in the preceding inftances, " would be High Treafon in
" every one of the actors." †

After this laborious difcuffion, Chief Juftice Eyre is not yet fatisfied
that he has framed a conftruction, ftrong enough to enfnare the perfons
now under confinement. He has heaped diftinction upon diftinction.
He has promulgated at leaft five or fix different claffes of treafon, not
found in the direct provifions of 25 Edward III. or in the remoter
inftances of Fofter and Hale; not fupported, as he explicitly confeffes,
by any law, precedent or adjudged cafe. But all this he does in the
mere wantonnefs of his power. If any of the prifoners now under confinement had acted according to all the enumerations of his imaginary
cafes, it may fafely be affirmed, that, upon any fober trial upon a
charge of High Treafon, they muft infallibly be acquitted. But the
Chief Juftice implicitly confeffes, that they have not acted according
to any one of his cafes. All this profufion of fiction, hypothefis, and
prejudication, is brought forward for the fole purpofe, either of convincing us of the unparalleled ingenuity of the Lord Chief Juftice of
his Majefty's Court of Common Pleas, or to bewilder the imaginations, to throw duft in the eyes, and confound the underftandings of the
Grand Jury and the nation. If this laft be the purpofe conceived, and
if it could poffibly be fuppofed that it fhould be fuccefsful for a moment, early would be the repentance, deep the remorfe, and fevere, it
is to be feared, the retribution!

The Chief Juftice then, having hitherto talked of every thing that
is not to the purpofe, comes at laft to fpeak of the matter in hand.
Here he employs all his ingenuity, exerts all his arts, and difplays his
utmoft intrepidity of countenance. This part of the cafe is opened
as follows.

" Whether the project of a Convention, having for its object the
" collecting together a power, which fhould overawe the legiflative body,
" but not fufpend it, or entirely determine its functions, if acted upon,
" will alfo amount to High Treafon, and to the fpecific treafon of
" compaffing and imagining the King's death, is a more doubtful quef-

" tion. Thus far is clear: a *force*, upon the Parliament, muft be im-
" mediately directed againft the King. It muft reach the King, or it
" can have no effect at all.   The laws are enacted in Parliament by the
" King's Majefty, by and with the advice and confent of the Lords
" and Commons in Parliament affembled. A force meditated againft
" the Parliament therefore, is a force meditated againft the King, and
" *feems* to fall within the cafes defcribed *"

Nothing can be more grofs to the view of any one who will attentively
read this paragraph, than its total want of all definite and intelligible
meaning. The Chief Juftice talks of " collecting together a power,"
and of " a force" exercifed upon the Parliament. What is here intended
by the words *power* and *force?* Under the kindly ambiguity of thefe
words, the Chief Juftice feems very willing to flip upon us the idea of
an *armed power* and a *military force*. But this can fcarcely by any conftruction be reconciled to the idea of a Convention. An army of delegates was an idea referved for Chief Juftice Eyre to introduce into the
world. Well then : Let us fuppofe that arms and violence are not intended ; yet the Chief Juftice fays, that the project of a Convention
has for its object " the collecting together a power, which fhould *over-*
" *awe* the legiflative body." This word is ftill more ambiguous than
any of the reft. What are we to underftand by the phrafe " to over-
" awe ?" *Awe* in its true acceptation has always been underftood to
mean *deference* or *refpect*. It cannot mean any thing elfe here, fince, as
we have already feen, armed power and military force are out of the
queftion. But in this fenfe, what is the object of every fpecies of Convention or political affociation whatever ? It is always intended to
produce deference and refpect. Thus the Chief Juftice very properly
obferves, that " a Convention, having for its fole object a dutiful and
" peaceable application to Parliament," does not fail to find that application attended with " refpect and credit, in proportion to its uni-
" verfality."* Indeed there can be no doubt, that there are but two
ways of operating upon men's conduct, the one, by exhibiting arguments calculated to prevail upon their own inclinations and conviction,
the other a perceiving how much the thing required accords with the
fenfe of numerous bodies of men, and bodies of men intitled to eminent credit.

Such being the fubftance of the moft material paragraph in the charge

* P. 13.   † P. 14.

to the Grand Jury, let us fee in what manner this paragraph is concluded, and what are the inferences drawn from it. What is the treatment due to this *force* which is no *force*; this *collecting together a power*,
unarmed, and entitled to credit only for its univerfality ? What
fhall be done to the men who thus *overawe* the legiflative body, by exciting its deference and refpect ; or, failing this, do not overawe it
at all, inafmuch as they have no power to inforce their demands ?
" Whether or no," as Chief Juftice Eyre fagacioufly obferves, " the
" project of fuch a Convention will amount to High Treafon, is a
" more doubtful queftion."

He adds, " in this cafe it does not appear to me, that I am warranted
" by the authorities, to ftate to you as clear law, that the mere con-
" fpiracy to *raife fuch a force* [recollect what has been faid upon the
" nature of this *force*], and the entering into confultations refpecting
" it, will alone, and without actually *raifing the force*, conftitute the
" crime of High Treafon. What the law is in that cafe, and what
" will be the effect of the circumftance of the *force* being thus medi-
" tated, will be fit to be folemnly confidered and determined when
" the cafe fhall arife." *

Here the Chief Juftice fpeaks with a proper degree of modefty and
precaution, fo far as relates to the fuppofed guilt of the perfons under
confinement ; but when he has occafion to refume the fubject, he, in his
ufual manner, introduces a variation into the ftatement. " It may
" perhaps be fitting," fays he, " *if you find* thefe perfons involved in
" fuch a defign, and *if the charges* of High Treafon are offered to be
" maintained againft them upon that ground, that, in refpect of the ex-
" traordinary nature, the dangerous extent, and at the beft, the very
" criminal complexion of fuch a confpiracy, this cafe, which I ftate
" to you as a new and a doubtful cafe, fhould be *put into a judicial*
" *courfe of inquiry, that it may receive a folemn adjudication*, whether it will
" or will not amount to High Treafon." †

It is difficult to conceive of any thing more abhorrent to the genuine
principles of humanity, than the doctrine here delivered. The Chief
Juftice, after having enumerated various forts of treafon, refpecting
which he fpeaks diffidently at firft, and peremptorily at laft, but which
are all the mere creatures of his own imagination, comes to a cafe upon
which even he hefitates to decide. He dares not aver the proceeding

* P. 13.   † P. 15.

defcribed

166

described in it to be treason. Well, then; what is the remedy he proposes? Surely, a new Act of Parliament; the remedy prescribed by the act of Edward III. " in cases of treason, which may happen in time to " come, but which could not then be thought of or declared." No such thing. Upon this case, which he does not venture to pronounce to be treason, he directs the Grand Jury to *find the bills to be true bills !* He tells them, " that it is fitting that this case," which he " states as " new and doubtful, should be put *into a judicial course of enquiry, that* " *it may receive a solemn adjudication,* whether it will or will not amount to High Treason !"

The Chief Justice, in this instance, quits the character of a criminal judge and a civil magistrate, and assumes that of a natural philosopher, or experimental anatomist. He is willing to dissect the persons that shall be brought before him, the better to ascertain the truth or falsehood of his pre-conceived conjectures. The plain English of his recommendation is this : " Let these men be put upon trial for their lives; " let them and their friends, through the remotest strainers of con- " nection, be exposed to all the anxieties incident to so uncertain and " fearful a condition; let them be exposed to ignomy, to obloqv, to " the partialities, as it may happen, of a prejudiced judge, and the " perverseness of an ignorant jury; we shall then know how we ought " to conceive of similar cases. By trampling upon their peace, throw- " ing away their lives, or sporting with their innocence, we shall ob- " tain a basis upon which to proceed, and a precedent to guide our " judgment in future instances."

This is a sort of language which it is impossible to recollect without horror, and which seems worthy of the judicial ministers of Tiberius or Nero. It argues, if the speaker understood his own meaning, or if the paper before me has faithfully reported it, the most frigid indifference to human happiness and human life. According to this method of estimate, laws, precedents, cases and reports are of high value, and the hanging a few individuals is a very cheap, economical, and proper way of purchasing the decision of a doubtful speculation.

Surely it would be worthy, if not of the judges, at least of the immediate Ministers of the Sovereign, to consider whether, if they mean to put us under a new rule of criminal law, it be not better solemnly to originate that law in the two Houses of Parliament, than to suffer it

to

to be made out of new conftructions of old ftatutes, contrary to all law and precedent, and contrary to the fecurity and liberty of the fubject. In Ireland, fome time ago, it was thought proper to bring forward a Convention-Bill, declaring fuch proceedings, as are the fubjects of the forced conftructions of Chief Baron Eyre, to amount to High Treafon. When the *Habeas Corpus* act was fufpended in England, we were given to underftand that this proceeding was thought fufficient for the prefent, and that a Convention-Bill, fimilar to the Irifh, and other fevere meafures, were referved to be adopted, as the cafe might acquire. This fallacious fhow of lenity, now turns out to be the moft unprincipled tyranny. Mr. Dundas and others talked in the laft Seffion of Parliament, of bringing home the Scottifh principles of jurifprudence, if need were, to England, and rendering affociations and Conventions a fubject of tranfportation to Botany Bay. They have fince refined upon their plan, and carried the law of England, or what they are pleafed to call fo, into Scotland, rendering thefe offences, real or imanary, a fubject of the penalties of High Treafon. Such have been the incroachments upon the Conftitution, by men who have the audacity to call themfelves its champions, that a man who fhould have pretended to foretel, from fix months to fix months, the meafures they would think proper to purfue, would have been laughed at for the improbability and utter abfurdity of his tale. Britons will at length awake, and the effects of reafon and conviction upon them, will not be lefs formidable or lefs unacceptable to their oppreffors, than the effects that might flow from a courfe of violence.

I have hitherto abftained from faying any thing refpecting the perfonal characters of the men now under accufation. If their abilities be as rare, and their merits as high as their warmeft admirers can conceive them, it would ftill be foreign to the queftion I propofe to confider. If they be men, exceptionable in their character, ambiguous in their defigns, and mifchievous in their counfels, that alfo ought to be put out of the confideration. The Englifh Conftitution is ftrong enough to difarm all the adverfaries of the public peace, without its being neceffary for that purpofe to deftroy its very effence. Twelve men are apparently concerned, but the liberties and happinefs of all are at ftake.

If thefe new treafons be eftablifhed, we may fay, as the Parliament of Henry the Fourth did, fpeaking of the new-fangled treafons under Richard the Second, that " no man can know how he ought to behave himfelf

" himfelf, to do, fpeak, or fay, for doubt of the pains of treafon." *
The conftructions of Chief Juftice Eyre, and the Special Commiffion,
put a perpetual bar to all affociations, delegations, and confultings
refpecting any fpecies of grievance. Will any man venture to fay,
that we fhall never ftand in need of thefe expedients ; or fhall we confent for all time coming, to hold every poffible reform and amendment
at the mere will of the adminiftration ? If thefe principles be eftablifhed, utterly fubverfive as they are of the principles of the Englifh
government, who will fay that we fhall ftop here ? Chief Juftice Eyre
fays to-day, " all men may, nay, all men muft, if they poffefs the faculty
" of thinking, reafon upon every thing, that fufficiently interefts them
" to become an object of their attention ; and among the objects of
" attention of freemen, the principles of government, the conftitution
" of particular governments, and, above all, the conftitution of the go-
" vernment under which they live, will naturally engage attention,
" and provoke fpeculation." But who will fay how long this liberty
will be tolerated, if the principles, fo alarmingly opened in the charge
to the Grand Jury, fhall once be eftablifhed ? This is the moft important crifis, in the hiftory of Englifh liberty, that the world ever faw.
If men can be convicted of High Treafon, upon fuch conftructions and
implications as are contained in this charge, we may look with confcious fuperiority upon the republican fpeculations of France, but we
fhall certainly have reafon to envy the milder tyrannies of Turkey and
Ifpahan.

From what has been faid it appears, that the whole proceedings intended in the prefent cafe, are of the nature of an *ex poft facto* law.
This is completely admitted by the Chief Juftice. In fumming up the
different parts of his charge, he enumerates three cafes, in the firft of
which he directs the Grand Jury to throw out the bills, and in that of
the two laft to find them true bills. One of thefe two relates to Chief
Juftice Eyre's new treafon of " a confpiracy to fubvert the Monar-
" chy," a treafon which, he fays, is not declared by the ftatute of
Edward III. and no lawgiver in this country has ever ventured to contemplate. The other, " that of overawing Parliament," he ftates to
be a new and doubtful cafe, and recommends, that it fhould be " put
" into a judicial courfe of enquiry, that it may receive a folemn adju-
" dication whether it will or will not amount to High Treafon."

* Blackftone Book iv. chap. 6, p. 86.

Th

Thus it is fully admitted, refpecting the perfons now under accufation, that they could find no reafon, either in the books of our law, or of any commentators of received authority, to fuppofe that they were incurring the guilt of treafon. " The mark fet upon this crime, " the token by which it could be difcovered, lay entirely concealed ; " and no human prudence, no human innocence, could fave them " from the deftruction with which they are at prefent threatened.*"

It is pretty generally admitted, that feveral of thofe perfons, at leaft, were honeft and well-intentioned, though miftaken men. Punifhment is awarded in human Courts of Juftice, either according to the intention, or the mifchief committed. If the intention be alone to be confidered, then the men of whom I fpeak, however unguarded and prejudicial their conduct may be fuppofed to have been, muft on that ground be infallibly acquitted. If, on the other hand, the mifchief incurred be the fole meafure of the punifhment, we are bound by every thing that is facred to proceed with reluctance and regret. Let it be fuppofed, that there are cafes, where it fhall be neceffary, that a well defigning man fhould be cut off, for the fake of the whole. The leaft confideration that we can pay in fo deplorable a neceffity, is, to warn him of his danger, and not fuffer him to incur the penalty, without any previous caution, without fo much as the knowledge of its exiftence.

I anticipate the trials to which this Charge is the prelude. I know that the Judge will admit the good intention and honeft defign of feveral of the perfons arraigned : it will be impoffible to deny it ; it is notorious to the whole univerfe. He has already admitted, that there is no law or precedent for their condemnation. If therefore he addrefs them in the frank language of fincerity, he muft fay, " Six months " ago you engaged in meafures, which you believed conducive to the " public good. You examined them in the fincerity of your hearts, " and you admitted them with the full conviction of the underftand- " ing. You adopted them from this ruling motive, the love of your " country and mankind. You had no warning that the meafures in " which you engaged were acts of High Treafon : no law told you fo ; " no precedent recorded it ; no man exifting upon the face of the " earth could have predicted fuch an interpretation. You went to your " beds with a perfect and full conviction, that you had acted upon the

* Hume, vol. vi. ch. liv. p. 404.

D　　　　principles

" principles of immutable juſtice, and that you had offended no pro-
" viſion or ſtatute that was ever deviſed. I, the Judge ſitting upon
" the bench, you, Gentlemen of the Jury, every inhabitant of the iſland
" of Great Britain, had juſt as much reaſon to conceive they were in-
" curring the penalties of the law, as the priſoners at the bar. This
" is the nature of the crime ; theſe are the circumſtances of the caſe.

" And for this, the Sentence of the Court [but not of the law] is,
" *That you, and each of you, ſhall be taken from the bar, and conveyed to*
" *the place from whence you came, and from thence be drawn upon a hur-*
" *dle to the place of execution, there to be hanged by the neck, but not until*
" *you are dead ; you ſhall be taken down alive, your privy members ſhall be*
" *cut off, and your bowels ſhall be taken out and burnt before your faces ;*
" *your heads ſhall be ſevered from your bodies, and your bodies ſhall then be*
" *divided into four quarters, which are to be at the King's diſpoſal ; and*
" *the Lord have mercy on your ſouls !"*

APPENDIX. No. I.

A MORE minute attention appears to be due to Chief Juſtice Eyre's new treaſon of a " conſpiracy to ſubvert the monarchy." The terms in which the idea is conveyed are ſtrong and impreſſive; and many perſons, who ſhall be convinced by what has been already offered, that by the law of England this is no treaſon, will yet perhaps entertain a wiſh that a new law were framed for the purpoſe of making it treaſon. Thouſands, and tens of thouſands of the inhabitants of England, are deeply attached to that Conſtitution, under which our anceſtors made ſo conſpicuous a figure in the face of the world. The attachment they feel is no doubt a virtuous attachment; but it is not every method that can be propoſed for preſerving what we love that is entitled to our approbation.

Let us conſider a little this phraſe, a " conſpiracy to ſubvert the " Monarchy."

There are but two ways in which ſuch a ſubverſion can be attempted. The firſt, argument, all writing, and familiar ſpeaking, by which a man, by himſelf, and without confederacy with others, ſhall ſeek to prevail upon his countrymen to adopt ſentiments ſimilar to his own. This, by the very meaning of the term, cannot be *conſpiracy*.

Two obſervations will ſuffice to clear up this article. Firſt, it might be ſuppoſed that he who is attached to the Monarchy, believing, of courſe, that the Monarchy is a good thing, ſhould feel little reluctance to commit his opinions to the fair field of argument, and entertain ſmall doubt that truth muſt prove more vigorous, and of longer life, than falſehood. Secondly, if it ſhould be ſaid, that ſome writings may be exceedingly inflammatory, we have already Laws of Libel. Theſe laws might be made ſtill ſtronger; but at all events the inflammation conſtitutes the offence, and not the object propoſed, whether it

D 2 be

be the fubverfion of the Monarchy, or of the Athanafian creed. As to familiar and unconfederate converfation, there can be little danger of inflammation in that. The only offence committed, will be an offence againft decorum, Whether or no hanging men is the moft fuitable way of teaching them good manners, is a point that will remain to be confidered,

The fecond method that may be employed for the " fubverfion of " the Monarchy," is open force, But let this force be a little examined, Is it to be employed upon all the Members of the Conftitution at once; and is the prefent race of traitors, like Guy Fawkes of old, to blow up King, Lords, and Commons, with gunpowder, on the firft day of the Seffion of Parliament? If " war be levied againft the King " within the realm," this is already treafon by 25 Edward III. If the plan be " to depofe the King, to imprifon him, or to get his perfon " into the power of the confpirators," this alfo, if we are to credit the authorities of Fofter and Hale, is already High Treafon, But let us not be deceived with high founding words. An attempt to fubvert the Monarchy is nothing, if it be not definite, and capable of fome clear and precife explanation. An attempt to procure a Reform in the Commons' Houfe of Parliament, through the medium of affociations and Conventions, is not a confpiracy to fubvert the Monarchy. If it be a crime, it will not be lefs fo, for being called by its appropriate name. The attempt to involve a man in the penalties of High Treafon, by calling evidence to prove that he has done one action, and then beftowing upon that action another appellation, will be regarded with contempt by every man of common fenfe, and with the deepeft abhorrence by every man of common humanity.

APPENDIX. No. II.

HITHERTO I have confined myfelf to an examination of the Charge to the Grand Jury. But there is fomething fo peculiarly flagitious in the manner of preparing the indictment, and the lift of witceffes, that it feems improper to difmifs an Effay, the object of which is to call the attention of Englifhmen to the prefent ftate of the proceedings againft the prifoners in his Majefty's goals of Newgate and the Tower, without a few words upon the fubject.

The law of High Treafon differs from our other criminal laws, by allowing the perfons accufed an interval of ten days, between the de-delivery of the indictment and lift of witneffes, and the day of trial. The object of the law apparently is, that he may have adequate time, in a matter of fo extraordinary magnitude, to prepare his defence. This object is completely defeated in the prefent inftance. One indictment is preferred againft twelve of the moft eminent perfons involved in the accufation. It confifts of nine overt-acts, and it is well known, that feveral of the overt-acts will not be attempted to be proved againft the majority of the prifoners. Every man is left to pick out, as he can, the articles, which the fobriety or the wantonnefs of accufation may think proper to alledge againft him. In the fame manner one lift of witneffes is delivered to all. This lift confifts of more than two hundred perfons.

Thus are the lenity and humanity of this provifion baffled. For what reafon is this ? Shall we be told that it faves trouble to the Crown Lawyers ? This is perhaps the moft plaufible pretence that can be adduced. And yet, in that cafe, it would fcarcely have been lefs decent, to have faved trouble, by hanging the accufed without the form of trial.

But this is not the real reafon. The moft temperate and fcrupulous

man

man cannot fail to confefs, that the objeɛt is, to facilitate the conviction of perfons fo much the objeɛt of deteftation to the prefent Miniftry. Government haftily involved itfelf in a dilemma, by apprehending thefe men for the fake of propagating alarm; and it is thought better to hang a few innocent perfons, than that the Minifter fhould ftand deteɛted in an error, or that the arm of government fhould be weakened by an aɛt of juftice.

It is a memorable faɛt and well worthy to be revived, in the prefent crifis, that on the eighth of April 1793, Mr. Pitt openly and unhefitatingly delivered, in the face of the Houfe of Commons, the doctrine which he has now reduced to praɛtice. The report upon the bill for preventing traiterous correfpondence with France, was on that day read; and an amendment was moved by Mr. Adam, and fupported by Mr. Fox, to allow " the perfons, who fhould hereafter be arraigned " upon this aɛt, the fame interval of ten days, that is allowed to other " perfons accufed of the crime of High Treafon." This claufe was oppofed by the Chancellor of the Exchequer, who alleged, that " the " propofed allowance would be of little ufe to the culprit. A lift of " fuch a *cloud of witneffes* might be fent him, as would render it im- " poffible for him, with all the affiduity of his friends, to enquire into " their charaɛters in the fpace of ten days."

Mr. Fox profeffed " his utter aftonifhment at fuch language from " the Minifter of the Crown. It muft be in a great meafure by his ad- " vice that the law officers for the Crown are to conduɛt profecutions " for Treafon; and that fuch a perfon, in fuch a fituation, fhould fug- " geft even the poffibility, of a public accufer fwelling the number of " witneffes, for no other purpofe than that of baffling the law, was a " declaration of the moft alarming nature. He hoped no fuch infa- " mous trick would be attempted. But, if it were, he trufted there " was fpirit enough in the people to bring its authors to a proper ac- " count".*

From this citation it appears, that the prefent proceedings is by no means the fuggeftion of the hour; and that there is a man in his Majefty's councils, capable of brooding in the folitary malignity of his mind, upon the different modes of defeating, to the perfons he fhall feleɛt as the objeɛts of his vengeance, the purpofes of fubftantial juftice.

* Senator, vol. vii. p. 580. 588.

Reports

Reports have been propagated of a very extraordinary nature, refpecting the manner of forming the Jury. Thefe reports, if not legally
proved, have never been contradicted; and therefore ought to be
ftated, that, if falfe, they may be contradicted. It is faid, that the
Sheriffs, inftead of fuffering the Jury to be ftruck, at the place where
the book of the Freeholders is kept, and by the Officers to whom
that care ordinarily falls, fent for the books from the office, and took
the tafk upon themfelves. It is farther affirmed, that, in confequence,
various miftakes were made; the fame perfons were fummoned upon
the Grand Jury, and the Petty Jury; and letters of fummons fent to
the one, that ought to have been fent to the other. Officers of great
and important truft, ought not to content themfelves with acting from
pure and difinterefted motives, but fhould refrain from affording even
a colour of fufpicion. It is obvious to every perfon who cafts his eye
over the lifts, that it confifts of a moft extraordinary affemblage, King's
tradefmen, contractors, and perfons labouring under every kind of
bias and influence; very few indeed that can at all pretend to independence and impartiality; and perhaps thofe few to be ultimately challenged by the Officers of the Crown. Thus every part of the tranfaction appears to be uniform, and marks an adminiftration, callous to
public character, and determined to employ all means indifcriminately
to effect their fanguinary purpofes.

FINIS.

At the *Cock and Swine*, No. 74, Newgate-ftreet, London.

	£.	s.	d.

THE WORKS. OF OLD HUBERT.

	£.	s.	d.
The Village Affociation — —	0	1	6
The Knaves-Acre Affociation —	0	0	4
The Soldier's Tale — — —	0	0	1
The Budget of the People, 1ft and 2d part, each	0	0	1
Pearls caft before Swine — —	0	0	1
Maft and Acorns — — —	0	0	2
Revolution without Bloodfhed — —	0	0	1

THE WORKS OF CHARLES PIGOT, ESQ.

	£.	s.	d.
The Cafe of Charles Pigot — —	0	1	0
Treachery no Crime ; or, The Syftem of Courts	0	2	0
Strictures on Burke — — —	0	1	6
Political Claffics, in Weekly Numbers, — —	0	0	6
A Letter to the Hon. Charles James Fox			6
Age of Reafon, by Thomas Paine — —	0	1	6
Monarchy no Creature of God's making	0	2	0
Virtues of Hazel ; or Bleffings of Government. By Thomas Thomas, A. B.			
D. I. Eaton's Three Trials—for Rights of Man—Letter to the Addreffers—Politics for the People, each	0	1	6
A Convention the only Means of Saving us from Ruin. By Jofeph Gerald — — —	0	2	6
The Same — — — —	0	1	6
The Addrefs of the Britifh Convention, —	0	0	6
Confiderations on the French War : in a Letter to the Right Hon. W. Pitt. By a Britifh Merchant	0	1	6
Politics for the People, publifhing in Weekly Numbers	0	0	2
The *extraordinary* Indictment of D. I. Eaton, for publifhing a fuppofed Libel in the above Work	0	0	2
Pernicious Effects of the Art of Printing — —	0	0	2
The True Churchman — —	0	1	0
Life of Alfred compared with the prefent Corrupt Syftem — — — —	0	0	6
Letter to the Church of Scotland, by Mark Blake, Efq.	0	0	6
Addrefs to the Public, alias the Swinifh Multitude	0	0	1
Conftitution of America, and the Declaration of Reafons for feparating from this Country —	0	0	6
Defence of Burke — —	0	1	0
Meafures of Miniftry to prevent a Revolution are the certain Means of bringing it on — —	0	1	6

In the Prefs, and fhortly will be publifhed,

Pigot's Political Dictionary
And feveral others

ANSWER

TO

CURSORY STRICTURES

On a CHARGE delivered to the Grand Jury,

October 2, 1794.

By LORD CHIEF JUSTICE EYRE.

SAID TO BE WRITTEN BY JUDGE THUMB.

In the Ministerial Paper called the TIMES, *October* 25, 1794.

[By Sir Francis Buller ?]

LONDON:

Printed for, and Sold by D. I. EATON, at the COCK and SWINE, No. 74, Newgate-street.

1794.

IF it be one of the first privileges of an Englishmen, one of the first duties of a rational Being, to discuss with perfect freedom all principles proposed to be enforced upon general observance, when those principles are first disclosed, and before they have yet, by any solemn proceeding, been made part of a regular established system;* surely

* Cursory Strictures, p. 3.

A

it

it marks the character of the moft dangerous villain, and determined enemy to the Conftitution of his country, to endeavour, on the
eve of trials of the greateft importance to every Englifhmen, by a
publication the moft impudent, falfe, and unconftitutional (for fo I
call the publication entitled "Curfory Strictures, &c."), to influence and
deceive the minds of thofe Jurymen, who are to be engaged in the
inveftigation of them. It is impudent, becaufe it is an attack upon a
high Judicial Character, in the difcharge of a duty impofed upon
him by a fituation he holds in the adminiftration of the laws of this
country ; it is falfe, becaufe it proceeds on a miftatement of the learned Chief Juftice's pofitions, fupported by affertions and obfervations
equally unfounded in law and fact ; it is unconftitutional, becaufe I
affert, that every publication before a trial, the obvious tendency of
which is to influence the minds of the Jury, is in direct oppofition to
the known and eftablifhed laws of England, which have anxioufly endeavoured to fhield the minds of Jurors from every biafs, but that
arifing from an attentive confideration of the evidence delivered before them at the time of the trial. Such being the obvious tendency
of this publication, I muft confider it not as the offspring of an honeft,
well-intentioned, though miftaken mind, but of one from motives the
moft deteftable and malignant, endeavouring to corrupt the moft valuable part of the Englifh Conftitution, viz. the Trial by Jury. But
as I wifh not my affertions to pafs for proof, I will proceed to the
confideration of the different pofitions, obfervations, and infinuations
to be found in the publication. The chief objection made by the author of " Curfory Obfervations, &c." and which runs through the
whole of his pamphlet, to the charge of the Chief Juftice, proceeds
on a fuppofition that the learned Judge had laid it down as law, that a
confpiracy to fubvert the Monarchy was in itfelf a diftinct fpecies of
High Treafon, and from thence he argues, that as this was not a Treafon declared by the 25 of Edw. III. and the Chief Juftice had admitted
that to be the ftatute by which we are bound, to affert, notwithftanding,
that fuch a confpiracy was High Treafon, was a violation of the eftablifhed laws, and to contradict his own admiffions. The anfwer to
which is, that the fuppofition is wholly ungrounded, from any pofition
to be found in the charge ; but, as the author well knew, had he fairly
ftated, what was really advanced by the Learned Judge, he had neither
                                                              reafon

reason or law to support him; he prefers grounding his observations on a wilful miſtatement, in order, if poſſible, to inflame the public mind with an apprehenſion, that the Judges of the Special Commiſſion had violated their duty, in declaring that to be Treaſon, which was not made ſo by the 25th of Edw. III. The expreſſions in the charge are, " That, by the 25th of Edw. III. it is declared to be High Treaſon to compaſs or imagine the death of the King, provided ſuch compaſſing and imagination be manifeſted by ſome act or acts, proved by two wit-neſſes, to have been done by the party accuſed, in proſecution of that compaſſing and imagination;" * and it is no where aſſerted, that any other acts can amount to a diſtinct ſpecies of Treaſon, than thoſe de-clared by that ſtatute. It afterwards goes on to ſtate, " that theſe overt acts involve in them two diſtinct conſiderations; 1ſt, the matter of fact of which they conſiſt; 2dly, the relation of the fact to the de-ſign." The matter of fact, the Judge tells the Grand Jury, will be for them to enquire into the true ſtate of; but, with reſpect to the ſe-cond queſtion, whether the fact has relation to the deſign, ſo as to con-ſtitute an overt act of this ſpecies of Treaſon, it involved in it conſide-rations both of law and fact, and made it impoſſible that any poſitive rule ſhould be laid down for their government, *overt acts being, in their nature, all poſſible means which may be uſed in the proſecution of the end propoſed.* †

The Chief Juſtice then proceeds to ſtate from the writers on the Law of Treaſon, what overt acts ſhall be evidence of Treaſon in compaſſing and imagining the death of the King, and from theſe writers, he ſays, we learn, that not only acts of immediate and direct attempts againſt the King's life are overt acts of this Treaſon, but that all the remoter ſteps taken with a view to aſſiſt to bring about the actual attempt, are equally overt acts of the ſame Treaſon, and that not only they who aim directly at the King's life, but the entering into meaſures which, in the nature of things, or in the common experience of mankind, do ob-viouſly tend to bring the life of the King into danger, were alſo overt acts of compaſſing and imagining the death of the King. He then ſtates from Sir Matthew Hale and Mr. J Foſter, the inſtances on which there had been adjudged caſes which were of conſpiracies to depoſe the King;

* Charge, p. 4.   † Ibid, p. 5.

B 2

to

to imprifon him; to get his perfon into the power of the confpirators; and to procure an invafion of the kingdom. * And the conclufion of the Chief Juftice from thefe inftances, is, that if fuch overt acts have been held evidence of compaffing and imagining the death of the King, *will not a defign to overthrow the whole government of the country, to pull down and fubvert from its very foundations, the Britifh Monarchy,* in a much greater degree, be an over act, and evidence of fuch treafon. † So that we fee, fo far from the Chief Juftice laying down " that a confpiracy to fubvert the Monarchy," was a diftinct fpecies of treafon, he only confiders it as an overt act, and evidence of compaffing and imagining the death of the King, declared to be High Treafon by the 25th of Edw. III. This grofs miftatement being detected, the anfwer given to the paffages cited from Hume, and the extracts from Lord Strafford's Defence, is, that they do not apply to any thing afferted by the Chief Juftice, for the treafon imputed to the Earl of Strafford, by the articles of impeachment againft him, was, " that he had traitoroufly endeavoured to fubvert the eftablifhed laws of England, &c." not that he had compaffed and imagined the death of the King; fo that all the obfervations on that trial are perfectly proper, for the Earl was convicted of a Treafon unknown to the law; whereas the only fpecific Treafon the Chief Juftice mentions was, that of compaffing and imagining the death of the King, declared to be High Treafon by the 25th of Edw. III. The compaffing and imagining the death of the King being then the fpecific Treafon, ftated by the Chief Juftice to be declared by the 25th of Edw. III. and the " confpiring to fubvert the Monarchy," only to be confidered as an overt act of this fpecies of Treafon, the Chief Juftice, and the other Judges in the Special Commiffion, have not taken upon them the characters of Legiflators, or borrowed reafonings from the axioms and dictums of moralifts and metaphyficians, ‡ but merely ftated the law of Treafon as declared by 25 of Edw. IIId. The claufe in the above Stat. " That if in any future time, it might be neceffary to declare any new Treafons, that fhould only be done by a direct proceeding in Parliament for that fpecial purpofe," has not been infringed. The Chief Juftice has declared no new Treafon, but only what amounted to overt acts, as evidence to prove the Treafon contained in the Statute, which is ftrictly conftitutional; for neither that,

* Charge, p. 6. † Ibid, p. 7. ‡ Curfory Strictures, p. 8.

or

or any other Statute, have pretended to lay down, what fhall amount to overt acts of Treafon. The wifdom of the Legiflature has only faid, that the Treafon muft be proved by an overt act, knowing the im. poffibility of defining the infinitely various means that may be made ufe of in the profecution of any Treafon propofed. Has then the Chief Juftice done wrong in ftating " a confpiracy to fubvert the monarchy," to be an overt act of Treafon in compaffing, and imagining the death of the King? becaufe no fuch inftance had happened before, or has he ftrained the fair inference to be deduced from fuch overt act.

If fuch argument was to prevail, the confequence would have been, though the 25th of Edward III. had exprefsly declared compaffing and imagining the Death of the King to be High Treafon, yet if there could be no overt act of fuch treafon unfupported by an adjudged cafe, no perfon could have been convicted of treafon under that Statute; for as there could be no overt act without an adjudged cafe, fo alfo there could be no adjudged cafe without an overt act, and of courfe a con- viction could never take place. But there have been adjudged cafes, which have been before ftated. What then is the fair way of reafon- ing? To confider whether a confpiracy to fubvert the Monarchy, be an overt act, coming within the fame principle under which thofe cafes have been held overt acts of compaffing and imagining the death of the King, and if fo, the Chief Juftice has not ftrained the fair inference to be deduced from fuch an act. What has been the principle! That fuch acts have an obvious tendency to endanger the perfon of the King*. If fuch acts then have an obvious tendency to endanger the perfon of the King, can it be argued for a moment, that a confpiracy to fubvert the Monarchy muft not have the like effect?

Another argument made ufe of is, that the Chief Juftice, in his Charge, having ftated that the Statute of the 25th of Edward III. by which we are bound, not having declared a confpiracy to fubvert the Monarchy to be a fpecific High Treafon, it followed by the moft irrefiftible evi- dence, that it cannot be conftrued Treafon till all law is annihilated. The anfwer is, that the conclufion which is drawn is a true one, but it does not therefore follow, that it is not an overt act of Treafon in com-

* Forf. Cr. L. fol. edit. 197.

paffing

paffing and imagining the Death of the King, in the fame way as a confpiracy to levy war, though not a diftinct Treafon in itfelf, has neverthelefs been held an overt act of Treafon in compaffing and imagining
the Death of the King, which is all that is contended for in the Chief
Juftice's Charge. " The Chief Juftice's Charge," fays the author of
the Curfory Strictures, " confifts of three parts; the firft five pages contain principally a found and conftitutional expofition of the Law of Treafon. In the two following pages we are prefented with this portentous
fpeculation, this new Treafon of confpiring to fubvert the Monarchy.
The remainder of the Charge is made up of hypothefis, prefumption,
prejudication, and conjecture *. Let us fee the foundation for this affertion. The Chief Juftice, in the eighth page of his Charge, ftates,
" that as the particular nature of the confpiracy, alledged to have been
formed againft the State, had been difclofed, &c. he was apprehenfive
he fhould not fulfil the duty which a Judge owes to a Grand Jury, when
queftions in Criminal Law arife on new and extraordinary cafes of fact,
if he did not plainly and diftinctly ftate what he conceived the law
to be, or what doubts he conceived might arife in the law, upon the
facts likely to be laid before them, &c." Was not this ftrictly within
the character of a Judge, to inftruct the Grand Jury in matter of law?
And how is it poffible to do fo, otherwife than by ftating the probable
facts on which the law may arife? By fo little juftice is this accufation
fupported, that in a part of his charge the Chief Juftice † tells the Jury,
" that though it has been exprefsly declared by the higheft authority, that
there do exift in this country men capable of meditating the deftruction
of the Conftitution under which we live, that declaration, being extrajudicial, was not a ground on which they ought to proceed"—for cautious is he to prevent all " pre-judication" which might arife in the
minds of the Jury. In ftating the different cafes, which by the ftation
he filled he was bound to do, which would amount to a confpiracy to
fubvert the Monarchy, and be overt acts of compaffing and imagining
the death of the King, the Juftice fays, " If you find the perfons accufed involved in, and proceeding upon a defign to collect the people
together againft the Legiflative Authority of the country, for the purpofe, not of ufurping the functions of the Legiflature, but of overawing Parliament, and fo," &c. perhaps it may be fitting, that in re-

* Curfory Strictures, p. 10.   † Charge, p. 8.

fpect

fpect of the extraordinary nature, dangerous extent, and very criminal complexion of fuch a confpiracy, &c. it fhould be put into a judicial courfe of inveftigation, that it may receive a folemn adjudication, whe-ther it will or will not amount to High Treafon: in order to which, the Bills muft be found 'True Bills *. This, according to the Author of the Curfory Strictures, is a flagrant breach of duty; and he conftrues the plain Englifh of this declaration to † " Let thefe men be put upon trial for their lives: let them and their friends, tho' the remoteft ftrain-ers of connection, be expofed to all the anxieties, incident to fo un-certain and fearful a condition: let them be expofed to ignominy, to obloquy, to the partialities, as it may happen, of a prejudiced Judge, and the perverfenefs of an ignorant Jury, we fhall then know how we ought to conceive of fimilar cafes. By trampling upon their peace, throwing away their lives, or fporting with their innocence, we fhall obtain a bafis on which to proceed, and a precedent to guide our judg-ment in future inftances." One hardly knows how to anfwer fo impu-dent and falfe an accufation, mixed with fuch malignant infinuations, without the fmalleft argument to fupport them.—If the Author had not been moft ftupidly ignorant of the laws of his country, or wilfully mif-apprehended them, he would have known that it hath been the univer-fal practice of ages, in all cafes of legal doubt, for Judges not rafhly to decide, but to leave fuch cafes to be maturely confidered, and dif-cuffed, and to receive a folemn adjudication by the Judges of the land. So that the fum of the accufation is, that a Judge has been wicked enough to ufe caution, and not immediately to decide a doubtful queftion. Such are the chief objections made by the author of Curfory Strictures againft the charge of the Chief Juftice, founded upon miftatement, and fupported by every falfe and fcandalous affertion and imputation that the moft malignant heart could frame. I have not time to animadvert on the matters contained in the fecond appendix, purpofely calculated to inflame and delude; they are mere affertions conveyed to the public obfervation at firft thro' the channel of a public Newfpaper. The Conftitution has pointed out a legal mode for the inveftigation of the truth of them, and, if they were fo, the known abilities, knowledge, and experience of the defenders of the accufed perfons would not fuffer fuch conduct to pafs unnoticed, but that an officious and unprincipled

* Charge, p. 15.   † Curfory Strictures, p. 22.

scribler

(8)

scribler should dare to scatter such imputations on the eve of such important trials, to blacken the characters of the Judges who are to preside at them, and traduce the constituted authorities of the country, by the imputation of the worst motives and actions, from surmise, from report, I hope will not lose its reward; and that the Attorney General, by a public prosecution of the author of the pamphlet entitled " Cursory Strictures, &c." will rescue the judicial character, and the trial by jury, from any future attacks of the same nature.

A

REPLY

TO

AN ANSWER

TO CURSORY STRICTURES,

SUPPOSED TO BE WROTE BY JUDGE BULLER,

By the AUTHOR of CURSORY STRICTURES.

LONDON:

Printed for, and Sold by D. I. EATON, at the COCK and SWINE,
No. 74, Newgate-ftreet.

1794.

T HERE appeared in the TIMES of Saturday, October the 25th, a paper entitled, " An Anfwer to Curfory Strictures on the Charge delivered by Lord Chief Juftice Eyre," which firft appeared in your paper * of the preceding Tuefday.

I faw this Anfwer on the day it was publifhed. It will, I think, readily be believed, by the majority of the readers of the Strictures, that no man is more anxious than I am, that the law of Treafon, as

* Intended for the MORNING CHRONICLE, but refufed infertion.

A   eftablifhed

established in Great Britain, should be fully understood, at this tremendous and unexampled crisis. But the Answer appeared to me so extremely unsatisfactory and superficial, that all the anxiety I felt, was not sufficient to induce me to trouble the public with the slightest animadversion upon it. I conceived, and still conceive, that, if the title were taken away from the paper printed in the Times, the Strictures might, with much greater propriety, be considered as an Answer to the paper, than the paper as an Answer to the Strictures. I am firmly persuaded in my own mind, that, upon supposition this charge were made, and the Strictures were read last, few persons would hesitate to admit, that the publication I have mentioned has there received a full confutation.

But names, however trivial in themselves, frequently produce a considerable effect. The paper laying before me, is called an Answer; and I understand that some persons have been misled into the idea, that it is really such. A rumour has also been whispered, that this paper originates with a person of no small eminence in the legal profession. In deference to these circumstances, I am willing to take a brief survey of what I had first intended to have past by in silence.

I can find but two things in this paper, upon which I suppose any one can bestow the name of argument.

First, the author says, that the Strictures have misrepresented the meaning of the Chief Justice; and that " the learned Judge did not " lay it down as law, that a conspiracy to subvert the Monarchy was " in itself a distinct *species of High Treason.*"

It is true, the Chief Justice does not employ the same precise words as his Apologist. But what are we to suppose him to mean, when he affirms, that " *the statute of Edw. III. by which we are bound, has not* " *declared this,* which undoubtedly in all just theory of Treason is the " greatest of all Treasons, *to be a specific* HIGH TREASON" ?

Is not this the same thing as affirming, that the theory of Treason, which the Chief Justice wishes to establish, is not founded in the statute 25 Edward III. ? What does he mean, when he twice over informs

us,

us, that this is " such a crime, as *no lawgiver in this country has ever*
" *ventured to contemplate in its whole extent?*

His Apologist would have us understand, that " a conspiracy to sub-
" vert the Monarchy" is not a new species of Treason, but a new overt
act of Treason ; and that, of consequence, it is to be determined on,
not by a new act of Parliament, but by solemn adjudication in the
courts below. If that were the case, what, in the name of common
sense, has a LAWGIVER to do with it?

Nothing can be more clear to any person, who will look over
the paper I am now considering, than that, the Cursory Strictures
having compleatly exposed and confuted the Chief Justice's doctrine,
so as to make it impossible for any reader of the pamphlet not to assent
to the confutation, his Apologist has thought proper to bring forward a
new doctrine, and wholly to desert the ground upon which the Chief
Justice builds his *just theory of Treason.* The Chief Justice tells us twice
in the space of a single page, that " no *lawgiver* had ever ventured to
" contemplate this crime in its whole extent." The Apologist tells us,
that the meaning of his leader is, that no lawgiver ought to have contemplated it ; that it would have been absurd even to dream of such a
thing ; and that the attempt would have argued a compleat ignorance
of the nature of human actions. The Chief Justice, if he have any
pleasure in it, is extremely welcome to accept of this explanation.

Let us recollect another part of the Chief Justice's Charge. He says,
that " they who aim directly at the life of the King, are not the only
" persons, who may be said to compass or imagine his death," Here
are other remoter cases, in which a man may incur the guilt of High
Treason ; and there he cites from the authorities of Foster and Hale,
whom he stiles " some of the wisest and most enlightened men of their
" time, where integrity has always been considered as the most pro-
" minent feature of their character, and whose doctrines do now form
" great land-marks, by which posterity will be enabled to trace, with
" considerable certainty, the boundary line between High Treason,
" and offences of a lower order and degree. It is a fortunate circum-
" stance," continues the Chief Justice, " that we are thus assisted. I
" can easily conceive, that it must be a great relief to Jurors, placed in

A 2   the

" the refponfible fituation in which you now ftand ; and fure I am, that
" it is a confolation and comfort to us, who have upon us the refpon-
" fibility of declaring what the law is, in cafes, in which the public
" and the individual are fo deeply interefted."

Let this paffage be compared with the theory of the Apologift. According to him, a confpiracy to fubvert the Monarchy is not High
Treafon by the ftatute ; but an overt act of High Treafon, not founded
upon any precedent or adjudged cafe, but which, he pioufly hopes, will
be fo adjudged. What then does the Chief Juftice fay upon this fubject ? He obferves, " it is a great relief to Jurors, that Hale and
Fofter have decided as to the fpecific acts of High Treafon," becaufe
Hale and Fofter, nor indeed any other author upon Englifh law, has
ever faid a fingle word refpecting the only queftion then before the
Jury. He fays, " It is a confolation and comfort to us, as we now
" ftand ;" becaufe we can derive no light from thefe authors upon the
fubject before us. Few perfons, I believe, will envy the confolations
and comforts of the Chief Juftice Eyre.

With refpect to the Apologift's new doctrine, that a confpiracy to
fubvert the Monarchy ought to be confidered as an overt act of High
Treafon, this is fully anfwered in the Appendix, No. I. affixed to the
Strictures.

The Chief Juftice's Apologift further fays, that " it has been the uni-
" verfal practice of ages, in all cafes of legal doubt, for Judges not
" rafhly to decide, but to leave fuch cafes to be maturely confidered
" and difcuffed, and to receive a folemn adjudication by the Judges of
" the land."

I will not at prefent enter into this queftion with him; but I defire
to repeat my proteft againft it, as an act more fuitable to a natural philofopher or experimental anatomift, than to a civil magiftrate. I repeat, that every man condemned upon an adjudication of this fort, is
condemned upon an *ex poft facto* law; and that a more nefarious proceeding can fcarcely be imagined, than that a man fhould be hanged
upon an action which he did not know to be High Treafon, which he
could not know to be High Treafon, which the Judges of the land did

not

not know to be High Treason, and which was not High Treason till it was made so by the adjudication under which he is executed!

The second objection which the Chief Justice's Apologist makes to the Cursory Strictures is, that they constitute " an endeavour, on the " eve of trials of the greatest importance to every Englishman, to in- " fluence and deceive the minds of those Jurymen who are to be en- " gaged in the investigation of them." To this there is a plain answer.

For the sake of illustration, let me suppose the Attorney General to have brought a prosecution against the Strictures, and that I was de- fending myself in full court. The following are some of the arguments I should probably employ.

" First, the Chief Justice promised, and has actually given, a publi- " cation of his Charge. I have not therefore attacked an high Magi- " strate in the exercise of his functions; I have simply reviewed the " pamphlet of an author. For the Chief Justice to publish his Charge, " was an extrajudicial proceeding, and calculated irregularly to ' influ- " ence and deceive the minds of those Jurymen, who were to sit upon " the approaching trials.' If the Chief Justice becomes an author, he " cannot claim, any more than other authors, the privilege of not be- " ing answered. If the Chief Justice irregularly influence the minds " of a Jury, it is impossible that it should be a crime to counteract " that influence. This is a case that has already been partly ad- " judged, in the matter of the King against Stockdale, upon Hasting's " trial.

" Secondly, it is impossible that this court, or you, Gentlemen of the " Jury, should seriously imagine, that an investigation of truth in a " most important crisis, can be mischievous. The Strictures are, upon " the whole, a composition of close, severe, and accurate investigation. " Can it be a thing to be deplored, that, when twelve men are in- " dicted of High Treason, the law upon which they are tried should " be fully understood ? The Chief Justice has not gone uncontradic- " ted. No. It is well known, that every man's story is good till " another man's story has been told. The Strictures brought out the
" paper

190

190 190

(**6**)

" paper to which I am replying. The Strictures were the subject of
" animadversion for one full hour to the Attorney-General, on the first
" day of Hardy's trial. The public therefore is indebted to the Au-
" thor of the Strictures for both these advantages. The whole case is
" an obvious dilemma. Either the Strictures contain found argument,
" and then, if they are condemned, it can only be for having told
" unseasonable truths : or their reasonings are false, and then they have
" obtained for the public the inestimable benefit, of causing the law of
" Treason to be more accurately understood, in consequence of the ar-
" guments to which they have given occasion.

" Thirdly, The ground upon which they are to be condemned, is,
" that they ' tend to influence the minds of the Jury, upon the eve of
" trials of the greatest importance.' In answering this, I will leave
" out of the question Chief Justice Eyre's Charge, which, in its pre-
" sent form, tends not less irregularly to influence the minds of the
" Jury. I will leave out of the question the reports of the parliamen-
" tary committees, which have been so universally circulated, and
" which also prejudge the case of the prisoners. But I will lay upon
" your table the libels of all kinds, which for the last six months have
" been published against the persons now under accusation. Alas,
" your table will not hold the fiftieth part of them ! No means have
" been left untried. Bills, hand-bills, songs, pamphlets, and even
" printed pocket handkerchiefs. The mouth of every hawker has
" been incessantly filled with their crimes. I will not suppose that this
" industry has been countenanced by Government or the dependents of
" Government. But they have not been prosecuted. Begone then
" from the court, you who attempt to prosecute me, and hide your
" heads with shame ! Will you suffer it to be said that men were well-
" come, in every possible mode to create prejudice against the persons
" accused, and insure their destruction; but that, the moment one hu-
" mane individual lifts his voice in their favour, he, and he only, is
" selected for your vengeance ; Is it the spirit of the English Constitution
" that calumnies of all kinds may be spread against persons appre-
" hended for High Treason, and that he only is a libeller who shall
" utter one word to counteract their malice ?"

I have

I have anfwered every thing that appears to me argumentative in the paper in queſtion. I have taken no notice of the epithets, which are plentifully beſtowed on me. The author of the Striĉures is called, again and again, " impudent, malignant, deteſtable, ſtupidly igno-" rant, wilfully miſtaken, an officious and unprincipled ſcribbler, and " a moſt dangerous villain." The writer of the paper, for ought I know may complain of theſe omiſſions, as the things omitted perhaps conſtitute the main eſſence of his argument. But I have no pleaſure in tranſcribing ſuch language. The public will judge between us, which of us argues with candour, and which is guilty of malignity. I am totally unconſcious of any of his epithets belonging to me; and there-fore hereby return them untouched upon his hands, to be employed in the next argument in which he ſhall have equal occaſion for them.

THE AUTHOR OF

CURSORY STRICTURES.

CONSIDERATIONS

ON

LORD GRENVILLE's AND MR. PITT's

BILLS,

CONCERNING

TREASONABLE AND SEDITIOUS

PRACTICES,

AND

UNLAWFUL ASSEMBLIES.

———

BY A LOVER OF ORDER.

———

LONDON:

Printed for J. JOHNSON, No. 72, St. Paul's Church-Yard.

———

[PRICE 1s. 6d.]

CONSIDERATIONS, &c.

IN the prefent irritated and unnatural ftate of political affairs, while one party will not endure to hear of any cautionary reftraints upon freedom, and another party, impreffed with apprehenfions of anarchy, conceives that fcarcely any reftraint can be too vigilant or fevere; it is the object of the following examination of the bills lately introduced into Parliament by Lord Grenville and Mr. Pitt, to eftimate their merits with the ftricteft impartiality. It is much to be defired, in moments pregnant with fo important confequences, that an individual fhould be found, who could preferve his mind untainted with the headlong rage of faction, whether for men in power or againft them; could judge, with

B   the

the fobriety of diſtant poſterity, and the ſagacity of an enlightened hiſtorian ; and could be happy enough to make his voice heard, by all thoſe directly or remotely intereſted in the event.

The great problem of political knowledge, is, how to preſerve to mankind the advantages of freedom, together with an authority, ſtrong enough to controul every daring violation of general ſecurity and peace. The prize of political wiſdom is due to the man, who ſhall afford us the beſt comment upon that fundamental principle of civilization, Liberty without Licentiouſneſs.

Great is the error, or ſiniſter and alarming the policy, of thoſe, who tell us that politics is a ſimple ſcience, where the plaineſt underſtanding is in no danger of a fatal miſtake. Politics, eſpecially if we underſtand that term as relating to ſuch ſocieties of men as at preſent divide the earth, is the maſterpiece of human ſagacity.

To govern individuals in a petty and limited circle, is eaſy. They may be governed, if ſufficient judgment be exerciſed upon the ſubject, by reaſon alone. But it is far otherwiſe with nations, with millions of men united

under

under a fingle head. In a petty and limited circle, all exercife an infpection over all. There are no deeds that are concealed; the general cenfure or applaufe, follows immediately in the rear of every action that is performed. But, in nations of men, there is no eye penetrating enough to detect every mifchief in its commencement; craft is fuccefsful in efcaping thofe confequences which juftice would annex to injury. Men take pleafure in this fpecies of dexterity, and the web of fociety is rent by the fallies of wantonnefs.

No variety can be more endlefs, than that which is to be found among the difpofitions of mankind. Public intereft and fecurity require from men, to a certain degree, an uniformity of action, and an uniformity of fubmiffion. How is this uniformity to be found among the countlefs caprices of human character? Reafon and expoftulation here are not fufficient: there muft be an arm to reprefs; a coercion, ftrict, but forbearing and mild. In all numerous collections of men, there will be individuals difpofed to offend. No fyftem of political arrangement can be fo wife, but that fome men will difapprove of

B 2   it.

(4)

it. No fyftem of equal adminiftration can be fo perfect, but that fome men will be urged by neceffity, and aggravated by diftrefs. If offence be difcountenanced by the fober and judicious, there will always be turbulent fpirits who will purfue a contrary conduct; they will confirm the offender in his error, inftead of recalling him to reafon; they will harden him in his deviation, and encourage him to hold inoffenfive remonftrance in contempt.

Human fociety is a wonderful machine. How great are the inequalities that prevail in every country in Europe! How powerful is the incitement held out to the poor man, to commit hoftility on the property of the rich, to commit it in detail, each man for himfelf, or by one great and irrefiftible effort to reduce every thing to univerfal chaos! Political wifdom, when it is found fuch as it ought to be, is the great and venerable power, that prefides in the midft of turbulent and conflicting paffions, that gives to all this confufion the principles of order, and that extracts univerfal advantage from a nearly univerfal felfifhnefs.

He that deliberately views the machine of human fociety, will, even in his fpeculations, approach

approach it with awe. He will recollect, with alarm, that in this scene,

—Fools ruſh in, where angels fear to tread.

The fabric that we contemplate is a ſort of fairy edifice, and, though it conſiſt of innumerable parts, and hide its head among the clouds, the hand of a child almoſt, if ſuffered with neglect, may ſhake it into ruins.

There is no good reaſon to conclude, that ſpeculative enquiries ought not to be tolerated, or even that they may not, if conſulted with ſoberneſs, afford materials for general utility. But it is with ſoberneſs and caution that the practical politician will alone venture to conſult them. Do you tell me, " that there are great abuſes in ſociety?" No wiſe man will diſpute it. But theſe abuſes are woven into the very web and ſubſtance of ſociety; and he that touches them with a ſacrilegious hand, will run the riſk of producing the wideſt and moſt tremendous ruin. Do you tell me, " that theſe abuſes ought to be corrected?" Every impartial friend to mankind will confirm your deciſion with his ſuffrage, and lend his hand to the ſalutary work.

Yes,

(6)

Yes, my countrymen, abuſes ought to be correĉted. The effort to correĉt them ought to be inceſſant. But they muſt be correĉted with judgment and deliberation. We muſt not, for the ſake of a problematical future, part with the advantages we already poſſeſs; we muſt not deſtroy, faſter than we rear.

There are perſons indeed, to whom the edifice of ſociety appears as nothing but one maſs of deformity. With ſuch perſons it is not neceſſary here to enter into any regular argument. Is all that diſtinguiſhes the moſt enlightened genius of modern Europe from the American ſavage, nothing? Is the admirable progreſs of light and knowledge, that has been going on almoſt uniformly for centuries, and that promiſes to go on to an unlimited extent, —is this nothing? Where is the man hardy and brutiſh enough to put all this to peril, to ſet this immenſe and long earned treaſure upon a ſingle throw, for the chance, if univerſal anarchy and barbariſm be introduced, of the more generous and auſpicious ſcenes that will grow out of this barbariſm?

Theſe univerſal principles of political ſcience it ſeemed neceſſary to premiſe, to a ſober examination of the bills now depending in parliament.

parliament. Every one will fee, without the neceffity of a direct application, how thefe principles are connected with the fubject to be difcuffed. The perfons at prefent concerned in the government of Great Britain, have a delicate and momentous tafk impofed upon them. Of all their duties, that which is perhaps paramount to the reft, is to preferve the bleffings we already poffefs, from the rafhnefs of prefumptuous experiment. General fecurity is the bafis of all thofe things which fociety has to give, that are worthy the acceptance of mankind. In fecurity only the cultivator plows his field, the manufacturer exercifes his ingenuity, and the merchant brings home the produce of every diftant climate. Without fecurity all thefe would be neglected, would be done with an irrefolute and nervelefs temper, and would fall gradually into ruin. In fecurity only fcience is extended, arts are cultivated, and the virtues expand themfelves. Without fecurity mankind would fpeedily become ignorant and blood-thirfty favages. To the governors of the earth, therefore, the flender band of wife and judicious citizens would fay, " Give us fecurity, we will provide for ourfelves all other advantages."

If

(8)

If the moſt important duty of thoſe who hold the reins of government, be, at all times, to take care of the public ſecurity, it is peculiarly ſo in the preſent criſis. We are never ſo well inſured againſt anarchy and tumult, but that it is incumbent upon government to be vigilant. But the dangers of anarchy and tumult are greater now, than at any ordinary period. The foundations of ſociety have been broken up in the moſt conſiderable kingdom of Europe. Dreadful calamities have followed. A great experiment has been made, and the happineſs of mankind is eminently involved in the iſſue of the experiment. But there is ſomething ſo beautiful and faſcinating, to a ſuperficial obſervation, in the principles that produced the French revolution, that great numbers of men are eager to adopt and to act upon them. The calamities that have attended their operation in France, do not deter them.

In the mean time, the ſucceſs of the experiment of the French revolution has not been ſo unmixed and brilliant, but that a man of reflection will deliberate long, before he deſires to ſee the experiment repeated in any other country. It is the duty of the governors of the earth, particularly at this time, to ſet

their

their faces againſt raſh and premature experiments. They will not ſeek to preclude men
from the exerciſe of private judgment. They
will not involve in an undiſtinguiſhing cenſure all projeсts of better œconomy and mode
rate reform. But, if they remark with a certain degree of applauſe the high blood and impetuous mettle of the racer, they will, at
ļeaſt, look to the boundary poſts, and endeavour to prevent his running out of the courſe.

Let us apply theſe common and unanſwer-
able topics of reaſoning to the objeсts embraced in Lord Grenville's and Mr. Pitt's bills.
Theſe objeсts are, the influx of French principles, and the danger accruing from theſe
principles to public ſecurity. There are two
points, in which this influx of principles and
their concomitant dangers have been more
particularly conſpicuous.

It is the purpoſe of theſe pages to enquire
impartially. In the part of the ſubjeсt upon
which we enter in this place, what we undertake is, to probe recent evils. The evil
muſt be probed, or the proper remedy can
never be diſcovered. It would be baſe and
unmanly in the inveſtigator, to intend to give
offence to any man, or any body of men.

C				But,

But, far from harbouring any such intention, it is not lefs his duty, not to be deterred by the fear of offence. In the progrefs of the inveftigation he will be obliged alternately to deliver truths unpalatable to every fet of men. He will be forry to hurt the felf-applaufe or the prejudices of any; but, if he give pain to individuals, he is encouraged in this ungracious part of his tafk, by a hope of contributing his mite to the welfare of all. He will confole himfelf, whatever may be the event, with having intended that welfare.

A farther preliminary remark is neceffary in this place to obviate the danger of mifconftruction. The duties of the ftatefman, and the duties of the minifter of criminal juftice, have often been confounded. The ftatefman has conceived himfelf to be bound by the rigid maxims of a court of judicature, and the lawyer has expatiated in the conjectural ftyle, and among the moral probabilities, to which the ftatefman is bound to give attention. This confufion has in both inftances been attended with fatal confequences. No two claffes of duties can be more diftinct.

In the obfervations to be here delivered, the reafonings muft be of a political, and not

of

of a judicial kind. Where the life of a man is at ftake, or where coercive penalties of any fort are to be inflicted, the maxims of evidence cannot be too rigid ; we ought not to pronounce a man guilty, when it is poffible to find him innocent. Hiftorical difquifition, on the other hand, yields no deference to fuch a diftinction. Guilt or innocence are matters of indifference at her bar, fhe brings together all the evidence, fhe weighs the oppofite probabilities, and fhe pronounces a verdict upon the flighteft turning of the balance. She pronounces a man guilty, when it is in many ways poffible that he may be innocent.

Political difquifition partakes in many refpects of the nature of hiftorical. The concern of the politician, ftrictly fpeaking, is with precaution, and not with punifhment. He is not therefore bound to the rigour of judicial maxims. I may not proceed againft the life of a man without the moft irrefiftible evidence. But in calculating refpecting the probable future, in endeavouring to mould that future in the way moft conducive to general welfare, in anticipating diforder, and keeping out the influx of calamity, it is allowable, nay it is neceffary, to proceed upon much flighter grounds. I muft content my-

C 2   felf,

felf, like a philofopher, with analyfing the human mind, and afcertaining the confequences it is moft reafonable to expect. I could do nothing with refpect to future events, if I adopted a different mode of proceeding. Trufting to the reafonablenefs of thefe remarks, we will now proceed to examine the irregularities intended to be corrected by Lord Grenville's and Mr. Pitt's bills.

The firft of the two points to which we alluded above, is the inftitution of the London Correfponding Society. Refpecting the nature of extenfive political focieties we have received a memorable inftruction, which no lover of the happinefs of mankind will eafily perfuade himfelf to forget, in the inftitution of the Jacobin Society in Paris. It is too notorious to admit of being reafonably queftioned, that the London Correfponding Society has in feveral refpects formed itfelf upon the model of the focieties which have produced fuch memorable effects in France. They have adopted the language of thefe focieties. They have copied their actions. They may, without the imputation of uncharitable conftruction, be fufpected of a leaning

to

to republican principles. But, what is moſt material, they have endeavoured, like the ſociety of Jacobins, to form leſſer affiliated ſocieties in all parts of the iſland ; and they have profeſſed to ſend miſſionaries to inſtruct them. The very name indeed of London Correſponding Society preſents to us this idea.

Let us conſider what idea we ought to form of this extraordinary inſtitution. It is extremely numerous in the metropolis, ſplit and divided into a variety of ſections. It boaſts, that it weekly gains an acceſſion of numbers. Its recruits are chiefly levied from the poorer claſſes of the community. It has abundance of impetuous and ardent activity, and very little of the ballaſt, the unwieldy dulneſs, of property.

Political enquirers might have been induced to pay leſs attention to this extraordinary machine, than its magnitude deſerves. But it has forced itſelf upon public notice, by the immenſe multitudes it has collected together in the neighbourhood of the metropolis, at what have been ſtiled its general meetings. The ſpeeches delivered at theſe meetings, and the reſolutions adopted, have not always been

2   of

of the moft temperate kind. The collecting of immenfe multitudes of men into one affem- bly, particularly when there have been no perfons of eminence, diftinction, and import- ance in the country, that have mixed with them, and been ready to temper their efforts, is always fufficiently alarming. We had a fpecimen of what might be the fequel of fuch collecting, in the riots introduced by Lord George Gordon and the Proteftant Affocia- tion in the year 1780.

Let us put together the different circum- ftances already enumerated. Let us confider the largenefs of this fociety, their numerous meetings, their inceffant activity, their po- verty, the abundance of their zeal, and their numerous affiliations whether in act, in ex- pectation, or in defire. It may be precipitate to pronounce what are the ideas of its leading members, and how far they underftand the magnitude of the machine they profefs to go- vern. But it is eafy to fee what fuch a machine is able to effect.

From this delineation of the London Cor- refponding Society, it follows, that the go- vernment of this country would be unpardon- able, if it did not yield a very careful and uninterrupted

interrupted attention to their operations. In this decifion, it is wholly unneceffary to mix any confideration of the intention of the individuals concerned. Their intentions, for any thing that is of moment in this argument, may be of a purity that is more than human. To rail againft men's intentions, is to take an undue advantage of popular prejudices. There is no man fo pure, but that fomething of felfifh mixes with his actions. There is probably no man fo bafe, as not to have fome regard for morality, and juftice, and the general welfare of mankind. But the ftatefman reafons about men, as the manufacturer reafons about his tools and the different parts of his machines. He cenfures the unwieldy, the blunt, the jagged, the flawed, and the corrofive, without an atom of bitternefs or refentment againft any one of thefe. He merely finds them not fit for his purpofe. He fears the ill effects they may produce in the working of the machine. To fpeak only of that part of the parallel that relates to men, the real ftatefman will love, will compaffionate, will fympathife with thofe individuals, whofe conduct he concludes upon the beft evidence, to be hoftile to the general welfare. He regrets

their

their errors, he defires their reformation and improvement. It is unneceffary to his pur-pofe that he fhould impute to them any ill defign. He knows that the conduct of men with the beft difpofitions, has often been pro-ductive of horrible mifchief. Such was pro-bably the fublime and difinterefted enthufiaft that ftabbed Henry the Great, and fuch the authors of the Gunpowder Treafon.

Thefe are then the conclufions that, it fhould feem, we ought to form refpecting the London Correfponding Society. The fecond article that feems to conftitute the prefent ground of alarm, are the Political Lectures that have been delivered for near two years at Beaufort Buildings, in the Strand; to which perhaps we may add fome of the difcuffions that have taken place in certain crowded af-femblies, called Debating Societies. To con-ceive the judgment we ought to form refpect-ing thefe Political Lectures, we have only to recollect what has been already obferved, re-fpecting the profoundnefs of political fcience as it relates to the cafe of great nations, and the delicate fabric of human fociety.

Whether or no political lectures, upon the fundamental principles of politics, to be de-livered

livered to a mixed and crowded audience, be entitled to the approbation of an enlightened ſtateſman, it is ſomewhat difficult to pronounce. It is not, for the moſt part, in crowded audiences, that truth is ſuccefsfully inveſtigated, and the principles of ſcience luminouſly conceived. But it is not difficult to pronounce whether the political lectures that are likely to be delivered by an impatient and headlong reformer, are entitled to approbation.

" We muſt reform," ſay the advocates of theſe lectures. True, we muſt reform. There is ſcarcely a man in Great Britain ſo ſtupid, ſo bigoted, or ſo ſelfiſh, but that, if the queſtion were brought fairly before him, he would give his ſuffrage to the ſyſtem of reform. But reform is a delicate and an awful taſk. No ſacrilegious hand muſt be put forth to this ſacred work. It muſt be carried on by ſlow, almoſt inſenſible ſteps, and by juſt degrees. The public mind muſt firſt be enlightened ; the public ſentiment muſt next become unequivocal ; there muſt be a grand and magnificent harmony, expanding itſelf through the whole community. There muſt be a conſent of wills, that no miniſter and no monopoliſt
D   would

would be frantic enough to withſtand. This is the genuine image of reform ; this is the lovely and angelic figure that needs only to be ſhewn, in order to be univerſally adored. Oh, Reform ! Genial and benignant power ! how often has thy name been polluted by profane and unhallowed lips ! How often has thy ſtandard been unfurled by demagogues, and by aſſaſſins been drenched and disfigured with human gore !

Proceeding then upon this conception of the ſubject, it is eaſy to perceive, that the en-lightened advocates of reform will proceed with wary and cautious ſteps ; that they will endeavour to inform the underſtandings of others, to invigorate their benevolence, and to appeaſe the tumult of their paſſions. Their labour ought to be inceſſant; their progreſs ought to be conſtant; the effects ought to be ſublime, but not terrible. Let us contraſt this with the ordinary and prevailing ideas of political lecturers.

It may happen, that a political lecturer ſhall commence his career with uncommon purity of intentions. I believe this has been the caſe with the political lecturer in Beau-fort Buildings. But there are two things ne-ceſſary

ceffary befide this favourable preliminary.
The lecturer ought to have a mind calmed,
and, if I may be allowed the expreffion, confecrated by the mild fpirit of philofophy. He
ought to come forth with no undifciplined paffions, in the firft inftance; and he ought to have
a temper unyielding to the corrupt influence
of a noify and admiring audience. It almoft
univerfally happens to public fpeakers, that,
though they may begin with the intention
of communicating to their auditors the tone
of their own minds, they finifh with the
reality of bartering this tone for the tone of
the auditors. Do the audience clap their
hands, or employ other demonftrations of applaufe? There is fcarcely a Stoic upon the
face of the earth fo rigid, but he feels his own
heart titillated and delighted with thefe fenfible tokens of complacence. He obferves what
paffages they are in his difcourfe that produce
the loudeft tumults of applaufe; he aims at
the frequent recurrence of fuch paffages; he
feels difcontented, if for any length of time
he is merely liftened to in filence. Add to
this, he well knows that the moft furious
applauders are the moft affiduous frequenters.
It would be inconfiftent with his purpofe, if

he delivered fuch difcourfes as tended to drive away his hearers, or if he did not deliver fuch as tended to bring them in ftill augmenting multitudes.

To what end does this intellectual progrefs in the mind of the lecturer ultimately lead? Quiet difquifition and mere fpeculative enquiry will not anfwer his purpofe. Strict difquifition, efpecially to perfons not much in the habits of regular thinking, is difficult to underftand: it requires too active and laborious an attention. Add to this, that it does not fuit the tone of collected multitudes. Sober inquiry may pafs well enough with a man in his clofet, or in the domeftic tranquillity of his own fire-fide: but it will not fuffice in theatres and halls of affembly. Here men require a due mixture of fpices and feafoning. All oratorical feafoning is an appeal to the paffions. The moft obvious feafoning of this fort is perfonality. The lecturer infallibly learns in a fhort time, to quit the thorny paths of fcience, and to inveigh againft the individuals that exercife the functions of government. Their vices are painted in caricature; their actions are disfigured, and uniformly traced to the blackeft motives; a horrible

groupe

groupe is exhibited; all the indignant emotions of the human mind are excited. The
audience do not haften from the lecture-room,
and hurry the minifter to the lamp-poft;
their paffions are only in training for deftruction. The cauldron of civil contention fim-
mers, but is not yet worked up into the in-
quietude of a tempeft.

It would be ludicrous, if it did not excite
a more painful fenfation, to liften to the faving
claufes that are, from time to time, introduced
into the difcourfe, to perfuade men to unbounded and univerfal benevolence. It is
lord George Gordon preaching peace to the
rioters in Weftminfter-Hall. " Commit no
" violence," faid his lordfhip, " but be fure
" you do not feparate, till you have effected
" your purpofe." It is Iago adjuring Othello
not to difhonour himfelf by giving harbour to
a thought of jealoufy.

Good God! is this the preparation that be-
fits us, in a time of crifis, and amidft the moft
irrefiftible neceffity for a reform? I can do
juftice to the individual; I can fee talents in
him that might be ripened for the moft valuable
purpofes : but I deplore the feeing them thus
arrefted in their growth, and thus employed.

We

We have now taken a view of the principal features of that fituation which has furnifhed the occafion for introducing lord Grenville's and Mr. Pitt's bills. The commentary upon the fituation is eafy. The London Correfponding Society is a formidable machine; the fyftem of political lecturing is a hot-bed, perhaps too well adapted to ripen men for purpofes, more or lefs fimilar to thofe of the Jacobin Society of Paris. Both branches of the fituation are well deferving the attention of the members of the government of Great Britain.

If, then, they be deferving of attention, it is here that we are bound to recollect the fort of attention which a wife ftatefman, in thefe cafes, ought to employ. He is no true ftatefman; he is a formidable and atrocious enemy of human kind, who, while exercifing the functions of government, fuffers himfelf to be made angry. Minifters of Great Britain, attend! You ought to do fo. You would be delinquents, if you did otherwife. But let your attention be calm; let your remedies be mild.

The great problem of political fcience, is not to know how to lay an iron hand upon popular

popular irregularities. If that were the cafe, Draco was the moft fuccefsful ftudent that ever exifted ; unlefs his merits were perhaps eclipfed by the profounder policy of Tiberius and Caligula. The great problem of political fcience, as we have already faid, is to know how to anticipate the injurious confequences of irregularity by the mildeft and leaft perceptible antidote ; to preferve liberty in all its vigour, while we effectually difcountenance licentioufnefs. This fundamental axiom will hardly be difputed with us. By this axiom therefore we proceed to try Lord Grenville's and Mr. Pitt's bills.

If ever a delicate and fkilful hand were neceffary in managing the public concerns, it was peculiarly neceffary upon the prefent occafion. Lord Grenville's bill relates to the moft important of all human affairs, the liberty of the prefs. Mr. Pitt's bill touches upon one of the grand characteriftics of Englifh liberty, the fundamental provifion of the bill of rights, the right of the fubject to confult refpecting grievances, and to demand redrefs

One word more, before we proceed. No two human underftandings are alike. No

two

two human underſtandings perhaps would pre-
ſcribe exactly the ſame conduct, under circumſtances that are in any degree complicated.
Let us not then, cenſure lord Grenville and
Mr. Pitt for trifles. They had an arduous
taſk to perform, let us grant them a liberal
allowance. They may have ſuggeſted a plan,
a little better or a little worſe than would
have occurred to the ſtudent in his cloſet: we
will not differ with them for that. If they
have diſcharged their taſk upon the whole
with ſucceſs; if they have offered only a promiſing remedy for the evil, and preſerved un-
injured the great palladiums of all that is in-
tereſting to man, they ought not to incur our
cenſure; they ought to receive a generous
applauſe.

The title of Lord Grenville's bill is, *An
Act for the ſafety and preſervation of his majeſty's perſon and government, againſt treaſon-
able and ſeditious practices and attempts.* Its
profeſſed object is to provide additional ſecu-
rities, for the ſafety of the royal perſon, and
againſt ſuch proceedings and language, as
may lead to popular tumult and inſurrection.
It conſiſts of two parts, one enacting new
treaſons, or definitions of treaſon, and the

other

other providing againſt ſeditious practices under the denomination of miſdemeanours.

The liberty of the preſs! If any thing
human be to be approached with awe, it is
this. If other men deſerve cenſure for trifling with public ſecurity, what cenſure do not
miniſters deſerve, if they have ſo trifled? If
leſſer offences, if a train of perſonal ſcurrili-
ties, ought not in ſome caſes to be paſſed over
without notice, what denomination ſhall we
give to his offence, who offends againſt the
liberty of the preſs, and who, while he offends, poſſeſſes the functions of government,
can ſtrike as ſoon as threaten?

If in reality any proviſions be neceſſary
againſt ſeditious writings, Heavens! with
what caution, with what almoſt morbid ſenſibility ought ſuch proviſions to be conſtruct-
ed? I would ſay to the author of ſuch a bill,
" Conſider well what it is that you are doing.
You enter upon the moſt ſacred of all human
functions. Do not, while you pretend to be
a friend to the public welfare, ſtab the frame
of the public welfare to the very heart!"

The manner in which the proviſions of
lord Grenville's bill are worded, may be ſa-
tisfactorily illuſtrated. For that purpoſe, I

E   will

will fuppofe thefe very pages to be conftrued
by the king's minifter to have a tendency " to
incite or ftir up the people to hatred or diflike" [What a word is this diflike! What
malignant genius introduced it into the bill?
What a fweeping term, that may mean any
thing or every thing that the profecutor fhall
be pleafed to underftand by it!]—" to incite
or ftir up the people to hatred or diflike of
the perfon of his majefty, his heirs or fucceffors, or the eftablifhed government and
conftitution [where is the philologift that will
give me a fecure definition of thefe two
words?] of this realm." Well, in that cafe,
I am to be " liable to fuch punifhment as may
by law be inflicted in cafes of high mifdemeanours;" and " for the fecond offence, I
am to be tranfported for feven years." The
only fecurity I have againft the infliction
of thefe penalties, the moment a profecution
is commenced againft me, confifts in the
hope, that the judge may be unbiaffed and
impartial; that the arguments of my counfel
may be found in the experiment to be irrefiftible; or that my jury in whole or in part may
be perfons of a firm, independent, and intrepid temper. In the mean time the profecution
com-

commenced againft me is a crown profecution ; it is attended in the courfe of it with the
popular clamour againft republicans and levellers ; and people are to be reminded every
day in the treafury prints, that, upon the conviction of fuch perfons as I am, depends the
fecurity of property, and all that is valuable in
focial exiftence.

Who does not fee, that, if I write a pamphlet or book in which any political queftion
is treated or incidentally mentioned, I may fuffer the penalties of this act ? Who does not fee,
that, if the king's minifter do not like my pamphlet, or do not like my face, if he have an old
grudge againft me for any paft proceeding, if
I have not proved a fortunate candidate for his
general good-will, or if, by any diftortion of
underftanding, or exceffivenefs of alarm, he be
led to fee in my pamphlet things it does not
contain, I may fuffer the penalties of this act ?
My after hopes are in the judge, that he fhall
have no inclination to gratify his majefty's
minifter; in my counfel, that he fhall be able
to convince men who may be predetermined
againft conviction ; or in the jury, that they
fhall be undecided by hopes or fears, from government, or any of the intemperate and indif-

criminate

criminate friends of government; or that the honeft part of them fhall be more enlightened, more determined, and better able to endure hunger and fatigue, than thofe who are difpofed to confult only the voice of intereft? This is the lottery, from which I am to draw my ticket. This is the game, at which I am to play for the liberties of an Englifhman. The words of the bill are exprefsly calculated to afford the wideft field for fophiftry, and the moft convenient recipe for quieting the awakened confcience of a delinquent jury or judge.

Surely, lord Grenville, you might have found milder penalties, that would have been equal to cure the mifchief in queftion, if in reality any new law and any penalties were neceffary for that purpofe! But the cafe is too plain. Minifters have indeed ftudied in the fchool of Draco. Did they feek to difcover by how mild or by how fmall an interference the evil might be adequately prevented? No, no: he muft be weaker than an idiot that can yield to fuch an impofition. On the contrary, minifters gladly feized the opportunity to provide a remedy ten times larger than the evil in queftion; to provide a remedy that would fuit all their purpofes; that would fuit all the

purpofes

purpofes of private revenge or fanguinary alarm : a remedy fo large, as fhould render them fecure that they would never need to come to parliament again, however much any future evil might differ from the evil now to be provided againft.

The fpirit of this bill is evidently to put an engine into the hands of minifters, calculated for their ufe in every imaginable emergency. There is no cafe to which this bill may not be ftretched ; there is no offence, prefent or future, definite or indefinite, real or fictitious, that it may not be made to include.

A ftriking illuftrarion of this is afforded us in one of the claufes, which is well calculated by its conftruction to explain and develop the intention of the whole.   Lord Grenville ftated in the houfe of lords, " that all the claufes, except the two principal claufes, the object of which is to define the new treafons created by this bill, and the crime of fedition, are calcu-lated for the benefit of fuch perfons as may be fuppofed to have offended againft it."   The firft of thefe claufes enacts, " that no perfon fhall be profecuted by virtue of this act, unlefs it be by order of the king, his heirs or fuccef-fors, under his or their fign manual, or by order

der of the privy council." What is the spirit
of this clause? To a superficial observer, or
to him who shall be disposed to give implicit credit to the assertion of a secretary
of state, the clause may indeed seem favourable to the subject: it tends to limit and super-
sede vexatious prosecutions. But, if we consider it more profoundly, it will not be found
to authorise so gentle a construction. The clause
in fact amounts to no less than an explicit ac-
knowledgment of the iniquity of the bill.
Other acts of parliament are directed against real
offences : other acts of parliaments profess to
describe and define the objects they have in
view. They may therefore be trusted to
the ordinary course of justice, every man is
free to execute and inforce them. But this
bill is a sacred instrument. No ordinary hand
may touch it. As it is equally adapted for
every purpose that the wantonness of power,
or the wantonness of malice can desire ; it is
therefore not to be confided to the discretion
of an ordinary subject. Private men are to
know nothing of it, except as they may happen to suffer under its penalties. It is the
consecrated engine of tyranny ; it is the open
and avowed enaction of an arbitrary power.

Another

Another ufe has been fuggefted for this extraordinary claufe. There is a numerous body
of men, who have lately been fuppofed infeparable from the maintenance of the prefent
conftitution of things in this country ; a body
better known in France before its late revolution : I mean the army of fpies and informers. Thefe men, if the execution of the
law had been trufted to vulgar hands, might
have been expofed to vexatious fuits under
fome of its provifions. Government, by
taking the whole into its own management,
and preventing ordinary individuals from touch-
ing this confecrated palladium of the new order of Englifh politics, have guarded againft
this evil. Seditious and turbulent reformers
may be punifhed under this act; but men,
whatever they be, that are fheltered by adminiftration, cannot be vexed.

A farther circumftance may deferve to be
mentioned, as calculated to illuftrate the generalities of lord Grenville's bill. This will
be rendered particularly confpicuous by a reference to the fpeech of bifhop Horfley, in
the committee upon this bill in the houfe of
lords, Wednefday, November 11th. This
fpeech is memorable for more reafons than

I   one.

one. In it, his lordſhip delivered a very con-
ciſe maxim, which upon ſecond thoughts he
was pleaſed to endeavour to qualify and explain, though he refuſed to retraƈt. The
maxim was, that he " did not know what the
" maſs of the people in any country had to do
" with the laws, but to obey them." But it
is not for the ſake of this paſſage, that the
mention of biſhop Horſley's ſpeech is introduced in this place. The following expreſſion, which appears to have fallen from him,
is particularly worthy of animadverſion :
" Common ſpeculative and philoſophical diſ-
" quiſitions might be ſtill written and pub-
" liſhed, though he always thought they did
" more harm than good ; for the bill was
" merely direƈted againſt thoſe idle and ſedi-
" tious public meetings for the diſcuſſion of
" the laws, where the people were not com-
" petent to decide upon them."

No topic can be more important, than that
which is ſtarted by the reverend prelate in
theſe remarks. It is a queſtion that well may
" give us pauſe." The diſtinƈtion of his
lordſhip is well and judiciouſly taken. It is
no doubt one thing to diſcuſs political queſtions in mixed and fortuitous aſſemblies ; it is

one thing to enquire into the ill confequences
that may refult from fuch tumultuary and
paffionate difcuffions; it is one thing to enquire into the reftraints that may reafonably
be put upon affemblies and proceedings of
this fort; and it is a thing fomewhat different, to enquire whether we fhall contribute, to the extent of our power, once for
all, to extinguifh the future profpects and
hope of mankind ; to put a violent termination upon the boundlefs progrefs of fcience,
of that fcience in particular which is moft
immediately and profoundly interefting to the
whole human race. It would be a project
indeed of gigantic dimenfions, that, in this
advanced period of human improvement,
fhould command us to banifh all the profef-
fors and cultivators of fcience, or to affaffinate
them. Lord Grenville, in that cafe, would
no doubt ftand forward to the lateft pofterity
as one of the moft diftinguifhed names, one of
the moft daring and hardy adventurers, in the
records of hiftory. Omar, the conqueror of
Alexandria, would be but a fool to him.
Omar did not execute the wantonnefs of his
tyranny upon the perfons of men of letters;
he only deftroyed their works. Robefpierre

F   is

is accufed of having harboured a mortal animofity againft men of letters : but this is probably a calumny, and we fhould fcorn to ca-
lumniate even Robefpierre. But affuming
the faƈt, lord Grenville would appear, but
for the explanation of bifhop Horfley, to
have far outftepped the tyrant of France.
Robefpierre merely made ufe of exifting
maxims, and applied them to the gratification
of his paffions. He perfecuted men of letters in an indireƈt manner. But lord Grenville, upon this fuppofition, would have introduced a bill in which they were clearly defcribed, and have faid, " It is only neceffary
" for you to have cultivated the moft im-
" portant of all fciences, to make you liable
" to the penalties of my bill." Much gratitude is due to bifhop Horfley, for having, in
the paffage above cited, fo clearly marked out
the diftinƈtion between the idle and inflammatory preachers of fedition, and the great
apoftles and champions of human intelleƈt,
and explained to us to whom the law did and
did not apply.

Here let us paufe a little. Is bifhop
Horfley's commentary in reality a juft one ?
Who is this celebrated prelate ? Let us fup-
                                        pofe

pofe him, for the fake of argument, to be the greateft man in exiftence : are his doctrines to be received as upon a level with the laws of the land, with enactions of king, lords, and commons, in parliament affembled ? What the bifhop fays is good, found reafon and juftice. True : but what then ? I look through the act of parliament, and I cannot find it there. Like Shylock, " I cannot find it in " the inftrument: It is not fo nominated in " the bond !"

Bifhop Horfley is an excellent moralift and politician. No doubt of it : but what of that ? Can he grant me a *noli profequi* ? Can I bring his fpeech into court, and offer it as a writ " to fhew why judgment fhould not pafs " upon me ?"

Lord Grenville, and the authors of the bill mean exactly what bifhop Horfley has expreffed. We will grant that; we will not ftay to debate about trifles. But this affumption only exhibits in a more atrocious light the iniquity of the bill.

Was the omiffion of every provifion for this purpofe an affair of accident ? We may hence learn what value they fet upon the liberties of

F 2   Englifhmen,

Englifhmen, and the moft important interefts of mankind.

Was it defign ? Did they intend to have all the literature of England, original or tranflated, and all its votaries at their mercy ?

But the matter lies deeper than we have yet feen. It is worth our while to enquire what would be the penalty awarded to the author of Hume's Idea of a Perfect Commonwealth, or Rouffeau's Treatife of the Social Compact, if they were living, and if thefe works were publifhed during the operation of Lord Grenville's bill.

Hume and Rouffeau appear in thefe treatifes to have been republicans. Republicanifm is a doctrine mifchievous and falfe. Be it fo. But there can be no enquiry and no fcience, if I am to be told at the commencement of my ftudies, in what inference they muft all terminate. Labouring under this reftraint, I cannot examine ; labouring under this reftraint, I cannot, ftrictly fpeaking, even attempt to examine. No matter how decifive are the arguments in favour of monarchical government ; if men enter freely upon the difcuffion, there will be fome, from fingularity of temper, or peculiarity of prejudices

dices which they are unable to correct, who will determine in favour of republicanifm. The idea of combining uniformity of opinion in the fequel, with liberty of enquiry in the commencement, is the moft impoffible and frantic notion that ever entered into the mind of man.

What men imagine they fee in the way of argument, they can fcarcely refrain from fpeaking, and they ought to be permitted to publifh. All republican writers (Hume is an eminent example) do not appeal to our paffions; all appeals to our paffions do not menace us with the introduction of univerfal anarchy. Confidering how triumphant the arguments in favour of monarchy are affirmed to be, we furely ought not to be terrified with every philofophical debate. It is a well known maxim of literature, that no principle upon any controverfial fubject, can be fo fecurely eftablifhed, as when its adverfaries are permitted to attack it, and it is found fuperior to every objection. A fober and confiderate obferver will have ftrange thoughts that fuggeft themfelves to him, refpecting the moft venerable and generally received maxims, if he find that every perfon who ventures to

enter

enter upon an impartial examination of them,
is threatened with the pillory.

A few words are due to thofe perfons who,
imbued with the fcepticifm incident to inqui-
fitive habits, may be in doubt whether the monarchical or republican opinion will ultimately
appear to be the moft found, or which of
them will ultimately prove victorious. A
doctrine oppofite to the maxims of the exifting government may be dangerous in the
hands of agitators, but it cannot produce
very fatal confequences in the hands of philofophers. If it undermine the received fyftem,
it will undermine it gradually and infenfibly ;
it will merely fall in with that gradual principle of decay and renovation, which is
perpetually at work in every part of the
univerfe.

Having here endeavoured to define the tendency of what bifhop Horfley calls " common
" fpeculative and philofophical difquifitions,"
let us fee whether they fall within the provifions of this bill, and what is the punifhment adjudged againft them. Under the feditious branch of the bill, we find thefe words:
" If any perfon or perfons fhall malicioufly
" and advifedly, by writing, printing, preach-
" ing,

" ing, or other speaking, express, publish,
" utter, or declare, any words, sentences, or
" other thing or things, to excite or stir up
" the people to hatred or dislike of the per-
" son of his majesty, his heirs or successors,
" or the established government and consti-
" tution of this realm, then he or they shall
" be liable to such punishment as may by law
" be inflicted in cases of high misdemeanours."
This clause needs no comment. Whatever
were the intentions of the authors of the bill,
into which perhaps it would be profane for us
to enquire, nothing is more certain than that
the clause may easily be wrested to include
" common speculative and philosophical dis-
" quisitions."

Well then, the author of every speculative and philosophical disquisition, is at the
mercy of the minister for his first offence—
[let it be recollected, that by offence is here
understood every enquiry, however temperate;
every argument, however solid and acute;
every instruction to mankind; however salutary and beneficial, for all these may, at the
mercy of the minister for the time being, be
brought within the provisions of this act]—
he is liable, I say, for his first proceeding of

this

this fort, to fine, imprifonment, and pillory; and for the fecond to be tranfported to Botany Bay.

This is fomething; this might fatisfy the moft inordinate appetite for arbitrary power. Philofophy and fcience, in all their moft eminent branches, though venerable as the pillars of the world, are by this act fent to fchool to lord Grenville. He is to teach them good manners; he is to brandifh over them the rod of correction; he is to fubject them to the rigours of fuch difcipline as to his judgment fhall feem meet.

Philofophy and fcience, we might imagine, are in this claufe amply provided for. But there is no end to the paternal attention of his majefty's minifters. Let us pafs from the inferior branch of lord Grenville's bill to the principal, *viz.* that which relates to the crime of high treafon. Here it is provided, that " if any perfon or perfons fhall compafs, ima- " gine, invent, devife, or intend, death or de- " ftruction, or any bodily harm, tending to " death or deftruction, maim or wounding, " imprifonment or reftraint of the perfon of " our fovereign lord the king, his heirs " and fucceffors, or to deprive or depofe him

3   " or

" or them from the ftyle, honour, or kingly
" name of the imperial crown of this realm,
" then fuch perfon or perfons fhall be ad-
" judged guilty of high treafon."

This claufe is fufficiently complicated in its
ftructure.   It is neceffary to read it more than
once, before we can completely underftand
it, or perceive to what fubftantives the government of the different verbs and partici-
ples it contains, are to be conftrued to extend.
But we will pafs over this circumftance.   Unhappily lord Grenville's bill, if it pafs into
a law, will not be fingular in this refpect.
We too often fee the lives and liberties of
men fufpended upon hair-breadth conftructions, upon diftinctions of grammar, and
fubtle, philological difcuffions refpecting the
meaning of words.   This is a fpectacle to
which we have been too long accuftomed,
for it to be capable of exciting in us any degree of wonder.

The immediate purpofe for which we
quoted this claufe, was to enquire whether or
no, in fober certainty, " common fpeculative
" and philofophical difquifitions," fell within the letter of this definition of high treafon.
Hume's Idea of a Perfect Commonwealth,

G   contains

contains principles that are either true or falſe. We will ſuppoſe this wonderful genius, the great ornament of Engliſh literature, who gave new delicacy to human language, new profoundneſs to hiſtorical compoſition, and new luſtre to the events of the Britiſh annals ; this genius, who dived into the depths of intellectual ſcience, who diſcovered new treaſures where the greateſt men of every age had ſearched before, and who, whether his concluſions ſhall ultimately be admitted as true or rejected as falſe, has certainly given that additional acuteneſs to philoſophical reaſoning by which mankind will be benefited as long as literature ſhall endure—we will ſuppoſe, I ſay, this wonderful genius to be arraigned as the author of the compoſition juſt mentioned.

What ſhall be his behaviour at the bar ? Shall he deſcend to the pitiful artifice of diſowning this able production, and truſt that government will not be able to bring it home to him in the way of legal proof? Shall he allege, " the principles of my performance " are falſe, they will be eaſily refuted, and " will never produce any perceptible effect ?" Or ſhall he affirm at once, " the performance

" is

" is mine, and its principles are true ?" In that cafe, the attorney-general retorts upon him, " they are calculated to produce an effect ; they tend " to incite and ftir up the " people to hatred or *diflike* of the perfon of " his majefty, *his heirs or fucceffors,* or the " eftablifhed *government and conftitution* of " this realm :" nothing more plain. They tend fooner or later to the diffemination of republican principles." Hume then upon this charge is to be fined, imprifoned, and fet in the pillory ; and, if he afterwards authorize the republication of his effay, he is to be tranfported to Botany Bay.

Stop a moment. This was not the purpofe for which the queftion was here introduced. The bufinefs was to enquire, under lord Grenville's bill, whether or no he were guilty of high treafon. Hume, for publifhing his Idea of a Perfect Commonwealth, guilty of high treafon ! conducted to the place of execution, and there hanged, drawn, and quartered !

Nothing is more indifputable, than that he might, with equal propriety, be profecuted under the firft, as under the fecond branch of lord Grenville's bill. There is no need of a laboured proof to fhew, that, in publifh-

G 2   ing

ing his Idea of a Perfect Commonwealth, he had some intention. His intention was to reconcile men by degrees to republican principles, or at least to wean them from the prevailing prepossessions against these principles. He is guilty therefore under the clause of " com-
" passing, imagining, devising, inventing, or
" intending, to deprive or depose our sovereign
"·· lord the king, or his heirs and successors,
" from the style, honour, or kingly name
" of the imperial crown of this realm."

But there is a more extraordinary circumstance behind. The authors of the bill, as if fearful that some lenient, or over-merciful judge might imagine that the publication of such a book as Hume's Idea of a Perfect Commonwealth, was not high treason, have proceeded more precisely to limit and define the meaning of the clause, which they do in the following words: "And [if such person or per-
" sons] such compassings and imaginations,
" inventions, desires or intentions, or any of
" them shall express, utter, or declare, by any
" *printing, writing,* preaching, or malicious and
" advised speaking, then every such person or
" persons shall be adjudged guilty of high
" treason." Thus " common speculative and
" philoso-

" philofophical difquifitions" are exprefsly declared to come within the defcription of high
treafon ; and, what is more curious, nothing
but printing, writing, preaching, or fpeaking,
is high treafon within the conftruction of this
act.

I am perfectly aware that lord Grenville
and the other authors of this bill, will ftart
with aftonifhment at the explanation I have
given. They are innocent ; they never had
it in contemplation to involve philofophical
writers, who fhould fcientifically difcufs the
nature of the human mind, or the operations
of man in a ftate of fociety, in the pains of
high treafon. I have no doubt of it. But
what follows from this ? Obferve, Englifhmen, " what manner of men" are your legiflators ! Obferve " what manner of men"
are felected for the king's minifters, and whofe
peculiar office it is to make laws, upon which
the tenure of human life is fufpended ! " They
" know not what they do." Is this a fufficient
apology ? When they have made laws, no
men fo much aftonifhed as they, if a fober
enquirer comes and tells them the meaning of
them. They " breath out threatenings and
" flaughter," they " throw about firebrands,"
and

and rifk at every moment a conflagration of
the edifice of our liberties; and they " fay,
" Are we not in fport ?" Such is the government under which we live. They fhut
up a magazine, containing an extract of every
human evil, in the fmalleft compafs, and then
prefent it to us as an advantage. If at fome
future time Pandora's box be unclofed, then,
and not till then, they will know, that what
they paffed for an odoriferous perfume, is in
reality the moft deadly poifon.

One obfervation more upon lord Grenville's bill, and it fhall then, for the prefent,
be difmiffed. Under both branches of the
bill, "fpeaking," "expreffing, publifhing, ut-
" tering, or declaring any words, fentences, or
" other thing or things," make a part of the
defcription of the offence hereby created. In
the firft claufe indeed it is underftood that
minifters, in their extreme benignity, intended
to withdraw fpeaking from the enumerations
of the bill; and I am no longer to be liable,
for faying in the courfe of a cafual converfation
by my own fire-fide, that, " in the abftract,
" I like a republican government better
" than monarchy," to be hanged, drawn, and
quartered. I am only, firft, to be pilloried, and
afterwards

afterwards tranfported to Botany Bay. " The " tender mercies of the wicked" are inftructive. Nor is it lefs effential to the rightly underftanding thefe bills, that we fhould confider them as they originally ftood, than as they may be fubfequently altered.

It is not eafy to pronounce whether this claufe, I mean the claufe fubjecting a man, for all manner of fpeaking, to imprifonment and tranfportation, is to be confidered as more or lefs atrocious than the claufes reftraining the liberty of the prefs. In one refpect it is worfe. It extends to every man, and no man can pretend fuccefsfully to guard himfelf againft its fanctions. But in other refpects it is lefs iniquitous. It is impoffible to be carried into general execution. It does not reach fo high, or wound fo effectually. Common converfation indeed may, at firft fight, appear to be more emphatically the general intereft and concern of mankind. But perhaps, upon farther confideration, we fhall retract that opinion. It is not upon common converfation, but upon fcience and the art of writing, that all that is dignified, all that is ennobling, all that is exquifite and admirable in human nature, depends. Brutes have a

fort

fort of common converfation; and, if we had
nothing higher to depend upon for our welfare but common converfation, we fhould
fpeedily degenerate into a fpecies of brutes.

Having thus endeavoured to guard againft
the laying too much ftrefs upon this prohibi-
tory claufe, againft fpeaking; or rather having
endeavoured to fhew, that it is not the worft
of the *overfights* of lord Grenville's bill, let
us attend a little diftinctly to its operation.
It might moft properly be termed, a claufe
for creating a national militia of fpies and informers. Henceforward it will be idle to fuppofe, that any man (efpecially any man who
is unacceptable to his majefty's minifters) is
fafe. He may be unalterably determined
againft every fpecies of confpiracy or political
confultation. He may throw away his ink
and his pens, and determine never to commit
another word to paper. He may refolve
never, upon any account, to fell, give, or lend
any book, paper or writing. Thefe are no
trifling precautions; thefe are precautions that
ought, in all reafon, to indemnify a man
againft the penal provifions of a political act
of parliament. He may go farther than this;
he may determine never more to open his

3   mouth

mouth upon any political topic, direct or indirect. He may confine himself to directions
to his servants, and counting the clock. Nay,
if that shall not be thought refining too idly,
he may enter into a vow not to utter any ar-
ticulate found; yet he is not safe. If he speak,
his words may be diftorted; and, if he be
filent, he may be proved, by legal evidence,
to have damned the king, and may be fent
to Botany Bay.

Againft this laft fuppofition perhaps it
may be alleged, " that the defect of lord
" Grenville's bill, is a defect that it poffeffes
" in common with every penal Act of Parlia-
" ment. Any innocent man may be proved
" by legal evidence, to be guilty of any crime,
" and may be punifhed accordingly." But
no : lord Grenville's bill is not upon a level
with every penal Act of Parliament. It is not
eafy to prove any man guilty of any crime;
and exculpatory circumftances, of various kinds,
and of the moft fatisfactory nature, may be
collected, to refute a calumniatory accufation.
But fpeaking is a crime that requires no ingenuity to invent, and no contrivance to fupport;
and it is a crime [Good God! fpeaking in any

H			manner

manner, a crime!] the moſt difficult of all others to be diſproved.

It will perhaps be thought too trite, if we were to dwell, in this place, upon the ill conſequences to reſult from inſtituting a national militia of ſpies and informers. What kind of a man is a ſpy? He is a man that inſinuates himſelf into your confidence in order to betray you. He pretends to be uncommonly vehement and intemperate, that he may excite you to be the ſame. He watches your unguarded moments, he plies you with wine, that he may excite you to ſpeak without reſtraint. He undertakes to remember words, and he has an invincible bias upon his mind, inducing him to conſtrue them in a particular way, and inſenſibly to change them for words more definite and injurious. His very income depends upon the frequency of his tales, and he is paid in proportion as the tales that he brings, whether true or falſe, tend to the deſtruction of the perſons to whom they relate.

Miſerable beyond compare muſt be the ſtate of that country, where ſuch men as this are to be found in every town, in every ſtreet, in every village, and in every houſe. " Evil
" communications

" communications corrupt good manners." It
is impoffible that I fhould continually affoci-
ate with knaves, without lofing fomething of
the unfullied luftre of my virtue.   Two virtues are moft important in civil fociety;
franknefs, that I fhould practife no duplicity,
that I fhould play no part under a mafk; and
mutual truft and confidence.   Now, what
confidence can there be, when men are furrounded with fpies and informers? When,
from the frequency of the phenomenon, I am
unable certainly to tell, whether my friend or
my brother be not a man, whofe trade is accufation, and who will one day caufe me to be
be tranfported or hanged? In a country where
the exiftence of fpies and informers is frequent,
the whole nation muft, of neceffity, be made
up of two claffes of hypocrites: hypocrites,
who hold out a falfe appearance, the better
to enfnare; and hypocrites, who hold out a
falfe appearance, that they may not be en-
fnared.

So much, for the prefent, for lord Grenville's bill.

We will now proceed to the confideration
of Mr. Pitt's bill.   Lord Grenville's bill is
probably the moft atrocious, becaufe writing

and the publication of fcience, are probably, of all imaginable things, the moft effential to the welfare of mankind.

Mr. Pitt's bill however is of no trivial importance. It is, as we have already faid, a direct attack upon the moft effential provifion of the Bill of Rights, the provifion, that authorizes the inhabitants of Great Britain, to confult refpecting their grievances, and to demand redrefs.

This is, in many refpects, like moft of the fundamental topics of government as they relate to a great nation, a fubject of extreme delicacy. For men to affemble in confiderable numbers, particularly with a view to the reformation of abufes, is perilous, and may lead to violence. To prohibit them from affembling, may lead to the fame thing in a worfe form. The longer difcontents are pent up and concealed, the more furioufly they may be expected to break out at laft. The Bill of Rights has folved this ænigma in political fcience, fo far as relates to the people of Great Britain, and has authorized the people to meet, of courfe expecting from government a vigilant attention to their fubfequent proceedings.

The

The firſt ſtrong meaſure that was taken, reſtraining, within narrower limits than thoſe of the Bill of Rights, the right of the inhabitants of this country to aſſemble, was the act of 1 George the Firſt, cap. v. commonly called the Riot Act. That act has been thought by ſome of the beſt judges and ſtateſmen who have ex- iſted ſince that period, to be the capital ble- miſh of the Engliſh ſtatute book. It was the fifth public act of the firſt year of George the Firſt; and the period at which it was made, is to be conſidered as perfectly unique. The king landed from Hanover on the 18th of September; and his predeceſſor, queen Anne, died on the firſt of Auguſt preceding. At the moment of her death it was a matter of com- plete uncertainty, whether the ſon of king James the Second, or the elector of Hanover, would be her ſucceſſor. Men's minds were divided between the two claimants; and it is commonly ſuppoſed that the majority of the nation was in favour of the repreſentative of the houſe of Stuart. At this period the Riot Act was paſſed, when king George was not yet warm in his throne, when it was uncer- tain how long he would remain the acknow- ledged ſovereign of Great Britain, and when a

rebellion

rebellion was already fermenting in the kingdom, which broke out a few months after.
The exprefs and avowed purpofe of this law
was to counteract the alarming fpirit of difaffection; but it unfortunately happened that the
proper claufe for declaring the act to be temporary was omitted, and it followed in this, as
in other memorable inftances, that an act,
made to provide againft a tranfitory emergency, has been, in a blind and indirect way,
placed in perpetuity upon the ftatute books.
Mr. Pitt's bill however goes infinitely farther
than the Riot Act. I fhall only infift upon a
few leading particulars and not go into the
fame detail refpecting it, that I have done refpecting lord Grenville's bill.

The moft ftriking provifion of Mr. Pitt's
bill, relates to the neceffity under which every
perfon is placed, of directly fummoning a
magiftrate to attend the meeting which he has
called together ; and to the powers to be exercifed by that magiftrate, when prefent.
The magiftrate is empowered to filence any
fpeaker in any part of his fpeech, and to dif-
perfe the meeting in any ftep of its proceedings. He is to employ his own judgment
and difcretion, as to whether that part of the
fpeech

fpeech, or ftep of the proceedings, is in any way dangerous or unauthorized, and every perfon, who is purpofely, or cafually prefent at the meeting, is required, under heavy penalties, to yield him implicit and inftant obedience, and repair to his own home at the word of command.

It is improbable that a greater infult was ever put upon any thing appearing in human form, than is contained in thefe enactments. Was ever an authority created more defpotic, more difgraceful, and that it was lefs practicable to endure? Better, much better, and infinitely more manly, would it have been, totally to have prohibited all meetings out of the ordinary courfe, than thus impudently to have exhibited the mockery of permitting them. What fort of materials muft that man be made of, who will refort to any meeting under fuch reftrictions? It is impoffible to conceive that any perfon upon reflection will, after the paffing of this bill, refort to any meeting of a political nature, unlefs it be one of thofe portentous meetings, of which we have fometimes heard, where men come together with the refolution to " fucceed or die."

Who will anfwer for himfelf that, in the act

2   of

of fpeaking, he fhall confent to ceafe, at the moment the auctioneering magiftrate fhall give the
fignal with his hammer? Who will anfwer for
himfelf that, though not fpeaking, his thoughts
fhall be under fuch fevere difcipline, as to
leave him in readinefs to depart the inftant he
is bid to do fo? Who will anfwer for himfelf
that the folly, the mifconftruction or the malice of this infolent magiftrate [even magiftrates
have been known to be infolent] fhall not excite in him the fmalleft indignation? No ftate
of a human being can be devifed more flavifh,
than where he is told, that he muft not expoftulate; he muft not anfwer; the mafter claps a
padlock upon his lips and he muft be filent; he
muft not have an opinion of his own. Even
fuppofing a man to be imbued in the higheft
degree with the principles of paffive obedience, if the whole affembly be not fo drilled
as to obey the word of command, he may be
hemmed in, in fpite of his efforts, and committed for trial, or fhot by the military.

Let us pafs from the enactment of the bill
in this refpect, to the penalty by which it is to
be inforced. Three days' imprifonment would
be too great a punifhment in this cafe, and
would be altogether intolerable to a man of a
lofty

lofty and independent fpirit. What then muft
be the feelings of any man imbued with the
principles of morality or humanity, when he
finds that the penalty, as ftated by Mr. Pitt in
opening the nature of the bill, is that of felony
without benefit of clergy? What fort of hearts
are thefe men endued with? What fort of underftandings? They fcatter about punifhments
upon every occafion, and the punifhment of
the flighteft offence is death. They know
no principles of comparifon, they are dead to
every feeling of the heart, they pronounce with
total indifference the punifhment of death
upon multitudes yet unborn; In the fpirit of
king Richard in the play, " I will not dine,
" until his head be brought me!"

Well may thefe men be the enemies of fcience, well may they declare every philofopher
who inveftigates the nature of man or fociety
fubject to the pains of high treafon; well may
they emulate the irruptions of the Goths and
Vandals, who fpread barbarifm and intellectual darknefs over the whole face of the earth!
They know no touch of civilization; they
were never humanized by fcience or art; they
come forth in all the pride of ignorance; laugh
at the fcruples of human kindnefs, and tram-

I   ple

ple upon all the barriers by which civil fociety can alone be preferved.

Having commented upon the principal branch of Mr. Pitt's bill, it feems as unneceffary as it would be odious, to follow him through all its detail. I will not attend him through all his fplittings and diftinctions, of fixpences to be paid at the door, or tickets to be delivered or fhewn; of the number of perfons that may be prefent in any one houfe without a licence; or the claufes and riders by which he will perhaps hereafter endeavour to fave card-clubs and ladies' routes from the general devaftation. It would, no doubt, be inftructive to purfue him through all thefe labyrinths; it would detect his fterility, and uncover his nakednefs. But this office will be performed by fkilful hands; and it is neceffary to the purpofe of thefe pages, that the argument they contain fhould be compreffed and ftriking.

We have now gone through, as far as feems to be neceffary upon the prefent occafion, the direct confideration of the two bills. There is however one hiftorical confideration, to which it is material to turn our attention, before we proceed to fum up the different parts of the

the argument. Lord Grenville, in opening the nature of his bill in the houfe of lords, ob-ferved, that it was founded in the precedents of other times, and therefore could not be re-garded as an innovation. The precedents to which he referred, were from the reign of queen Elizabeth and of king Charles the Se-cond. In this ftatement he was, no doubt, for the moft part well founded. The bill he in-troduced is, in feveral important refpects, a tranfcript of a temporary act cf 13 Elizabeth, and 13 Charles the Second.

In referring us to thefe precedents, lord Grenville is to be regarded as the vehicle of an important inftruction. When the meafures of the prefent day are borrowed from former times, it is one of our indifpenfible duties, to look to thofe times, and confider the fpirit in which the meafures originated.

One of the firft confiderations that fuggefts itfelf refpecting the precedents of lord Gren-ville is, that they are drawn from times an-terior to the revolution. They are not there-fore fuperior to all fufpicion. It was once the mode to talk of " the Englifh conftitution " as fettled by the glorious revolution." Whe-ther it be the purpofe of lord Grenville and

Mr.

Mr. Pitt to cure us of this antiquated prejudice, time will effectually shew. I remember to have heard lord chief baron Macdonald, then attorney-general, upon the trial of
Thomas Paine, observe, " that our glo-
" rious and incomparable conftitution exifted
" from the earlieft accounts of time, and
" was recognized by Julius Cæfar." But
other men, better informed, or more modeft
than lord chief baron Macdonald, will probably acknowledge, that England, like the
other countries of Europe, was, at a period
greatly fubfequent to Julius Cæfar, fubject to
the feudal tyranny; that all thefe countries
about the fame time endeavoured to fhake off
the yoke; that the ftruggles of fome were
more fuccefsful than of others; and that it
was not till after frequent viciffitudes of
anarchy and oppreffion, that England acquired her " conftitution as fettled at the glo-
" rious revolution."

Let us confider the fpirit of the times of
queen Elizabeth and king Charles the Second.
The liberty of the commons of England began
to affume fome faint appearance of a definite
form, about the time of king Edward the Firft.
The progrefs, though fmall, was neverthelefs

progrefs,

progress, nearly down to the clofe of the fifteenth century. The improvements indeed
were flight, they were attended with ftrong
contradictions and fymptoms of defpotifm,
fuch as will for ever be incident to a barbarous
age ; but ftill they accumulated. The bloody
contentions however of the houfes of Lan-
cafter and York, feemed to have deftroyed
the moft valuable principles and inftitutions of
a regular fociety. Henry the Seventh was defpotic; Henry the Eighth was ftill more fo. The
very name of liberty feemed to be forgotten,
and the only contefts that are of importance in our hiftory, were upon the fubject of
religion, and were produced by the reformation. With the puritans commenced the revival of ideas of liberty. They oppofed the
defpotifm of the eftablifhed church ; civil liberty " lay immediately in their path, and
" they found it." The firft regular oppofition in parliament under the houfe of Tudor,
appeared in the reign of queen Elizabeth. It
will be a matter both of curiofity and importance, to recur to Hume's account of the
feffion of parliament in which that bill was
drawn, which lord Grenville has attempted to
revive upon the prefent occafion.

" A

" A new parliament, after five years in-
" terval, was affembled at Weftminfter. We
" fhall be fomewhat particular in relating the
" tranfactions of this feffion, becaufe they
" fhew, as well the extent of the royal
" power during that age, as the character of
" Elizabeth, and the genius of her govern-
" ment. It will be curious alfo to obferve,
" the faint dawn of the fpirit of liberty among
" the Englifh, the jealoufy with which that
" fpirit was repreffed by the fovereign, the
" imperious conduct which was maintained
" in oppofition to it, and the eafe with which
" it was fubdued by this arbitrary princefs."
Vol, V. ch. xl. page 173.

" A motion made by Robert Bell, a pu-
" ritan, againft an exclufive patent granted
" to a company of merchants in Briftol, gave
" occafion to feveral remarkable incidents.—
" Sir Humphrey Gilbert, the gallant and re-
" nowned fea-adventurer, endeavoured to
" prove the motion made by Bell to be a
" vain device, and perilous to be treated of;
" fince it tended to the derogation of the pre-
" rogative imperial, which whoever fhould
" attempt, fo much as in fancy, could not, he
" faid, be otherwife accounted than an open
" enemy.

" enemy. For what difference is there be-
" tween saying that the queen is not to use
" the privilege of the crown, and saying that
" she is not queen ? And though experience
" has shewn so much clemency in her ma-
" jesty, as might, perhaps, make subjects
" forget their duty, it is not good to sport or
" venture too much with princes. He re-
" minded them of the fable of the hare, who,
" upon the proclamation that all horned beasts
" should depart the court, immediately fled, lest
" his ears should be construed to be horns;
" and by this apologue he seems to insinuate,
" that even those who heard or permitted
" such dangerous speeches, would not them-
" selves be entirely free from danger. He
" desired them to beware, lest, if they meddled
" farther with these matters, the queen
" might look to her own power ; and finding
" herself able to suppress their challenged li-
" berty, and to erect an arbitrary authority,
" might imitate the example of Lewis the
" Eleventh of France, who, as he termed it,
" delivered the crown from wardship.

" Though this speech gave some disgust, no-
" body at the time replied any thing ; but that
" sir Humphrey mistook the meaning of the
I   " house,

" houfe, and of the member who made the
" motion : They never had any other purpofe,
" than to reprefent their grievances, in due and
" feemly form, unto her majefty. But in a
" fubfequent debate, Peter Wentworth, a man
" of a fuperior free fpirit, called that fpeech an
" infult on the houfe ; noted fir Humphrey's
" difpofition to flatter and fawn on the prince;
" compared him to the cameleon, which can
" change itfelf into all colours, except white ;
" and recommended to the houfe a due care
" of liberty of fpeech, and of the privileges of
" parliament. It appears, on the whole, that
" the motion againft the exclufive patent had
" no effect. Bell, the member who firft intro-
" duced it, was fent for by the council, and
" was feverely reprimanded for his temerity.
" He returned to the houfe with fuch an
" amazed countenance, that all the members,
" well informed of the reafon, were ftruck
" with terror, and during fome time no one
" durft rife to fpeak of any matter of import-
" ance, for fear of giving offence to the queen
" and the council. Even after the fears of the
" commons were fomewhat abated, the mem-
" bers fpoke with extreme precaution ; and by
" employing moft of their difcourfe in pre-
" ambles and apologies, they fhewed their
                              " confcious

" confcious terror of the rod which hung
" over them.—It is remarkable, that the
" patent, which the queen defended with
" fuch imperious violence, was contrived for
" the profit of four courtiers, and was atten-
" ded with the utter ruin of feven or eight
" thoufand of her induftrious fubjects.

" Thus every thing which paffed the two
" houfes was extremely refpectful and fub-
" miffive; yet did the queen think it incum-
" bent on her, at the conclufion of the fef-
" fion, to check, and that with great feve-
" rity, thofe feeble efforts of liberty, which
" had appeared in the motions and fpeeches
" of fome members. The lord keeper told
" the commons, in her majefty's name, that,
" though the majority of the lower houfe
" had fhewn themfelves in their proceedings
" difcreet and dutiful, yet a few of them had
" difcovered a contrary character, and had
" juftly merited the reproach of audacious,
" arrogant, and prefumptuous : Contrary to
" their duty as fubjects and parliament-men,
" nay, contrary to the exprefs injunctions
" given them from the throne at the begin-
" ning of the feffion, injunctions which it
" might well become them better to have at-
" tended to, they had prefumed to call in
                    K   " queftion

" queftion her majefty's grants and preroga-
" tives. But her majefty warns them, that
" fince they thus wilfully forget themfelves,
" they are otherwife to be admonifhed :
" Some other fpecies of correction muft be
" found for them; fince neither the com-
" mands of her majefty, nor the example of
" their wifer brethren, can reclaim their
" audacious, arrogant, and prefumptuous folly,
" by which they are thus led to meddle with
" what nowife belongs to them, and what lies
" beyond the compafs of their underftand-
" ing." P. 178, 179, 180, 181.

" [Her arbitrary] maxims of government
" were not kept fecret by Elizabeth, or
" fmoothed over by any fair appearances or
" plaufible pretences. They were openly
" avowed in her fpeeches and meffages to
" parliament; and were accompanied with
" all the haughtinefs, nay fometimes bit-
" ternefs, of expreffion, which the meaneft
" fervant could look for from his offend-
" ed mafter. Yet notwithftanding this
" conduct, Elizabeth continued to be the
" moft popular fovereign that ever fwayed
" the fceptre of England; becaufe the max-
" ims of her reign were conformable to the
                                  " principles

" principles of the times, and to the opinion
" generally entertained with regard to the
" conftitution. The continued encroach-
" ments of popular affemblies in Elizabeth's
" fucceffors have fo changed our ideas on thefe
" matters, that the paffages above-mention-
" ed appear to us extremely curious, and even
" at firft furprizing; but they were fo little
" remarked during the time, that neither
" Camden, though a contemporary writer,
" nor any other hiftorian, has taken any notice
" of them. So abfolute indeed was the au-
" thority of the crown, that the precious
" fpark of liberty had been kindled, and was
" preferved, by the puritans alone; and it was
" to this fect, whofe principles appear fo fri-
" volous, and habits fo ridiculous, that the
" Englifh owe the whole freedom of their
" conftitution." P. 182, 183.

These paffages are full of materials for falutary reflection. The fpeeches themfelves are
extracted by Hume, from Sir Simon d'Ewes's
Hiftory of the Proceedings of Parliament.
They difcover to us, in an irrefiftible manner,
the principles by which his majefty's minifters
defire to have the government of this country

conducted, and the fources to which they refort for conftitutional authority.

The act of queen Elizabeth was revived in
about two years after the reftoration of king
Charles the Second. The events which had
preceded, were, what Clarendon calls, the
Great Rebellion, the beheading of king Charles
the Firft, the ufurpation of Cromwel, and
the anarchy which followed upon his deceafe.
Men were tired with the unfuccefsful experiments that had been made of the principles
of republicanifm; and, when the king's reftoration was once determined, the tide of loyalty
became uncontrolable. Such was the impatience of all ranks of people, that the negociations refpecting the terms upon which he
fhould be reftored, were abruptly terminated,
and the people threw themfelves, without
treaty or condition, into the arms of the fovereign.

Thus it has been feen, in the firft place,
that the precedents of lord Grenville, as being drawn from a period anterior to the revolution, do not belong to the Englifh conftitution, and that he might, with as much real
propriety, have drawn them from the tranfactions, equally remote, of France or Spain.
Secondly,

Secondly, it has appeared, that, in addition to the precedents' poffeffing no intrinfic authority, they are drawn from periods by no means compatible with the principles of liberty. But the objection has not yet been put in its ftrongeft light.

The moft important object of lord Grenville's bill, is to impofe certain reftraints upon the liberty of the prefs. To what period does he recur for inftruction upon that fubject? What authorities does he confult? The reign of queen Elizabeth; the year 1571. Is this the confummation of ignorance, or are we to regard it in the light of unblufhing fophiftry? I will fuppofe that the reign of queen Elizabeth, had been as much diftinguifhed by maxims of liberty, as it was by the maxims of arbitrary power. Lord Grenville's argument will gain nothing by that fuppofition.

In the year 1571, literature was not yet emancipated from its cradle: the liberty of the prefs had not yet been heard of. This important doctrine, fo invaluable to times of knowledge and illumination, had not yet been invented. Men might have loved all other kinds of liberty, but this they could not love, for they could not underftand. The prefs,

that

that great engine for raifing men to the dignity
of gods, for expanding and impregnating the
human underſtanding, for annihilating, by
the moſt gentle and ſalubrious methods, all the
arts of oppreſſion, was a machine thruſt into
an obſcure corner, and which, for its unpo-
liſhed plainneſs and want of exterior attraction,
was almoſt regarded with contempt. Men
knew ſcarcely more of the real powers of the
preſs, and its genuine uſes, than the ſavage
would ſuſpect of the uſes of the alphabet, if
you threw the four and twenty letters into
his lap.

And now, in the cloſe of the eighteenth
century, lord Grenville would bring us back
to the ſtandard of 1571. Does he think we
are to be thus led? Does he believe that he
will be permitted to treat men arrived at years
of maturity, in the manner they were treated
while children? Is the *imprimatur* of government to be a neceſſary preliminary to every
publication? Are we to have an *Index Ex-
purgatorius*, teaching us what books we may
read, and what books muſt on no account be
opened? Is government to appoint certain
perſons to draw up for us catechiſms and
primers, Whole Duties of Man, and elemen-

3   tary

tary treatifes of every fcience? And are we, by thefe publications from authority, to model our creed and fafhion our underftandings?

Little indeed do thefe minifters apprehend of the nature of human intellect! Little indeed have they followed its growth, to the vigorous fublimity of its prefent ftature! They are ftrangers come from afar, and cannot underftand the language of the country. They are like the feven fleepers, that we read of in the Roman hiftory, who, after having flumbered for three hundred years, knew not that a month had elapfed, and expected to fee their old contemporaries, their wives ftill beautiful, and their children ftill in arms. But they will be taught the magnitude of their error. This giant, the underftanding, will roufe himfelf in his might, and will break their fetters, " as a thread of tow is broken, " when it toucheth the fire."

We have now taken a view of the provifions and fpirit of the propofed bills, and nothing remains for us, but to fum up the arguments on either fide, and attend to the refult. We have ftated the emergency of the cafe upon which minifters acted, with as much candour and accuracy as we could exert,

ert, and certainly with a defire, very oppofite
to that of fuppreffing or difguifing any of its
circumftances. This would, in our apprehenfion, have been unpardonable. We agree
with minifters in the principle of their bills,
if the admiffion of certain facts, and of the
neceffity of fome vigilance, perhaps of fome
exertion, can be called the principle of the
bills.

We are now to compare the difeafe and
the remedy together, to afcertain in what degree they are proportioned to each other, or
how far it can be expected that that, which
is offered us as a remedy, will prove a remedy.

The firft of thefe queftions may be difmiffed in a few words. The evil is to be confidered as an embryo evil. The operations
of the London Correfponding Society, and
its adherents, if not oppofed, muft have terminated in one or two ways. Either they
would have burft out prematurely, and then
it would have been a mere common tumult
or fedition ; it would have been eafily quelled;
its authors would have been its victims; and
they would have left, as a legacy to their
countrymen, an infallible pretext for new feverity and affumption on the part of government.

ment. Or the tendency of their operations
would have been more formidable ; and, by
continually gaining ftrength, they would at
laft have been able to overturn the conftitution. But, to accomplifh that purpofe, it
would have been neceffary, that they fhould
have been peculiarly tranquil and orderly
in their appearance ; that they fhould have
watched their opportunity with unalterable
patience; and that they fhould have fuffered
years to elapfe before they broke out into
act.

It may well be doubted, whether an evil
thus diftant, though unqueftionably entitled
to the attention of minifters, required the introduction of any new act of parliament to
encounter it. It may well be believed, that
the laws already in exiftence, fagacioufly ad-
miniftered, would have been abundantly fufficient for the purpofe. I think this would have
been the cafe, even if we had torn the Riot
Act from our ftatute book, and introduced
fome more humane and wholfome regulation
in its place.

The nature of the proper remedy was generally delineated in the firft pages of this
enquiry. But it may not be ufelefs, to reca-

L					pitulate

pitulate and expand what was there delivered. The circumftance, as we then obferved, principally to be regretted was, that the proceedings of the London Correfponding Society and its partizans, were of fuch a nature, that, in endeavouring to check them, the ftatefman would be perpetually in danger of intrenching upon the freehold of our liberties. In this cafe it would be incumbent upon him, to tread with wary fteps, and to handle every thing that related to the tranfaction with a tender hand, and a religious fear. Before he fet out upon his expedition, he would fwear upon the altar of his country, that, in dealing with her internal foe, he would not infringe upon her liberties.

It is no eafy matter to lay down the precife conduct he would purfue. It would be idly to detract from the ufefulnefs of thefe pages, to offer any undigefted opinion upon that fubject. Undoubtedly he would fit down, with the matureft deliberation, with the moft unalterable conftancy, with the moft perfect coolnefs of temper, and with the pureft kindnefs towards all the parties concerned, to meditate upon this critical queftion. He would certainly prefer means of conciliation to means

of

of force. Means of conciliation will always offer themſelves in abundance, to the man of ſtrong underſtanding, and of ardent benevolence.

Such then is the nature of the preliminary circumſtances, and ſuch the general nature of the remedy to be applied. It will not be neceſſary to enter into a long recapitulation of the meaſures propoſed by lord Grenville and Mr. Pitt, in order to ſhew how far they correſpond with the conditions of the remedy. It is not probable that their warmeſt advocates will pretend, that they have proceeded with a very cautious ſtep; that they have ſhewn any uncommon ſolicitude for the preſervation of our liberties, through all their minuteſt particles, and their wideſt and tendereſt ramifications. Their warmeſt advocates will not pretend, that they have not advanced to this buſineſs with a ſort of youthful alacrity; and that they have not rather ſeized a pretext, than been preſſed into the ſervice by an occaſion. They have no ſympathy with the friends of liberty. They conſult not the coolneſs of philoſophy, but the madneſs of paſſion. When the time calls upon them to reaſon, they begin to rail. Their profeſſion is that of invec-

tive;

tive; and invective has been their principal medium for working on the minds of their countrymen, for the laft three years. They act with the unfteadinefs and vehemence of paffion; and, if they produce a falutary effect, it will be by the fame kind of accident, as the painter, who produced upon his canvas the appearance he wifhed, by throwing his brufh at it from the impulfe of impatience and defpair.

Such are the minifters to whom the affairs of a great country are confided; and fuch is the fhallow policy, mifnamed exquifite and profound, by which the interefts of mankind have been managed, in too many inftances, in all ages of the world.

There is a curious fact relative to this fubject, which deferves to be ftated, and upon which the reader will make his own reflections. From the beginning of the prefent reign, there have been two parties conftantly concerned in the government of this country; certain individuals in habits of perfonal intimacy with the king; and his oftenfible advifers. Between thefe two parties it has been neceffary that there fhould be a conftant fpirit of compromife; the king's minifters would

not

not confent to be the nominal conductors of
affairs, without having an occafional voice in
the meafures they undertook to recommend
and to vindicate. This compromife has been
a matter of increafing difficulty and delicacy,
during that part of the king's reign which is
now elapfing. In earlier periods, it was
thought proper for him to maintain a certain
fort of indifference for his minifters, and, if a
prefent fet were not found fufficiently com-
plying, to have recourfe to others. During
the adminiftration of Mr. Pitt, he has fcarcely
at any time had the choice of fuch an alternative. Of confequence, the commerce has
been carried on upon more equitable terms.
As the minifter has often zealoufly exerted
himfelf to perfuade parliament into the adoption of meafures which he perfonally difap-
proved, fo the king has been obliged repeatedly to make a fimilar conceffion. Thus two
men, one of whom at leaft is fuppofed to entertain a mortal antipathy to the other, have
found the fecret of going on very amicably
together. In the inftance to which this pamphlet relates, it has it feems been the king's
turn to concede. His moft intimate and confidential advifers have been hoftile to the prefent

sent measure. They have conceived that it tended to create danger, where it professed to communicate security. Thus ministers have, with a consistency and candour sufficiently memorable, brought in a bill, the entire and exclusive purpose of which is to secure themselves in their places, under the title of *An Act for the safety and preservation of his majesty's person and government, against treasonable and seditious practices and attempts.* Mr. Pitt stands upon so high ground in the cabinet upon the present occasion, that it was not thought safe, on the part of the king's friends, to refuse their acquiescence to the bills. Lord Thurlow alone has displayed a sort of ambiguous opposition, just sufficient to shew, that he did not consider the present measures as by any means entitled to his approbation.

An idea will inevitably suggest itself in this place to one class of readers. They will confess, " that they are not very solicitous, as to " whether the bills of lord Grenville and " Mr. Pitt be somewhat stronger than the " occasion demanded. They are not abso- " lutely determined against all ideas of li- " berty; but they conceive that, in the pre-
" sent

" fent times at leaft, liberty muft be viewed
" as a fubordinate confideration. A grand
" iffue is now depending, between the
" ftrengthening the powers of government,
" and extending what is called, our liberties;
" and they prefer without hefitation an eftab-
" lifhed defpotifm to the apprehenfions of
" anarchy. The only queftion about which
" they are folicitous, is, Will thefe bills,
" granting that they are fuperfluoufly ftrong,
" anfwer their oftenfible purpofe, keep out
" innovation, and perpetuate the domeftic
" peace of Great Britain ?"

This is a queftion to which we cannot turn
without fome degree of pain; but it is neceffary that it fhould be examined. The following reafons induce us to think, that the
bills will not anfwer their oftenfible purpofe.

The human fpecies, as has already been
obferved, is arrived, in a certain fenfe, at years
of maturity. It can no longer be treated with
the rigours of infantine difcipline, nor can it
be moulded into every form that its governors
fhall pleafe to prefcribe. The materials have
already affumed a decided character, and government has nothing left but to make the
beft of thefe materials. Cardinal Wolfey
faid

said in the reign of king Henry the Eighth, speaking of the papal superstition, " If we do " not destroy the press, the press will destroy " us." It will be doubted by a careful reasoner, whether cardinal Wolsey spoke in time, and whether the daring project at which he hinted could, even then, have been execute d. But it cannot now be executed. The press is " a stone against which whosoever stumbles, " shall be broken ; but whosoever shall pull it " upon his own head, shall be crushed in " pieces."

No infatuation can be more extraordinary than that which at present prevails among the alarmed adversaries of reform. Reform must come. It is a resistless tide ; and, if we endeavour to keep it out too long, it will overwhelm us. You are friends to the peace and tranquillity of human society. So is every reasonable and conscientious man that lives. But, take heed lest your mistaken friendship should produce the effects of hatred, In order to maintain the peace and tranquillity of society, it is necessary to temporize. We must both accommodate ourselves to the empire of old prejudices, and to the strong and decisive influx of new opinions. We

must

muft look far before us. To promote greatly our own interest, we must think a little of the interest of pofterity. We muft not fpend the whole capital of our eftate, in the firft year that we come into poffeffion. If we would preferve in the community any reverence for authority, we muft exercife it over them with frugality. We muft not ftretch the ftrings of our inftrument fo far, as to put them in inftant danger to fnap.

The London Correfponding Society has been thoughtlefsly purfuing a conduct, which was calculated fooner or later to bring on fcenes of confufion. They have been to blame. But it is fcarcely poffible for a ferious enquirer to pronounce, that the king's ministers, and the opulent and titled alarmifts, are not much more to blame. Thefe were men who, by their fituation and influence in the country, were peculiarly bound to hold the balance even, and confult for the interefts of the whole. But, they have been the first to violate the general compact. They have thrown down the gauntlet. They have had recourfe to every kind of irritation. They have laid afide the robes and infignia of authority; and leaped, like a common

M wreftler,

wrestler, upon the stage. They have been loudest in increasing the broil; they have urged on the animosity of the combatants; and they have called for blood. Neither the present times nor posterity will forget the trials for high treason last year at the Old Bailey; a measure which, for precipitation, folly, and an unscrupulous and sanguinary spirit, has never been exceeded. This was one of the early measures, by which government conspicuously forced the moderate and the neutral, to take their station in the ranks of the enemy.

But the present bills will have still more strongly, and, if they pass into a law, much more permanently, the same effect. What is it that we are called upon to part with, and what to admit, that we may enter into a treaty, offensive and defensive, with the present ministers? We must part with the Bill of Rights, with the liberty of the press, and the liberty of speech. We must place ourselves in the situation, which is described in the preamble of the Act, 1 Henry IV, when, " no man could know " how he ought to behave himself, to do, " speak or say, for doubt of the pains of " treason,"

Treafon." We must admit a national militia of fpies and informers. This is a price
that fcarcely any man will be content to pay.
If it be paid for want of reflection at first,
men will full furely awake ; they will
loudly reclaim their birth right ; and the indignation they will conceive at having been
thus overreached, will probably produce a
convulfion. The prefent bills force men
into the extremest state of hostility ; they
leave no opening for treaty ; they offer no
compromife ; they inculcate an obstinate
and impracticable temper upon both parties.
At a time when conciliation is most neceffary, they most deeply infpire into us fentiments of animofity.

The nature of Mr. Pitt's bill deferves
particularly to be recollected in this place.
It abrogates the fundamental provifion of
the Bill of Rights. When the Bill of Rights
authorized men to confult refpecting grievances, and to demand redrefs, it is not probable that its authors were unaware of the
danger attendant upon crowded affemblings
of the people. But they reafoned upon the
nature of the cafe, and they thought the
legal permiffion of thefe affemblies, under

M 2   certain

certain conditions, the leaft evil. They
knew that, when the people thought themfelves aggrieved, they muft be redreffed.
They knew that difcontent was one of the
moft undefirable ftates of the public mind.
They knew that difcontent, when fhut up,
grew ftronger and more menacing ; and they
conceived that it was true political wifdom
to provide it a channel by which to exprefs
itfelf. Mr. Pitt is determined that there
fhall be no difcontent. At leaft he is determined, that difcontent fhall not declare
itfelf, and that no clamours fhall be heard.
He fhuts up every avenue, of open confulting, of political publications, and of private
converfation. Minifters will be found perhaps, to be fufficiently ignorant at prefent
of the ftate of the public mind. It is one
of the great problems of political government to be adequately acquainted with it.
The moft fatal effeɗs have always followed
from this ignorance. The American war
was begun, from a perfuafion that the majority of the people were loyalifts : and the
prefent war would probably never have
been undertaken, if the Englifh government had not believed, that the great mafs
of

of the inhabitants of France were concealed adherents of the dethroned fovereign. The prefent bills are calculated to fwell this fpecies of ignorance to its greateft dimenfions. Mr. Pitt is determined that we fhall not hear the tempeft, till it burft upon us in a hurricane, and level every thing with the duft.

Having, in this inftance, affigned reafons why thofe perfons, who are under no apprehenfions from the extenfion of authority, ought yet to difapprove of the prefent bills, we will conclude, in conformity to the moderate and conciliating fpirit with refpect to the two oppofite political fyftems, that we hope has pervaded thefe fheets, with offering a few confiderations to perfuade thofe perfons who are enthufiaftic advocates for the extenfion of liberty, that they ought not to conceive too vehement an animofity, and to be poffeffed with too profound a defpair, if thefe bills fhould ultimately pafs into law. The enthufiaftic advocates for liberty are too apt to exclaim upon every new encroachment, " This is the laft degree of hoftility ; " every thing depends upon our prefent fuccefs; " if we mifcarry now, the triumph of defpotifm " is final, and there is no longer any hope that " remains

" remains to us." The precifely oppofite of this is the true inference in the prefent inftance. Thefe bills are *an unwilling homage, that the too eager advocates of authority pay to the rifing genius of freedom.* Why will you always fhut your eyes upon the real nature of your fituation? Why will you believe, while every thing is aufpicious, that every thing is defperate? If you cannot fee how deeply more liberal principles of freedom have ftruck their root into the foil of Britain, how widely they have diffufed themfelves, and how faft they are ripening for the purpofes of reform, you have here the testimony of your enemies to convince you. You are mistaken: the prefent effort of intemperate alarm, is not the act of of prefumptuous confidence; it is dictated by a fentiment of dejection and defpair. Be tranquil. Indulge in the most flattering profpects. Be firm, be active, be temperate. If alarmifts are refolved no longer to keep any terms with you, you then, in all just confideration, fucceed to the double office, of the advocates of reform, and the moderators of contending and unruly animofities.

THE END.

THOUGHTS.

OCCASIONED BY THE PERUSAL OF

DR. PARR'S SPITAL SERMON,

PREACHED AT CHRIST CHURCH,

APRIL 15, 1800;

BEING A REPLY TO THE ATTACKS OF DR. PARR,
MR. MACKINTOSH, THE AUTHOR OF
AN ESSAY ON POPULATION,
AND OTHERS.

―――――◆―――――

BY WILLIAM GODWIN.

―――――◆―――――

LONDON:

PRINTED BY TAYLOR AND WILKS, CHANCERY-LANE;
AND SOLD BY G. G. AND J. ROBINSON, PATERNOSTER-ROW.

1801.

THOUGHTS

OCCASIONED, &c.

I HAVE now continued for some years a silent, not an inattentive, spectator of the flood of ribaldry, invective and intolerance which has been poured out against me and my writings. The work which has principally afforded a topic for the exercise of this malignity, has been the Enquiry Concerning Political Justice. This book made its appearance in February 1793; its reception with the public was favourable much beyond my conception of its merits; it was the specific and avowed occasion of procuring me the favour and countenance of many persons of the highest note in society and literature, of some of those who have since lent themselves to increase the clamour, which personal views and the contagion of fashion have created against me. For more than four years it remained before the public, without any man's having made the slightest attempt for its refutation; it was repeatedly said that it was invulnerable and unanswerable in its fundamental topics; high encomiums were passed on the supposed talents of the writer; and, so far as I have been able

B

to learn, every man of the flighteft impartiality was ready to give his verdict to the honeft fentiments and integrity of fpirit in which it was written.

If the temper and tone in which this publication has been treated have undergone a change, it has been only that I was deftined to fuffer a part, in the great revolution which has operated in nations, parties, political creeds, and the views and interefts of ambitious men. I have fallen (if I have fallen) in one common grave with the caufe and the love of liberty ; and in this fenfe have been more honoured and illuftrated in my decline from general favour, than I ever was in the higheft tide of my fuccefs.

My book, as was announced by me in the preface, was the child of the French revolution. It is eafy to underftand what has been the operation of many men's minds on the fubject of that great event. Almoft every man entertains in his bofom fome love for the public: there is, I fuppofe, no man that lives who has not fome love for himfelf. Both thefe fentiments were extenfively exercifed, in the various European nations who were fpectators of the French revolution. Where was the ingenuous heart which did not beat with exultation, at feeing a great and cultivated people fhake off the chains of one of the moft oppreffive political fyftems in the world, the moft replenifhed with abufes, the leaft mollified and relieved by any infufion of liberty? Thus far we were all of us difinterefted and generous. But the reflex act of the mind is fo effential a part of our nature,

nature, that it was impoffible men fhould not, in the firft interval of leifure, enquire how they would be affected by this event in their perfonal fortunes. The reafonings which guided the perfons alluded to in this particular, are obvious. They believed that liberty could not be thus acquired by a moft refpected and confiderable nation in the centre of Europe, without producing confequences favourable to liberty in every furrounding country. They inferred therefore that, while each man was indulging his enthufiafm and philanthropy, each man would find himfelf moft effectually promoting his private intereft. They worfhipped the rifing fun. They applauded their fagacity and long-fightednefs, while they thus heaped up for themfelves the merit of being the virtuous and early champions of infant, and as yet powerlefs liberty.

But thefe expectations and this fagacity have been miferably difappointed. The perfons however who acted under their influence, were flow and unwilling in giving up their hopes. They had felt a real and honeft paffion for the French revolution : but honefty is a principle of an unaccommodating fort ; and paffion, once fet in motion, will not be fubdued in a moment. Befide, thefe perfons, confiding in

their fagacity, had declared themfelves in a very peremptory and decifive manner. Shame therefore for
a long time held them to their point. They faw
that their retreat would come with a very ill grace;
they would not retire upon the firft fymptoms of

B 2   mifcar-

mifcarriage; they cheered themfelves and one another with affurances that thefe fymptoms would
fpeedily fubfide ; they hoped to add to the praife of
long-fightednefs, the nobler praife of magnanimous
perfeverance in fpite of adverfe and difcouraging
appearances.

What was the confequence of this? Mr. Burke
publifhed his celebrated book againft the French revolution in 1790: they were unmoved. The
powers of Europe began to concert hoftile meafures
upon this fubject in 1791: they were unmoved.
Louis was depofed; monarchical government was
profcribed in France: they were unmoved. In September 1792 fcenes of execrable and unprecedented
murder were perpetrated in the capital and many of
the provinces: they fcorned for the fake of a few
private mifdeeds to give up a great public principle.
The head of Louis fell upon the fcaffold: ftill they
were confiftent. The atrocious and inhuman reign
of Robefpierre commenced ; it continued from May
1793 to July 1794; almoft every day was marked
with blood; almoft all that was greateft and moft
venerable in France was immolated at the monfter's
fhrine, the queen, madame Elizabeth, Vergniaud,
Genfonné, Roland, madame Roland, Bailli, La-
voifier; it were endlefs to recollect a tithe of the
bloody catalogue: ftill thefe advocates of the French
revolution were confiftent. Down to the fpring of
1797, when petitions were fent up from fo many
parts of England for the removal of the king's minifters,

nifters, fcarcely one of thofe perfons who had declared themfelves ardently and affectionately interefted for the fuccefs of the French, deferted their caufe.

I am willing to yield to thefe men confiderable praife for the conftancy with which they perfevered fo long; as long perhaps as worldly prudence could in any degree countenance. But why, becaufe I have not been fo prudent as they, fhould I be made the object of their invective? I never went fo far, in my partiality for the practical principles of the French revolution, as many of thofe with whom I was accuftomed to converfe. I uniformly declared myfelf an enemy to revolutions. Many perfons cenfured me for this lukewarmnefs; I willingly endured the cenfure. Several of thofe perfons are now gone into the oppofite extreme. They muft excufe me; they have wandered wide of me on the one fide and on the other; I did not follow them before; I cannot follow them now.

But, though I commend thefe perfons for having perfevered fo long, I can be at no lofs to affign the principal caufe why they have perfevered no longer. What has happened fince the fpring of 1797 to juftify their revolt? Has any new fyftem of diforganifation been adopted in France? Have the French embrued their hands in further maffacres? Has another Robefpierre rifen, to fright the world with fyftematical, cool-blooded, never-fatiated murder? No, none of thefe things. How then has it happened, that men who remained unaltered fpite of thefe terrible events, now profefs their conviction that the hope of melioration in human fociety muſt be given up; and, not contented with that, virulently abufe thofe by whom the hope is ſtill cheriſhed? To the government of Robefpierre fucceeded what was called an Executive Directory, a fet of men whofe principles and actions fo nearly refembled thofe of the regular governments of Europe, that it is with an ill grace the advocates of thofe governments can pronounce a cenfure againſt them. Upon the diffolution of the Directory, we have feen an aufpicious and beneficent genius arife, who without violence to the principles of the French revolution, has fufpended their morbid activity, and given time for the fever which threatened to confume the human race, to fubfide. All the great points embraced by the revolution remain entire: hereditary government is gone; hereditary nobility is extinguiſhed; the hierarchy of the Gallican church is no more; the feudal rights, the oppreffive immunities of a mighty ariftocracy,

are banished never to return. Every thing promises that the future government of France will be
popular, and her people free. It follows therefore,
almost with the force of a demonstration, that it is
nothing which has happened in France that has produced this general apostacy from the principles of
her revolution.

(7)

But the perfons for whofe conduct I am account-
ing, while they have looked with lefs folicitude than
before at what is paffing in France, have looked
very attentively at what is paffing at home. Not that
in our own country events have happened, to juftify
any better, in the way of argument, this transformation of their opinions, than the events in France.
The revolutionary focieties in this metropolis were
once numerous; they had fpread their ramifications
through almoft every county in England; revolu-

tionary lectures were publicly read here and elsewhere with tumults of applause; almost every alehouse had its artisans haranguing in favour of republicanism and equality: at this time the persons
of whom I am speaking conceived no alarm. The
societies have perished, or, where they have not,
have shrunk to a skeleton; the days of democra-
tical declamation are no more; even the starving la-
bourer in the alehouse is become a champion of
aristocracy. Yet it is now that these persons come
forth to sound the alarm; now they tread upon the
neck of the monster whom they regard as expir-

ing; now they hold it neceſſary to ſhow themſelves intemperate and inceſſant in their hoſtilities againſt the ſpirit of innovation.

We muſt look therefore elſewhere than in the naked convictions of the underſtanding, for the prin-ciple of their conduct. Like the patriarch of old, they watched narrowly to ſee a day of auſpicious tidings to the people; and, if they could have ſeen

I remember how *happy*s in ancient modern *reading* till ending our *first* philosophy in afterwards, *create of beauty* *fiction* till the fire (8) following *shapes*.

they

reflect

equal

there

on

portion

hear

it, like the patriarch, they would have been glad. But, while they expected the burſting of a glorious sunſhine, the ſky around them became darker and more unpromiſing—It is not to my preſent purpoſe to enquire how far recent events have tended , to confirm and give ſtability to the old governments of Europe, and that of our own country in particular; but at leaſt theſe perſons have ſeen them in that point of view. They are willing to make their peace; nor would they chaffer too obstinately, though it should be neceſſary to make a sacrifice or two at the ſhrine of the divinity againſt whoſe worſhip they had too irreverently railed.

But it is not my diſpoſition to ſee the characters and actions of men in the worſt point of view. I can diſcern other human weakneſſes concerned in this converſion of my neighbours, leſs offenſive to the moral feelings than bare worldly wiſdom and perſonal intereſt. It is not in the nature of man to like to ſtand alone in his ſentiments or his creed.

We ought not to be too much surprised, when we perceive our neighbours watching the seasons, and floating with the tide. Nor is this fickleness by which they are influenced, altogether an affair of design. It is seldom that we are persuaded to adopt opinions, or repersuaded to abandon them, by the mere force of arguments. The change is generally produced silently, and unperceived except in its ultimate result, by him who suffers it. Our creed is, ninety-nine times in a hundred, the pure growth of

our

our temper and focial feelings. The human intellect is a fort of barometer, directed in its variations by the atmofphere which furrounds it. Add to this, that the opinion which has its principle in paffion (and this was generally the cafe with the opinions of men on the topic of the French revolution) includes in its effence the caufe of its deftruction. " Hope deferred makes the heart fick." Zeal, though it be as hot as Nebuchadnezzar's furnace, without a connual fupply of fuel will fpeedily cool.

I feel little refentment againft thofe perfons who, without any frefh reafons to juftify their change, think it now neceffary to plead for eftablifhments, and exprefs their horror at theories and innovation, though I recollect the time when they took an oppofite part. But this I muft fay, that they act againft all nature and reafon when, inftead of modeftly confeffing their frailty and the transformation of their fentiments, they rail at me becaufe I have not equally changed. If I had expreffed a certain degree of difpleafure at their conduct, I fhould have had a very forcible excufe. But I was not prepared with a word of reproach : I would have been filent, if they would have permitted me to be fo.

Down to about the middle of the year 1797, as I have faid, the champions of the French revolution in England appeared to retain their pofition, and I remained unattacked. About that time a forlorn hope of two little fkirmifhing pamphlets began the war. But the writers of thefe pamphlets appear to

have

have been uninftrudted in the fchool of the new converts I have attempted to defcribe, and their productions were without fcurrility. The next and grand
attack was opened in Mr. Mackintofh's Lectures. A
book was publifhed about the fame time, profeffing
to contain remarks upon fome fpeculations of mine,
entitled an Effay upon Population. Of this book
and the fpirit in which it is written I can never
fpeak but with unfeigned refpect. Soon after followed a much vaunted Sermon by Mr. Hall of Cambridge, in which every notion of toleration or decorum was treated with infuriated contempt. I difdain to dwell on the rabble of fcurrilities which followed : the vulgar contumelies of the author of the
Purfuits of Literature, novels of buffoonery and fcan-
dal to the amount of half a fcore, and Britifh Critics,
Anti-Jacobin Newfpapers, and Anti-Jacobin Magazines without number. Laft of all, for the prefent
at leaft, for I am not idle enough to flatter myfelf that the tide is gone by, Dr. Parr, with his
Spital Sermon before the Lord Mayor, brings up
the rear of my affailants. I take occafion from
this firft avowed and refpectable publication*, to
offer the little I think it neceffary to offer in my
defence.

But, before I enter upon particulars, let me ftop
a moment to obferve upon the fingular and perverfe
deftiny which has attended me on this occafion. I

---

* The main attack of the Effay on Population is not directed
againft the principles of my book, but its conclufions.

wrote

wrote my Enquiry Concerning Political Juſtice in the innocence of my heart. I ſought no overt effects; I abhorred all tumult; I entered my proteſt againſt revolutions. Every impartial perſon who knows me, or has attentively conſidered my writings, will acknowledge that it is the fault of my character, rather to be too ſceptical, than to incline too much to play the dogmatiſt. I was by no means aſſured of the truth of my own ſyſtem. I wrote indeed with ardour; but I publiſhed with diffidence. I knew that my ſpeculations had led me out of the beaten track; and I waited to be inſtructed by the comment of others as to the degree of value which ſhould be ſtamped upon them. That comment in the firſt inſtance was highly flattering; yet I was not ſatisfied. I did not ceaſe to reviſe, to reconſider, or to enquire.

I had learned indeed that enquiry was the pilot who might be expected to ſteer me into the haven of truth. I had heard a thouſand times, and I believed, that whoever gave his ſpeculations on general queſtions to the public with fairneſs and temper, was a public benefactor: and I muſt add, that I have never yet heard the fairneſs or temper of my publication called into doubt. If my doctrines were formed to abide the teſt of ſcrutiny, it was well: if they were refuted, I ſhould ſtill have occaſion to rejoice, in having procured to the public the benefit of that refutation, of ſo much additional diſquiſition

and

and knowledge. Unprophetic as I was, I refted in perfect tranquillity, and fufpected not that I fhould be dragged to public odium, and made an example to deter all future enquirers from the practice of unfhackled fpeculation. I was no man of the world; I was a mere ftudent, connected with no party, elected into no club, exempt from every imputation of political confpiracy or cabal. I therefore believed that, if my fpeculations were oppofed, and if my opponent were a man of the leaft pretenfion to character and decorum, I fhould be at leaft oppofed in that ftyle of fairnefs and refpect which is fo eminently due from one literary enquirer to another.

My attention was not much excited by what I have already called the preliminaries of the combat. Mr. Mackintofh was the firft perfon who awakened me to any ftrictnefs of attention. How much then was I furprifed at finding his printed preliminary Difcourfe written, in fuch parts as had any allufion to my doctrines, in a fpirit lofty, overbearing and fcornful, fuch as that I fcarcely recollected its parallel in the publications of the eighteenth century! I had been for fome years in habits of friendly intercourfe with Mr. Mackintofh; the franknefs of my difpofition led me therefore immediately to addrefs him with a letter of expoftulation.

DEAR

302

January 27, 1799.

I HAVE juft read with mingled emotions of pleafure and pain your Difcourfe of the Law of Nature and Nations. My emotions of pleafure you will take, and you are well entitled to do fo, as the juft tribute of my admiration for the comprehenfivenefs of your talent and the profoundnefs of your difcernment. An enquiry into the fource of my emotions of pain* will probably not be very interefting to you, and I therefore (except in one incidental particular) pafs it over in filence.

Will you give me leave to enquire (I hope you will not impute to an impertinence of difpofition, a queftion I fhould fcarcely have deigned to addrefs to a lefs man than yourfelf) who are the fpeculators whom you defignate by the following epithets?—
" Superficial and moft mifchievous fciolifts, *p.* 24—mooters of fatal controverfies, *p.* 30—men who, in purfuit of a tranfient popularity, have exerted their art to difguife the moft miferable common-places in the fhape of paradox, *p.* 32—promulgators of abfurd and monftrous fyftems, *p.* 35—of abominable and peftilential paradoxes, *p.* 36—fhallow metaphyficians —fophifts fwelled with infolent conceit, *p.* 36—favage defolators, *p.* 38†."

If

* I knew not before the extent of the change in Mr. Mackintofh's fyftem of politics.

† Of this writer, Dr. Parr ftates it as one prominent characteriftic,

If thefe epithets are meant to apply to Rouffeau, Turgot, or Condorcet, will you condefcend to inform me how it is you have difcovered, that their motives were lefs pure or lefs philanthropical, than thofe of Grotius, Puffendorff, Wolff, Burlamaqui or Vattel, who are the fubjects of your applaufe? It would perhaps be prefumption in me to fuppofe that any portion of this invective was defigned to light upon myfelf; but, if it were, I muft be allowed to anfwer that, however weak my fpeculations may be, I am not confcious of their difhonefty.

Again, fuppofing the motives of the authors you feem difpofed to treat as heterodox were lefs pure than thofe of the orthodox (and I hold no motives to be unmixed), is it the foundeft and moft manly way of refuting an author's paradoxes, to load his character with odium, and his doctrines with a frightful catalogue of confequences, pernicious and immoral? I am the more furprifed at this in the Difcourfe before me, as, in the perfonal intercourfe which for years I have been fo fortunate as to hold with you, I have always found you the clofeft, the moft difpaffionate and candid difputant I ever encountered.
. . . . I fhould really be happy to meet you as a literary antagonift; for 1 fhould rejoice to have the miftakes

teriflic, to " refute without acrimony, *p.* 114." Whether he refutes or not, for obvious reafons I do not take upon me to determine; but that he is acrimonious, no one reader, I believe, of thefe pages, not excepting Mr. Mackintofh himfelf, will pretend to deny.

into

into which I may have fallen corrected, and I know no man so competent to the task as yourself. But, if you condescend to refute my errors, I should very earnestly wish that you would console me, by the liberality and generosity of your manner, for the philosophical patience which the task of seeing his systems demolished would require from any human being. It would be a consolation, not to my personal feelings merely, but upon general principles. No man, who, after having meditated upon philosophical subjects, gives the result of his reflections to the world, believes that, for having done so, he deserves to be treated like a highwayman or an assassin : and this sort of invective, I think, upon further consideration, you will not deny, contributes much more effectually to the spread of malignity and persecution, than of science and truth.

I am, with great regard, yours, &c.

This letter, as being in the first instance my own, and in its application relating merely to the letter-writer and the person to whom it is addressed, in a sort of public capacity, I hold myself at liberty to insert here for the purpose of illustrating the present argument. I do not feel that I am equally free upon the point of Mr. Mackintosh's answer. I shall therefore only say that, if it were inserted, it would not fail, provided it had been followed by a correspondent conduct, to redound in the highest degree to the credit of the writer.

I soon

I foon found however that what I had written totally failed of the effect, of moderating the indecorum and violence of Mr. Mackintofh's ftyle. I was not prefent at the firft of the Lectures delivered in Lincoln's Inn Hall. I attended the two or three following ; and I fhould have continued my attendance, had it not been that the expreffions, which I believed to be perfonal in the fpeaker, and which I faw were underftood as perfonal to me by many of the hearers, were fo continual, and had fo little moderation, as made it utterly improper for me to be the filent fpectator and witnefs of an attack, to which from its nature and circumftances I could not reply.

But, though I ceafed to be an auditor of Mr. Mackintofh's Lectures, I did not ceafe to hear of the fpirit and temper with which they were marked. One perfon in particular, upon the accuracy of whofe obfervation and the fidelity of whofe memory I could entirely rely, reported to me, not conftantly, but from time to time, the ftyle in which they went on. From his report, and that of many others, I found that they were in a ftate of continual improvement, in every thing that could do honour to a Dominican or an inquifitor.

One fentence, though in reality there was little room for the exercife of choice, ftruck me fo forcibly that I inftantly took it down from the mouth of this perfon, who had as inftantly vifited me after the Lecture was over. By an accident not worth mentioning

tioning I loft this minute from my poffeffion, fome time after it was made. Were it now before me, I fhould have no hefitation fo vouch for its accuracy to the minuteft fyllable. Quoting, as I am now compelled to do, from my own memory of its contents, I can only anfwer for giving a faithful reprefentation of its fpirit and fentiment. "Gentlemen," faid Mr. Mackintofh, " may be affured that, if thefe felf-called philofophers once came to have power in their hands, it would fpeedily be feen that the oonfequences I draw from their doctrines, are not, as they would have us believe, far-fetched inferences; they would be feen to be realized in action; and thofe who maintain them would be found as ferocious, as blood-thirfty, and full of perfonal ambition, as the worft of thofe men who fheltered themfelves under fimilar pretenfions in a neighbouring country."— I do not mean to rebuke any fingle expreffion in Mr. Mackintofh's Lectures; I enter my proteft againft the whole fpirit with which they were animated, and by which almoft every fingle Lecture was in a greater or lefs degree characterifed.

Among many objections that I felt againft this fpecies of declamation, one was as follows. Mr. Mackintofh's plan, it feems, did not admit of his naming fpecifically any individual political writer of the prefent day. What was the confequence of this? If he had named me, for inftance, old habits of familiarity and intercourfe would have obliged him to interpofe fomething kind and confiderate,

refpecting

refpecting a man who had been, and who wifhed ftill to continue his friend. If he had named me, or any one circumftanced as I was, he would have been obliged to make fome conceffion to the intellectual powers of a man, whom he judged worthy to be taken as the eternal fubject of his refutation. But, fheltering himfelf in generalities, he thought himfelf entitled to revolve inceffantly between the extremes of contempt and abhorrence, without one interval to fhow that he regarded his adverfary as poffeffing the form or characteriftics of a human creature.

It was my fortune to be, among Englifh writers, the moft confpicuous and generally known of thofe whom Mr. Mackintofh and his friends have nicknamed advocates of the New Philofophy. This is no boaft; it is on the prefent occafion, and in the circle of the auditory in Lincoln's Inn Hall, like the fituation of Milton's devil in Pandæmonium, a " painful preheminence." The confequence was however, that every fentence of invective againft the New Philofophy, was by many of Mr. Mackintofh's hearers as faithfully applied to me, as if the lecturer had fpoken of me by name.

There are two things, efpecially worthy of notice, as infeparable from this mode of attack upon a political writer in a feries of Lectures. Firft, the attack proceeds in a uniform and uninterrupted ftyle without admitting of an anfwer. Three times a week did Mr. Mackintofh addrefs an audience of one hundred

perfons,

perfons, diffecting and mangling my fentiments and reafonings as he pleafed, without the poffibility of my in any way checking his career. If Mr. Mackintofh had printed his animadverfions as I printed my Enquiry, I might have examined them deliberately, and replied or not, accordingly as I judged they called for reply. Now, having ventured only to quote a fingle fentence, Mr. Mackintofh may fhelter himfelf under the confeffed inaccuracy with which I have reprefented the words of his fentence, and from thence may conclude, if he pleafes, that I have mifreprefented the fpirit. But further; if Mr. Mackintofh had printed, inftead of fpoken his animadverfions, he would have found himfelf, in fpite of his new-born zeal, checked in fome of his fublimeft flights, and reduced in a certain degree within the bounds of propriety and decency.

Another feature, infeparable from an attack, which is at leaft generally conftrued as perfonal, in a feries of public Lectures, is to be found in this known fact, the contagioufnefs of human paffions when expreffed in fociety. Of this at all events an Anti-Jacobin ought to have been completely aware. When Mr. Mackintofh was three times a week expreffing uncontradicted in all the richnefs of his varied phrafeology his contempt and abhorrence of me and my writings, and reprefenting me as a wretch, who only wanted the power, in order to prove himfelf as infernal as Robefpierre, how did he know that he was not inciting his audience to perfonal outrage, to the tear-

ing

ing me to pieces? Or, let it be granted that his audience were by their education and condition in life fecured from thefe exceffes, he was at leaft induftrioufly planting, as far as was in his power, a diflike and abhorrence towards me in every one of their breafts. I am not much in the habit of indulging perfonal alarms; but, where the public is concerned, I confefs I have no great affection for a mob, either vulgar or polite.

From Mr. Mackintofh I proceed to Dr. Parr.

And here I muft firft remark, that feveral of the obfervations I had occafion to make in attempting to delineate the hiftory of apoftacy, do not apply to Dr. Parr. He is not an apoftate, or not an apoftate in the fenfe in which the perfons there referred to are fuch. His head and his logic have, I believe, fcarcely ever been favourable to experiments, or to fpeculations which might lead to experiments, for meliorating the political condition of mankind. I have always found him the advocate of old eftablifh-ments, and what appeared to me old abufes. But in this refpect his heart feemed to my apprehenfion much better than his logic. The generofity of his fentiments and the warmth of his temper have often led him to exprefs partialities as honourable to him, and wifhes as little likely to pleafe our political fu-periors, as if his creed had been more favourable to thofe objects I am accuftomed to love.

But, though I do not accufe Dr. Parr of tergiver-fation, or tergiverfation of the fame fort as theirs
whofe

whofe conduct he is now imitating, yet (if he will
permit me fo far to compliment his talents as to
compare them to whatever is moft awful in the elements of nature) I will accufe him, as king Lear
reproaches the angry fkies, that, if he were not of
my political kindred, and " owed me no fubfcrip-
tion, yet I call him fervile" auxiliary, that he has
" joined his high-engendred battles" to theirs.

All that I am now commenting upon, is the time
which Dr. Parr has chofen for his attack. There is
nothing which I can perceive in the public fituation
of things that required it. Jacobinifm was deftroyed; its party, as a party, was extinguifhed; its
tenets were involved in almoft univerfal unpopularity
and odium; they were deferted by almoft every
man, high or low, in the ifland of Great Britain.
This is the time Dr. Parr has chofen, to mufter his
troops, and found the trumpet of war.

Thus ftands the public view of the period. As to
myfelf, after having for four years heard little elfe
than the voice of commendation, I was at length attacked from every fide, and in a ftyle which defied
all moderation and decency. No vehicle was too
mean, no language too coarfe and infulting, by
which to convey the venom of my adverfaries. The
abufe was fo often repeated, that at length the by-
ftanders, and perhaps the parties themfelves, began
to believe what they had fo vehemently afferted.
The cry fpread like a general infection, and I have
been told that not even a petty novel for board-

ing-

ing-fchool miffes now ventures to afpire to favour,
unlefs it contain fome expreffions of diflike and abhorrence to the new philofophy, and its chief (or
fhall I fay its moft voluminous?) Englifh adherent.
I do then accufe Dr. Parr that, inftead of attempting
to give the tone to his contemporaries, as his abilities well entitle him to do, he has condefcended to
join a cry, after it had already become loud and
numerous.

In what I fhall think proper to fay exprefsly on
the topic of Dr. Parr's Spital Sermon, I fhall firft lay
before the reader a fpecimen of the ftyle and fpirit in
which it is written, and then comment upon fo much
of the argument of it, as I may chance to feel myfelf
particularly interefted in.

It may appear at firft fight a little furprifing, that
all there is of gall, intolerance and contempt in Dr.
Parr's publication, is contained in that part of it
which was delivered by him from the pulpit in the
character of a Chriftian preacher, and that whatever
is gentlemanlike, liberal or candid is thrown back
into the Notes. It would not perhaps be very difficult, if it were neceffary to my difquifition, to account for this. I cannot however avoid ufing this
circumftance in illuftration of my argument refpecting Mr. Mackintofh: that, while men intrench themfelves in generalities, the eloquence of invective is too
apt to find a ready way to their lips ; but, when they
name individuals, they will neceffarily, if not dead to
every feeling of ingenuoufnefs, yield fome attention

to

to the dictates of good temper and decency. In Dr. Parr's publication, I am not directly spoken of in the Sermon, but, when he comes to the Notes, he, in a way which is entitled to my commendation, names the individual whom the reference concerns, and quotes his words.

The following expressions therefore are drawn exclusively from the body of the Sermon. " The philanthropic system is accompanied by a long and portentous train of evils, which have been negligently overlooked, or insidiously disguised by its panegyrists, *p.* 2.—In the motives by which the philanthropist is impelled, the kind affections may be so writhed round the unsocial,—that, if our common sense did not revolt from the incongruous mass, scarcely any process could separate affectation from hypocrisy, delusion from malignity, that which deserves only contempt or pity from that which calls aloud for reprobation, *p.* 3."—The champions of this system are " men, neither altogether asleep in folly, nor sufficiently awake in the true light of understanding, *p.* 5.—To fill the capacious mind of a modern sage, who is rapt in beatific visions of universal benevolence, *p.* 9.—If the representations we have lately heard of universal philanthropy served only to amuse the fancy, we might be tempted to smile at them as groundless and harmless, *p.* 10.—Whether we are induced by ——, or by a supposed proficiency in philosophy, to think more highly of ourselves than we ought to think, and to seek the

praise

praife of men by affecting to be righteous over-much, the haughtinefs of our pretenfions will awaken fufpicion in, &c. *p.* 11.—Socrates did not mifemploy his talents in wily infinuations, or declamatory harangues, to the difcredit of gratitude or patriotifm, *ditto.*"

I now difmifs the direct confideration of what is perfonal and illiberal in Dr. Parr's Sermon, and proceed to a fhort comment upon the train of his argument.

Perfons not verfed in the myfteries of this controverfy, may perhaps be at a lofs to underftand, why what Dr. Parr calls the doctrine of " univerfal philanthropy" fhould awaken in lawyers and divines, in reviewers and fcribblers for the circulating libraries, fuch fiercenefs of invective, and fuch vehemence of reprobation. I proceed to examine how far it deferves the treatment it has experienced.

And here, that the queftion may be placed at once in the cleareft light to the moft uninformed reader, I will fet out with tranfcribing a paffage from the preface to a book, publifhed by me in December 1799, and entitled, " St. Leon : a Tale of the Sixteenth Century ;" which paffage is alfo tranfcribed by Dr. Parr, in the Notes to his Sermon, *p.* 52, though, from fome caufe, he has not fpecified the book from which the quotation is taken.

" Some readers of my graver productions will perhaps, in perufing thefe little volumes, accufe me of inconfiftency; the affections and charities of private
life

life being every where in this publication a topic of the warmeſt eulogium, while in the Enquiry Concerning Political Juſtice they ſeemed to be treated with no degree of indulgence and favour. In anſwer to this objection all I think it neceſſary to ſay on the preſent occaſion, is that, for more than four years, I have been anxious for opportunity and leiſure to modify ſome of the earlier chapters of that work in conformity to the ſentiments inculcated in this. Not that I ſee cauſe to make any change reſpecting the principle of juſtice, or any thing elſe fundamental to the ſyſtem there deliv red; but that I apprehend domeſtic and private affections inſeparable from the nature of man, and from what may be ſtyled the culture of the heart, and am fully perſuaded that they are not incompatible with a profound and active ſenſe of juſtice in the mind of him that cheriſhes them. The way in which theſe ſeemingly jarring principles may be reconciled, is in part pointed out in a recent publication of mine [*Memoirs of the Author of a Vindication of the Rights of Woman, cb. vi. p. 90. ſecond edition*], the words of which I will here therefore take the liberty to repeat. They are theſe:

" A ſound morality requires that *nothing human ſhould be regarded by us as indifferent;* but it is impoſſible we ſhould not feel the ſtrongeſt intereſt for thoſe perſons whom we know moſt intimately, and whoſe welfare and ſympathies are united to our own.

True

True wifdom will recommend to us individual attachments ; for with them our minds are more thoroughly maintained in activity and life than they can
be under the privation of them, and it is better that
man fhould be a living being, than a flock or a
flone.   True virtue will fanction this recommendation ; fince it is the object of virtue to produce
happinefs ; and fince the man who lives in the midft
of domeflic relations, will have many opportunities
of conferring pleafure, minute in the detail, yet not
trivial in the amount, without interfering with the
purpofes of general benevolence.   Nay, by kindling
his fenfibility, and harmonifing his foul, they may
be expected, if he is endowed with a liberal and
manly fpirit, to render him more prompt in the fervice of ftrangers and the public."

St. Leon, Preface, p. viii.

Here is a full and explicit avowal of all I acknowledge or perceive to be erroneous upon this point in
the Enquiry Concerning Political Juftice; and this
is the point, and the only point, which Dr. Parr, after
he knew of my avowed purpofe to introduce into it
certain effential modifications, has attempted to refute, with fuch fupercilioufnefs of rebuke, and vehemence of invective.   In fact it feems to me to be by
a very nice fhade that Dr. Parr and I differ upon this
point : but this is not the firft time in which the well-
known maxim has been illuftrated, that " the fmaller

is

is the fpace by which a man is divided from you in opinion, with the more fury and intemperance will he often contend about it."

I will now, firft, attempt to afcertain the quantity of *peftilential and deftructive* confequences which were like to have flowed from this error in my Enquiry Concerning Political Juftice, " for fuch offences I am charged withal ;" and, fecondly, 1 will enquire into the foundnefs of what Dr. Parr has " heard remarked by perfons well fkilled in the tactics of controverfy, that, after the furrender of fo many outworks [as are contained in the point above fpecified], the citadel itfelf [the great purpofe aimed at in the Enquiry Concerning Political Juftice] is fcarcely tenable." *Sermon, p. 52.*

In entering on the firft of thefe queftions it is right we fhould have a clear idea how far my admiffions already recited militate with any thing advanced in my original treatife. The idea of juftice there contained is, that it is a rule requiring from us fuch an application of " our talents, our underftanding, our ftrength and our time *," as fhall, in the refult, produce the greateft fum of pleafure, to the fum of thofe beings who are capable of enjoying the fenfation of pleafure.—Now, if I divide my time into portions, and confider how the majority of the fmaller portions may be fo employed, as moft effectually to procure pleafure to others, nothing is more

* Political Juftice, Book II. Chap. II. p. 135, third edition.

obvious,

obvious, than that many of thefe portions cannot be
employed fo effectually in procuring pleafure, as to
my immediate connections and familiars : he therefore who would be the beft moral economift of his
time, muft employ much of it in feeking the advantage and content of thofe, with whom he has moft
frequent intercourfe. Accordingly it is there maintained, that the external action recommended by
this, and by the commonly received fyftems of morality, will in the generality of cafes be the fame, all
the difference lying in this, that the motives exciting
to action, upon the one principle, and the other, will
be effentially different.

Here, according to my prefent admiffion, lies all
the error of which I am confcious, in the original
ftatement in the Enquiry Concerning Political Juftice: I would now fay that, " in the generality of
cafes," not only the external action, but the motive,
ought to be nearly the fame as in the commonly received fyftems of morality; that I ought not only,
" in ordinary cafes, to provide for my wife and
children, my brothers and relations, before I provide for ftrangers, *p*. 132," but that it would be well
that my doing fo, fhould arife from the operation
of thofe private and domeftic affections, by which
through all ages of the world the conduct of mankind has been excited and directed.

There is a diftinction to be introduced here, with
which I am perfuaded Dr. Parr is well acquainted,
though for fome reafon he has chofen to pafs over

one fide of this diftinction entirely in filence in his
Sermon, between the motive from which a virtuous
action is to arife, and the criterion by which it is to
be determined to be virtuous. The motives of human actions are feelings, or paffions, or habits. Without feeling we cannot act at all; and without paffion
we cannot act greatly. But, when we proceed to
afcertain whether our actions are entitled to the name
of virtue, this can only be done by examining into
their effects, by bringing them to a ftandard, and
comparing them with a criterion.

I cannot be miftaken in affirming that Dr. Parr
and I are agreed about this criterion. All the difference is that Dr. Parr is moft inclined to call this criterion by the name of " utility," and that I have
ofteneft called it by the name of " juftice." Nor is
the difference here complete; fince I have frequently
ufed his name for it, though I believe he has never
employed mine. We are agreed however, as I have
faid, in this interefting and leading propofition, that
" that action or principle which does not tend to produce a general overbalance of pleafurable fenfation,
is not virtuous."

What then is the moft effential difference between
us as to the principle of morals? Simply this, that
Dr. Parr is inclined to lay moft emphafis, and moft
frequently to remind thofe he would inftruct, of the
motive from which as human beings their moral
actions muft fpring, and that I would ofteneft and
moft earneftly remind them of the criterion by which
they

they muſt aſcertain whether their actions are virtuous. This is the great ſource of all Dr. Parr's declamation. This is the ſufficient reaſon why I am to be treated as a " wily inſinuator, the child of affectation, entitled at beſt only to contempt or pity, a man to be ſmiled at as dealing in groundleſs and unauthoriſed hypotheſes," to be ſneered at, as only " not altogether aſleep in folly, as a modern ſage of capacious mind, rapt in beatific viſions of benevolence ;" and my tenets, as " accompanied with a long and portentous train of evils, which have been negligently overlooked, or inſidiouſly diſguiſed," by their author.

I grant however that there is a real difference between Dr. Parr and me in the point now ſtated. He, for ſome reaſon or other, has not once mentioned utility, the criterion of virtue, in his whole Sermon. I had been told indeed by one of his hearers that he had expreſsly contradicted and oppoſed that principle. I find in peruſing the Sermon, that it is only paſſed over in ſilence ; and I therefore take it for granted, that his real opinion on that point is juſt what it was accuſtomed to be.   Dr. Parr in the mean time, certainly upon this, and probably upon moſt occaſions, is inclined to lay his principal ſtreſs upon the motives of virtue : I on the contrary regard it as the proper and eminent buſineſs of the moraliſt, to call the attention of his fellow men to the criterion of virtue. My mind indeed, in writing the Enquiry Concerning Juſtice, was ſo deeply and earneſtly bent upon this,

as

as to lead me to throw an undue degree of flight and
difcredit upon the ordinary, and what I would now
call the moft practicable, motives of virtue. I am certainly forry that the treatife I wrote is affected by this
error; I feel, fince Dr. Parr is fo pleafed to exprefs
it, " fome degree of contrition," that the detection
of this overfight " had not occurred to the writer
before" the book was given to the world*. Yet my
contrition is confiderably the lefs, 1. becaufe I never
intended to fet up for a dictator, or to form a party,
who were to take my fayings for infallible : 2. becaufe, though it would be well that no fingle treatife
of morality or politics fhould be blotted with a fingle
error, yet the exiftence and difcovery of fuch errors
has at leaft the falutary effect of teaching the reader,
that he muft exercife his own underftanding, and not
refign it into the hands of another : and 3. becaufe I
do not believe, that the error into which I fell, is accompanied with thofe tremendous and appalling confequences, that " long and portentous train of evils,"
which Dr. Parr and his coadjutors have been pleafed
to afcribe to it.—The reafons for my not believing fo
are thefe.

The human mind is fo conftituted, as to render our
actions in almoft every cafe much more the creatures
of fentiment and affection, than of the underftanding. We all of us have, twifted with our very natures, the principles of parental and filial affection,

of

of love, attachment and friendſhip. I do therefore not think it the primordial duty of the moraliſt to draw forth all the powers of his wit in the recommendation of theſe.

Parental and filial affection, and the ſentiments of love, attachment and friendſhip, are moſt admirable inſtruments in the execution of the purpoſes of virtue. But to each of them, in the great chart of a juſt moral conduct, muſt be aſſigned its ſphere. They are all liable to exceſs. Each muſt be kept within its bounds, and have rigorous limits aſſigned it. I muſt take care not ſo to love, or ſo to obey my love to my parent or child, as to intrench upon an important and paramount public good.

Parental and filial affection, and the other principles above enumerated, are ſo far from compoſing the great topics by which the doctrine of virtue is to be taught, that they are the proper characteriſtics of a mind, which has as yet remained an utter ſtranger to doctrine. The moſt ignorant parent, whoſe lips were never refreſhed from the well of knowledge, whoſe mind was never expanded by ſympathy with the diſintereſted and illuſtrious dead, or by a generous anxiety for the welfare of diſtant climes and unborn ages, will ſcarcely ever fail to love his child. He will often love him ſo much, even though he ſhould be an idiot, deformed and odious to the ſight; or imbued with the baſeſt and moſt hateful propenſities, that he will perhaps rather conſent that millions ſhould periſh, than that this miſerable minion of his dotage
ſhould

should suffer a moment's displeasure. I do not regard a parent of this sort with any strong feeling of approbation.

Patriotism, or the love of our country, will frequently operate in a similar way. With the majority perhaps of the human species, a kind of selfish impulse of pride and vain-glory, which assumes the form of patriotism, and represents to our imagination whatever is gained to our country as so much gained to our darling selves, leads to a spirit of hatred and all uncharitableness towards the countries around us. We rejoice in their oppression, and make a jubilee, venting our joy in a hundred forms of extravagance, when the bleeding carcasses of thousands of their miserable natives are strewed upon the plain. This sort of patriotism, in its simplest and most uninstructed exhibition, vents itself in uttering hisses, and perhaps casting stones at the unprotected foreigner as he passes along our streets. I do not regard a patriotism of this kind with much feeling of approbation.

A truly virtuous character is the combined result of regulated affections. These sentiments, of which scarcely any human being is destitute, and of which we have much more frequent occasion to observe the excess than the defect,—the cultivation of these sentiments, I say, does not appear to me the principal office of moral discipline. For, after all, though I admit that the assiduities we employ for our children

D ought

8

ought to be, and muſt be, the reſult of private and
domeſtic affections, yet it is not theſe affections that
determine them to be virtuous. They muſt, as has
been already ſaid, be brought to a ſtandard, and
tried by a criterion of virtue.

This criterion has been above deſcribed, and it is
not perhaps of the utmoſt importance whether we
call it utility, or juſtice, or, more periphraſtically,
the production of the greateſt general good, the
greateſt public ſum of pleaſurable ſenſation. Call
it by what name you pleaſe, it will ſtill be true that
this is the law by which our actions muſt be tried.
I muſt be attentive to the welfare of my child ; becauſe he is one in the great congregation of the
family of the whole earth. I muſt be attentive to the
welfare of my child ; becauſe I can in many portions
of the never-ceaſing current of human life, be conferring pleaſure and benefit on him, when I cannot
be directly employed in conferring benefit on others.
I beſt underſtand his character and his wants ; I
poſſeſs a greater power of modelling his diſpoſition
and influencing his fortune ; and, as was obſerved
in Political Juſtice, (*p.* 132.) he is the individual,
in the great " diſtribution of the claſs needing ſuper-
intendence and ſupply among the claſs capable of
affording them," whom it falls to my lot to protect
and cheriſh.—I do not require that, when a man is
employed in benefiting his child, he ſhould con-
ſtantly recollect the abſtract principle of utility,
but

but I do maintain that his actions in profecuting that benefit are no further virtuous than in proportion as they fquare with that principle.

Confidering the fubject in this light, it appears to me to follow with irrefiftible evidence, that the crown of a virtuous character confifts in a very frequent and a very energetic recollection of the criterion, by which all his actions are to be tried, "whether they are of good, or whether they are of evil." It is this point, and this point alone, that leads to the diftinction between fuch a man, and a man of the moft vulgar character, of a character the leaft entitled to our approbation. The perfon, who has been well inftructed and accomplifhed in the great fchool of human excellence, has paffions and affections like other men. But he is aware that all thefe affections tend to excefs, and muft be taught each to know its order and its fphere. He therefore continually holds in mind the principles by which their boundaries are to be fixed.

I fhould think fuch a man would be the more perfect, in proportion as he endeavoured to elevate philanthropy into a paffion. There appears to me to be little danger on that fide. That we are all of us the creatures of fenfible impreffions, is a great and momentous truth. Let a man then try, as much as he will, to cultivate a love for his fpecies, we may, I conceive, be very fecure that occafions enough will prefent themfelves, to pull him down

from

from his enthufiaftic eminence, and remind him of his concerns as an individual.

I certainly regard thofe examples, in which men, ftruggling with the deareft and moft powerful fentiments of their nature, have facrificed their own lives, or the lives of their children, to the imperious demands of public good, as the moft glorious inftances of the degree of excellence to which human beings are capable of afcending. I contemplate with tranfports of admiration the conduct of a Decius and a Regulus. If the ftory of thefe men is a fable, I am proud that I belong to a fpecies, of which fome individuals have been capable of imagining fuch excellence, and thoufands have felt " that within" them, that embryo generofity and noblenefs of nature, which prompted them to credit this excellence as a member of genuine hiftory. Brutus probably did well, when he put his fons to death, as the only alternative for preferving and perpetuating the rifing liberties of the Roman republic.

But I conceive that there are not only extraordinary cafes in which men fhould recollect and act upon views of general philanthropy. I would ftate thefe views as a part of the ordinary bufinefs of our lives, and would maintain that we ought to recollect and imprefs them upon our minds, as often as pious men repeat their prayers. I would defire to love my children; yet I would not defire fo to love them, as to forget that I have what we were accuftomed to

call,

call, before the hoarfe and favage cry of Jacobinifm !
had frighted all moral language from its propriety,
higher duties. I would wifh fo to employ a portion
of every day, as to qualify me for being a benefactor
to the ftranger and the man whom I know not ; and
I would have men, in proportion to the faculties
they poffefs, not omit to devote part of their energies
to the natives of diftant climates, and to ages yet
unborn.

Let us confider here for a moment the cafe, fo
often attacked with all the weapons of argument
and ridicule, of Fenelon and the valet, and afk how
far the decifion of this cafe will be affected, by the
admiffion of the domeftic affections.

" In a loofe and general view," fays the Enquiry
Concerning Political Juftice, " I and my neighbour
are both of us men ; and of confequence entitled
to equal attention. But, in reality, it is probable
that one of us is a being of more worth and importance than the other. A man is of more worth
than a beaft ; becaufe, being poffeffed of higher
faculties, he is capable of a more refined and genuine
happinefs. In the fame manner the illuftrious
archbifhop of Cambray, was of more worth than his
valet, and there are few of us that would hefitate to
pronounce, if his palace were in flames, and the life
of only one of them could be preferved, which of
the two ought to be preferred.

" But there is another ground of preference, befide the private confideration of one of them being

further

further removed from the ftate of a mere animal. We are not connected with one or two percipient beings, but with a fociety, a nation, and in fome fenfe with the whole family of mankind. Of confequence that life ought to be preferred, which will moft conduce to the general good. In faving the life of Fenelon, fuppofe at the moment he conceived the project of his immortal Telemachus, I fhould have been promoting the welfare of thoufand̃s, who have been cured by the perufal of that work, of fome error, vice and confequent unhappinefs. Nay, my benefit would extend further than this; for every individual, thus cured, has become a better member of fociety, and has contributed in his turn to the happinefs, information and improvement of others.

" Suppofe I had been myfelf the valet; I ought to have chofen to die, rather than Fenelon fhould have died.——

" Suppofe the valet had been my brother, my father or my benefactor. This would not alter the truth of the propofition.————My brother or my father may be a fool or a profligate, malicious, lying or difhoneft. If they be, of what confequence is it that they are mine?" *Political Juftice, Book II, Chap. II. p.* 126.

Dr. Parr well obferves that this is a queftion of " unufual duties," and a cafe, " imaginary" he calls it, I would fay, that perhaps will fcarcely happen once in the hiftory of an age. That it is not
imaginary,

imaginary, will be evident to every man who recollects
that a decision precisely on the same principles
happened in the life of Timoleon, and a second
time in that of Lucius Junius Brutus, to confine
myself to instances of the most consummate notoriety.
The reader however is bound in fairness to recollect
the unusualness of the case, and to bear in mind
that, whichever way it is decided, it can have no
tendency to shake the domestic affections in the ordinary intercourses of life. Dr. Parr indeed, because it is unusual and extreme, treats it as criminal to have called towards it the attention of
mankind. In this I do not agree with him. It
is a question which must be tried by the criterion
of all virtue. If indeed, as Dr. Parr seems to think
(judging from the sacred silence he has preserved
concerning it in the course of an argument where it
must have obtruded itself on his mind a thousand
times), this criterion by which all our actions are to
be tried, this book of life by which must be decided
the merits and demerits of every day of our existence,
must slumber in awful repose to the resurrection of
the dead, then it may be a crime to enquire into
the respective claims of Fenelon and his valet. But,
as has already appeared, I hold, that this criterion
cannot be consulted too often, that the recollection
or non-recollection of it constitutes the main difference between the Livonian peasant and the sage, and
that it would be well for mankind and the generation
of an accomplished moral character, that justice and

philan-

philanthropy fhould be converted into a paffion
and made one of the ftirring and living thoughts of
our bofom. I conceive that there muft lurk a fecret
contradiction in terms, in the idea of a criterion
which is never to be confulted; and I do not know
how our acquaintance with, and facility in the application of, this criterion can be fo effectually improved, as by frequently confulting it, and applying
it to cafes of a certain nicenefs and delicacy,——
To return.

In revifing the queftion of Fenelon and the valet,
in its relation to the facrednefs, the beauty and utility
of the domeftic affections, three things are principally to be obferved.

Firft, I will fuppofe that I fave in preference, the
life of the valet, who is my father, and in fo doing
intrench upon the principle of utility. Few perfons
even upon that fuppofition will be difpofed feverely
to blame my conduct. We are accuftomed and
rightly accuftomed, to confider every man in the
aggregate, as a machine calculated to produce many
benefits or many evils, and not to take his actions
into our examination in a disjointed and feparate
manner. If, without paufe or hefitation, I proceed
to fave the life of my father in preference to that of
any human being, every man will refpect in me the
fentiment of filial affection, will acknowledge that
the feeling by which I am governed is a feeling
pregnant with a thoufand good and commendable
actions, and will confefs, according to a trite, but
ex-

exprefsive, phrafe, that at leaft I have *my heart in the right place*, that I have within me thofe precious and ineftimable materials out of which all virtuous and honourable deeds are made.

But, fecondly, the confideration of the domeftic affections, and their infinite importance to "the culture of the heart," does effentially modify the queftion of utility, and affect the application of the criterion of virtue. The action, viz., the faving of the life of Fenelon, is to be fet againft the habit, and it will come to be ferioufly confidered, whether, in proportion to the inequality of the alternative propofed to my choice, it will contribute moft to the mafs of human happinefs, that I fhould act upon the utility of the cafe feparately taken, or fhould refufe to proceed in violation of a habit, which is fraught with a feries of fucceffive utilities.

Thirdly, it is proper to notice the deception which Dr. Parr and his coadjutors put upon themfelves and others, in conftantly fuppofing that, if the father is faved, this will be the effort of paffion, but if Fenelon is faved, the act will arife only from cool, phlegmatic, arithmetical calculation. No great and honourable deed can be atchieved, but from paffion. If I fave the life of Fenelon, unprompted to do fo by an ardent love of the wondrous excellence of the man, and a fublime eagernefs to atchieve and fecure the welfare and improvement of millions, I am a monfter, unworthy of the appellation of a

man,

man, and the fociety of beings fo " fearfully and wonderfully made," as men are.

I perceive that I did not fufficiently take into mind the prejudices and habits of men, when I put the cafe of Fenelon, the writer of certain books of reafoning and invention. The benefit to accrue from the writing of books is too remote an idea, to ftrike and fill the imagination. If I had put the cafe of Brutus, and fuppofed that upon the prefervation of his life, againft which his fons appear fo bafely to have confpired, hung all the long feries of Roman freedom and Roman virtue,—if I had put the cafe of Bonaparte, upon the affumption that his exiftence was neceffary to avert the reftoration of defpotifm on the one hand, or the revival of all the horrors of anarchy on the other, few perfons, I believe, would have felt any difficulty in deciding. It would eafily have been feen, that to have facrificed any life, rather than fuffer the deftruction of a man who could alone preferve his contemporaries and future ages from barbarifm and flavery, was a proper theme for paffion, for the exercife of that illuftrious and godlike philanthropy, which conftitutes the higheft merit the human heart is able to conceive.

An expreffion has efcaped Dr. Parr, in his zeal againft the doctrine of univerfal philanthropy, which is perhaps remarkable enough, to deferve to find a place in the procefs of this difcuffion. He fays, "the good Samaritan haftened to the fuccour of the

the man fallen among thieves, and the bleſſed Author
of Chriſtianity has *juſtified* the deed, *p. 5*." If Dr.
Parr will permit me for a moment to play the divine, a trade for which I am not altogether without
diſcipline. I will anſwer him that Chriſt did not
" juſtify the deed." He did ſomething infinitely
different. He applauded ; he has, I believe, immor-
taliſed it ; he has bid all his followers go and imitate
that deed, which Dr. Parr thinks he has barely.
juſtified. Indeed, whatever becomes of the doctrine
of univerſal philanthropy, I am perſuaded that, to the
extent in which I have above explained it, the author
of Chriſtianity will be found among its moſt conſpicuous advocates. He has ſtated the love of God,
and of our neighbour, that is, of our fellow-men, as
the ſum of morality, or, to uſe his own expreſſion, as
the " two commandments on which hang all the
law and the prophets :" ſo much ſtreſs did he place
upon that maxim of utility, which Dr. Parr in his
Spital Sermon has thought proper to paſs in total
ſilence. He has again and again expreſſed himſelf
in diſparagement of the private affections. Not that I
mean to affirm he intended wholly to proſcribe them ;
but certainly, if there is meaning in words, he meant
to aſſign to them a very ſubordinate ſituation.

But Dr. Parr ſays, that the doctrine of univerſal
philanthropy " may be uſed as a cloke to us for in-
ſenſibility where other men feel, and for negligence
where other men act with viſible and uſeful, though
limited, effect, *p. 10*." Certainly it may, like the

beſt

beſt principles of morality, or the moſt vaunted in-
ſtitutions of religion, be uſed by bad men as a pretence and juſtification of the moſt hateful proceedings. But I ſhould think it little likely; as it is not
probable, at leaſt in our days, that it will have ſufficient popularity, to become a formidable rival to
pretended devotion, or patriotiſm, or any other of
thoſe ſpecious ſeemings, by which knaves have been
accuſtomed to impoſe upon fools time out of mind.
But to whatever bad purpoſes the pretence of univerſal philanthropy may be uſed, certainly none can be
more hoſtile to the reality, than that which Dr. Parr
ſpecifies. Philanthropy is a bank in which every
creature that lives has an intereſt, the firſt and pre-
ferable allies being, by the very nature of the caſe,
in poſſeſſion of thoſe who are neareſt to us, and
whom we have moſt frequent opportunity to benefit.
The doctrine of philanthropy countenances no negligence, but requires of us diligently to devote " our
talents, our underſtanding, our ſtrength and our
time, to the production of the greateſt quantity of
general good." So as long as we continue under
the influence of this principle, we cannot be inattentive to any of the claims of benevolence; and,
when it relaxes its empire over us, as from the frailty
of our nature it will frequently do, I believe we ſhall
fall back into the great maſs of our fellow-men, and
be governed by ſuch motives, paſſions and affections,
as they are accuſtomed to obey.

There is one ſuperficial and ſomewhat ludicrous
objection,

objection, which I have often heard in the mouths of the vulgar, but which I certainly did not expect to meet with in a compofition from the pen of Dr. Parr. In the language of Dr. Parr's Sermon it is as follows : " What would become of fociety, if" they who are called on to relieve our neceffities, " fhould ponder, ere they ftretch forth their hands to refcue us from wretchednefs, and paufe, left peradventure fome other human being might be found a little more virtuous, and a little more miferable than ourfelves? *p.* 10."—Undoubtedly, all the actions of our lives muft be, in a greater or lefs degree, a compromife between the niceties of deliberation and the rapid progrefs of time. Undoubtedly, we muft often fubmit, in the urgency of the cafes which come before us, to the chance of being miftaken in the preferences we make. He muft be an idiot, and not a moralift, who would require of us to give fo much time to confideration, as would eventually take away from us the occafion to act. This is not a qualification upon the doctrine of philanthropy; it is a direct inference from, and an effential member of it. By this doctrine, as has been ftated again and again, we are required to employ " our talents, our underftanding, our ftrength, and our *time*," in conferring on our fellow-men the greateft fum of advantage.

I have done with all I think it neceffary to fay to the general argument of Dr. Parr's Sermon. I conceive I have fufficiently proved that the doctrine of

univerfal

universal philanthropy (even as it is stated in Political Justice, with somewhat too much disparagement and too little toleration to the private affections) is not " accompanied with so long and portentous a train of evils," as Dr. Parr is willing to ascribe to it. I feel myself obliged to infer, that it was some extraordinary perturbation of Dr. Parr's intellectual perspicacity, and not a cool and unruffled view of the subject, which led him to combine it with such nameless horrors.

The second thing I proposed, was to enquire into the soundness of what Dr. Parr has " heard remarked by persons well skilled in the tactics of controversy, that after the surrender of so many outworks (viz., the question of the private and domestic affections), the citadel itself (the great purpose aimed at in the Enquiry Concerning Political Justice) is scarcely tenable." Upon this point I shall be very short.

The great doctrine of the treatise in question is what I have there called (adopting a term I found ready coined in the French language) the perfectibility, but what I would now wish to call, changing the term, without changing a particle of the meaning, the progressive nature of man, in knowledge, in virtuous propensities, and in social institutions.

Upon the face of the question it is not easy to see, how the admission of the private and domestic affections operates to put a period to the progress of hu-

man

man improvement. Our advances in knowledge, I believe it will be admitted, will not be materially and fatally interrupted by the due exercise of these affections.

Our improvement in virtuous propensities, is intimately connected with our improvement in knowledge. There is no condition of mind so favourable to the rank and poisonous vegetation of vice, as ignorance. It is only short-sightedness and folly which persuade men that, while they are over-reaching and defrauding their neighbours, they are promoting their own interests. Extravagant expence and ostentation are the playthings of the infancy of mind; and when, in consequence of the continued and perennial influx of knowledge, the human species, or great societies of men are past their infancy, we shall cease to admire and applaud these things in one another, and they will insensibly become antiquated and perish. The progress of knowledge will render familiar to every mind the criterion of virtue, or, in other words, this terrible doctrine of universal philanthropy. We shall be astonished to see in how many instances interests, supposed incompatible, perfectly coincide; shall find that what is good for you, is advantageous to me; that, while I educate my child judiciously for himself, I am rendering him a valuable acquisition to society; and that, by contributing to the improvement of my countrymen, I am preparing for my child a society in which it will be desirable for him to live.

I cannot

I cannot purfue this argument to its juft extent. Were I to enter further into it in this curfory way, I fhould inflict an injury upon its beauty and force. It has already been amply difcuffed in the Enquiry Concerning Political Juftice; and it is obvious that none of the confiderations here touched on, are in the flighteft degree invalidated by the admiffion of the domeftic affections.

I know that Dr. Parr and Mr. Mackintofh look with horror upon this doctrine of the progreffive nature of man. They cling with all the fervours of affection, to the opinion that the vices, the weakneffes and the follies which have hitherto exifted in our fpecies, will continue undiminifhed as long as the earth fhall endure. I do not envy them their feelings. I love to contemplate the yet unexpanded powers and capabilities of our nature, and to believe that they will one day be unfolded to the infinite advantage and happinefs of the inhabitants of the globe. Long habit has fo trained me to bow to the manifeftations of truth wherever I recognize them, that, if arguments were prefented to me fufficient to eftablifh the uncomfortable doctrine of my antagonifts, I would weigh, I would revolve them, and I hope I fhould not fail to fubmit to their authority. But, if my own doctrine is an error, and if I am fated to die in it, I cannot afflict myfelf greatly with the apprehenfion of a miftake, which cheers my folitude, which I carry with me into crowds, and which adds fomewhat

what to the pleafure and peace of every day of my
exiftence.

Refpecting the point of the improvement of our
focial inftitutions, that cannot be fundamentally affected by any confideration to arife out of the domeftic affections. Politics is nothing elfe, but one
chapter extracted out of the great code of morality.
While therefore the criterion of virtue remains un-
changed, the conduct which ought to be held by
ftates, by governments and fubjects, and the principles of judicial proceeding between man and man
will for ever remain the fame.   In the Enquiry Concerning Political Juftice it is endeavoured to be
proved, that in morality each man is entitled to a
certain fphere for the exercife of his difcretion ; that
it is to be defired that in this fphere he fhould be directed by a free, an inftructed and independent judgment ; and that it is neceffary for the improvement of
mankind, that no man or body of men fhould intrench upon this fphere but in cafes of the moft irrefiftible urgency. The inference drawn from thefe
particulars is, that the lefs government we had, and
the fewer were the inftances in which government
interfered with the proceedings of individuals, confiftently with the prefervation of the focial ftate, the
better would it prove for the welfare and happinefs
of man. Nothing which has been admitted on the
fubject of the domeftic affections, in the flighteft degree interferes with thefe reafonings. As to the quantity of improvement which may from time to time

E   be

be introduced into the focial condition of man, and
the extent to which the interferences of government
may ultimately be profcribed, the decifion of that
queftion depends upon the degree in which the human fpecies is fufceptible of improvement in virtuous
propenfities.

I have been obliged to treat the propofition of
the progreffive nature of man in a very flight and
imperfect manner in this place. I have rather furnifhed hints, which the reader may, as he feels inclined, apply to the doctrines and reafonings delivered
in Political Juftice. I thought fo much due to fuch
readers as may be difpofed to attach a value to the
theories delivered in that work; but I cannot do
more, confiftently with the plan and defign of the
prefent effay.

I know not whether it is of fufficient importance
to notice the ftrictures Dr. Parr has made upon my
marginal reference to Jonathan Edwards, in Political Juftice, p. 129. *See Spital Sermon, p. 74.* Every
candid reader will perceive that the reference is not
made for the purpofe of giving authority to what is
there ftated by me on the fubject of gratitude. The
name of Jonathan Edwards is much too far removed
from general eminence and notoriety in Englifh literature, to anfwer any fuch purpofe. I affixed his
name to the page, merely from a fpirit of franknefs,
becaufe in reality it was Jonathan Edwards's Effay
there referred to, which firft led me into the train of
thinking on that point exhibited in Political Juftice;

and

and I believed it would be unmanly to fupprefs the name of my benefactor. If any perfon is either amufed or inftructed by Dr. Parr's diftinction between virtue and true virtue, in order to prove that, though Jonathan Edwards denied gratitude to be true virtue, he admitted it to be virtue fimply taken, I confefs I have too much humanity to be willing to difturb his enjoyments.

The firft pamphlet, I believe, which ufhered in this tremendous war againft philanthropy, is entitled an Examination of the Leading Principle of the New Syftem of Morals, and was, fome time after its publication, avowed as the production of Thomas Green, efq. I was confiderably amufed, and, as far as fuch a trifle could operate, confirmed in the way of thinking expreffed in Political Juftice, by the perufal of this effay; though I could not accept the compliment which Mr. Green pays me in the outfet, where he fays, " Nothing can be more thoroughly confiftent," than the doctrines of this work. " Allow the firft pofition (and it has every prepoffeffion in its favour), and all the inferences follow fo clearly and irrefiftibly, that it feems impoffible to elude their force." He goes on, in a fort of attempt to imitate the ftyle of Mr. Burke, " All was found, all was water-tight ; not a cranny, not a chink for truth to flip out, or error to creep in," *Examination, p.* 13, 15. I could not, I fay, accept this compliment ; I never flattered myfelf that a work, fo multifarious in its difquifitions, could be without

E 2   inconfift-

inconfiftencies; nor, to fpeak ingenuoufly, though I was not vain enough to prefume that every thing I had faid was truth, neither was I modeft enough to imagine that my book, from beginning to end, contained no line but what was error.

My curiofity however was fomewhat excited to know what my antagonift regarded as the leading principle of my fyftem, which muft be removed, under penalty of fuffering the whole fyftem to ftand invulnerable and impregnable to the lateft ages. This principle is ftated by the author with great explicitnefs, *p.* 16. It is " the opinion which has lately prevailed, that virtue confifts altogether in utility ; that it is the beneficial or pernicious tendency of an action, which alone conftitutes it virtuous or vicious. If virtue is indeed only another name for the utility of an action, I am bound to look to utility, and to utility only, as a teft of moral rectitude."

I remember, the firft idea which arofe to my mind, in that tone of careleffnefs and fecurity which fuch an attack produced, was, I may leave this gentleman to be anfwered by Dr. Parr. I knew, if I knew any thing, that Dr. Parr regarded " utility, and utility only, as a teft of moral rectitude," in common, as Mr. Green very juftly obferves, with " Law, Brown, Paley, Helvetius and Hume, *Exam. p.* 20." I knew that Dr. Parr held this principle in high reverence, and made it the very frequent topic of his panegyric. Yet to my aftonifhment, in the Notes to the Spital Sermon, *p.* 86, I find Mr. Green very warmly recom-

8   mended

mended for his " penetration, taste, and large
views in philosophy," without the least notice of his
having fallen, in the pamphlet applauded, into any
considerable error.   I can no otherwise account
for this, than by suppofing that whatever attacks
the pernicious system of universal philanthropy,
though at the expence of the leading article of Dr.
Parr's creed, the very test and criterion of all virtue,
is acceptable.——Dr. Parr has indeed gone further
than this.   He has undertaken to effect a consolida-
tion of Mr. Green's doctrine to his own.   He has
inserted in his Notes, *p.* 72, the very passage of the
Examination, above recited ; and, by the help of not
quoting the second sentence, and of throwing an
emphasis upon the words " altogether" and " alone"
in the first, has attempted to extract a meaning out
of the passage, of which I believe every impartial
reader will pronounce it incapable.

I am loth to labour too much so irresistible a
point as the opposition between Dr. Parr and Mr.
Green, though I own I should be sorry to leave a
loop-hole in the argument, out of which for Dr.
Parr to escape.   I add therefore a very few words.
Mr. Green says, just after the passage above referred
to, *p.* 17, " I am fairly at issue with the advocates of
the New System of Morals, by directly denying,——
that it is practicable, as a project, to deduce moral
distinction from this source," *viz.*, " the tendency of
its objects to promote or thwart the general good."
Can any thing be less equivocal than this ? Again:

Mr. Green very fairly and spiritedly owns, that the authors to whom his reasonings are adverse, are "Law, Brown, Paley, Helvetius and Hume." Dr. Parr must therefore show how his opinion on the subject of utility differs from theirs, before he can make out that Mr. Green's pamphlet is not in as direct hostility to his creed, as to the leading principle of the Enquiry Concerning Political Justice.

The remainder of these pages shall be dedicated to an examination of so much of the reasoning in the Essay on the Principle of Population, as has been supposed by some persons to be subversive of the favourite doctrine of the Political Justice, the progressive nature of man. Dr. Parr says that the author of this treatise has " *demonstrated,* that Mr. Godwin's scheme of equality can never be realised, and that, were it realised, it soon would cease, and drive us back, from the transient blessings of an ill-directed and overstrained benevolence, to all the terrible evils of the most corrupt and ferocious selfishness, *Spital Sermon, p.* 143."—The word in italics is so marked by Dr. Parr.

And, independently of Dr. Parr's sanction, which is too easily gained, and too easily forfeited, for me to be disposed to lay much stress upon it, I had several reasons for wishing to pay a certain attention to the Essay on Population. Many persons who have been well disposed towards the theories of Political Justice, and whose ardent benevolence led them to contemplate with delight the prospects of unlimited improvement,

provement, have expreffed themfelves exceedingly perplexed with the reafonings of this treatife, and have invited and urged me to enter into the dif- cuffion of its principles. Perhaps I owed to thefe perfons to have written fomething exprefsly on that point. But I own I never could perfuade myfelf to fee any adequate reafon for doing fo. It ftood out fo obvious and glaring to my mind, that the reafonings of the Effay on Population did not bear with any particular ftrefs upon my hypothefis, that I thought other men, who had any confiderable motive to wifh for information, ought to be able to make out the point for themfelves, without calling on the original affertor of the hypothefis for affiftance. I am happy however to have this opportunity obtruded on me, to make a few brief obfervations on an argument, which I was by no means fure did not call on me for fome explanation, independently of the occurrence of fuch an opportunity.

I approach, as I have already faid, the author of the Effay on Population with a fentiment of un- feigned approbation and refpect. The general ftrain of his argument does the higheft honour to the libe- rality of his mind. He has neither laboured to excite hatred nor contempt againft me or my tenets : he has argued the queftions between us, juft as if they had never been made a theme for political party and the intrigues of faction : he has argued, juft as if he had no end in view, but the inveftigation of evidence, and the development of truth.

E 4

This

This author has a claim, perhaps ftill higher, upon my refpect. With the moft unaffected fimplicity of manner, and difdaining every parade of fcience, he appears to me to have made as unqueftionable an addition to the theory of political economy, as any writer for a century paft. The grand propofitions and outline of his work will, I believe, be found not lefs conclufive and certain, than they are new. For myfelf I cannot refufe to take fome pride, in fo far as by my writings I gave the occafion, and furnifhed an incentive, to the producing fo valuable a treatife.

Dr. Franklin feems firft to have collected the facts upon which our author's hypothefis proceeds ; but he has not given the flighteft hint of thofe inferences which are drawn from them in the Effay on Population.

The foundations of the difcovery contained in this treatife are exceedingly fimple. Every one, whofe attention is for a moment called to the fubject, will immediately perceive, that the principle of multiplication in the human fpecies is without limits, and that, if it tends to any increafe in the numbers of mankind, it muft have that tendency, independently of any extrinfic caufes checking the growth of population, for ever.

Dr. Franklin has found, in the refult of a feries of enquiries fet on foot in the new-fettled colonies of North-America, that the increafe of population among them is fo rapid, that they conftantly
double

double the number of their inhabitants in twenty or five-and-twenty years. Under the long established governments of Europe, population in some instances is at a stand, and in others is thought rather to tend to diminution. The only cause of this difference is probably to be traced to this circumstance, that, in old-settled countries, an increase in the number of children is found in almost all instances to be a burthen to the parents, and, in countries which are on the point of being settled for the first time, they are the most precious wealth which the settler can have to his lot. The genuine and unadulterated operation of the principle of population is therefore to be taken from new-settled countries. Hence it appears that the progress is in the nature of a geometrical ratio, or 2, 4, 8, 16, 32, 64, doubling itself every twenty years.

Having thus ascertained and fixed the principle of population, we come next to consider the measures of subsistence. If the latter do not keep pace with, or at least press closely on the footsteps of the former, the most dreadful calamities and disorders must be expected to ensue. To ascertain this point then, let us suppose the actual produce of the soil of England precisely capable of feeding its present inhabitants, and let us suppose that the number of those inhabitants is eight millions. It has already appeared that, in twenty years, the principle of population, if operating without a check, would cause those inhabitants to double their present number, that is,

to

to be fixteen millions. Well, fays the author of the Effay on Population, let us be liberal in our conceffions, let us not rifk the inforcing our principle with too great ftrictnefs, and let us fuppofe that, by a more enlightened ftudy of agriculture, by the breaking up of wafte lands, and by various other expedients, the foil of England fhall, twenty years hence, be able to fubfift this vaft acceffion of inhabitants.

Let us go on again and again in the fame liberal ftyle of conceffion in which we fet out. We are far from being able to anticipate all the expedients man is able to difcover, and the refources of his ingenuity. Let us imagine that, as the firft twenty years produced additional fubfiftence adequate to the fupport of eight millions of added inhabitants, the next twenty years fhall produce fubfiftence for eight millions more, and fo on, in arithmetical ratio, or the ratio of addition, for ever. This is an ample allowance, as the foil of England, as well as the furface of the globe, is limited, and contains only an affignable number of acres. But this conclufion prefents to us in the moft ftriking light, the inadequatenefs of the principle of fubfiftence to meet and bear up againft the principle of population. Population, left to itfelf, would go in the ratio of 2, 4, 8, 16, 32, 64, and fubfiftence, upon a fuppofition certainly fufficiently favourable, only in the ratio of 2, 4, 6, 8, 10, 12, for every twenty years fucceffively.

I have

I have found it moſt convenient, both for the ſake of clearneſs and brevity, to ſtate the main doctrine of the Eſſay on Population in my own words. I hope I have done juſtice to the meaning of the author: I am ſure I have not deſignedly miſrepreſented it. It is a doctrine too full of ſerious reflections to the political ſpeculator, and of too much importance to the beſt intereſts of mankind, not to impoſe upon every one who meddles with it, a rigid duty of fairneſs, impartiality and candour.

The way in which the author of this treatiſe endeavours to bring his arguments to bear upon the doctrines of Political Juſtice is as follows. How is it, he is led to enquire, that the principle of population, which has ſo perpetual a tendency to proceed beyond the limits of the means of ſubſiſtence, is kept down in this and other countries, ſo as to be attended ſcarcely with any perceptible increaſe? And his anſwer cannot be accuſed of not being broad and ample enough to cover the difficulty. He ſtates it to be " the grinding law of neceſſity ; miſery, and the fear of miſery, *p.* 176." And elſewhere he appears willing to aſſign two cauſes, which undoubtedly can never exiſt ſeparately from each other, vice and miſery.

The inference from theſe poſitions is, that the political ſuperintendents of a community are bound to exerciſe a paternal vigilance and care over theſe two great means of advantage and ſafety to mankind ; and that no evil is more to be dreaded, than that we

ſhould

should have too little vice and misery in the world to confine the principle of population within its proper sphere. Of consequence every attempt greatly to improve the condition of mankind is to be viewed with an eye of jealousy; and, above all, a scheme, such as in the fervour of my heart I endeavoured to delineate, the tendency of which is to drive all vice and misery from the face of the earth, would, if it could be realised, prove to be one of the most intolerable calamities with which the human species can be afflicted. The author does not exult in this view of the subject. He is pleased to say, " The system which Mr. Godwin proposes is, without doubt, the most beautiful and engaging of any that has yet appeared.—In short, it is impossible to contemplate the whole of this fair structure, without emotions of delight and admiration, accompanied with an ardent longing for the period of its accomplishment, *Essay*, *p.* 174, 5." And he can only express his regret, that " the great obstacle in the way to any extraordinary improvement in society, is of a nature that we can never hope to overcome, *p.* 346." The author therefore cannot be displeased with me for attempting the relief of so " disheartening" a consideration.

The chief, perhaps I might say the only, difficulty I feel in entering upon this subject, is that I must consider myself as addressing readers, many of whom never bestowed a perusal upon the Enquiry Concerning Political Justice, and the rest, if they ever entered

with

with ardour into the feelings that book was intended
to excite, have doubtlefs, in the interval which has
fince elapfed, had their ardour cooled by the operation
of time.   The intercourfe of the world has a powerful tendency to blunt in us the fentiments of enthufiafm, and the fpirit of romance ; and, whatever
truth we may fuppofe there to be in the doctrine of
the progreffive nature of man, it is fo far remote
from the tranfactions of ordinary life, and the feelings which impel us in fuch tranfactions to bend to
the routine of circumfcribed and unfpeculative men,
that it can with difficulty preferve its authority in
the midft of fo ftrong a contagion.   Yet I am now
obliged to recur to the romantic and unpractifed
theories of the Political Juftice, nakedly, abruptly,
without any preparation or interval to mitigate the
prejudices of the reader.   I can therefore only in-
treat him to recollect, that the queftion how far they
are romantic or impracticable in other views does
not now fall under our confideration, but that we
are fimply to enquire in what degree they are affected, by the difcoveries of the author of this Effay refpecting the principle of population.

Let it be recollected, that I admit the ratios of the
author in their full extent, and that I do not attempt
in the flighteft degree to vitiate the great foundations
of his theory.   My undertaking confines itfelf to the
tafk of repelling his conclufions.

I admit fully that the principle of population in the
human fpecies is in its own nature energetic and
unlimited,

Strange, that S. should be hastily to disbelieve in themselves, and so undoubtedly contribute to their own ruin. How strit is so hard... [illegible]... to Malthus, that on enough I hope [illegible] ... anxiety from Physical (62) accepts without...

immorality unlimited, and that the safety of the world can no

or that otherwise be maintained, but by a constant and

hardly powerful check upon this principle. This idea de-
was

etc. of molishes at once many maxims which have been

long and unsuspectedly received into the vulgar code

Yet I of morality, such as, that it is the first duty of princes
hope
(continued) to watch for the multiplication of their subjects, and

to him that a man or woman, who passes the term of life

in a condition of celibacy, is to be considered as

having failed to discharge one of the principal obligations they owe to the community. On the contrary it now appears to be rather the man who rears /!! a numerous family, that has in some degree transgressed the confidence he owes to the public welfare. Population is always, as this author observes, in all old-settled countries (putting out of our view the temporary occurrence of extraordinary calamities, which however may be expected to be rapidly repaired), in some degree of excess beyond the means of subsistence : there is constantly a smaller quantity of provisions, than would be requisite for the comfortable and vigorous support of all the inhabitants.

The checks upon population which are honoured with the patronage of the author of this Effay, are vice and mifery. Here it is obvious to the remark of every man, that we can fcarcely felect checks which fhall have a lefs feducing and agreeable ap-pearance, or fewer intrinfic recommendations to plead in their behalf. Thus the author, in corre-fpondence to the habitual fairnefs of his difquifitions, affords

affords every advantage to fuch as fhall feel difpofed to enquire into the doctrine of fubftitutes.

Is it neceffary that we fhould always preferve the precife portion of vice and mifery which are now to be found in the world, under pain of being fub-jected to the moft terrible calamities? The author very truly fays, that his inferences are in a ftate of open war againft every " extraordinary improvement in fo-ciety." Not only what Mr. Mackintofh ftyles the " abominable and peftilential paradoxes" of Political Juftice, but every generous attempt for any import-ant melioration of the condition of mankind, is here at ftake. The advocates of old eftablifhments and old abufes, could not have found a doctrine, more to their heart's content, more effectual to fhut out all reform and improvement for ever. Let then every ardent and philanthropical friend to the beft interefts of mankind, whatever may be his particular fpecu-lation and favourite project, go along with me in the inveftigation of our author's conclufions.

To difcover whether exactly the fame proportions of vice and mifery which now obtain, are requifite for the prefervation of the great ftructure of human fociety, let us open our eyes to furvey the records of ancient hiftory, and to confider what is perhaps now taking place in different parts of the globe. One of the greateft evils which can infeft political difqui-fition, is the imagination that what takes place in the fpot and period in which we live, is effential to the general regulation and well-being of mankind.

What

(64)

What was called the expofing of children prevailed to a very extenfive degree in the ancient world. The fame practice continues to this hour in China.

I know that the prejudices and habits of modern Europe are ftrongly in arms againft this inftitution. I grant that it is very painful and repulfive to the imagination of perfons educated as I and my countrymen have been. And I hope, and truft, that no fuch expedient will be neceffary to be reforted to, in any ftate of fociety which fhall ever be introduced in this or the furrounding countries.

Yet, if we compare it with mifery and vice, the checks pleaded for in the Effay on Population, what fhall we fay? I contemplate my fpecies with admiration and reverence. When I think of Socrates, Solon and Ariftides among the Greeks, when I think of Fabricius, Cincinnatus and Cicero among the Romans, above all, when I think of Milton, Shakefpear, Bacon and Burke, and when I reflect on the faculties and capacities every where, in different degrees, inherent in the human form, I am obliged to confefs,—that I know not of how extraordinary productions the myfterious principle to which we owe our exiftence is capable, but that my imagination is able to reprefent to itfelf nothing more illuftrious and excellent than man. But it is not man, fuch as I frequently fee him, that excites much of my veneration. I know that the majority of thofe I fee, are corrupt, low-minded, befotted, prepared for degradation and vice, and with fcarcely any veftige about
them

them of their high deſtination. Their hold therefore is rather upon my compaſſion and general benevolence, than upon my eſteem. Neither do I regard
a new-born child with any ſuperſtitious reverence.
If the alternative were complete, I had rather ſuch a
child ſhould periſh in the firſt hour of its exiſtence,
than that a man ſhould ſpend ſeventy years of life
in a ſtate of miſery and vice. I know that the globe
of earth affords room for only a certain number of
human beings to be trained to any degree of perfection ; and I had rather witneſs the exiſtence of a
thouſand ſuch beings, than a million of millions of
creatures, burthenſome to themſelves, and contemptible to each other.

It has been ſuggeſted to me, that the expoſing of
children has never been found to anſwer the purpoſe
of keeping down the principle of population ; and I
have been referred to Hume, Eſſays, Part ii, Eſſay
xi, where he ſays, " Perhaps, by an odd connection
of cauſes, the barbarous practice of the ancients
might rather render thoſe times more populous. By
removing the terrors of too numerous a family it
would engage many people in marriage; and ſuch
is the force of natural affection, that very few, in
compariſon, would have reſolution enough, when it
came to the puſh, to carry into execution their
former intentions. China, the only country where
this practice of expoſing children prevails at preſent,
is the moſt populous country we know of; and
every man is married before he is twenty. Such

F   early

early marriages could fcarcely be general, had not
men the profpect of fo eafy a method of getting rid
of their children."

I do not think there is any truth in thefe conclufions. They are in direct hoftility to the main
theory of the Effay on Population. According to
that theory population is always held clofely in check
by the meafures of fubfiftence, and nothing can caufe
a nation greatly to increafe in numbers, but a profpect
of an obvious and eafy enlargement of thofe meafures. Lycurgus limited the number of citizens in
his republic. Something of a fimilar nature took
place in Athens. If China, as late obfervers have
informed us, is, and has long been fo populous, that
every inch of ground is highly cultivated, and the
very furface of the rivers is covered with beds of
earth, and compelled to yield its contribution to the
ftock of fubfiftence, it is impoffible but that, in fuch
a country, population muft be at a ftand.

But, if the conclufions of Hume were as correct,
as they appear to me to be loofe and unfounded, the
remark would not be effential. It would ftill be
true that the expofing of children is in its own nature an expedient perfectly adequate to the end for
which it has been cited.

This was the expedient reforted to by the ancients
and the Chinefe as a check upon the principle of
population. Other expedients may be found in the
defcriptions and records of other parts of the world.
In the ifland of Ceylon for example, it appears to be

5   a part

a part of the common law of the country, that no woman shall be a mother before she is thirty, and they accordingly have their methods for procuring abortions, which, we are told, are perfectly innoxious. I do not love to enter into the minutiæ of these expedients. Those who are curious on the subject may refer to what travellers have related on this article.

I have not introduced these particulars, as seeming to me necessary to the solution of the difficulty proposed. It was just however to give a comprehensive, though compendious, view of the subject. This catalogue might be further enlarged.

It is right however that, in addition to these particulars, we should hypothetically take into the account, the resources of the human mind; the inventions and discoveries with which almost every period of literature and refinement is pregnant, rendering familiar and obvious to every understanding, what previously to such discoveries presumption and ignorance had pronounced to be impossible; and the vast multitude of such discoveries which may be expected, before we arrive at the chance of making experiment of a state of equality and universal benevolence. Were it not for the impression which the ingenuousness of this author and some of his readers has made upon me, I should certainly have pronounced, that a man must be strangely indifferent or averse to schemes of extraordinary improvement in society, who made this a conclusive argument against them,

F 2   that,

that, when they were realifed, they might peradventure be of no permanence and duration.

Let us however confider the cafe, fuch as in the
prefent ftate of political fcience we are able to make
it, and putting out of our view thofe harfh and dif-
pleafing remedies, which have no further recommendation than that they are better than mifery
and vice.

Many perfons with whom I have converfed, adverting on the one hand to the boundlefs power of
the principle of population, and on the other recol-
lecting that, in a ftate of continual advance in liberty and juftice, the period muft come, when public fafety would imperioufly require that the principle of increafe fhould be fufpended, have feen the
neceffary checks under a more frightful afpect, and
as more nearly and urgently preffing and hemming
us round, than is by any means the cafe. This error
may eafily be corrected.

Let us fuppofe that population was at this moment, in England or elfewhere, fo far advanced, that
the public welfare demanded that it fhould no further
increafe. Under thefe circumftances it is plain, that
every man and woman in the community might be
permitted to marry, and that every marriage might
be allowed to produce two children. This would
merely keep up the population to its prefent ftandard.
In reality more than this might be allowed. Of the
children born into the world in the moft favourable
circumftances, I believe not more than two out of
three

three may be expected to be reared to maturity. Every marriage then might be permitted to produce three children. But further than this. Every marriage is not found to be prolific. There will be natural defects on the side of the man, or on that of the woman. Again; every man and woman in the community will not marry. The prejudice which at present prevails against a single life, and the notion so generally received, that a man or woman without progeny, has failed in discharging one of their unquestionable duties to society, frightens many men and women into an inclination towards the marriage state. This prejudice the doctrines of the Essay on Population, when they shall come to be generally diffused and admitted, will tend to remove. Add to this, that every mind will not meet with its mate. Some men will not be gross enough to marry from mere appetite, and too delicate easily to believe that they have met with the woman, whose mind claims kindred and equality with theirs. If this subject were further pursued it would lead to many observations and details, curious and important in their own nature, but which would prove repulsive to the general reader, and would more properly find place in a treatise of medicine or animal economy. From these added particulars it appears, that the average of three children to every prolific marriage would not keep up the present state of population. I believe we might allow four. Hence it follows that, whatever becomes of the general question of checks, the case is not alto-

gether

gether fo alarming and tremendous, as by fome perfons it has been apprehended to be.

It is not neceffary to regard the calculation here
prefented as a rule to be laid down for the conduct of
the individual members of a happy community. I am
anfwering a book of calculation, and therefore muft
repel its doctrines by the fame means with which
they are inforced. All I propofe by the eftimate here
prefented is to fhow, that the evil is not fo urgent, nor
the limitation fo narrow, as a terrified imagination
might lead us to conceive.

The general doctrine of the Effay on Population
is fo clear, and refts on fuch irrefiftible evidence, that
this circumftance, together with its novel and unexpected tenour, is apt to hurry away the mind, and
take from us all power of expoftulation and diftinction. When however we have recovered from our
earlieft impreffion of aftonifhment, the firft thing
which is likely to ftrike every reflecting mind is, that
this excefs of power in the principle of population
over the principle of fubfiftence, has never in any paft
inftance, in any quarter or age of the world, produced thofe great and aftonifhing effects, that total
breaking up of all the ftructures and maxims of fociety, which the Effay leads us to expect from it in
certain cafes in future. Its operation has been filent,
graduated and unremarked; fo much fo, that no former political writer has touched upon it but by incident, and it was referved to the year of the Chriftian
era 1798 fully and adequately to call our attention

to

to its effects. Yet, as the author of the Eſſay on Population very properly remarks, this is no new caſe or remote ſpeculation. In all old-ſettled countries, the meaſure of population continually trenches on the meaſure of ſubſiſtence, and the actual quantity of proviſions falls ſomewhat ſhort of what would be neceſſary for the vigorous and comfortable ſupport of the inhabitants.

It is therefore well worthy of our attention to enquire, reſpecting ſuch a country as England, where, according to the majority of political calculators, population has long been at a ſtand, by what checks it is kept down within the limits it is found to obſerve.

One of the checks continually operating is, that great numbers of the children who are born in this country, are half deſtroyed by neglect and improper food, and that, after pining away a few weeks, or a year or two of exiſtence, they periſh miſerably without any chance of approaching maturity. The parents, in many claſſes of the community, ſcarcely able to maintain themſelves in life, if they provide food in ſufficient quantity for their children, can at leaſt pay no attention to its being properly adapted to their age or conſtitution. The married woman, whoſe only ſhelter is a hovel or a garret, if ſhe is unfortunate enough to be prolific, is ſo harraſſed by the continual labour which her circumſtances require of her, that her penury becomes viſible to every ſpectator in

F 4   the

the meagrenefs of her fhattered frame. She can pay no regularity of attention to the infants fhe brings into the world. They are dragged about by children a little older than themfelves, or thruft into fome neglected corner, unable to call, or to feek, for the fupply of their wants. They are bruifed, they are maimed, their bodies diftorted into horrible deformity, or their internal ftructure fuffering fome unfeen injury, which renders them miferable while they live, and ordinarily hurries them to an early grave. This is undoubtedly a fufficient check upon increafing population. But there is nothing in this which any political reafoner will recommend to imitation. This is probably the principal of thofe checks arifing from mifery and vice, which the writer of the treatife before us had in his contemplation.

Another check upon increafing population which operates very powerfully and extenfively in the country we inhabit, is that fentiment, whether virtue, prudence or pride, which continually reftrains the univerfality and frequent repetition of the marriage contract. Early marriages in this country between a grown up boy and girl are of uncommon occurrence. Every one, poffeffed in the moft ordinary degree of the gift of forefight, deliberates long before he engages in fo momentous a tranfaction. He afks himfelf again and again how he fhall be able to fubfift the offspring of his union. I am perfuaded it very rarely happens in England that a marriage takes place, without
this

this queftion having firft undergone a repeated examination. There is a very numerous clafs in every great town, clerks to merchants and lawyers, journeymen in fhops, and others, who either never marry, or refrain from marriage till they have rifen through the different gradations of their ftation to that degree of comparative opulence, which they think authorifes them to take upon themfelves the burthen of a family. It is needlefs to remark that, where marriage takes place at a later period of life, the progeny may be expected to be lefs numerous. If the check from virtue, prudence or pride operates lefs in the lower claffes of life than in the clafs laft defcribed, it is that the members of thofe claffes are rendered defperate by the oppreffion under which they groan ; they have no character of prudence or reflection to fupport, and they have nothing of that pride, arifing from what is called the decent and refpectable appearance a man makes among his neighbours, which fhould enable them to fupprefs the firft fallies of paffion, and the effervefcence of a warm conftitution.

Let us apply thefe remarks to that condition of fociety, which forms the only important queftion between me and the author of the Effay on Population, a condition of fociety in which a great degree of equality and an ardent fpirit of benevolence are affumed to prevail. We have found that, in the community in which we live, one of the great operative checks upon an increafing population arifes from virtue, prudence or pride. Will there be lefs of virtue,

tue, prudence and honourable pride in fuch a condition of fociety, than there is at prefent ? It is true, the ill confequences of a numerous family will not come fo coarfely home to each man's individual intereft, as they do at prefent. It is true, a man in fuch a ftate of fociety might fay, If my children cannot fubfift at my expence, let them fubfift at the expence of my neighbour. But it is not in the human character to reafon after this manner in fuch a fituation. The more men are raifed above poverty and a life of expedients, the more decency will prevail in their conduct, and fobriety in their fentiments. Where every one has a character, no one will be willing to diftinguifh himfelf by headftrong imprudence. Where a man poffeffes every reafonable means of pleafure and happinefs, he will not be in a hurry to deftroy his own tranquillity or that of others by thoughtlefs excefs.

Nor, in fuch a ftate of fociety as that which now employs our reafonings, will it be poffible for a man to fall into the error upon which we are commenting, from inadvertence. The doctrines of the Effay on Population, if they be true as I have no doubt that they are, will be fully underftood. Society will not fall into clans as at prefent, nor be puzzled and made intricate by the complexity of its ftructure. Such regularity and equity will prevail, as to enable every man to fee a vaft way before and around him. Every man will underftand the interefts of the community, and be mafter of the outline of its political ftate.

ftate. As fcarcely any man will have, or imagine he has, feparate interefts of his own, every man will be much influenced in his conduct by the interefts of the general. He will love his brethren. He will conceive of the whole fociety as one extenfive houf-hold. He will feel his own happinefs fo entirely dependent on the inftitutions which prevail, as will remove far from him all temptation to touch the ark with a facrilegious hand. He will not be able to live without character and the refpect of his neigh-bours, and no confideration on earth will induce him to forfeit them.

I do not imagine that I have here exhaufted the fubject which the author of the Effay on Population has led me to confider. I will not pretend that I have fo linked together my arguments, and in fuch manner fenced them againft uncertainty and exception, as to have made out an abfolute demon-ftration that we have nothing to fear, from that fource of ruin with which this writer menaces us. But I think, to fay the leaft, I have collected fuch ftrong prefumptions, as may well lead us to believe, that there is no imminent danger to be apprehended from that fide. I truft I have put down fuch hints of what muft be in the higheft degree gratifying to every lover of virtue and of man, as to convince the majority of impartial readers, that there is no fuch " obftacle in the way to any extraordinary im-provement in fociety," as fhould oblige us to fit down for ever under the whole mafs of exifting

moral

moral evils, and to deprecate every generous attempt
to improve the condition of mankind, as leading,
under specious appearances, to the reality of great
and intolerable mischief.

Let me conclude this review of the Essay on Population with a brief recollection of its principal
doctrines, so far as we have been concerned with
them. The basis of our author's work, the ratios
of population and subsistence, I regard as unassailable,
and as constituting a valuable acquisition to the
science of political economy. His conclusions from
these premises are, that vice and misery are the only
sufficient checks upon increasing population, and
that there is an obstacle of such a nature in the way
to any extraordinary improvement in society, as we
can never entertain the hope to overcome. I do not
regard these conclusions with any complacency. It
is not, I hope, a taste absolutely singular in me, that
I entertain no vehement partialities for vice and
misery, and that I view the prospect of extraordinary
improvement in society, of some kind or other, to
take place hereafter, with pleasure and affection. I
do not think the conclusions of our author powerfully connected with his premises. If I look to
the past history of the world, I do not see that increasing population has produced such convulsions
as he predicts from it, or that vice and misery alone
have controled and confined it; and, if I look to
the future, I cannot so despair of the virtues of man
to submit to the most obvious rules of prudence, or

of the faculties of man to ftrike out remedies as yet
unknown, as to convince me that we ought to fit
down for ever contented with all the oppreffion,
abufes and inequality, which we now find faftened
on the necks, and withering the hearts, of fo great
a portion of our fpecies.

In thefe fheets, among other topics, I have
thought proper to develop the perfonalities which
have been directed againft me, and the treatment I
have endured. But I am fully aware that there is
nothing fingular in my cafe. It is part of a great
plan. It is on this account the more fitting in me
to have called the public attention to it. The
maxims, upon the difcovery and eftablifhment of
which our fathers of the laft century prided themfelves, are reverfed. Difcuffion is no longer regarded as one of the great fources of benefit to man.
The principle and practice of toleration among us
hang by a very flender thread. All declamation, and
all licenfed argument, muft be on one fide. The
queftions now propofed to a reafoner, are not, Do
you argue well? Are the principles on which your
theory refts found? Do your premifes fufficiently
fuftain and make out your conclufions? But, Are your
arguments caft in the mould of Ariftotle, Bacon and
Hooker, of Grotius, Puffendorff and Vattel?

This proceeding undoubtedly comes with fufficient grace from the adverfaries of the progreffive
nature of man. By placing a barrier againft difcuffion, and by branding with abhorrence and obloquy

loquy thofe who have not fworn themfelves in at any
fchool or under any mafter, they, to the beft of
their power, fufpend the improvement of human intellect. He cannot vigoroufly underftand or explain any
fyftem, who has not allowed himfelf with an unbiaffed
mind to inveftigate one fyftem and another. He
cannot truly and firmly be convinced of the truth
of any doctrine, who has not dared intrepidly to
analyfe its evidence. The man who enters the
fchool of fcience, pre-determined and pre-engaged
as to the conclufions in which his enquiries muft terminate, makes a mock at fcience, and tramples upon
the divinity of the human mind. As the parties
now ftand arranged, the advocates of the progreffive
nature of man are the champions of refinement and
cultivation and politenefs, which their adverfaries
would without mitigation or remorfe exchange for
the favage ftate.

Let it be granted (in the way of argument), that
the French revolution has been prolific of mifchief
to mankind. Let it be further granted, that it was
enquiry, and difcuffion, and the undaunted affertion
and pleading for all opinions without referve, which
afforded the occafion and the means to thefe evils.
May it not yet be worth our while to enquire,
whether the difcuffion might not be permitted, and
the mifchiefs which in this inftance have been grafted
on it, prevented? whether men might not be permitted to difpute in their fchools, and in theoretical
and fcientific difquifition, without being allowed to
fally

fally forth with firebrands in their hands, and devaftation and ruin in their intentions? It is a ferious
thing to fay, that men muft neither argue nor write,
till they have firft fubdued the free-born nature of
their fouls to the trammels of fome fortunate and
highly patronifed creed, which is to be received as
orthodox. If the nature of man is not altogether fo
progreffive, fo full of profpect and promife, as I,
and thofe who think with me, have imagined; is it
quite certain we can never get beyond what Grotius
and Puffendorff, or even Ariftotle and Bacon have
digefted to our hands? At prefent it is only attempted to deter men from rebellion againft thefe
great literary authorities, by obloquy and abufe, by
the contempt of the authorifed inftructor and his
followers, and by an ill-will and animofity to be
generated and diffufed through as wide a circle as
poffible. I believe there is fomewhat in the nature
of man, and of his attainments already realifed, ftrong
enough to baffle the prefent deep-laid project of defpotifm and intolerance. But, if they are not thus
checked, I am perfuaded that the contempt, the fcurrilities and the obloquy which are now circulated,
will fpeedily be exchanged for thofe more formidable adverfaries of difcuffion, imprifonment and
pillory, banifhment, and what its promulgators will
denominate an ignominious, death. No one, acquainted with the nature of man, can fail to perceive by how eafy a gradation one of thefe leads to
the other, and that, when you have fuccefsfully held

up

up a perfon for years to general derifion and abhorrence, you rather comply with, than outrun, the fentiments of mankind, by dooming him to deftruction.

I would not have given myfelf the trouble
of throwing together thefe few obfervations, were it
not the general purpofe of my adverfaries to undermine a great public intereft, through the medium of
the errors and abfurdities they have fo liberally imputed to me. In the commencement of thefe pages,
I have allowed myfelf to fpeak a little perfonally of
my own fituation, and the injuftice I have experienced; and, after the immenfe volume of abufe,
ludicrous and grave, which for years has been poured
out againft me, this departure from the great queftion we are examining (if it be indeed a departure) will be forgiven to me by the good-
natured reader. But I am nothing, in comparifon of the important caufe the Political Juftice was
intended to plead. A queftion indeed of higher
magnitude was never brought before the tribunal of
the public. In this view, and confidering the fo-
lemnity of the tafk I had undertaken, I am willing,
if Dr. Parr pleafes, to be the victim of " contrition," and to take fhame to myfelf for all the overfights committed by me in that book, and which
have been fo eagerly feized, and fo emuloufly taken
advantage of, by my opponents. The queftion at
iffue is whether " any extraordinary improvement
can ever be expected to take place in fociety." The
human imagination is capable of reprefenting to
itfelf

itfelf a virtuous community, a little heaven on earth. The human underftanding is capable of developing the bright idea, and conftructing a model of it, where " every thing fhall be confiftent; where, granting its firft pofition, a pofition which has every prepoffeffion in its favour, all the inferences fhall follow fo clearly, that it feems impoffible to elude their force." Shall this idea ever be realifed; or, do we " walk in a vain fhow, and difquiet ourfelves in vain?" Are vice and mifery, as my antagonifts fo earneftly maintain, in all their extent, and with all their difguftful circumftances as they now exift in the world, entailed on us for ever; or may we hope ultimately to throw off, or greatly diminifh, the burthen? In other cafes of an eminent nature, what the heart of man is able to conceive, the hand of man is ftrong enough to perform. There is no beauty of literary and poetical compofition which we can fo much as guefs at, that excels what we find executed in the divineft paffages of Milton or Shakefpear. There is no virtuous action which we can figure to ourfelves, that furpaffes that virtue and elevation of mind which we find over and over again recorded in the faithful page of hiftory. Fiction here labours in vain ; it never equals what men have acted and felt, in the great vifion and awe-creating prefence of reality. Imagination only treads the round of man; and, whatever myfterious being we may reverence without comprehending him, every individual image of excellence which we are

G   capable

capable of vividly and impreffively reprefenting to ourfelves, we may fafely claim as the lawful endowment and birthright of our nature. Let us then learn to refpect man, and to be proud of ourfelves that we belong to a fpecies capable of fo high atchievements. Let us not, from the vain faftidioufnefs of mifanthropy, be led to blafpheme againft the caufe of virtue. For myfelf I firmly believe that days of greater virtue and more ample juftice will defcend upon the earth; and in the mean time, I will not hold it for my confolation and luxury, fondly to imagine that the throne of ignorance and vice is placed on fo firm a bafis that it can never be removed.

THE END.

WILKS and TAYLOR ⎱
Printers, Chancery-lane. ⎰

To the Editor of the Monthly Magazine.

SIR, *Nov.* 10, 1801.

I FIND that a mifreprefentation of *Mr. Godwin's Reply to Dr. Parr,* has crept into your laft month's Magazine. I therefore requeft your immediate infertion of the following letter from that gentleman, addreffed to a friend, which feems, to me, to contain the only proper anfwer that can be given to fuch afperfions.

"DEAR SIR, *Aug.* 29, 1801.

"I thank you moft fincerely for the kindnefs of your letter. Human creatures living in the circle of their intimates and friends are too apt to remain in ignorance of the comments and conftructions which may be made of what they fay and do, in the world at large. I entertain a great horror of this ignorance. I do not love to be deceived, and to fpend my days in a fcene of delufions and chimera. I feel it as an act of unequivocal friendfhip, that you have communicated to me a fact in which I muft hold myfelf interefted, though you deemed the communication to be ungracious.

" Good God! and so you heard me gravely represented in a large company yesterday, as an advocate of infanticide! I have been so much accustomed to be the object of misrepresentation in all its forms, that I did not think I could be surprised with any thing of that sort. The advocates of those abuses and that oppression against which I have declared myself, have chosen it as their favourite revenge to distort every word I have ever written, and every proposition I have ever maintained. But there is a malignity in this accusation, which, I confess, exceeds all my former calculations of human perverseness.

" They build the accusation, it seems, upon a few pages in my Reply to Dr. Parr, &c. where I am considering the hypotheses of the author of the Essay on Population. They eagerly confound two things so utterly dissimilar, as hypothetical reasoning upon a state of society never yet realised, and the sentiments and feelings which I, and every one whom it is possible for me to love or respect, must carry with us into the society and the transactions in which we are personally engaged. Because I have spoken of a certain practice prevailing in distant ages and countries, which I deprecate, and respecting which I aver my persuasion, that in no improved state of society will it ever be necessary to have recourse to it, they represent me as the recommender and admirer of this practice, as a man who is eager to perfuade every woman who, under unfortunate and opprobious circumftances, becomes a mother, to be the murderer of her own child.

"Really, my friend, I am fomewhat at a lofs whether to laugh at the impudence of this accufation, or to be indignant at the brutal atrocity and outrageous fentiment of perfecution it argues in the man who uttered it. I fee that there is a fettled and fyftematical plan in certain perfons, to render me an object of averfion and horror to my fellow-men : they think that when they have done this, they will have fufficiently overthrown my arguments. Their project excites in me no terror. As the attack is a perfonal one, it is only by a retrofpect to my individual felf that it can be anfwered.

"My character is fufficiently known to you and the friends in whofe habitual intercourfe I live. Am I a man likely to be inattentive to the feelings, the pleafures, or the interefts of thofe about me ? Do I dwell in that fublime and impaffive fphere of philofophy, that fhould teach me to look down with contempt on the little individual concerns of the meaneft creature I behold ? To come immediately to the point in queftion, am I, or am I not, a lover of children ? My own domeftic fcene is planned and conducted folely with a view to the improvement and gratification of children. Does my character, as a father, merit reprehensions? Are not my children my favourite companions and most chosen friends?

In this sense the charge is too ridiculous. How can such men as the calumniator you describe, be confident or weak enough to flatter themselves that, by their obscure and reptile efforts, they can change the character of a man in the apprehension of his contemporaries, into the reverse of all that it is? What man of a sober and decent mind will credit such accusations, without first endeavouring to seek out the truth? What man of a sober and decent mind, having, in the slightest degree, investigated my temper and habits, will suffer so execrable a supposition, as that I should be the advocate of an unnatural disposition, the inciter and persuader of acts of horrible enormity, to pass unbranded by his condemnation? Let then these men go on in their despicable task of misrepresentation and calumny.—Let them endeavour to exhibit me as the advocate of every thing cruel, assassinating and inhuman. You and I, my friend, I firmly persuade myself, shall live to see whether their malignant artifices, or the simple and unalterable truth, shall prove triumphant.

LETTERS

OF

VERAX,

TO

The Editor of The Morning Chronicle,

ON

THE QUESTION OF A WAR TO BE COMMENCED
FOR THE PURPOSE OF PUTTING AN END
TO THE POSSESSION OF THE SU-
PREME POWER IN FRANCE BY
NAPOLEON BONAPARTE.

———

By WILLIAM GODWIN.

———

LONDON:

PRINTED BY RICHARD AND ARTHUR TAYLOR,

SHOE-LANE.

———

1815.

PREFACE.

—————

I HAVE always considered myself as a citizen of the great commonwealths of England and mankind, and have believed that it was my duty to offer my contribution from time to time, for the benefit of the generation of men among which I live. As I have spent a great portion of my days in retirement, the pen was the means with which I could principally hope to effect any thing for the welfare of others. I am now drawing toward the close of human existence. I can foresee the time, when I shall be no longer a spectator, or a party, however small, to this mortal scene; but I cannot foresee the termination of the war which seems now ready to burst upon us. It will not improbably last longer than I shall; and that is a consideration that gives it a peculiar solemnity to my mind,

No occasion of so great magnitude to the interests of human nature and the civilized world, will perhaps occur again during the short remainder of my life; and I felt as if I ought not to close the book of my little annals, without pouring out the sentiments with which my heart is at this moment full.

LETTERS

TO

THE EDITOR

OF

𝔗𝔥𝔢 𝔐𝔬𝔯𝔫𝔦𝔫𝔤 𝔠𝔥𝔯𝔬𝔫𝔦𝔠𝔩𝔢,

LETTER I.

MR. EDITOR,

I HAVE lived long enough to see my country four times involved in the miseries, the prodigality, and the guilt of war. I am scarcely sixty years of age, and of that period thirty-six years have been passed by my country in a belligerent state. To men considerably younger than myself the case is more striking, and the proportion of years of war to years of peace still greater. I would not be understood from this statement to argue in favour of a pusillanimous temper; but I would be understood to argue in favour of deliberation, and that, when we have brought on ourselves and mankind mischiefs incalculable, we should not at last be re-

B

duced to Christ's intercession for his murderers—
" Father, forgive them, they know not what they
do !"

I am aware that some of your readers will be
disposed to stop me in the outset, and to say, War
is already resolved, and deliberation is vain; we
are engaged with our Allies ; there would be neither
honour nor safety in deserting them ; and they
have signed a Treaty for the destruction of Bonaparte.

I will not enter into that objection in this place.
For the present I will concede the point they
claim, and say, Be it so ! Yet it is well we should
understand the nature of the act in which we are
engaged, whether it be the conspiracy of a gang of
robbers, of men who undertook, like Brutus, an
unhallowed act for the salvation of their country,
or of men like Junius Brutus, his predecessor, who
gave birth to the most glorious series of years that
almost any where illustrates the annals of mankind.
I would say to my countrymen, Unsheath your
swords!

> Fight, Gentlemen of England ! fight, bold Yeomen !
> Spur your proud coursers hard, and ride in blood !

But yet consider that you are beings endowed with
a rational nature ; yet let me expostulate with you
the true character of the business in which you are

committed ; do not resolve to be blind, because
you are fierce ; and then act with all the energy you
are able, and extricate yourselves as you can from
the miserable dilemma in which you are plunged.

It is true indeed, that we arc in some sort engaged, engaged with a precipitance to which it
would be difficult to find a parallel in the history
of the civilised world ; first, by the Declaration,
signed by the Ministers of the different powers who
happened to be at Vienna on the 13th of March,
the moment they heard that Bonaparte was landed
in France, which contains, among others, the unhallowed expressions, that he "has placed himself
" without the pale of civil and social relations, and
" destroyed the only legal title upon which his exist-
" ence depends." In signing this Declaration, the
Ministers disdained to wait for instructions from
their respective Courts ; the question was too trivial
to need the ordinary forms of diplomacy ; and they
cared not to enquire or reflect whether Bonaparte
had landed merely like a desperate man, as a chief
of banditti, or, as immediately after appeared to
be the case, he came invited, and was at that moment virtually the head of the most powerful nation in the world. The second step by which we
are thus entangled, is the Treaty of Vienna signed
twelve days after, founded on the above precipitate
Declaration, and concluded, as Lord Liverpool

well observed in debate, before the parties yet knew of Bonaparte's triumphant entry into Paris, and that Louis the Eighteenth, instead of being able to retain his position in the capital, could not keep possession of one foot of his dominions. Of all follies those of Courts and Ministers are the greatest. If Guicciardini were alive now, he would cease to search in the subtleties of political logic for the springs of public affairs, and would look only into the frensy of the passions. An ordinary tradesman, before he engages in an enterprise, is obliged to calculate whether he shall be able to meet the cost; but these plenipotentiaries, in an affair in which the existence of Europe, as it is, is committed, dismiss all forecast, and refuse to enquire how things now are, or in what they promise to terminate. The whole is a plunge in the dark, that bids defiance to credibility.

I proceed to consider the true character of the deed upon which we are entering. It is a first principle in the law of nations, that no state or confederacy of states has a right to interfere in the internal government of another state. How does the Government of Great Britain endeavour to evade the force of this law in the present instance? By a Memorandum, that " the contracting parties to the " Treaty of Vienna are bound to a common effort " against the power of Napoleon Bonaparte, but that

" they are not bound to prosecute the war with a view " of imposing upon France any particular govern- " ment." It is true, " the Contracting Parties" forgot this in digesting the heads of the Treaty; but the Prince Regent of England knows their mind on the point, and has undertaken to explain it for them; and it must be confessed that Napoleon Bonaparte makes a most conspicuous figure both in the Declaration of March the 13th and the Treaty, while his most Christian Majesty is barely mentioned by the bye.

But how does this soften the breach of public law which it is intended to heal? On the contrary, I affirm it is a refinement, rendering the interference of foreign powers in the internal affairs of a nation ten thousand times more odious and intolerable than if it had been brought forward in any other form. The Contracting Parties might have issued a Declaration, stating, beside the hereditary, indefeasible right of the Bourbons, that they are the choice of the whole French nation, that they have been expelled by an insignificant faction with arms in their hands, and that the Allies accordingly march to rescue thirty millions of men from an ignominious yoke, and to preserve them from being dragooned by a military despotism into subjection to a tyrant who is detestable in their eyes : and such a Declaration, though containing many falsehoods, would be less contrary to rule, and would undoubtedly be infinitely less insulting, than that which the Memorandum of the Prince Regent announces. Suppose Louis the Fourteenth, at the time of the English Revolution, had said to our ancestors—Choose any Government you please; I do not pretend to impose James the Second and his son upon you; but I forbid you to confer the crown on King William, the inexorable adversary to my views of universal empire;—What would have been the feelings of Englishmen on that memorable occasion?

A general proposition interfering with the affairs of another, must at all times be much less galling and repulsive to a noble spirit, than when it is pointed at one individual proceeding, action, or man. This barbs the arrow, and dips its point in the most corroding poison. The language of the supposed declaration is—" Frenchmen, your de-" cisions and your acts are free as air; we allow it;" we sanction it; there is only one act that you " shall not do; one man that you shall not choose." Good God! how must the heart of every generous and independent being swell against such a mandate!

Why is this man selected as the individual they may not choose? The selection is not made at random the name is not brought forward because the person is indifferent. He is named, because the Allies find the greatest reason to fear that he will be the man of their choice, and that a large majority of the French people are eager to adhere to him. Never did a sovereign ascend the throne of any nation under such astonishing evidences of general favour, as Bonaparte has just now ascended the throne of France. The Allies therefore say to the French people, Take any course you please, we promise not to interfere; only there is one course upon which your hearts appear to be bent, and that we interdict you.

Is it possible that such a Declaration should not render Bonaparte infinitely more dear to the people of France, than he ever could be before? Does it not shew them their honour as bound up with him, and their independence and character as a nation as invaded by a pretended attack upon him? Does it not shew them that they have but one path left to preserve themselves from being struck out of the roll of Sovereign nations, and that is by making common cause with the man whom the Allies so brutally proscribe?

But let us turn from the consideration of the alleged principle of the war, as applying to the law of nations, and examine it in a moral view, in that view in which it must necessarily be seen by rational and accountable agents, who had never heard of the technicalities of law. The first impulse of moral wisdom is, when we are about to touch the beginning of a chain consisting of innumerable links, what sort of consequences are we likely, by so doing, to pull down upon the heads of those who have no part in the act, but must abide the awful results?

By the Memorandum of the Prince Regent, the French nation is called upon, and by the supposed Declaration of the Allies they will be called upon, " to judge for themselves, and to choose what " Government they please, but to throw off sub- " jection to Bonaparte."—Will the Allies condescend to explain how this is to be done? Or, are they too much wrapped up in their imaginary elevation, to deign to think of the practicability of executing their despotic mandates? Is the existing Government of a nation so literally a spider's web, as such a Declaration ought, by just inference, to imply?—Oh, that it were indeed so! Then would there be no such thing as tyranny and despotism existing on the face of the earth! then would the generous successors of Brutus and Cassius, Cremutius Cordus, Thrasea Pœtus, and their friends, have shaken off the yoke of the Roman Emperors, and such names as Tiberius, Caligula, and Nero, would never have stained the page of history.

Bonaparte is at this moment in full possession of

the powers of Government in France; and the
Allies, with a sober face, and an indifferent temper,
call upon the nation to renounce their subjection to
him, upon pain of being visited in their fields and
their hearths with the bitterest and the worst calamities of war. Is it possible in the compass of human imagination to conceive any thing more barbarous and insulting than this? Again I ask, and I
call upon our Legislators who are this day to pronounce their vote of war against France*, to consider, how this is to be done? A nation is an artificial
individual, the creature of the reasoning faculty
merely. The inhabitants of France are in reality
thirty millions of souls, scattered over a wide extent of territory, acquainted only in small knots
and circles with each other's faces, and still less
acquainted with each other's judgments and inmost
desires. Every step then to be taken, is a step in
the dark; every step is beset with the pains and
penalties of treason. Each man is to communicate with his neighbour, with his township, with
his department, to learn whether they are disposed, or to incline them to be disposed, to
shake off the dominion of their present Go-

* This Letter was intended to appear in the Morning Chronicle on May 23; it did appear on May 25: the War was
voted in the House of Lords on the former, and in the House
of Commons on the latter of these days.

vernment. The inhabitants of London, and the people of England, were nearly unanimous, a short time ago, for the rejection of the Corn Law. Could they, for that, effect their purpose? No—the two Houses of Parliament and the Constituent Members of the Government were organized, and the sense of the nation had no organ by which it could be brought into act. The people of England, if it could now be put to the vote, would renounce the present commencement of war: but shall we for that be freed from its guilt, and obtain the blessings and the virtues of peace? We are told by the Ministers in both Houses of Parliament, that the armies of France, numerous and warlike as they are, are the supporters of Bonaparte; and yet they have the effrontery to call upon the nation to shake off their subjection to him, or expect the most exemplary sufferings. Well might the people of France reply—Visit us with all the evils you threaten, desolate our fields, violate our wives, massacre our children, but do not insult us in the midst of these miseries, by calling upon us to avoid them by doing that which it is impossible for us to do!

Oh, but, say the Allies, we do not thus leave you forlorn in your miserable state; our generous bands are collecting from every country of Europe, and will shortly be in the midst of you, to help you in this honourable task of choosing a Government for yourselves. Then shall the fetters of Bonaparte fall from your hands; and, free as air, you shall deliberate what Government you shall choose, whether a Monarchy, or a Republic, or a mixture of both. You shall not be deserted in your present calamity; all we call upon you for is, to prepare yourselves for the blessings of our visitation; form yourselves into knots and cabals; try secretly to gather a strength that may overcome the power that now reigns over you; spread anarchy and confusion from one end of your fertile land to the other; and then, in the midst of plots, and cabals, and conspiracies, and treasons, our Hulans and Cossacks shall pour down upon you; and under their humane auspices you shall choose a Government, the wisest, the noblest, and the most beneficent the world ever saw.

But the Allies know very well, that what they demand from the people of France, as the alternative to escape from their generous invasion, is impossible to be performed, and therefore they consider war as a thing absolutely decided on. We will not now examine what will be the consequence if they should be defeated; but we will recur to what will be the results if they should succeed, and by that means undertake to prove that the prayer of every friend to man must be for their miscarriage. To simplify this view of the subject, I will suppose the Allies to have already made their triumphal entry into Paris.

I will own that I was one of those persons who felt proud of the scenes that passed upon that theatre in the Spring of the former year. Though a friend to freedom, I was contented with the Restoration of the Bourbons. I was sufficiently disgusted with the character of Bonaparte, as it had been displayed up to his exile to Elba; how far his character or his circumstances are altered now, I do not precisely know; but I could have been well satisfied that things had remained as they were settled in 1814. I was delighted with the spectacle of victorious Monarchs yielding their homage to a people's choice, witnessing the assembly of the national representatives, and patiently waiting till they had pronounced, " Upon the ac- " ceptance of certain conditions favourable to gene- " ral freedom, the Bourbons shall be restored." I was delighted with the spectacle of a revolution flowing from so formidable a source, which yet was effected with such admirable tranquillity; no man disturbed in his possessions, no drop of blood shed on the scaffold, even the master-offender spared, and treated with moderation and liberality.

But I suppose no man is so deluded as to imagine that the second entry of the Allies into Paris will be like the first. The Allies have seen in one, instance how frail was the duration of that system, which with so much gentleness they established; and the first object of their deliberation will be, what securities they are to take for the permanence of the system they are now to set up. They have already repented of their humanity. They have pronounced that Bonaparte has forfeited " his " legal title to existence." His blood must therefore be shed. But he will not fall alone. If the security of the new system for France is to be effected by executions, multitudes must fall on the scaffold; and according to the letter of the first inaccurate translation of the Treaty of Vienna, the Allies will undertake to " bring to justice all such " as may have already joined, or shall hereafter " join, the party of Napoleon." All such more especially, will be construed his partisans, who conceived that he might be made the instrument of establishing on an immoveable basis the cause of freedom. All officers who shall serve in his army, all members of his legislature, all persons who shall officiate under him in the administration of justice, will be brought to the bar, to save their lives if they can, by proving that their obedience was not voluntary. What a tremendous state must that people be in, who cannot be protected in obeying a King *de facto,* and conforming themselves to a Government, which they cannot resist but under pain of immediate destruction! The Allies have already repented of their respect for property. They are convinced that no radical change can be made, and the people brought back to their old Sovereigns, without a change in this article, and the property being substantially vested in the staunch friends of the race of their Kings. I have been told that five-sixths of the landed property of France has changed hands in consequence of the successive events of the Revolution. We may conceive therefore what havock must be made, in order to obtain this species of security for the Government that is to be established.

The Allies have already repented of their respect for freedom. France, which is, all things considered, the most important country in Europe, must be prostrated and trampled in the dust, to effect the security which the Allies contemplate. All shadow of representation and a national voice must be taken away. France must be garrisoned with foreign armies. She must be committed to wardship; and the Austrians, and the Prussians, and the Russians must be made her guardians. France must be partitioned : less than this can never satisfy the vigilance and the jealousies of Allies who have so dearly repented of their liberality. France is too powerful for their fears; and nothing less than this can make them secure that she shall never hereafter recover her independence. In a word, France must be annihilated. The name will remain to adorn the page of history; but if the Allies obtain their will of her, she will never hereafter be a member of the commonwealth of Europe.

The pen drops from my hand. Oh that I had a warning voice, to make the people of England, the conscientious and reflecting part of this great community, consider the nature of the act to which they are about to be committed! War on the present occasion would then be impossible. The war at this moment proposed, has but one parent, Talleyrand, the most unprincipled, the most perfidious, and the most venal Statesman I am able to name. Urged by his coward fears, the moment he heard that Bonaparte was landed in France, he drew up the memorable paper by which this astonishing man was declared to be " without the pale of civil " and social relations," and to have forfeited " the " only legal title on which his existence depended;" and this crafty diplomatist drew in the honourable, but unsuspecting Wellington, to blemish his name for ever by setting his hand to this paper. Twelve days afterward he consummated his atrocity, by the signature of the Treaty of Vienna, by which the Allies engage " not to lay down their arms, until

" Bonaparte shall have been rendered absolutely
" unable to create disturbance, or to attempt the
" possession of the supreme power in France."

The war that is meditated differs from all other
wars in the history of the civilised world, by the
perfidious irony with which it addresses the people
against whom it is to be directed, and the crime it
proposes to perpetrate, the entire destruction as a
nation, of one of the most eminent nations on the
face of the whole earth. It differs from all wars
in the profligate principle which it takes for its
basis, and which is unblushingly avowed—that the
sword shall never again be sheathed, till the Government, now in full operation, and presiding
over the enemy, shall cease to exist.

I have confined myself in this letter to consider
what will be the consequences, if the war that is
threatened shall be absolutely commenced, and if
the Allies shall succeed in their purposes; and I
have restrained my pen to one single train of reasoning, in the hope by that means to render so
awful an expostulation the more impressive. There
are several other views of the subject that offer
themselves, and particularly what may be the result if the Allies should fail in obtaining their object, upon which I may possibly be induced to
treat on some future occasion.

VERAX.

LETTER II.

Mr. Editor,

In my former letter I expressly treated of the question, What will be the result of the war about to be commenced, in case the Allies succeed in accomplishing their purposes? This ought always to be the first point of view in any discussion respecting human actions. In every deliberate act, we propose to ourselves a certain object; and we are bound seriously to consider whether that object, with its inseparable concomitants, is such, as in justice, in sound policy, and in humanity, we ought to choose. The second question, which I propose to treat in this letter, is, What will be the consequence if we fail? It is not enough in any moral consideration, that the object we propose to ourselves is good and desirable (though that is far otherwise on the present occasion); it is also necessary that we should take into our view those consequences of our determination, which do not enter into the motives of our choosing, which may often be the very reverse of our desires, but which may be the real, nay, perhaps the most probable, results of our interference.

c

Let us indeed pause for a moment, and consider what are the chances of success. To the probability of success a good cause is necessary. This was never more strikingly illustrated than in the history of recent events. While the French fought, in the beginning of their Revolution, to preserve their independence against a combination of Sovereigns, who said, " France shall not be free ; France shall " not have a government which we fear will prove " an ill example to our own subjects,"—the feeling of the cause enabled her to overcome every obstacle, and rendered her irresistible in the contest. After a lapse of years, the goodness of the cause changed sides, France was listed under the banners of an insatiable ambition, and the armies of the Allies contended against incroachments that knew no bounds, and that threatened to subject the independence of all other nations to the domineering spirit of one unbridled individual. The Allies fought from the same sacred impulse that had before animated the French, and their success was no less complete.

Now what is the cause and principle of the war about to be commenced ? " Bonaparte has " broken the Treaty ; Bonaparte is a man with " whom no faith can be kept ; Bonaparte is a " creature of unconquerable ambition, and no peace " can be concluded with France, till he shall cease

" to possess the supreme authority in that
" country."

" Bonaparte has broken the Treaty, and there-
" fore we are at war with him. He agreed to ab-
" dicate the throne of France, and to retire to
" Elba; and he has now in defiance of his engage-
" ments returned to France, and reascended the
" throne." That here is a Treaty broken is past
all doubt; but it is reasonable to enquire, before
we proceed to extremities on this breach, to which
party the guilt belongs. I will not insist upon those
breaches of the Treaty which consisted in not pay-
ing to Bonaparte his stipulated income, and in with-
holding from his wife and son the principalities in
Italy, which by the Treaty were assigned them.
These, we are told, were subjects for negociation
and remonstrance. I well know what sort of negociations they were likely to be, between this memorable exile and the Allied Sovereigns, and with
what attention his remonstrances would have been
received. But I will take the simple fact of the
purposed compulsory removal of Bonaparte from
the island to which he had been exiled. Earl Ba-
thurst tells us in the debate of 22 May, " Whether
" any design existed to remove him is another ques-
" tion ; but certainly no demonstration of such an
" intention had been given." Is it possible to conceive a greater insult to the common sense of man-

kind than this statement? "A design existed to re-
" move him;" *that is not denied.* But no overt
steps were taken for that purpose; the removal
was not effected. Bonaparte should have waited
for that; if he had been actually taken and shut
up for life in some strong castle, or exiled to Sibe-
ria, he would then have had a right to complain;
if from thence he had reascended the throne of
France, we could not have charged him with the
infraction of a Treaty. No; an unprofitable right
it is a mockery to confer on a man. If a compulsory removal would have conferred on him a right
which would then have been useless, he had a right
to anticipate that event; and it is an execrable sophistry to call upon him, as in the ordinary courts
of justice, to make out his case, and establish his
fact by evidence within the rules. It is enough, if
we affirm that a design existed to take him from his
retreat; and that no state and no minister of the
Allies has yet had the audacity to deny it.

" But we go to war with him, because he is not
" to be trusted, because on various occasions he
" has shown himself sufficiently disposed to break
" his engagements, and violate his plighted faith."
Alas, if this is an adequate ground of war, Europe, it is to be feared, will know no peace for ages
to come. Who is there so little read in history, as
not to know, that interest, and not fidelity to en-

gagements, is the ruling principle in all governments in their conduct towards each other? Since
treaties and engagements between nation and nation have been so common, no war has ever commenced between independent states, without a violation of plighted faith on one side. They then
fight till one or both finds it ruinous or impracticable to contend any longer; and afterwards they
enter into engagements, to be observed for a time,
to afford to the defeated party a respite enabling
it to renew its strength, and when circumstances
alter, then the engagement to be treated as out of
date, and a state of peace to be changed for a state
of war. This above all is the history of modern
Europe; no treaty is made, without a clear fore-
sight in all but children and fools, that it is sooner
or later to be broken. Nations do not defend their
going to war with each other, from the existence
on either part of immoral dispositions that may
lead to mischief; but because actual incroachment
has been made, or in the mildest statement, that
incroachment has been so clearly prepared, as to
oblige the other party in prudence to anticipate the
blow.

" We go to war with Bonaparte," we are told,
" because we see something in his dispositions that
" we by no means approve." Was ever such a
cause of war heard of? Was ever the morality

subsisting between nations sunk to so low an ebb? Was ever war, with all its countless calamities, treated with such insufferable levity, as a thing respecting which it was scarcely of any moment, whether we chose that or its opposite? Doubtless the dispositions of Louis the Fourteenth were one of the impelling motives of the hostilities against him; and our ancestors in the close of the seventeenth and commencement of the eighteenth centuries, had not a sufficient repugnance to a state of war: but they did not say as we do: "We view " with alarm the persisting ambition of Louis, and " we will not sheathe our swords so long as he re- " mains on the throne."

It is a bitter aggravation of our present calamities, when we recollect that in the spring of 1814, it almost depended upon the turn of a feather, whether peace should be made with Bonaparte or with the Bourbons. On the 1st of December 1813, the Allies issued a Declaration at Frankfort, in which they assert, that the " first use they have " made of their victories has been to offer peace " to the Emperor of the French, that they desire " that France may be great, powerful, and happy, " and that they are ready to *confirm to the French* " *Empire an extent of territory that France un-* " *der her Kings never knew.*" What indications has Bonaparte given since the 1st of December

1813, of a spirit of incroachment, that renders the individual to whom they were willing then to concede so great an extent of territory, now incapable of all political relations? The negociations continued between him and the Allies up to the 22d of March, nine days before they entered Paris. We do not perhaps exactly know what were the terms that Bonaparte that day rejected; but there can be no doubt they were terms which would have left him in quiet possession of the throne of France; and it was his obstinacy only, and persisting confidence in the ascendancy of his fortune, that defeated these negociations. Shall we draw the sword now in rejection of those terms, in contemplation of which we were then willing to sheathe it? It is said, in the preamble to the Treaty of Paris, signed May 30, 1814, that the Allies no longer found it necessary to " exact from the " Bourbons conditions and guarantees, which they " with regret demanded from France under the " government of Bonaparte." I dare not insinuate against the Confederated Sovereigns that this was true on the 1st of December 1813, in the face of their Declaration at Frankfort. But be it so, that it was true a few weeks later. This immediately affords us a subject of negociation. Let us propose our conditions. If they are reasonable, and are rejected, that will unquestionably give us a right to have recourse to the sword. Oh, for a legitimate cause of war, that will not arm every reflecting and deep-reaching mind, that will not arm all posterity, and every Frenchman against us! Let us go to war for some motive that we can avow, and not for a principle [that it is to be feared the enemy may not prove in all cases faithful to his engagements], which if generally acted upon, would immediately put every government, now existing in Europe, out of the pale of the law of nations!

It is in vain, therefore, that ministers and their abettors endeavour to film over the present question with the webs and meshes of a plausible sophistry. Oh, that men in office and public men should be so hardened, as to endure the thought that those quibbles and vicious syllogisms that are tolerated in some insignificant question of an assault or trespass in our courts of law, should be applied in an enquiry, where the well-being of all mankind, and the safety of generations to come, are at stake! The common sense of the human species in this case rises against them. They know that the French nation contends, because she will not be controled in the choice of her rulers, because she will not suffer the Emperor of Russia and the Prince Regent of England to say to her, " You have got a government with which you

" appear to be satisfied ; your satisfaction has been
" cogently indicated by the way in which your
" present ruler proceeded triumphantly, and almost
" alone, from Frejus to Paris ; but that government
" you shall not be permitted to retain." On the
other hand the motives of the Allies are not less
palpably displayed, to the apprehension of every
man not trained in the present corrupt school of
politics, than the sacred principle that must animate
the French. He has seen in the transactions of the
Congress of Vienna, that if the Allies were inspired
by a liberal principle for a time, while they stood
in the awful presence of the nation they had hum-
bled, they had at least no sooner retreated from
that scene, than they fell to partitioning, taking so
many hundred thousand souls from one Sovereign
and giving them to another, counting for nothing
the sentiments and desires of the people thus given
away, and trampling upon the hopes and expectations of the Italian States, expectations built on the
promises the Allies had authentically promulgated.

The Confederated Sovereigns have gained one
point, as they think, (if indeed their gain is not
a loss,) in the present crisis. Every reasonable
man knew that their object was at all times to dictate a Government to France. They could not
bear that any thing should rise that looked like

liberty; they could not endure that any change
should be made in the persons or families possess-
ing the sovereignty; they were for old measures of
government, and old dynasties. But they dared
not avow this; they covered their designs with a
mask, in deference to the indefeasible sentiments of
the human heart. They have now thrown away
the mask; they now say,—what their unauthen-
ticated followers always said for them,—" Our de-
" sign is to interfere with the internal government
" of the nation against which we arm." Is any
man deceived with the insolent pretence, " Choose
" a government for yourselves; but let it be one
" which we do not reprobate: throw off the as-
" cendancy of Bonaparte (which they know will
" never be done without five foreign armies can-
" toned on France); and then, oh then! you shall
" feel that you are free?"

Is any man infatuated enough to believe that the
armies of the Allies will advance against France in
the same spirit, as in the end of the year 1813?
That was indeed a memorable occasion! That
was a sacred reaction! The insolent conqueror,
after having robbed the King of Prussia and the
Emperor of Germany, after having kidnapped the
Sovereigns of Spain, and, to crown his enormities,
having marched his Myrmidons to Moscow, was

driven back with confusion upon his own territories. That was a moment to follow up the blow, to dictate terms to the invader, and to take reasonable securities that the same crimes should not be repeated. Whatever was in the hearts of the conductors of that scene, their actions were glorious. They declared themselves " ready to " confirm to the French Empire an extent of ter- " ritory that France under her Kings never " knew ;" and when they entered Paris, the Sovereign of ruined Moscow, acted as not remembering with sentiments of revenge the retaliation that was now in his power. Did not the heart of every genuine man advance in fancy on the French soil, as the Allies advanced ; and were not the prayers of every pure spirit, that they might be able to humble the late invader, and prescribe bounds to his ambition?

And now in what spirit will the bands of the Allies advance, and will the bystanders contemplate their march? The ministers of the Allies have just risen from the unhallowed meeting where they were dividing the spoils; and forsooth they are grievously disappointed, that a spirit should any where manifest itself in discordance to their behests. They are seized with terror, and they express themselves in the language of fear, with virulence, with abusive terms, and without thought and deliberation. In December 1813, they believed that Bonaparte, defeated in his legions, lowered in his military character, driven back upon France itself, expelled from Spain, stripped of Holland and Switzerland, and with the Rhine for his boundary, was no longer a subject of restless and incessant alarm, and might be trusted with " a ter-" ritory more extensive than France under her " Kings ever knew." They thought so then, because they felt like men, and were engaged in the prosecution of a great, a salutary, and an eternal principle. They think differently now, because they feel like that non-descript monster, called a statesman. Then they were brave; now they are cowards: then they felt with the heart of a soldier; now they feel with the heart of Talleyrand; and they have the poltroonery to propose to march the hundred thousands of united Europe for the destruction of a single individual.

They attack him now, not because he is stronger, but because he is weaker. In December 1813, they had the virtue to say, You are enough reduced for our safety; you may now be admitted into the roll of European states with impunity: we have shorn your strength; we have weakened the magic of your name; we have convinced France, and we have convinced yourself, that schemes so void of all reason and right must be

attended with a bitter retribution; we are strong
enough not to apprehend that we cannot keep you
in check: but if our magnanimity deceive us in
this, at least it will be years before you can be
sufficiently formidable to think of acting over again
the scenes you have acted; and we can appreciate
too well the crimes and the miseries of war, to
feel justified in creating or protracting it, in anticipation of a mischief that may never arrive. The
Revolution of 1814 has marvellously weakened
the strength of Bonaparte: before he reigned
without a competitor; now a pretender has started
up, who was till then forgotten, and without a party
in France; but a reality has by this event been
given to his pretensions, for Louis the Eighteenth
has been actually seated on the throne. The Allies know this; and they think that this is the time
to devour the weak, and to reduce France, and the
spirit of independence she has dared to cultivate,
to the lowest pitch of abject misery and desolation.

But they are wofully mistaken. With such a
cause as theirs, proceeding on the principle of
punishing thirty millions of men for daring to dislike the puppet the Allies had set over them, acting with indifference, and worse than indifference,
to the fate of a nation which, for twenty-six years,
has solely occupied the attention of the world,

stimulated at once with a cowardice, that thinks no conditions can secure them while one man lives, and with a dastard spirit that resolves, now that it believes itself able, to obliterate all vestiges of improvement that has taken place on the earth since the gloomy ascendancy of Philip the Second and Mary Tudor;—with such a cause, I say, it needs no great degree of sagacity to foresee what will be the issue. The Allied armies will be told that they fight, as in 1813, for the deliverance of Europe; but the human mind is not so blunted and so blind as to believe this. They will not perhaps throw down their arms; but a secret murmur of discontent will run along their ranks : they will move like machines; but they will be animated with no enthusiasm. Even Kings themselves are not so divested of humanity, as to contend with equal energy in a bad cause, as a good one; for spoil as for the common welfare; to suppress the last spark of liberty, as to arrest and disarm the man who openly professed the design of subjecting all other nations, and who had just been driven back from the farthest North, whither he had marched in pursuit of this unhallowed purpose. The cause of 1813 necessarily included in it a vital principle of union; the cause of 1815 includes in it a principle of self-destruction. The Confederated Sovereigns will soon fall out (they were very near doing so at the

Congress of Vienna) about the division of the spoil: one party will think that France, and Bonaparte who now is France, should be altogether extinguished, and another, that some vestige of the presiding nation of Europe should be preserved.

But, if this is the spirit in which the Allies will proceed to the contest, let us consider what spirit will animate the French. Bonaparte was never conquered but by himself; and it cost even him infinite pains to effect this conclusion. He marched twice to Vienna, he proceeded to Berlin, to Poland, to Tilsit; all these were steps towards his ruin. He endeavoured to impose his own brother as a Sovereign on Spain; still perhaps he might have recovered his error, and been safe. It required something more extravagant than all this, to undermine the foundations of his throne: he fulfilled his destiny, and marched to Moscow. How different is his condition now! He has expiated his offences, and has entered on a new career. He has ascended the throne on new conditions, and assembled about him a veteran army collected from all the prisons in Europe. Will any man believe that France, if she had been contented to defend her own borders, would not have proved invulnerable? Will any man believe, that adopting that system now, she will not be found equally invulnerable? Before, she wanted a motive to call forth her energies. Her tyrant was driven back from attempting the most unjustifiable objects that ever entered into the mind of man; and France was astonished, appalled, deprived altogether of self-possession. Yet even then Bonaparte, but for an ill-timed inflexibility, might have preserved himself on the throne. Now the continuity of the march of the Allies, so to express myself, is broken; and it is impossible that France should not see, that she only is aimed at, that she is first to be insulted in the grave irony of Declarations, and next to have a government fastened about her neck, such as the Allies in their mercy shall appoint, and with such securities of partitioning, and the permanent establishment of foreign garrisons, as shall tranquillise the coward fears of her assailants.

In a question like this, I feel we cannot succeed; and I frankly confess I do not even wish we should succeed. I am too much the friend of man, and too little the citizen of a particular country, shut up within the pale of all its prejudices, to breathe one prayer for the prosperity of so base a pretension. It carries in its very vitals a principle of confusion and ruin to all its abettors. I still trust, for the credit of human nature, and the salvation of the human species in general, that France will continue to be France, obeying the impulses of her own judgment, not dictated to, and

desolated, and trampled under foot, by the loving-
kindnesses of the Allies of the Bourbons. The
heart of man revolts against the principle of this
war; and the sword of man will never be found
to contend resolutely for its success.

Since then—I was going to say—it is so clear
and entirely certain that the purposes of the Allies
will fail—but I check myself—This is a question
of infinitely too momentous a nature, for me voluntarily to submit to any, the least approach to
self-delusion. Nothing here shall be done by me,
" in pride, or in presumption." I know that " the
" race is not always to the swift, nor the battle to
" the strong." I know that the best calculations,
where moral considerations intervene, and the varieties of mental energies and resolves affect the
issues of things, may fail.

Since then,—as far as I am able to look into the
darkness of the future, it appears certain that the
purposes of the Allies will fail,—let us enquire into
the consequences that will attend that failure. If
we left Bonaparte to himself, he is at present surrounded with the best patriots and republicans of
France, with Carnot, with Constant, with La
Fayette, and they are a pledge to the world that
he shall conduct himself with propriety. He holds
his sceptre at this moment only by the tenure of
professing his repentance of his past usurpations on

other states and on the liberty of his own, and of shewing himself the earnest votary of peace. But let us suppose that all these securities, *in addition to those with which the Allies were satisfied in the spring of* 1814, *with his offences yet unexpiated,* are insufficient : what proceeding do sober reason and calm consideration prescribe? We are told, that the French Nation are secretly averse to him, and that his enemies within his own borders are innumerable. Why then do we not leave him to himself, and not force the nation, by the invasion of foreign armies, to make common cause with him? Either the French agree to approve him as their Sovereign, or they do not. If they do, then it is madness in us to assail him; if they do not, then his power, if not interfered with, is precarious; the nation has been surprised by him, not won; the gloss of his new-acquired success will wear off; and his present greatness will crumble into nothing. As if the Allies were inspired with madness, they now propose to attack him, in the first brilliancy of a scene that the world cannot parallel, instead of allowing him time to make false steps, to alienate the indifferent and even his present supporters, and instead of permitting the French to repent, in the undisturbed moments of reflection, of the welcome they have unwarily bestowed upon him.

It is said, that we fight against the French, because they are become a warlike nation, and therefore under a warlike leader are too formidable for the tranquillity of Europe. This is a way of putting the question, that one would think should make the most frivolous and light-hearted man serious. If by war we are to cure the French of being warlike, it must be by humbling them, by subjugation, by partitioning, by extermination. But if we do not succeed, we then inevitably render them more warlike. We rouse into ferment the propensities we fear; we put their activity in march, and in all human calculation it must go on; we apprehend the effects their powers render them capable of producing, and we at the same time stimulate those powers into madness; we apprehend the insatiable ambition of their chief, and we force him into the direction of armies, that will in that event be victorious, and prepared to execute whatever he may command.

Bonaparte now holds his sceptre upon the condition of peace. His ministers, or his masters, call them which you please, require this of him. They are at present his masters, for they have made him sing the recantation of his principle of dictating to independent powers; they have extorted from him the abolition of the slave-trade, and the establishment of a free press; and they are in the very act of putting upon him the restraint of a limited constitution.

Bonaparte is at this moment reduced to a narrower territory, than was prescribed by the jealousy of the Allies. in the spring of 1814 : he does not enjoy " *a dominion greater than the French nation* " *ever knew under its Kings.*" But, if the Allies force him into a war, and if they rouse the people of France as one man, by their cruel ironies, and the scenes which their pusillanimous fears may induce them to act, who shall say how so tremendous a reaction is to be arrested? It was thus that the French once before were raised into a condition of military energy and success, that threatened the utter subjugation of Europe. They sought no war; but the Duke of Brunswick at the head of an Allied army advanced into their provinces, and demanded the abolition of the government which then subsisted among them. The efforts that expelled the Duke of Brunswick, went on in a progressive series; and the fields of St. Menehoud led to the fields of Moscow.

Bonaparte is at this moment in the hands of men, who will not allow him to take one step that has an aspect towards war. Be it, that he will one day escape out of the guardianship under which he is at present placed, and that he will be willing to act over again all those follies which have once before terminated in his ruin. This at least depends on a thousand coincidencies. Are the Allies so fearful that it will not happen, that they are deter-mined to cut off all the accidents that might pre-vent it? Is it their interest to thrust the sword into Bonaparte's grasp,—to convince the French nation that they cannot dispense with the services of this great military leader?

Bonaparte is at present, as I have said, in the hands of the republicans ; he wears his crown upon the condition of conducting himself sincerely on the system of peace. In what manner the expla-nation has been conducted between himself and his present illustrious advisers I know not; but vir-tually they have said to him, " Napoleon ! hereto-" fore a scholar of the Royal Military Academy " of Paris, afterwards a general, First Consul of " France, Emperor of the French people ! look " back on the career you have run, and learn wis-" dom ! You have affected the name of a great " conqueror, an Alexander, a Charlemagne, mas-" ter of the civilised world. The object you set " before your eyes, was a vain and unsubstantial " phantom, never to be secured by you. We will " not talk to you of the calamity and the crime " with which such a scheme is pregnant ; we will " simply tell you, that it was and ever will be im-" practicable for you. Yet, for this empty phan-" tom, you have oppressed and trampled upon " every state within your reach, you have played

" the part of an unfeeling despot to the French to
" whom you owed every thing, you have left hun-
" dreds of thousands of your people dying and
" dead amidst the snows of Russia and Poland,
" and returned discomfited to your palace of the
" Thuilleries with scarcely the skeleton of an
" army. You have played this part as far as it
" would bear ; it at length arrived at its natural
" close. Go back then into the recesses of your
" own heart, and consult yourself. Are you con-
" tented to abjure these follies for ever ? We want
" a leader, who shall think only of rendering France
" flourishing in the arts of peace, who shall be as
" distinguished towards foreign powers by measures
" of conciliation, as you have hitherto been by
" the language of despotism and insolent ambi-
" tion, and who shall co-operate with us to nur-
" ture and cherish the principles of equity, inde-
" pendence and liberty. We cannot find this
" leader among the Bourbons; a thousand pre-
" judices among our countrymen point to you;
" your talents are pre-eminent; your energies are
" unrivalled; you have already filled our throne.
" We believe you capable of sustaining the part
" we tender for your acceptance. While you do
" so, we will support you against every attack, se-
" cret or warlike, that can be made on you. But
" we are pledged to our characters, to our senti-

" ments, to our country, and to Heaven, that such
" and no other shall be the prince that shall reign
" over us."

Such was the contract, and such were the professions that accompanied Bonaparte at his entry into
Paris on the twentieth of March. Is not this a
character, are not these principles, no less conducive
to the welfare of Europe in general, than of France
in particular? Would to God the ill-omened incan-
tations of Talleyrand at Vienna had never been
heard! Would to God the Allies would have
waited for the developement of this system, and the
operation of this contract! But they, no less than
Talleyrand, had their reasons why they thought it
dangerous that such a commencement should remain unbroken in upon and uninvaded.

Such was the situation of Bonaparte; and this
situation (for the general interests of Europe, as
they say) the Allies have thought proper to put an
end to. Daily we see the enumeration of the hundreds of thousands, that from Russia, from Prussia,
from Austria, and from other quarters, are to in-
vade France on every side. Troops, it is said, will
be embattled, more numerous than Europe ever
witnessed on any former occasion. It is no matter that all their weapons will fall pointless upon
France. It is no matter that such a country must,
in all moral speculation, rise superior to every as-

sault. Yet much blood must be shed. Think
then, with what sentiments France will behold these
enemies, at length, amidst a thousand slaughters,
retiring from her territories ! At present, the best
men in France are at the head of her councils. But
at that moment the mild voice of La Fayette will
not be heard. The French are men; and they
will ruminate with fearful resentments upon the
unprovoked attack that has been made upon them,
upon the tyranny that has been meditated against
them as a people, upon the vengeance that was in
reserve for them, because they dared to take the
ruler of their own choice, upon the extermination
that was decreed against them as a nation, in
case the Allies had succeeded in their purposes.
All these sentiments inevitably grow up in the
blood-stained field. The minds of men are there
necessarily heated, their tempers grow ferocious,
and their passions uncontrolable. In the midst of
the madness of victory, they will cry out to Bonaparte, " Lead us forward! This is no time for mo-
" deration and philosophy. The Allies compounded
" a draught of complicated mischiefs for us; they
" shall themselves drink of the cup they had pre-
" pared; they shall be disabled for ever from re-
" peating the enormity of their crimes; we will
" leave to posterity an imperishable example of
" what it is to conspire to rob a nation like France

" of her independence."—The Allies must depend, in case of this event, upon the inflexible moderation with which Bonaparte, the man whom they have declared to be " out of the pale of civil and " social relations," and to have " forfeited the only " legal title upon which his existence depends," shall resist these exhortations to conquest and revenge.

How glorious was the victory of 1814! Never did Confederated Sovereigns appear so lovely as on that occasion. The rights of all appeared to be respected; and the Allies professed, as they had reason, to be indifferent whether a Bonaparte or a Bourbon sat upon the throne of France. A new æra was opened upon the exhausted world. A long reign of peace promised to succeed; commerce was destined to flourish, science and intellect to be cultivated, and men to learn to love each other, not who belonged to this or that particular country, but who were fellow-inhabitants of civilised Europe. The spectacle was the more enchanting, because it was novel, and because it succeeded to a world of devastation. I for one, Mr. Editor, who had been painfully compelled to witness so many convulsions, rejoiced, words cannot tell how much, that I was now to spend the remnant of my days in scenes of tranquillity, and of brotherly and unsuspecting intercourse of nation

with nation. Let this fair face of serenity be remembered to successive ages! Then came the
insignificant change, insignificant to the public interests of Europe, if the Allies would have allowed
it to be so, of the individual ruler of France,
accompanied with no change in its dominions, its
treasures, its armies, or its professions. For this
shall every thing, that has been so gloriously
achieved, be subverted? For this shall the worst
principle be obtruded on the scene, that of interfering with the internal government of an independent state, and the most dastardly, that of saying Europe cannot be at rest while one man is in
power? For such a change shall hell-gates be
again thrown open, and a bridge be made by which
every thing that is pestiferous may enter the fair
scene of the world?

How glorious was the victory of 1814! It came
in the conclusion of a war, which had been carried on, with little intermission, for fourteen years
against the incroachments of Bonaparte, not to
count in the incroachments of the French governments that preceded his, which had also been
years of war. It was a cold contention of the
finances of Great Britain, often single-handed,
against the greatest genius for war that had arisen
in the civilised world since the commencement of
the Christian æra. His successes and his con-

quests had gone on in a career, which nothing seemed to interrupt. It was like the fragment of a rock, descending from an exceedingly high mountain, which we could distinctly observe as it proceeded, but without almost a hope that it would fail to overwhelm the independence of Europe. At length, contrary to all human expectation, by a concurrence of circumstances the most unlikely, the danger was averted. It seemed as if a special Providence had watched over us, to snatch from destruction the energies of the mind of Europe. Are we so in love with ruin, that we would, on the heels of so wonderful a deliverance, invite, and as far as depends on us, compel a repetition of this scene? Would any man, just escaped from the most terrible eruption of Mount Vesuvius, build up his mansion for the next following years on the declivity of the mountain?

The characteristic of the present war, distinguishing it in some measure from all former wars, is that it is undertaken without the semblance of reflection. The sanguinary Declaration against Bonaparte was issued the instant it was understood that he had landed in France, and the Treaty of Vienna was signed, before it was known that he had made his triumphal entry into Paris. The war was therefore determined on in profound ignorance of what the Contracting Parties undertook, and was dictated purely by that fire of virtuous indignation in Talleyrand and the other negociators, which was lighted up by the abstract love of truth, and could not wait, in so just a cause, to count the cost, or anticipate the results. Just so, the English administration has plunged into the war, without once adverting to the state of our finances, and what they are able to effect. I grant, that when nations are attacked, they must perhaps defend themselves, however desperate may be their prospect of success. But in this case we are not attacked; we refuse to negociate; nothing will content us but the absolute destruction of the hostile government; we go to war, merely because (as we say) we have the right to do so. The deepest proficients in political economy are inclined to believe that Great Britain is nearly at the end of her resources : the most zealous advocates for the independence of Europe returned thanks to Providence, that, by means of the march to Moscow, the struggle was brought within a limited period, to which the means of our country might fortunately extend. Every man must allow that, unless the government of France can be overturned by a *coup de main*, it is difficult to predict within what compass of time the object of the war is to be effected. And we enter upon this war without the least consideration to what year of the contest our system may be made to last. We care not, in comparison with our generous hatred of Bonaparte, what destruction we may bring upon our finances, or upon the hundred thousands of families that exist upon the interest of our national debt. Nor is it merely that our widows, and our orphans, and our men of mean estate, must perish: if they fall, the point for which we contend is also lost. But we are prepared voluntarily to sacrifice ourselves to this great issue, and content, if such should be our fate, to pull down the vast edifice of the polilitical fabric upon the heads of all!

VERAX.

THE END.

Printed by Richard and Arthur Taylor, Shoe-Lane, London.

LETTER

OF

ADVICE

TO

A YOUNG AMERICAN:

ON

THE COURSE OF STUDIES IT MIGHT BE MOST ADVANTAGEOUS FOR HIM TO PURSUE.

———

By WILLIAM GODWIN.

———

London:

PRINTED FOR M. J. GODWIN AND CO. SKINNER-STREET,

BY RICHARD AND ARTHUR TAYLOR, SHOE-LANE.

———

1818.

LETTER.

MY DEAR SIR,

I HAVE thought, at least twenty times since you left
London, of the promise I made you, and was at first inclined to consider it, as you appear to have done, as
wholly unconditional, and to be performed out of hand.
And I should perhaps have proceeded in that way; but
that my situation often draws me with an imperious sum-
mons in a thousand different directions, and thus the first
heat of my engagement subsided. I then altered my mind,
and made a resolution, that you should never have the
thing you asked for, unless you wrote to remind me of
my promise. I thought within myself, that if the advice
was not worth that, it was not worth my trouble in digesting. From the first moment I saw you in this house,
I conceived a partiality for you, founded on physiognomy
in an extensive sense, as comprehending countenance,
voice, figure, gesture, and demeanour; but if you forgot
me as soon as I was out of your sight, I determined that
this partiality should not prove a source of trouble to me.

And, now that you have discharged your part of the
condition I secretly prescribed, I am very apprehensive
that you have formed an exaggerated idea of what I can
do for you in this respect. I am a man of very limited
observation and enquiry, and know little but of such

things as lie within those limits. If I wished to form a universal library, I should feel myself in conscience obliged to resort to those persons who knew more in one and another class of literature than I did, and to lay their knowledge in whatever they understood best, under contribution. But this I do not mean to undertake for you I will reason but of what I know; and I shall leave you to learn of the professors themselves, as to the things to which I have never dedicated myself.

You will find many of my ideas of the studies to be pursued, and the books to be read, by young persons, in the Enquirer, and more to the same purpose in the Preface to a small book for children, entitled, " Scripture Histories, given in the words of the original," in two volumes, 18mo.

It is my opinion, that the imagination is to be cultivated in education, more than the dry accumulation of science and natural facts. The noblest part of man is his moral nature; and I hold morality principally to depend, agreeably to the admirable maxim of Jesus, upon our putting ourselves in the place of another, feeling his feelings, and apprehending his desires; in a word, doing to others, as we would wish, were we they, to be done unto.

Another thing that may be a great and most essential aid to our cultivating moral sentiments,will consist in our studying the best models, and figuring to ourselves the most excellent things of which human nature is capable. For this purpose there is nothing so valuable as the histories of Greece and Rome. There are certain cold-blooded reasoners who say, that the ancients were in nothing better than ourselves, that their stature of mind was no taller,

and their feelings in nothing more elevated, and that
human nature in all ages and countries is the same. I do
not myself believe this. But, if it is so, certainly ancient
history is the bravest and sublimest fiction that it ever
entered into the mind of man to create. No poets, or
romance-writers, or story-tellers, have ever been able to
feign such models of an erect and generous and public-
spirited and self-postponing mind, as are to be found in
Livy and Dionysius of Halicarnassus. If the story be a
falsehood, the emotions, and in many readers the never-
to-be-destroyed impressions it produces, are real : and I
am firmly of opinion, that the man that has not been imbued with these tales in his earliest youth, can never be
so noble a creature, as the man with whom they have made
a part of his education stands a chance to be.

To study the Greek and Roman history it were undoubtedly best to read it in their own historians. To do
this we must have a competent mastery of the Greek and
Latin languages. But it would be a dangerous delusion
to put off the study long, under the idea that a few years
hence we will read these things in the originals. You
will find the story told with a decent portion of congenial
feeling in Rollin's Ancient History, and Vertot's Revolutions of Rome. You should also read Plutarch's Lives,
and a translation into English or French, of Dionysius's
Antiquities. Mitford for the History of Greece, and
Hooke for that of Rome, are writers of some degree of
critical judgment ; but Hooke has a baleful scepticism
about, and a pernicious lust to dispute, the virtues of illustrious men, and Mitford is almost frantic with the love
of despotism and oppression. Middleton's Life of Cicero,

and Blackwell's Court of Augustus, are books written in the right spirit. And, if you do not soon read Thucydides in the original, you will soon feel yourself disposed to read Sallust, and Livy, and perhaps Tacitus, in the genuine language in which these glorious men have clothed their thoughts.

The aim of my meditation at this moment is to devise that course of study, that shall make him who pursues it independent and generous. For a similar reason therefore to that which has induced me to recommend the histories of Greece and Rome, I would next call the attention of my pupil to the age of chivalry. This also is a generous age, though of a very different cast from that of the best period of ancient history. Each has its beauty. Considered in relation to man as a species of being divided into two sexes, the age of chivalry has greatly the advantage over the purest ages of antiquity. How far their several excellencies may be united and blended together in future time, may be a matter for after consideration. You may begin your acquaintance with the age of chivalry with Ste Palaye's *Memoires sur l'Ancienne Chevalerie*, and Southey's Chronicle of the Cid. Cervantes's admirable romance of Don Quixote, if read with a deep feeling of its contents, and that high veneration for and strong sympathy with its hero, which it is calculated to excite in every ingenuous mind, is one of the noblest records of the principles of chivalry. I am not anxious to recommend a complete cycle of the best writers on any subject. You cannot do better perhaps in that respect, than I have done before you. I always found one writer in his occasional remembrances and references leading to another, till I

might, if I had chosen it, have collected a complete library
of the best books on any given topic, without almost being
obliged to recur to any one living counsellor for his advice.

We can never get at the sort of man that I am con-
templating, and that I would, if I could, create, without
making him also a reader and lover of Poetry. I require
from him the glow of intellect and sentiment, as well as
the glow of a social being. I would have him have his
occasional moods of sublimity; and if I may so call it,
literary tenderness, as well as a constant determination of
mind to habits of philanthropy. You will find some good
ideas on the value of poetry in Sir Philip Sidney's Defense
of Poesy, and the last part of Sir William Temple's
Miscellanies.

The subject of poetry is intimately connected with the
last subject I mentioned, the age of chivalry. It is in the
institutions of chivalry that the great characteristics, which
distinguish ancient from modern poetry, originate. The
soul of modern poetry, separately considered, lies in the
importance which the spirit of chivalry has given to the
female sex. The ancients pitted a man against a man,
and thought much of his thews and sinews, and the graces
and energy which nature has given to his corporeal frame.
This was the state of things in the time of Homer. In a
more refined age they added all those excellencies which
grow out of the most fervid and entire love of country.
Antiquity taught her men to love women, and that not
in the purest sense; the age of chivalry taught hers
to adore them. I think, quite contrary to the vulgar
maxim on the subject, that love is never love in its best

spirit, but among unequals.   The love of parent and child
is its highest model, and most permanent effect.   It is
therefore an excellent invention of modern times, that,
while woman by the nature of things must look up to
man, teaches us in our turn to regard woman, not merely
as a convenience to be made use of, but as a being to be
treated with courtship and consideration and fealty.

Agreeably to the difference between what we call the
heroic times, and the times of chivalry, are the characteristic features of ancient and modern poetry.   The ancient is simple and manly and distinct, full of severe
graces and heroic enthusiasm.   The modern excels more
in tenderness, and the indulgence of a tone of magnificent
obscurity.   The ancient upon the whole had more energy ;
we have more of the wantoning of the imagination, and
the conjuring up a fairy vision

> " Of some gay creatures of the element,
>   That in the colours of the rainbow live,
>   And play in the plighted clouds."

It is not necessary to decide whether the ancient or the
modern poetry is best; both are above all price; but it
is certain that the excellencies that are all our own,
have a grandeur and a beauty and a thrilling character,
that nothing can surpass.   The best English poets are
Shakespear and Milton and Chaucer and Spenser.   Ariosto
is above all others the poet of chivalry.   The Greek and
Latin poets it is hardly necessary to enumerate.   There
is one book of criticism, and perhaps only one, that I
would recommend to you, Schlegel's Lectures on Dra-

matic Literature. The book is deformed indeed with a pretty copious sprinkling of German mysticism, but it is fraught with a great multitude of admirable observations.

The mention of criticism leads me to a thought which I will immediately put down. I would advise a young person to be very moderate in his attention to new books. In all the world I think there is scarcely any thing more despicable, than the man that confines his reading to the publications of the day : he is next in rank to the boarding-school miss who devours every novel that is spawned forth from the press of the season. If you look into Reviews, let it be principally to wonder at the stolidity of your contemporaries who regard them as the oracles of learning.

One other course of reading I would earnestly recommend to you; and many persons would vehemently exclaim against me for doing so,—Metaphysics. It excels perhaps all other studies in the world, in the character of a practical logic, a disciplining and subtilising of the rational faculties. Metaphysics we are told, is a mere jargon, where men dispute for ever without gaining a single step; it is nothing but specious obscurity and ignorance. This is not my opinion. In the first place, metaphysics is the theoretical science of the human mind; and it would be strange if mind was the only science not worth studying, or the only science in which real knowledge could not be acquired. Secondly, it is the theoretical science of the universe and of causation, and must settle, if ever they can be settled, the first principles of natural religion. As to its uncertainty, I cannot conceive that any one with an unprejudiced mind can read what has been best written on free-will and necessity, on self-love and benevolence, and other grand questions, and then say that nothing has been attained, and that all this is impertinent and senseless waste of words. I would particularly recommend bishop Berkley, especially his Principles of Human Knowledge, and Hume's Treatise of Human Nature, and Hartley's Observations on Man. Your own Jonathan Edwards has written excellently on free-will; and Hutcheson and Hazlit on self-love and benevolence. The title of Hutcheson's book is an Essay on the Nature and Conduct of the Passions and Affections, and of Hazlit's an Enquiry into the Principles of Human Action. No young man can read Andrew Baxter's Enquiry into the Nature of the Human Soul, without being the better for it.

It is time that I should now come to the consideration of Language. Language is as necessary an instrument for conducting the operations of the mind, as the hands are for conducting the operations of the body; and the most obvious way of acquiring the power of weighing and judging words aright, is by enabling ourselves to compare the words and forms of different languages. I therefore highly approve of classical education. It has often been said by the wise men of the world, What a miserable waste of time it is, that boys should be occupied for successive year after year, in acquiring the Greek and Latin tongues! How much more usefully would these years be employed, in learning the knowledge of things, and making a substantial acquaintance with the studies of men! I totally dissent from this. As to the knowledge of things, young men will soon enough be plunged in the mire of cold and sordid realities, such things as it is the calamity of man that he should be condemned to consume so much of his mature life upon; and I could wish that those who can afford the leisure of education, should begin with acquiring something a little generous and elevated. As to the studies of men, if boys begin with them before they are capable of weighing them, they will acquire nothing but prejudices, which it will be their greatest interest and highest happiness, with infinite labour to unlearn. Words are happily a knowledge, to the acquisition of which the faculties of boys are perfectly competent, and which can do them nothing but good. Nature has decreed that human beings should be so long in a state of nonage, that it demands some ingenuity to discover how the years of boys of a certain condition in life, may be employed innocently, in acquiring good habits, and none of that appearance of reason and wisdom, which in boys surpasses in nothing the instructions we bestow on parrots and monkies. One of the best maxims of the eloquent Rousseau, is where he says, The master-piece of a good education is to know how to lose time profitably.

Every man has a language that is peculiarly his own; and it should be a great object with him to learn whatever may give illustration to the genius of that. Our language is the English. For this purpose then, I would recommend to every young man who has leisure, to acquire some knowledge of the Saxon, and one or two other northern languages. Horne Tooke, in his Diversions of Purley, is the only man that has done much towards analysing the elements of the English tongue. But another, and perhaps still more important way to acquire a knowledge and true relish of the genius of the English tongue, is by studying its successive authors from age to age. It is an eminent happiness we possess, that our authors from generation to generation are so much worth studying. The first resplendent genius in our literary annals is Chaucer. From this age to that of Elizabeth we have not much; but it will be good not entirely to drop any of the links of the chain. The period of Elizabeth is perfectly admirable. Roger Ascham, and Golding's version of Mornay's Trewnesse of Christian Religion, are among the best canonical books of genuine English. Next come the translators of the classics in that age, who are worthy to be studied day and night, by those who would perfectly feel the genius of our language. Among these, Phaer's Virgil, Chapman's Homer, and Sir Thomas North's Plutarch, are perhaps the best, and are in my opinion incomparably superior to the later translations of those authors. Of course I hardly need say, that Lord Bacon is one of the first writers that has appeared in the catalogue of human creatures, and one of those who is most worthy to be studied. I might have brought him in among the metaphysicians; but I preferred putting him here. Nothing can be more magnificent and impressive than his language: it is rather that of a God, than a man. I would also specially recommend Burton's Anatomy of Melancholy, and the writings of Sir Thomas Browne. No man I suppose is to be told, that the dramatic writers of the age of Elizabeth are among the most astonishing specimens of human intellect. Shakespear is the greatest, and stands at an immense distance from all the rest. But though he outshines them, he does not put out their light. Ben Jonson is himself a host: of Beaumont and Fletcher I cannot think without enthusiasm: and Ford, and Massin-

ger well deserve to be studied. Even French literature
was worthy of some notice in these times; and Montaigne
is entitled to rank with some of the best English prose-
writers his contemporaries.

In looking over what I have written, I think I have not
said enough on the subject of Modern History. Your language is English; the frame of your laws and your law-
courts is essentially English. Therefore, and because the
English moral and intellectual character ranks the first of
modern times, I think English history is entitled to your
preference. Whoever reads English history must take Hume
for his text. The subtlety of his mind, the depth of his
conceptions, and the surpassing graces of his composition,
must always place him in the first class of writers. His
work is tarnished with a worthless partiality to the race of
kings that Scotland sent to reign over us; and is wofully
destitute of that energetic moral and public feeling that di-
stinguishes the Latin historians. Yet we have nothing else
on the subject, that deserves the name of composition. I
have already spoken of the emphatic attention that is due
to the age of chivalry. The feudal system is one of the
most extraordinary productions of the human mind. It is
a great mistake to say, that these were dark ages. It was
about this period that logic was invented: for I will venture
to assert that the ancients knew nothing about close reasoning and an unbroken chain of argumentative deduction, in
comparison with the moderns. For all the excellence we
possess in this art we are indebted to the schoolmen, the
monks and friars in the solitude of their cloisters. It is true,
that they were too proud of their new acquisitions, and
subtilised and refined till occasionally they became truly

ridiculous. This does not extinguish their claim to our applause, though it has dreadfully tarnished the lustre of their memory in the vulgar eye. Hume passes over the feudal system and the age of chivalry, as if it were a dishonour to his pen to be employed on these subjects, while he enlarges with endless copiousness on the proofs of the sincerity of Charles the First, and the execrable public and private profligacies of Charles the Second.

Next to the age of feudality and chivalry the period of English history most worthy of our attention lies between the accession of Elizabeth and the Restoration. But let no man think that he learns any thing, particularly of modern history, by reading a single book. It fortunately happens, as far as the civil wars are concerned, that we have two excellent writers of the two opposite parties, Clarendon and Ludlow, beside many others worthy to be consulted. You should also have recourse to as many lives of eminent persons connected with the period then under your consideration, as you can conveniently procure. Letters of state, memorials, and public papers, are in this respect of inestimable value. They are, to a considerable degree, the principal actors in the scene writing their own history. He that would really understand history, should proceed in some degree as if he were composing a history. He should be surrounded with chronological tables and maps. He should compare one authority with another, and not put himself under the guidance of any. This is the difference I make between reading and study. He that confines himself to one book at a time, may be amused, but is no student. In order to study, I must sit in some measure in the middle of a library. Nor can any one truly study, without the perpetual use of a pen, to make notes, and abstracts, and arrangements of dates. The shorter the notes, and the more they can be looked through at a glance, the better. The only limit in this respect is that they should be so constructed, that if I do not look at them again till after an interval of seven years, I should understand them. Learn to read slow;—if you keep to your point, and do not suffer your thoughts, according to an old phrase, to go a wool-gathering, you will be in little danger of excess in this direction.

Accept in good part, my young friend, this attempt to answer your expectation, and be assured that, if I could have done better, it should not have been less at your service. Your dispositions appear to me to be excellent: and, as you will probably be enabled to make some figure, and, which is much better, to act the part of the real patriot and the friend of man, in your own country, you should resolve to bestow on your mind an assiduous cultivation. It is the truly enlightened man, that is best qualified to be truly useful; and, as Lord Bacon says, " It is almost without instance contradictory, that ever any government was disastrous, that was in the hands of learned governors. The wit of one man can no more countervail learning, than one man's means can hold way with a common purse."

My best wishes attend you.

February 12, 1818.

NAMED IN THE FOREGOING PAGES.

Printed by R. and A. Taylor, Shoe-lane, London.

No. II.

Skinner Street, March 19, 1818.

MY DEAR SIR,—Whatever was left imperfect in your second letter, as to my Paper of advice, is fully made up in your last, and I am more than satisfied.

The question you ask, why am I silent in this paper on the sub-ject of politics? is a very natural one, and I will give you an inge-nuous answer. The person who asked my advice as to the course of his studies, I naturally concluded had some respect for my lite-rary character; and I therefore thought it superfluous (as far as it could be avoided) to repeat any thing I had said in my public writings, or to refer directly or indirectly to any thing therein treat-ed. Even the person, who without ever having known me, should have sufficient respect for my advice to make it in any degree his compass to steer by, would hardly, I thought, be so indolent or indifferent, as not to inquire what I had myself written for the amusement, improvement, and instruction of my species generally. The species of composition denominated novel, a sort of prose-epic, and in my opinion a memorable addition to the stock of hu-man literature, which with a few exceptions, did not assume its present consummate form till the age of Fielding and Richardson: but I am a writer of novels; and for that reason principally I was silent under that head. I have also written on the science of po-litics; and though my work is twenty five years old, I am sorry to say, I am grown very little wiser under that article: if I had to write my work over again, I could correct many errors, but scarce-ly any thing that strikes my mind as fundamental. In my inquiry concerning Political Justice, I have not only laid down, as well as I was able, the principles of moral and political truth, but have al-so made a point of commemorating, and delivering a candid and sincere judgment respecting almost every considerable political writer that fell in my way. What therefore could I have added in my Letter of advice, to what in that work I have delivered?

I inclose you a copy of my letter, printed on a sheet of paper, which I caused to be so printed, merely because it has happened to me very many times to have the same request made to me by young men, which from you, occasioned the writing these pages; and I thought it might save some trouble, and be the means of some good, to have the paper always at hand, to give away to any person to whom I judged it might be desirable. This copy is sent merely to gratify your private curiosity: as I would not be the means, or appear to be the means, of checking any additional sale which the insertion of my letter might bring to Mr. Constable's magazine. * * * * *

No. III.

Skinner Street, April 27, 1818.

——————— You say that ' since the arrival of my paper, you have been sedulously engaged in the study of the old English authors, and of the classics.' I am not sure that this is right as to the first. I had some doubts on this point when I penned my advice; that is, I doubted whether it was right for readers in general, though I was sure that what I put down was reasonable for you. For I was obliged to consider in writing, though I did not name the consideration, that part of your object was to collect books, and that you could not suddenly add old and scarce books to your collection when you were once fixed in ————. I cannot better express the ground of my doubt above conveyed, than by a quotation from Ben Jonson's Discoveries. He says, ' Therefore youth ought to be instructed betimes, and in the best things; for we hold those longest we take soonest. And as it is fit to read the best authors to youth first, so let them be clearest; as, Livy before Sallust, Sidney before Donne. And beware of letting them taste Gower and Chaucer at first, lest falling too much in love with antiquity, and not apprehending the weight, they grow rough and barren in language only.' Now if there is any thing in this caution of Ben Jonson, he and his contemporaries are now somewhat obsolete to us, as Chaucer was to him. The best model perhaps for a modern English style, would be a due mixture and medium of Burke and Hume, adding, when you have gained this substratum, as much wealth from the elder writers, as may be consistent with this platform and system in building.

Again, as to what you say of the classics, I have some doubt about the indiscriminate use of your pen in making translations. I know it is good in part, for this is the sure way of discovering whether we perfectly understand our author. But, I know also, that we ought frequently, while we read books in another tongue, to forget for the time that there is any other language than that we are reading. It is thus we shall come to relish their idiom; while on the other hand, if we are continually seeking for equivalent phrases in English, we shall go on much as children do in beginning to talk or write French, whose phrases and construction are English, and the words only borrowed from our neighbour tongue.

I am also inclined to disapprove the very limited list of classics you now set down. Latin and Greek are not to be laid aside, as we lay aside our old clothes. My own method through the greater part of my life has been, to devote at least one hour of every day to the classics, and by this means I found the book-shelves of my brain enlarging, till at last the classics made an appearance not altogether despicable. I hope you do not mean to shut out the poets.

You say, ' Is there a condition of life more replete with enjoyment, than that of a young man, with moderately independent circumstances, &c. &c. &c.?' I say, in reply, ' Is there a condition of life more full of the noblest promise of honour and usefulness, and therefore more replete with enjoyment, than that of a young man, with certain qualities of the head and heart, *who no revenue has but his good spirits and inborn energies to feed and clothe him?*' I have tried the one; you are about to try the other. Both have their disadvantages and their temptations. But yours, I am afraid, is the most dangerous. Man is a creature of so frail and feeble a texture, that we want *all appliance and means to boot,* and even in some degree the stimulus of stern necessity, in addition to our own original good dispositions, to make us do our duty fully, and not sometimes be found like a faithless centinel, sleeping upon our post. See what you can do to counteract this evil! May your slumbers be short, conducing only to the infusion of new vigour, and not partaking of that lethargy, in which our powers, our honour, and ourselves, are momentarily in danger of being lost without remedy.

You will think it strange in me, if I mention a new book, and by an Aikin. The book is miss *Aikin's* Memoirs of the Court of Elizabeth. It is a book of no great strength and still less depth. But it contains a vast deal of interesting, and some curious information, that is brought together in no other book. * * * * *

No. IV.

Skinner Street, June 29, 1818.

———————— I congratulate you upon your good fortune, in being in the British Islands at the time of a general election. This is an instructive, and, in some respects, an animating spectacle. Perhaps I have not fully considered all the advantages and disadvantages of the two modes: but I dislike the French scheme of the people electing an elective body, and then these electors electing the legislature, and that other scheme of some of our reformers, that the members of a county shall be elected by a ballot to take place in every little district and market-town on the same day. I am pleased with the open avowal our electors make of their sentiments. I am pleased with the sympathy excited in their breasts by their general congregating to the place of election, thus reviving (though alas! but once in seven years) the practical and healthful feeling, that they are freemen. I am pleased with the scene of an election protracted for four or five days, and thus nourishing the love of what is right, by some degree of uncertainty and suspense respecting the event. I am an enemy to mobs; but this sort of mob, or confluence of mankind, expressly directed by the law, and terminating in a specific act, seems to me to be deprived of the sting, the terror, and the hot-blooded, savage, and dangerous feeling, attendant on bodies of men, called together at their own pleasure, and chusing for themselves the sort of exertion to which their power shall be directed.   *   *   *   *   *

No. V.

Skinner Street, July 24, 1818.

————————— You ask me my sentiments respecting the writers generally called the English classics. Let us see who they are. I suspect that at the head of them are Pope, Swift, and Addison. These were all admirable writers, though greatly inferior to the great writers of the age of Elizabeth. They are, however, worth studying, and are even in some respects entitled to a priority, as being to a great degree standards of the language now in use. It is perhaps impossible to excel Pope in his kind, that is, as a man delivering in metre the dictates of good sense, and a certain obvious species of observation on life and manners, seasoned and rendered acute by all the poignancy of an elegant sort of wit and sarcasm. Addison wants strength; but his deficiency in that respect is compensated, in a great degree, by his delicacy and refinement. His humour, wherever displayed, and most of all in his character of sir Roger de Coverly, is inimitable. The third of these men, Swift, is vastly the greatest. The depth of his observation, a quality very scarce in that age, is astonishing, and is most of all displayed in his Gulliver's Travels. There is not a page of that book, that you may not read six times, before you see all that is in it. And this is rendered more surprising by the unaffected simplicity and plainness with which he delivers himself there, and in all his writings. Congreve, the contemporary of Pope, Swift, and Addison, is also worth your attention. Dr. Conyers Middleton, though something later, is fully entitled to class with these, whom he exceedingly surpasses in copiousness and energy. These are the genuine standards of English style.

You may study the writers since that age, as you may study the writers before, as enlarging the stores of our tongue, but they are to be viewed with a certain caution. They are not our standards. Hume is in a high degree subtle and elegant. Burke is a profound thinker, and a powerful declaimer; but his declamation is over-ornamented and over-done. Johnson is the worst of this trio. We may read him however, sometimes for admiration, still oftener as a melancholy example of something, *not* to be imitated.

Rousseau is very nearly the best writer of the middle part of the last century; the writer from whose works we may derive the greatest degree of profit.

Montesquieu was a man of great talents. His best work is his Persian Letters, written in his youth. His Spirit of Laws is overrun with affectation. Every sentence is an epigram. And of him we say more truly, what Johnson says of Shakspeare's punning; ' An epigram is the Cleopatra for which he loses the world, and is content to lose it.'

I have answered your letter. I am at this moment incessantly occupied in my answer to Matthews on Population, which, I believe, I mentioned to you before you left London.

I think I ought to have named Bolingbroke and Shaftesbury with the authors of the age of Addison, though greatly inferior as standards to those already mentioned. Bolingbroke is manly, but the garden of his language has never felt the pruning hook: the branches of his eloquence choke each other like the branches of a forest. Shaftesbury is a most elegant and amiable thinker, but with perpetual affectation. He dances so much, that he is not able to walk.

No. VI.
Skinner Street, September 11, 1818.

———————— I have looked three times through the Letter of Advice, to endeavour to discover where I have said, ' Read the great English poets; but do not neglect any of the rest.' But as Shylock says, ' I cannot find it; it is not in the bond.' If your quotation had stood, ' Do not neglect the rest,' I should have said, ' I did not write it, but it is my sentiment.' But ' do not neglect *any* of the rest,' is certainly too much for me.

With respect to your choice of them, if you are guarded by common fame, you will not materially err; and it will be good that you should somewhat use your own independent judgment, in saying, ' This has been praised too much; and this not enough.' You will have much aid in your decision, if you make Shakspeare, and Milton, and Chaucer, and Spenser your standards. The old poets I should recommend for their language, their depth of thinking, and their strength of phrase. I have given you a tolerable list of dramatic poets; and if you grow fond of them, you will feel prompted to read their poetical compositions, not in the dramatic form, and those of the men they tell you they loved. You will hardly miss Dryden and Pope, or even the melancholy Cowley. Remember what I have said, that ' I have always found one writer in his occasional remembrances and references leading to another,' and trust yourself to that. The living poets I would wish to have some of your attention, but ' I would have a young person to be very moderate in his attention to new books.' That is the vice of your country.

You ask me for ' a summary view of the distinguished characteristics of the ages of Elizabeth, Anne, and George III. both for poetry and prose.' That is a large question; and I beg to postpone it. I have furnished some hints towards an answer in former letters.

I recommended the other day in a letter to a young author, whose talents I respect, to undertake a book, to be called the Lives of the Commonwealth Men. My list extended to ten names; Milton, Algernon Sidney, Martin, Vane, president Bradshaw, president Scott, his successor in office, Ludlow, Henry Nevil, Henry Ireton, Robert Blake. This would be a choice book for an American to read, though no American could write it as it ought to be written. England in all her annals has produced no men, as public characters, worthy to be ranked with these—not even an eleventh to be added to these ten. They were all to their last breath devoted to the principles of republicanism, and looked upon monarchy with that generous horror and contempt, which, abstractedly considered, every enlightened and impartial man must regard it. Now every reader that almost at all deserves the name, ought in some degree to play the part of an author, and collate the materials of a subject, nearly as if he were going to treat of it in a book. The materials of the Commonwealth History of England lie principally in a few authors; Clarendon, Ludlow, Whitlocke, Mrs. Hutchinson, Clement Walker, sir Henry Vane, Trials of the Regicides, and Noble. To be sure, he who would have his collection complete, should add to these, Rushworth's and Thurloe's Collection of State Papers, and as many of Milton's, and the other notable pamphlets of the time as he can meet with. The whole would not amount to fifty volumes.

I should have answered your letter dated August 20, sooner, but for other occupations, and still more for ill health.

Very truly and sincerely yours,
William Godwin.

P. S. I believe I ought to add, as a matter of taste, that you might apprehend my idea, that I confined the scheme of the book to one volume.—Of my heroes Scott was hanged, Bradshaw and Ireton were gibbetted after death, Algernon Sidney and Vane beheaded, Martin was a prisoner twenty years, and Ludlow an exile thirty years, at the end of which time they died.

List of books recommended to the same person by Stephen Lee, Esq. librarian to the Royal Society.

Mathematics.—Simson's Euclid, Robinson's Conic Sections, Bridge's Algebra, Trigonometry, Conic Sections, and Mechanics, Bonnycastle's Arithmetic, Le Croix, Cours de Mathematiques, Woodhouse's Trigonometry, Hutton's Mathematics,* Mathematical Tracts, and Mathematical Dictionary, Cagnoli's Trigonometry, Newton's Principia, La Place, Mecanique Celeste, Brook Taylor's Elements of the Linear Perspective, Robinson's Elements of Mechanical Philosophy,† Taylor's Logarithms, Callet's ditto, Hutton's ditto.

Physico-Mathematics, and Mechanical Arts.—Prony, Architecture Hydraulique, Nicholson's Carpenter's New Guide, Joiner's Assistant, Principles of Architecture, Mechanical Exercises, Student's Instructions in the Five Orders, Stalkart's Naval Architecture, Steed's ditto, Vince's Astronomy, Young's Lectures on Natural Philosophy, Biot, Precis (ou Traité) Elementaire de Physique Experimentale, Montucla, Histoire de Mathematiques, Smeeton's Works, Singer on Electricity, Berthoud, Traité d'Horlogerie, Paynant, Traité de Geoderie.

Natural History, Agriculture, &c.—Linnæus, Systema Naturæ, Shaw's Zoology, Miller's Gardener's Dictionary, Kaimes' Gentleman Farmer, Reports of the Board of Agriculture, Arthur Young's

* Dr. Hutton considers the American edition the best.
† Edition by Brewster.

Experimental Farmer, Cuvier, Anatomie Comparatif, Blumenbach's Comparative Anatomy by Lawrence, Kirby's Entomology, Wood's Conchology, Smith's Introduction to Botany, Block's Icthyology, Bakewell's Geology, Parkinson's Organic Remains of a Former World.

Miscellaneous.—Russel's History of Modern Europe, Pinkerton on Medals, Biographical Dictionary by Chalmers, Dictionnaire Historique, Blan's Chronology, Johnson's Dictionary, Lowth's Grammar, Murray's Grammar, Elegant Extracts, La Harpe, Lycée, Smith's Wealth of Nations, Macpherson's Annals of Commerce, Locke on the Human Understanding, Eustace's Classical Tour, Encyclopædia Britannica, Encyclopedie Methodique, published in parts.

Course of Law Study, by the late lord Ashburton (Mr. Dunning).

1. Hume's History of England, particularly observing the rise, progress, and declension of the feudal system. Minutely attend to the Saxon government that preceded it, and dwell on the reigns of Edward I, Henry VI, VII, and VIII, James I, Charles I, and II, and James II.

2. Blackstone. On second reading turn to the references.

3. Mr. Justice Wright's Tenures.

4. Coke upon Lyttleton, especially every word of Fee Simple, Fee Tail, Life, and Years.

5. Coke's First and Second Institutes, with serjeant Hawkin's Compendium.

6. Coke's Reports and Plowden's Commencing; and in succession the Modern Reporters.

Additions to this list, by an eminent Irish barrister.

Sullivan's Lectures on the Feudal Law, Cruise's Digest, Gwillim's edition of Bacon's Abridgment, particularly the head of leases for years, as explanatory of the different heads in Coke; Gilbert on Rents, and on Replevins, Phillips on Evidence, last edition, Reeves' History of the Common Law.

BIOGRAPHICAL SKETCH OF
THE LATE JOSEPH RITSON, ESQ.

Joseph Ritson was born October 2, 1752, at Stockton-upon-Tees, in the county of Durham, and was bred to the profession of the law. He was greatly distinguished for the acuteness of his judgment, and the profoundness of his researches, in the characters of a consulting barrister and a conveyancer. But his literary enquiries were by no means confined within the limits of his profession ; and he was, perhaps, the most successful of those persons by whom the investigation of old English literature and antiquities was cultivated in the latter part of the eighteenth century. His memory was so tenacious, that nothing he ever stored there was obliterated : the most astonishing labours and indefatigable enquiries were to him amusement ; and his penetration and judgment were so exact, that it is difficult, in his voluminous publications, to detect a single error of fact or of inference.

It is to be regretted that his style, and the mode in which he communicated his discoveries to the public, were by no means such as to adorn his discoveries. The language of his writings is harsh, rugged, and barren ; and his publications are further disfigured by the affected singularity of their orthography. But this, though it hindered them from obtaining that general success to which, by their essential merits, they were entitled, does not prevent them from being, to the learned and the studious, invaluable repositories of the science of which they treat. Mr. Ritson was fully sensible of the superiority he possessed in those points of learning which had engaged his attention, and was not accustomed to express himself on these subjects, with any degree of diffidence and reserve. Conscious of his own general exemption from error, he had no forbearance for the errors and misapprehensions of others. The style in which he attacked Malone, Warton, and other contemporary critics, was remarked for a greater degree of rudeness, bitterness, and insult, than is perhaps to be found in any other controversialist.—

He set somewhat too high a value on his own favourite pursuits, and defended his dogmas in a very magisterial tone. It was a favourite maxim of his that literary forgery was a crime, not less deserving the gallows, than the forgery which deprived a man of his property; and he expressed himself respecting those persons, who, whether gravely or by way of amusement, gave into practices of this sort, with a fierceness of resentment which was very surprising to those who did not enter into his particular habits of thinking.— Yet Mr. Ritson was not less uncommonly modest on all other subjects, than peremptory on those which he had industriously investigated; and was at all times forward to confess his ignorance of the learned languages, of the philosophy of mind, and the graces of composition; and ready to bow to the authority of those whom he deemed his superiors in these particulars. To the attainments which he has made in knowledge, Mr. Ritson added many excellent virtues of the heart. He was liberal in the disposition of his income, and ever ready to relieve merit in distress. He had great ingenuousness and integrity of disposition, never employing himself in any sort of pretence or imposition, practising rigidly in his conduct, the moral judgments of his understanding, and constantly abstaining from the commission of every thing he felt to be wrong.— One singular proof of this is, that having convinced himself that the use of animal food was a cruel and unjustifiable proceeding, he for more than twenty years adhered to the strictest abstinence in this respect.

The admirable sincerity of his character was also shewn in many other particulars. Having amply studied the laws and constitution of his country, he was on principle an enemy to the succession of the house of Hanover; and, without any prejudices of education to urge him, became a Jacobite from reasoning, at a time when the race of Jacobites, by descent, was nearly extinct in this country.— This unfortunate singularity he however discarded about the period of the French revolution, and till his death remained firmly attached to the principles of republicanism. Mr. Ritson purchased, about the year 1785, the office of high bailiff of the liberties of the Savoy. In this situation it was his singular fortune to be connected with Mr. Reeve.—Mr. Reeve was high steward of the Savoy, and, for his political conduct, was regarded with no less antipathy by Mr. Ritson, than Malone and Warton for their literary misdemeanors.— Mr. Reeve, a few years ago, resigned his office of high steward; and it was a favourite opinion of Mr. Ritson, that he, by his hostilities, had driven him from his station.

Whether it were owing to the original feebleness of his constitution, to the singular severity of his diet,* or to the not inferior
severity of his literary application, Mr. Ritson exhibited, at the age
of fifty, every mark of caducity and premature decay. His memory
failed him; his temper daily increased in moroseness, and his conversation betrayed tokens of dotage. He was seized with repeated
attacks of the palsy, and the last attack having fallen upon the
brain, produced a delirium, and terminated his existence in a fort-
night. One further singularity in this extraordinary man is, that,
after having laboured so incessantly for the information of the
world, he expressed a desire that he might be forgotten. He made
it his particular request that no stone might be placed over his
grave, and added a hope that nothing, good or ill, might be said of
his memory. Justice to his attainments and his virtues, and a desire to gratify the honest curiosity of the public, have, in the writer
of these lines, overpowered the whimsical caprice of the deceased,
whom the writer had long the honour to call his friend. The following is probably an accurate list of Mr. Ritson's publications:
1. Observations on Johnson's and Steeven's Edition of Shakspeare.—
2. Quiss Modest, in Defence of ditto.—3. Cursory Criticisms on
Malone's Edition of Shakspeare.—4. Observations on Warton's
History of English Poetry.—5. Descent of the Crown of England,
in a large sheet.—6. Spartan Manual.—7. Digest of the Proceedings of the Savoy Court.—8. Office of Constable explained.—9. Ju-
risdiction of the Court Leet.—10. A Collection of English Songs,
3 vols.—11. Ditto, Scottish Songs, 2 vols.—12. English Anthology,
3 vols.—13. Minot's Poems, 2 vols.—14. Metrical Romances, 3 vols.
—15. Bibliographia Poetica; and, 16. Treatise on Abstinence from
Animal Food.—Mr. Ritson had further projected an edition of
Shakspeare, and there are many valuable notes from his pen in the
latest editions of that author. He also proposed to publish several
etymological works, together with a treatise, in which his peculiar
system of orthography was to be vindicated and established. His

---

* Mr. Ritson not only abstained from animal food on principle, but, from his
habits, he abstained from almost every kind of aliment. A potatoe, a biscuit, or an
egg, generally constituted his whole support during the day, and his beverage was
either lemonade or tea. He was a total stranger to what, in family arrangements, is
called a regular meal. With a constitution naturally very weak, and with his practice
of intense study, it is then rather to be wondered that he lived so long, than, that at
fifty, after several attacks of disease, he should have had the appearance of being six
or seven years older than he was.

manuscript collections were extremely numerous; and it is an irreparable loss to the public that he committed the chief part of them to the flames, at the commencement of the delirium which terminated his existence.

THE LONDON CHRONICLE

for 1806. Nov. 22—25. 499

To the EDITOR *of the* LONDON CHRONICLE.

SIR,

YOU will, if you think proper, insert the inclosed in your paper, and subscribe it with my name. It is an unexaggerated statement of what I think of the character of our lately deceased Minister, taken in a single point of view. In writing it I have dismissed from my mind all temporary feelings of regret, and expressed myself with the severity and plainness of a distant posterity. I have nothing to do with Administration, and have scarcely a slight acquaintance with a few of its Members. My character, such as it is, and my disposition, are subjects of notoriety; and every one, capable of judging righteous judgment, has a tolerably found idea respecting them. Perhaps then even my testimony, individual and uninfluenced as it necessarily is, may not be an unacceptable tribute to the memory of the great man we deplore. I am, Sir, your obedient servant.
London, Oct. 21, 1806. W. GODWIN.

CHARACTER OF MR. FOX.

Charles James Fox was for thirty-two years a principal leader in the debates and difcuſſions of the Engliſh Houſe of Commons. The eminent tranſactions of his life lay within thoſe walls; and ſo many of his Countrymen as were accuſtomed to hear his ſpeeches there, or have habitually read the abſtracts which have been publiſhed of them, are in poſſeſſion of the principal materials by which this extraordinary man is to be judged.

Fox is the moſt illuſtrious model of a Parliamentary Leader on the ſide of liberty that this Country has produced. This character is the appropriate glory of England, and Fox is the proper example of this character.

England has been called, with great felicity of conception, " The land of liberty and good ſenſe." We have preſerved many of the advantages of a free people, which the Nations of the Continent have long ſince loſt. Some of them have made wild and intemperate ſallies for the recovery of all thoſe things which are moſt valuable to man in ſociety, but their efforts have not been attended with the happieſt ſucceſs. There is a ſobriety in the Engliſh People, particularly in accord with the poſſeſſion of freedom. We are ſomewhat ſlow, and ſomewhat ſilent; but beneath this outſide we have much of reflection, much of firmneſs, a conſciouſneſs of power and of worth, a ſpirit of frank dealing and plain ſpeaking, and a moderate and decent ſturdineſs of temper not eaſily to be deluded or ſubdued.

For thirty-two years Fox hardly ever opened his mouth in Parliament, but to aſſert, in ſome form or other, the cauſe of liberty and man-

kind, and to repel tyranny in its various
shapes, and protest against the incroachments
of power. In the American War, in the questions of reform at home, which grew out of the
American War, and in the succeffive scenes
which were produced by the French Revolution, Fox was still found the perpetual advocate of freedom. He endeavoured to secure
the privileges and the happiness of the people
of Afia, and the people of Africa. In Church
and State his principles were equally favourable
to the cause of liberty. Englishmen can no
where find the sentiments of freedom unfolded
and amplified in more animated language, or
in a more confistent tenor, than in the recorded
Parliamentary Debates of Fox. Many have
called in queftion his prudence, and the practicability of his politics in fome of their
branches: none have fucceeded in fixing a
ftain upon the truly English temper of his
heart.

The reafon why Fox fo much excelled in this
reign William Pulteney, and other eminent
leaders of Oppofition, in the reign of George
the Second, was, that his heart beat in accord
to fentiments of liberty. The character of the
English Nation has improved fince the year
1760. The two firft Kings of the Houfe of
Hanover, did not afpire to the praife of en-
couragers of English literature, and had no
paffion for the fine arts; and their Minifter, Sir
Robert Walpole, loved nothing, nor pretended
to underftand any thing but finance, commerce,
and peace. His opponents caught their tone
from his, and their debates rather refembled
thofe of the directors of a great trading company, than of men who were concerned with
the paffions, the morals, the ardent fentiments,

and the religion of a generous and enlightened
Nation. The Englifh feemed faft degenerating
into fuch a people as the Dutch ; but Burke
and Fox, and other eminent characters not neceffary to be mentioned here, redeemed us from
the imminent depravity, and lent their efforts
to make us the worthy inhabitants of a foil,
which had produced a Shakefpeare, a Bacon,
and a Milton.

Fox, in addition to the generous feelings of
his heart, poffeffed, in a fupreme degree, the
powers of an acute logician. He feized with
aftonifhing rapidity, the defects of his antagonift's arguments, and held them up in the moft
ftriking point of ridicule. He never mifreprefented what his opponent had faid, or attacked
his accidental overfights, but fairly met and
routed him when he thought himfelf ftrongeft.
Though he had at no time ftudied law as a
profeffion, he never entered the lifts in reafoning with a lawyer, that he did not fhew himfelf
fuperior to the gowned pleader at his own weapons. It was this fingular junction of the beft
feelings of the human heart, with the acuteft
powers of the human underftanding, that made
Fox the wonderful creature he was.

Let us compare William Pitt in office, and
Charles James Fox out of it, and endeavour to
decide upon their refpective claims to the gratitude of pofterity. Pitt was furrounded with
all that can dazzle the eye of a vulgar fpectator :
he poffeffed the plenitude of power ; during a
part of his reign, he was as nearly defpotic as
the Minifter of a mixed Government can be :
he difpenfed the gifts of the Crown ; he com-
manded the purfe of the Nation ; he wielded
the political ftrength of England. Fox during
almoft all his life had no part of thefe advantages.

It has been faid, that Pitt preferved his Country from the anarchy and confufion, which from
a neighbouring Nation threatened to infect us.
This is a very doubtful propofition. It is by
no means clear that the Englifh people could
ever have engaged in fo wild, indifcriminate,
ferocious, and fanguinary a train of conduct as
was exhibited by the people of France. It is
by no means clear that the end which Pitt is
faid to have gained, could not have been accomplifhed without fuch bloody wars, fuch formidable innovations on the liberties of Englifhmen, fuch duplicity, unhallowed dexterity and
treachery, and fo audacious a defertion of all
the principles with which the Minifter commenced his political life as Pitt employed.
Meanwhile, it was the fimple, ingenuous and
manly office of Fox to proteft againft the mad-
nefs and the defpotical proceedings of his rival
in adminiftration : and, if he could not fuccefsfully counteract the meafures of Pitt, the honour at leaft is due to him, to have brought
out the Englifh character not fundamentally
impaired, in the iffue of the moft arduous trial
it was ever called to fuftain.

The eloquence of thefe two renowned Statef-
men well correfponded with the different parts
they affumed in public life. The eloquence of
Pitt w a cold and artificial. The complicated,
yet harmonious, ftructure of his periods, be-
fpoke the man of contrivance and ftudy. No
man knew fo well as Pitt, how to envelope his
meaning in a cloud of words, whenever he
thought obfcurity beft adapted to his purpofe.
No man was fo fkilful as Pitt to anfwer the
queftions of his adverfary without communi-
cating the fmalleft information. He was never
taken off his guard. If Pitt ever appeared in

some eyes to grow warm as he proceeded, it was with a meafured warmth; there were not any ftarts and fallies, and fudden emanations of the foul; he feemed to be as much under the minuteft regulation in the moft vehement fwellings and apoftrophes of his fpeech, as in his coldeft calculations.

Fox, as an orator, appeared to come immediately from the forming hand of nature. He fpoke well, becaufe he felt ftrongly and earneftly. His oratory was impetuous as the current of the River Rhone; nothing could arreft its courfe. His voice would infenfibly rife to too high a key; he would run himfelf out of breath. Every thing fhewed how little artifice there was in his eloquence. Though on all great occafions he was throughout energetic, yet it was by fudden flafhes and emanations that he electrified the heart, and fhot through the blood of his hearer. I have feen his countenance lighten up with more than mortal ardour and goodnefs; I have been prefent when his voice has been fuffocated with the fudden burfting forth of a torrent of tears.

The love of freedom which marks the public proceedings of Fox, is exactly analogous to the natural temper of his mind: he feemed born for the caufe which his talents were employed to fupport. He was the moft unaffuming of mankind. He was fo far from dictating to others, that it was often imputed to him, though perhaps erroneoufly, that he fuffered others to dictate to him. No man ever exifted more fimple in his manners, more fingle-hearted, or lefs artificial in his carriage. The fet phrafes of what is called polifhed life, made no part of his ordinary fpeech; he courted no man; he practifed adulation to none. Nothing

was in more diametrical oppofition to the affected, than the whole of his behaviour. His
feelings in themfelves, and in the expreffion of
them, were, in the moft honourable fenfe of
the word, childlike. Various anecdotes might be
related of his innocent and defencelefs manners
in private and familiar life, which would form
the moft ftriking contraft with the vulgar notions of the ftudied and defigning demeanour
of a Statefman. This was the man that was
formed to defend the liberties of Englifhmen:
his public and his private life are beautiful parts
of a confiftent whole, and reflect mutual luftre
on each other.

To conclude, Fox is the great ornament of
the Kingdom of England during the latter part
of the eighteenth century. What he did is the
due refult of the illumination of the prefent
age, and of the character of our anceftors for
ages paft. Pitt (if I may be excufed for mentioning him once again) was merely a Statefman, he was formed to feize occafions, to poffefs himfelf of power, and to act with confummate craft upon every occurrence that arofe.—
He belonged to ancient Carthage—he belonged
to modern Italy—but there is nothing in him
that exprefsly belongs to England. Fox on the
contrary—mark how he outfhines his rival—
how little the acquifition of power adds to the
intrinfic character of the man!—is all our Englifh. He is the mifer of the national character
of the age in which he lived—its beft, its pureft,
its moft honourable reprefentative. No creature
that has the genuine feelings of an Englifhman,
can recollect, without emotions of exultation,
the temper, the endowments, and the public
conduct of Fox.

[JOHN PHILPOT CURRAN]

Shortly after Mr. Curran's death, several attestations to his character and powers appeared in the London newspapers. From these the two following are selected: the first, which appeared in The Morning Chronicle two days after his decease, was written by Mr. Godwin.

" Mr. Curran is almost the last of that brilliant phalanx, the cotemporaries and fellow-labourers of Mr. Fox, in the cause of general liberty. Lord Erskine in this country, and Mr. Grattan in Ireland, still survive.

" Mr. Curran is one of those characters which the lover of human nature and its intellectual capacities delights to contemplate : he rose from nothing; he derived no aid from rank and fortune ; he ascended by his own energies to an eminence which throws rank and fortune into comparative scorn. Mr. Curran was the great ornament of his time of the Irish bar, and in forensic eloquence has certainly never been exceeded in modern times. His rhetoric was the pure emanation of his spirit, a warming and lighting up of the soul, that poured conviction and astonishment on his hearers. It flashed in his eye, and revelled in the melodious and powerful accents of his voice. His thoughts almost always shaped themselves into imagery, and if his eloquence had any fault, it was that his images were too frequent; but they were at the same time so exquisitely beautiful, that he must have been a rigorous critic that could have determined which of them to part with. His wit was not less exuberant than his imagination, and it was the peculiarity of Mr. Curran's wit, that even when it took the form of a play on words, it acquired dignity from the vein of imagery that accompanied it. Every jest was a metaphor. But the great charm and power of Mr. Curran's eloquence lay in its fervour. It was by this that he animated his friends and appalled his enemies; and the admiration which he thus excited, was the child and the brother of love.

" It was impossible that a man whose mind was thus constituted should not be a patriot; and certainly no man, in modern times, ever loved his country more passionately than Mr. Curran loved Ireland. The services he sought to render her were coeval with his first appearance before the public, and an earnest desire for her advantage and happiness attended him to his latest breath. The same sincere and earnest heart attended Mr. Curran through all his attachments : he was constant and unalterable in his preferences and friendships, public and private. He began his political life in the connexion of Mr. Fox, and never swerved from it for a moment. Prosperity and adversity made no alteration in him; if he ever differed from that great man, it was that he sometimes thought his native country of Ireland was not sufficiently considered. There was nothing fickle or wavering in Mr. Curran's election of mind. The man that from an enlightened judgment, and a true inspiration of feeling, he chose, he never cooled towards, and never deserted.

" Mr. Curran had his foibles and his faults; which of us has not? At this awful moment it becomes us to dwell on his excellencies—and as his life has been illustrious, and will leave a trait of glory behind, this is the part of him that every man of a pure mind will choose to contemplate. We may any of us have his faults—it is his excellencies that we would wish, for the sake of human nature, to excite every man to copy in his proportion to do so."

[KEMBLE'S ACTING]

To the EDITOR of The MORNING CHRONICLE.
SIR,   *April* 3, 1809.

Perhaps at this time, in a Holiday week, you may not be unwilling to allow me to call the attention of your Readers for a few moments from scenes of warfare and political contention, and to appropriate a column of your excellent Paper to a question of English literature and taste.

I witnessed, a few weeks ago, the representation of Shakespear's historical Play of *King Henry the Eighth*, and experienced considerable delight from the exhibition. Nothing, in my opinion, can be finer than the *Queen Catharine* of Mrs. Siddons, and there is much entertainment and nature in the representation of the humourous *King*, and of *Bishop Gardiner*, by Pope and Blanchard. If the gestures and address of *King Harry* are a little over-charged, this must not be imputed to his present representative, as, I believe, such has been the traditional mode of exhibiting this character, perhaps from the hour the piece was brought on the Stage ; and if the representation is not exactly in accord with our ordinary notions of royal dignity, it cannot be accused of clashing, in any degree, with what I respect full as much within the walls of the Theatre, the text of Shakespear.

But I cannot say that I feel myself equally well satisfied with the representation of the character of *Cardinal Wolsey*, by my friend Kemble. From the hour I saw the play I conceived the idea of asking your assistance to enable me to discuss this question with him ; and seeing the piece announced for repetition in the course of the present week, has induced me to lay aside a little remainder of hesitation that I felt, and to take up the pen. I hope I shall succeed in carrying conviction to the good sense of this Gentleman ; but if I should fail in this, I do not despair, in spite of the well-earned fame of the Actor, of convincing the public that he is wrong in this instance, and so far rescuing Shakespear from misinterpretation.

Before I enter upon the question, I must premise, that I have nothing to do on this occasion with the historical and real character of *Henry's* Prime Minister. Shakespear might be right or wrong in his conception ; but on every supposition, this I hold for incontrovertible, the Actor has no right to correct his Author, and to make Shakespear say what Shakespear never thought. I have, therefore, no concern but with the text of the play ; and in the broad question, what sort of character *Cardinal Wolsey* exhibits in the work of the Poet, it would be great folly to enter into captious refinements, and to explain away the obvious sense of the speeches as they rise. I call upon no divinity to assist me in my present research, but the divinity of common sense.

I have but little to say to Mr. Kemble's exhibition of *Cardinal Wolsey* as long as he is the confidential Minister of the Sovereign. He must, undoubtedly, be fawning and obsequious ; though I should have been glad, even there, that the arrogant nature of the man peeped something more frequently and something more visibly. But, from the moment *Cardinal Wolsey* is in disgrace, Mr. Kemble and I divide entirely, and for ever, in this question, in our understanding of our Author.

In my apprehension, Shakespear seized with avidity the occasion of exhibiting a great man sustaining himself with dignity amidst the storm of his fortune.— Shakespear knew that greatness is not inseparable from goodness, and that a great villain (which *Cardinal Wolsey* was not) will sometimes be supported inflexibly to the very last by the fierceness and pride of his heart. In Mr. Kemble's apprehension (at least in his performance) *Cardinal Wolsey* is a poor, broken-hearted wretch, robbed of office and spirit at the same time, and whimpering and wailing in the most pitiful strain, and uninterruptedly, through two or three long scenes. I call on Shakespear then to be the umpire of our controversy, and am not afraid boldly to invoke the oracle to explain its meaning.

Cardinal Wolsey is for a short time confounded by the tokens of the *King's* displeasure, and by the Lords, who appear to announce to him in the most insulting terms, the change of his fortune. Yet even here his spirit breaks out at intervals, and we discover him to be a man " cast down, but not destroyed." When left alone by the *King*, he says, after a little reflection,

I know
A way, if it take right, in spite of fortune
Will bring me off again.

To the Lords he declares his resolution not to surrender the Great Seal but to the *King* in person ; he gives the lie to *Surrey* ; and, in other ways, expresses the firmness and inflexibility of his nature. The Lords no sooner depart than he breaks out into the celebrated soliloquy, which begins,

Farewel, a long farewel, to all my greatness.

Shakespear knew human nature better than to engage a man in moral declamation who was utterly dejected and overcome with had happened to him : this sort of moralizing is the trick of man, the natural effort we employ, when we are anxious to recover the poize and equability of our spirit. And it succeeds accordingly with *Cardinal Wolsey*: he presently breaks out into the exclamation,

Vain pomp, and glory of this world, I hate ye!
and, which is more to our purpose,
    I feel my heart new-opened.

He then goes on, like a man just escaped from a wreck, and looking back on the dangers he has passed :—

    Oh, how wretched
Is that poor man, that hangs on Princes' favours!

This Mr. Kemble will not deny is bravery ; it may be real ; it may be counterfeit: let us see whether it is any way belied by all that follows :—

" *Cromwel*," according to the stage direction, " enters amazedly," and his first words are—

    I have no power to speak, Sir.

To this the *Cardinal* replies,

    What, amaz'd
At my misfortunes? Can thy spirit wonder
A great man should decline ?

In the very language of a stoic philosopher, the faithful Secretary asks,

    How does your Grace?

To which the *Cardinal* answers,

    Why, well;
Never so truly happy, my good Cromwel,
I know myself now; and I feel within me
A peace above all earthly dignities,
A still and quiet conscience.

But Shakespear was not contented to exhibit in a general way the tranquillity of his hero's spirit ; he probes him in a truly dramatic vein in the tenderest points, and brings him off triumphant. *Cromwel* announces to him the appointment of *Sir Thomas Moore* as *Lord Chancellor* in his place ; that *Cranmer* is installed *Lord Archbishop of Canterbury*, and that *Ann Bullen* had that day been viewed openly as *Queen* ; to each of which particulars, *Wolsey* answers appropriately and with striking courage. At last, upon *Cromwel's* tender expressions of attachment in parting, the *Cardinal* exclaims,

    Cromwel, I did not think to shed a tear,
In all my miseries; but thou hast forc'd me,
Out of thy honest truth, to play the woman.

Yet, out of this momentary melting of the *Cardinal*, Shakespear has contrived to extract new proofs of his magnanimity. *Wolsey* instantly forgets his own misfortunes, is no longer stunned with his fall, thinks only of the interests of his faithful servant, and devotes himself to the giving him such cordial and considerate advice, as may best preserve him from all dangers, and prevent him from experiencing a reverse similar to his Master's. Shakespear does not, however, dismiss the *Cardinal* from the scene without one touch of human nature, or without showing that the most elevated philosopher is still a man. *Wolsey*, having wrapt himself up in his virtue, and proudly exclaimed

> My robe,
> And my integrity to Heaven, is all
> I dare now call my own:

is led by that thought into himself, and the secret chambers of his conscience; and breaks out,

> Oh, Cromwel, Cromwel,
> Had I but serv'd my God, with half the zeal
> I serv'd my King, he would not in my age
> Have left me naked to my enemies.

Cromwel is astonished with this sudden burst of soul, and mildly interposes,

> Good Sir, have patience.

Wolsey instantly recollects himself, and concludes with his wonted composure,

> So I have. Farewel
> The hopes of Court: my hopes in Heaven do dwell!

If so plain a text as this needed any comment, Shakespear has given it in the subsequent part of the play, where he concludes the eloquent and beautiful eulogy of *Wolsey*, pronounced in the sick chamber of *Queen Catharine*, in the following terms:—

> His overthrow heap'd happiness upon him;
> For then, and not till then, he felt himself,
> And found the blessedness of being little:
> And to add greater honours to his age
> Than man could give him, he died fearing God.

I cannot express my astonishment at the misconception of all this (as it appears to me) by Mr. Kemble. It not only subtracts in so far from his character as a critic, but it takes away most grievously in this instance from the display of his powers as an actor. Who cares for the pitiful, whining, broken-souled *Wolsey* of the Theatre Royal, in the Haymarket? Where through the whole of these scenes does he once gain the tribute of our applause? The abased, self-deserted character, that confesses he is nothing, but as royalty shines upon him, we are already to trample and spit upon. This misrepresentation is the more wonderful, as Mr. Kemble's natural powers eminently fit him for the exhibition of loftiness and disdain. How much has he been admired in the triumphant style of *Zanga*, the mere creature of the Poet's imagination! But *Wolsey* is no imaginary being : we all know and honour the high spirit of the man, which raised him (as tradition says) from a butcher's shambles to be the Arbiter of Europe : we all reverence the most eminent and magnificent of the revivers of literature that England ever boasted ; and the high soul of such a man, rising superior to a host of misfortunes, would, if properly exhibited, be welcomed with tumults of applause, and acquire such honour to the actor as would flourish even over his grave. There is no reason to doubt that *Cardinal Wolsey* might, if he pleased, *generously* trample upon the allurements of ambition, with much more effect than *Zanga in the career of his detestable passions* tramples on the body of *Alonzo*.

I know that a vulgar actor, who attempted to do justice to the true sense of Shakespear's *Wolsey*, would deviate into idle and senseless rant; but there is no danger of this with Mr. Kemble. He would not tear the passion to rags, to very tatters. He would clearly perceive that a magnanimous collectedness of soul works inwardly, and does not rave. He would command our applause by the depth of his tones and the significance of his looks. He would delight the souls of the audience, by making every one of them feel how much loftier and more elevated a soul breathed in *Wolsey*, than was probably ever experienced by any one of those who looked upon his mimic representative.

ARISTARCHUS.

THE MORNING CHRONICLE.

LONDON:
TUESDAY, DECEMBER 25, 1821.

IRELAND.

An intelligent Correspondent informs us that according to the late Census, which has not yet been published, the population of Ireland amounts to seven millions three hundred thousand. At the time of the revolution the population of that country was estimated at 1,200,000, nay, some writers set it down so low as 900,000, many of those writers expressing their regret that there were not people enough to cultivate the soil, whole tracts of which lay waste in consequence. But what an extraordinary change has since taken place. No nation in Europe has increased in population by any means in the same proportion —yet none of the causes to which such increase is usually attributed, have at any time operated in Ireland: for the people (we mean the peasantry) have generally been little more than half-fed. Poverty has uniformly been their lot—they have never enjoyed comfort, nor seldom any internal peace; and of oppression and exaction they have always complained, as they have had but too much occasion. No one at all acquainted with the country can, indeed, doubt that they have ample reason to complain at present, through the severe pressure of taxation, the intolerable exaction of rack-rents, the excessive burthen of tithes, the general supineness and occasional harshness of the magistracy, and the unremitting rancour of the Orangemen. How is it possible that six millions of people, of which at the least the Catholics consist, can patiently endure such an accumulation of insult and injury, and that they shall remain a proscribed class in their own native land?

But with hostility perpetually rankling in their breasts, and discontent inseparable from their condition, which is infinitely more wretched than that of the peasantry of any civilized nation upon earth, how do the British administration propose to govern or to manage with a mass of malcontents—whether by coercion or conciliation? The former has been tried for a series of ages, and the result has been only to enlarge the extent, and to aggravate the severity of the disease which it was meant to cure. Yet no experiment of conciliation has been resorted to, nor has ever even an overture of that nature been made to the Irish people, excepting in the kind professions and courteous demeanour of the King, upon his Majesty's late visit to Ireland. But paradoxical as it may seem, those professions and that demeanour have rather served to do mischief than to produce any material good; for from the *éclat* with which they were announced through the Irish press, the peasantry, who are unhappily in a state of comparative ignorance, never conceived that the Royal beneficence could consist merely in the suavity of a smile, the grace of a bow, or the exhibition of a shamrock. No; they, poor creatures, construed the King's professions into a pledge for the redress of grievances; which redress his Majesty has not in fact the power to grant, at least without the consent of Parliament. But amidst this redress, the peasantry calculated upon the reduction of their rent, their tithes, and their taxes. They experienced, however, no such result; but hearing that his Majesty's good wishes towards the great body of the Irish were thwarted in Dublin, by the Orangemen, the tenantry upon the immense estate of Lord Courtenay, in the county of Limerick, who have long complained most loudly of the oppression of middle men, his Lordship having been an absentee for several years, and likely to continue so for life, were actually heard to declare that they had no doubt their grievances would have been redressed, if the tyranny, which they attributed to their Landlords, did not intervene between them and the benevolent purposes of their Sovereign. Such is our information, to which it is added, that several of these poor misled peasants were heard to exclaim, " We will oppose these —— middle-men and proctors, and *the King will take our part.*" Hence the disturbances which have since taken such a wide range, are really said in Ireland to have originated; and those Gentlemen who may question the fact, must err very much in their judgment, if they apply the general rules for estimating probabilities to the perverted or feeble minds of a body of people, who are in fact in a state of the most barbarous ignorance.

But to return to a consideration of the means by which such minds are to be directed, and by which Ireland should in future be governed. If conciliation be the purpose of our Government, the emancipation of the Catholics and the commutation of tithes float upon the surface, as the first measures that ought to be adopted in order to satisfy the minds of the Irish people, and the necessity of resorting to the latter may be collected from the following fact, which has been communicated to us by the most unquestionable authority. A clergyman, who is the son of a Peer, and who holds a living of considerable value in one of the Munster counties, granted a lease of his tithes towards the close of the late war, at a certain pecuniary rent, according to the price of corn at that day, which it will be recollected was exceedingly high. To this clergyman an application was lately made by the lessees to reduce the terms of the commutation, or to cancel the lease. But this application was sternly rejected, the worthy Divine insisting upon the sum originally covenanted for, although since that covenant was entered into, every article of agricultural produce in the district has fallen off no less than 200 per cent. Several instances of a similar nature might, we understand, be readily quoted, and such conduct must be the more galling to the Irish farmers, as it proceeds from a Priesthood from whom they derive no instruction or advantage whatever, and with whom they can feel no sympathy.

But, if our Government determine upon continuing the old system of coercion and irritation in Ireland, how frightful the prospect for universal humanity, as well as for the particular interest of this country. Should the Bourbons be reconciled to the French people, or the French people be reconciled to the Bourbons, there can be little doubt that the old national antipathy of France to Great Britain would soon be set in motion, considerably inflamed, too, by a recollection of the events which led to the termination of the late war. The national pride of France received a wound upon that occasion which the French are but too generally anxious to heal by retaliation upon England ; and should they, in the event of war, be able only to convey 10,000 troops to Ireland, with a due supply of arms and ammunition, how can it be conceived difficult, with such an immense multiplication of starving, and consequently desperate beings, to produce a separation between Great Britain and Ireland? and how long could the gigantic power or imperial greatness of this country survive such a separation?

THE POPULATION QUESTION.

25 *Dec.* 1821.

Sir,—In the *Morning Chronicle* of this day I find the following passage :—

" The increase [of the population of Ireland] since 1791, is therefore upwards of three millions. When we consider that Ireland has sent nearly as many emigrants to the United States as the rest of Europe taken together, and that a large stream of emigration is besides constantly flowing into both parts of this island from it, we need not go further for a proof of all that Mr. Malthus has asserted with respect to the rate at which population may increase."

Now the assertion of Malthus with respect to population, is, that it increases in a geometrical ratio under favourable circumstances with regard to virtue and abundance ; and is kept from increasing by the agency of vice and misery. I should like to know therefore, supposing the above astounding statements of the increase in Ireland to be correct, which I take to be as extravagant as supposing that the writer in the Chronicle has any the smallest knowledge of this subject,—I should like to know, I say, how the state and population of Ireland prove the truth of Malthus's doctrine ? If virtue, or, to speak more properly with reference to this question, the absence of libertinism, or encouragements to marriage, together with abundance of food, set population a going at the geometrical pace, while vice and misery reduce it to a stand, or at least restrain its progress in a very great degree, it should follow, that in places where marriage was enjoined by law, and provision was made for the offspring, however numerous, as in Sparta, anciently, and with some little difference in Paraguay, in more modern times, population would flourish: while, on the other hand, in places which have been subject to every kind of misrule, where certainly no extraordinary incitements to marriage have existed, and where there has been a constant scarcity of the means of subsistence, such as in Ireland for many centuries, and more particularly since 1791, population would be stationary if not retrograde.

Godwin, in his Enquiry concerning Population, has disproved the assertion of Malthus, by reference to the actual history of Sparta, Paraguay, and other places similarly situated, and thus clearly shows that plenty and good government could never beget children in a geometrical ratio; and now comes a sagacious writer in the Chronicle to clinch the proof by reference to Ireland, and convince his readers, that nothing is so favourable to population as Vice and Misery, which, according to Malthus, are the universal and only efficient checks. "Unfortunate Chronicle! you have, as the Lawyers say, proved too much!" Nor can this be evaded by either the Chronicle or Malthus, for they are both agreed on the subject of existing Vice and Misery in Ireland; and, as to bad Government, though, from entirely opposite points, I believe they meet here, and join in thinking a different system necessary. If it is to be said that there has not been enough of Vice and Misery in Ireland, to keep population from increasing in a geometrical ratio, it would be worth while to inquire of Mr. Malthus or his friend in the Chronicle, what quantity is necessary for producing in a population, such as that of Ireland, this desirable effect; what are the proportions, in short, in which Vice and Misery must be compounded with mankind, to prevent the horrors (Vice and Misery) of a superabundant population.

With this short notice I leave them both. The nonsense of writers of this class might, indeed, pass unheeded; but it offends me, when a scribbler, for no other reason than that his party stand pledged as it were to a particular side of a question, perks himself forward with an air of self-sufficiency, and upon the strength of his plural number, treats with the assumed confidence of an adept, a matter of which it is plain that he is blindly ignorant ; and I feel a pleasure in pinning him to the spot, to be the laugh or scorn of every observer, just at the moment when his impudence has betrayed him into the most ludicrous absurdity.—I am, Sir, your obedient servant,   C.

POPULATION.

The subjoined Letter on the subject of Population, professes to be an answer to a Paragraph in *The Morning Chronicle* of the 25th ult. We wish to believe that a Letter in *The Examiner* of Sunday last, on the same subject, written with an asperity quite uncalled for, and which the conductor of that Journal will, we think, on reflection, regret that he inserted, did not proceed from the source to which we are indebted for the following. Upon the excursive principle adopted by our Correspondent, he might have filled a volume. On Mr. Malthus's work we pronounced no opinion; we confined ourselves in one paragraph, to the rate at which, according to him, population may increase. Our Correspondent has not quoted fairly what we said on that point. After the statement of the population of Ireland at various periods, we observed, " The increase since 1791 is, therefore, upwards of three millions. When we consider that Ireland has sent nearly as many emigrants to the United States all the rest of Europe taken together, and that a large stream of immigration is besides constantly flowing into both parts of this Island from it, we need not go further for a proof of all that Mr. Malthus has asserted with respect to the rate at which population may increase."

We shall not attempt to follow our Correspondent into the various subjects on which he has entered. The sum and substance of his reasoning with respect to Ireland, seems to be, that because we have no authentic enumeration of the population in former times, and because there is no regular evidence before the public of a Census having lately been authorised by Parliament, and because that Census *may* be inaccurate, we are not at liberty to infer that the population is greater at this moment than it was at any former period.

Now, without being able to prove to an exact nicety what the population of Ireland was formerly, or now is, we can adduce sufficient evidence at all events, to show that it is much higher now than it was at any former period since her connection with this country, and that the increase within the last century and a half has been very great indeed.

Giraldus Cambrensis represents Ireland in 1185 as almost un-inhabited. It had been conquered in 1172 by three bodies of men, amounting in all to 150 Knights, 90 Esquires, and 460 Archers. Froissart, vol. 4, c. 63, tells us, that Henry Castide, an Englishman, at the Court of King Kichard, who had been made prisoner by the Irish, lived seven years with Brian Costoret, an Irish Chieftain, whose daughter he married, who spoke the Irish language, and was well acquainted with the country and people, informed him that the Irish "vivent grossement et rudement pareillement comme bestes;" that the country in the interior was wild and full of forests, and " n'y sait on comment entrer, pour eux porter dommage et faire guerre; car quand ils veulent, on ne sait a qui parler, n'on n'y treuve nulle ville, et se recueillent Irlandois est bois: et demeurent en grotes faites des-sous arbres ou hayes, et en buissons, ainsi comme bêtes sau-vages." At that time we may safely affirm the population could not be very great.

But not to waste the time of our readers on these remote periods, we shall proceed to a time when we have something like authentic information.

Sir William Petty, a most acute and observing man, intimately acquainted with Ireland, the greatest part of which he had by contract surveyed, who landed at Waterford in 1652, states in 1672, that the population was about 1,110,000. He gives very minutely the data on which he made this statement. He in-ferred that the population in 1652 was about 850,000, and he gives also the grounds for his inference.

That he could err to any great extent is very improbable. He tells us again and again, that Ireland was a thinly peopled coun-try, and always gives it a lower population than that of Scot-land. " Ireland," he says, " being under peopled."—Tracts, p. 238. " Ireland containing not the tenth part as many Irish natives as there are English in both kingdoms."—P. 267. " As for thieving, it is affixt to all thin peopled countries, such as Ireland is, where there cannot be many eyes to prevent such crimes." In five Essays written in 1686, he says, " England hath seven millions of people, and Scotland, Ireland, with the Islands of Man, Jersey and Guernsey, but 2-5ths of the said number, or 2,800,000."

Sir William Temple also represents, from observation, Ireland as a very thinly peopled country. It were easy to multiply authorities to the same effect.

Now, without pledging ourselves to the accuracy of subsequent calculations and enumerations, it is enough for us to state that they all agree in exhibiting a great progressive increase; and that no one within the last twenty years has ever thought of representing the population at much less than five millions. All travellers, from Arthur Young downwards, agree also in representing Ireland to exhibit the appearance of a very thickly peopled country. Mr. Curwen, one of our latest travellers, who went over the greatest part of the country, was lost in *astonishment* at the marks of crowded population he every where saw. "In many districts," he says, "I am persuaded an inhabitant would be found for every acre."—A man must be very sceptical indeed who doubts that the population of Ireland has greatly increased within the last century and a half.

To THE EDITOR OF THE MORNING CHRONICLE.

SIR,   Dec. 29.

A paragraph has by some accident found its way into *The Morning Chronicle* of the 25th instant, which I saw with considerable pain. It relates to the question concerning the "power of increase in the numbers of mankind," and builds certain conclusions respecting it on the example of Ireland. I can hardly conceive a question more vital to the interests of the human race. According to Mr. Malthus, such are the "Laws of Nature, which are the Laws of God," that vice and misery are the inseparable concomitants of that power, which concomitants we can never hope, and ought not to desire, to see banished out of the world, or to see existing in it in a degree materially less than that in which they now prevail. Mr. Malthus reasons forcibly to this conclusion, nor do I know of any of his disciples who have successfully endeavoured to disarm its terrors. Upon this I would observe, that if Mr. Malthus's "Law of Nature" shall be found to be the true law, we must then submit, that a sound philosophy will not refuse a principle merely because it is unpalatable, but that neither does it become us blindly to rush into a system so much to be deplored, and which no friend of man can consistently admit but upon evidence that is irresistible. About twelve months ago Mr. Godwin, a name of some account among our living literati, produced an elaborate work in refutation of Mr. Malthus. It is therefore fair to consider this great question as upon its trial. The issue will be in favour of a beneficient administration of the system of the universe as it relates to man, or in favour of one that is less beneficent. In this state of the affair, I cannot but think it is to be regretted that any one should attempt to settle the question by a slight paragraph; and, after a very few lines of hints and figures, should conclude, as the writer of this paragraph does, " we need go no further for a proof of all that Mr. Malthus has asserted with respect to the rate at which population may increase."

My first feelings, as I have said, were those of considerable pain. But upon reflection these feelings abated. I have always been an advocate, as *The Morning Chronicle* has been, for unrestricted inquiry. The more any question is discussed, the more will its true merits become known. *The Morning Chronicle*, having inserted a paragraph in favour of a doctrine not altogether in unison with the wishes of the friend of man, will not, I am sure, refuse to admit a few observations intended to bring the contents of that paragraph to a st and infallible criterion. I proceed.

This paragraph relates entirely to the population of and. The circumstances of that population are ed by the writer as decisive of the question between Mr. Malthus and his antagonist ; he does not in the slightest degree advert to the evidence that Mr. Godwin has collected from the Histories of " Europe, Asia, Africa, and South America, in Ancient and Modern Times." Sparta, and Athens and Rome are nothing to him. The fact, so generally acknowledged from the times of Derham to our own, that the population of the earth is actually at a stand, is of no weight. The case of Paraguay, which alone to many fair judges appears to settle the question, must be forgotten.— Ireland, according to certain authorities, which I shall proceed to examine, has increased to an extraordinary degree, therefore, all the phenomena of all the rest of the world must yield to Ireland.

The writer of this paragraph says, " Sir William Petty, who had excellent means of knowing, affirms, that—

In 1652, the number of the People was . 850,000
According to Mr. South, the computation
  in 1695, gave 1,034.000
By a poll-tax return in 1731, it was . 2,010,221
In 1788, calculating from the numbers of
  houses, it was 3.728,904
In 1791 4,206,618

" Finally, an intelligent correspondent informs us, that according to the late census, which has not yet been published, the population of Ireland amounts to 7,300,000. We need go no further therefore for a proof of all that Mr. Malthus has asserted, &c."

Now the first authority that I beg leave to oppose to this is Mr. Malthus himself. He says, Book II. chap. x. " the details of the Population of Ireland are but little known;" evidently meaning that we know but little about its increase. And be it observed, that of the six stages of progress exhibited by this writer, Mr.

Malthus, who has employed twenty years on the subject, had as good an opportunity of being acquainted
with the first five, as any inquirer of the present day.—
Mr. Malthus, therefore, evidently gave little credit to
the random guesses of Sir William Petty.

The question of an increase is evidently a question
that lies between two or more terms to be compared.—
My principal answer to this writer shall therefore be,
that both the terms of his comparison are involved in
the utmost obscurity, and that therefore Mr. Malthus
was right in saying, " We know little about the population of Ireland."

Nothing is more easy than to affirm of any man, that
he had "excellent means" of informing himself; and,
when we find this assertion tacked to a great name, it
will not fail to pass current with a majority of readers.
Sir William Petty, a native of Hampshire, was at
about the age of thirty appointed physician to General
Fleetwood, Lord Deputy of Ireland, and afterwards
Clerk of the Council to Henry Cromwell. It is remarkable that his residence in Ireland commenced in
the very year in question, 1652.

But, before we can truly estimate the means he had
of informing himself, we must consider the then state
of Ireland. Ireland is a country that was never fully
subdued and reconciled to the English yoke. A vivid
picture of the state of Ireland about the beginning of
the seventeenth century, has been handed down by the
immortal pen of Spencer, in his Dialogue on that subject. The native princes struggled for their independence from the time of the invasion by Henry the
Second. They threw up one fortification and intrench-
ment behind another, and their main policy was to pre-

vent the English from becoming acquainted with the true
state of their country. Sir John Davies published, in
1612, " *A Discovery of the True Causes why Ireland was never Subdued.*" The fact of the country
having remained Catholic when the rest of the King's
dominions became Protestant, is itself an irresistible
evidence that Ireland has always been to a certain degree in a state of rebellion. The fury and devastation
of Cromwell's wars in Ireland are well known, and
these wars were concluded in the year 1651. The date
assigned to the enumeration of Sir Wm. Petty is 1652.
Now, how is it that the enumeration of a people is
to be taken? The mode in the United States is by a
proper officer appointed by the Congress, who goes
from house to house, and collects from the master of
the house, or some of its inhabitants, the number of inmates. What sort of account was likely to be given
by the Irish in 1652? Where was the officer who
would venture to take an account of their numbers?—
Was he to be attended in his circuit by the Peace
Officers of the district, or not rather by a military
force? Thus it appears that the account of Sir Wm.
Petty, as Mr. Malthus by implication admits, was a
mere random guess. The cue of the natives at that
time, was, it seems, to say, We are nothing.
Sir William Petty was a man, whose life was devoted to inquiry; but unfortunately he lived at a time
when the sciences on which he exercised his industry
were in their infancy. A striking instance of this is,
that he repeatedly states, in his Essay on the Growth
of London and elsewhere, the population of the world
at 320,000,000. Mr. Malthus sets down the population of China at 333,000,000 (Vol. i. p. 293), thirteen

millions more than Sir William Petty allows for the whole world.

Who shall decide when Doctors disagree?

With respect to an estimate founded on the numbers of houses, enough may be seen on the subject of the uncertainty of calculations built on a tax of that sort, in Dr. Price's Observations on Reversionary Payments.

I come, therefore, next to the "late census" of 7,300,000, taken, it seems, but "not yet published." I pass over the singularity of arguing from a report "not yet published," and the eagerness to plunge us into all the calamities exhibited by Mr. Malthus, which it appears to imply.

But how has this census been taken? Ireland, I will suppose, is in a state less disturbed now, than it was in 1652. But yet I should lke to know how the persons commissioned by Government were to penetrate into some of its districts? What reception would be given by the natives to such visitors? What dependence would be to be placed upon the report of one of these semi-rebels as to the numbers of his inmates? The cue of the Irish in 1652, subjugated and hopeless as they were from the severities of Cromwell, was to represent themselves as few as possible. The cue of the Irish at present, it seems, is to exaggerate their numbers. The question is, whether they are more numerous now than when they set down their numbers at the lowest rate?

The first observation I will make bearing upon this question is, that, according to Pinkerton, if Ireland contains three millions of inhabitants, this implies a proportion of 114 to the square mile. Hence it follows, that, if there are seven millions, this mounts the proportion to 226 to the square mile. Now, the population of England is at the rate of 200 to the square mile, and that of China 230 (Godwin, p. 256); consequently the population of Ireland, if this unpublished census is to be relied on, is greater than that of England, and even greater than that of China. Yet in Ireland the bogs are unreclaimed, and agriculture languishes. There must be an overpowering weight of evidence in the unpublished Census that should induce a sober man to believe this.

Having then sufficiently pointed out the obscurities that belong to both the terms of the comparison attempted to be instituted, let us next, for the sake of argument, assume them both to be accurate, and consider a little the sort of phenomenon thus set before us.

Ireland was in the year 1652, according to Sir William Petty, to whose authority this writer adds Sir William Temple, a desolate country. Ireland is one of the oldest established countries in the records of modern history. She flourished in arts and letters before the commencement of what are called *the dark ages*. She was governed by a long line of native Princes, in all the pomp of pride and independence. For centuries she defied all the forces that England could bring against her. How came she in 1652 to be in a state of desolation? The power of procreation, no doubt, was equally vigorous in her at all times. Had she always been thus desolate? Or, having had heretofore her seven millions, was she gradually reduced by wars and plagues to this melancholy condition?

Well; but from 850,000, she has recruited her numbers, and in 170 years has risen again to her seven millions. What is the cause of this?

The reason, we are told, why the United States of America have " doubled their numbers six times in 150 years," is, that it is an unplanted country, that thousands and millions of acres may be had in it for almost nothing, that peace and independence every where prevail, that the wages of labour are high, and that to have a large family there, is an infallible means of growing rich. In a word, virtue and happiness cause this rapid increase in North America, as vice and misery keep it down in all the rest of the world. This is the theme of every page of the Essay on Population.

The territory of the United States is computed to contain six hundred and forty millions of acres. Ireland reaches to about twenty millions. Yet the population of Ireland, according to the unpublished census, rather exceeds the population of the United States, according to the last published census for 1810.

I cannot help suspecting that the writer, upon whose statements I am commenting, while he professes to concur in the assertions of Mr. Malthus, is secretly an enemy. The main doctrines of that author, after his famous " enunciation" respecting the power of procreation in the United States, are, that vice and misery are the only *considerable* causes why the people of no other country in the known world increase, in any degree approaching to the people of America, and that an extraordinary facility in procuring the means of subsistence, is the indispensible condition on which a rapid increase can be founded. Now, though I think there is much error lurking in these positions of the Essay on Population, yet I am willing to admit that the converse of them appears absolutely untenable. Vice and misery cannot surely be the true and effectual causes of an increase of population, and a dreadful deficiency of the means of subsistence will not immediately render a country abundant in habitants.

Let us recur to Mr. Malthus's own statements respecting Ireland:—" The checks to the population of this country are chiefly of the positive kind, and arise from the diseases occasioned by squalid poverty, by damp and wretched cabins, by bad and insufficient clothing, by the filth of their persons, and occasional want. To these have been added, of late years, the vice and misery of intestine commotion, of civil war, and of martial law."—*Essay on Population*, Book II. Chap. X.

In another part of *The Morning Chronicle* of the 25th instant, I find observations similar to these:—" The people of Ireland (we mean the peasantry) have generally been little more than half fed. Poverty has uniformly been their lot : they have never enjoyed comfort, and seldom any internal peace ; of oppression and exaction they have always complained, as they have had but too much occasion. Hostility perpetually rankles in their hearts, and discontent is inseparable from their condition, which is infinitely more wretched than that of the peasantry of any civilized nation upon earth."

See then to what we shall be reduced, if the reasonings of this writer shall once be admitted for just. If Ireland, oppressed, rebellious, trampled upon, half-fed, half-starved, multiplies as fast as America, I am afraid

all schemes for keeping down population are gone for
ever. If Ireland thus multiplies, where shall we find
a country in which population ought to be at a stand, or
to decay? America is no longer (as Mr. Malthus
imagined) an exception: it is impossible, I suppose, to
assign a reason why Ireland should be an exception:
therefore the whole body of mankind is every where under the uncontrolable dominion of the geometrical ratio.
We may address our fellow-creatures on all sides in the
stile of *Macbeth*—

What is amiss?—You are, and do not know it:
the flood, the inundation, of increase is perpetual and
omnipotent, and in two thousand years we shall be
fully prepared to "people the whole visible universe at
the rate of four men to a square yard."

Be it remembered that the question I am here examining has comparatively little to do with Sir William Petty's numbers, or with the numbers of the unpublished census. Ireland may have contained only
850,000 inhabitants in 1652, or may contain 7,300,000
now. Either the one or the other may be true. All I
contend for is, that both cannot be true. It is practicable
in some cases, where a country is tranquil, and the
people are satisfied and confiding, to take the number
of its inhabitants. But, when we have done this, we
have done very little. The question between Mr. Malthus and his opponents is, not what are the absolute
numbers, but what is the increase? We must, as I
have remarked, have one census and another, and those
arranged under the proper heads of age, before we can
know any thing solid about the progress of population.

The question, so far as regards Ireland, is not what number of people it had at a given time, or what numbers it has now, but whether its population has at all increased, and, if so, at what rate it has increased?

As I believe it clearly appears from what has been said, that Ireland affords no documents enabling us to conclude respecting the power of increase in the numbers of mankind, I am entitled to infer that the question still stands where it did, and that the sincere friends of the human race are called upon to investigate the question with more application and care than have yet been employed upon it.

L'AMI DES HOMMES.

Since writing the above, I have examined the Act for taking an account of the population of Great Britain, passed 1820, in which there is no mention of Ireland, and have inquired in vain for a distinct Act for taking an account of the population of Ireland. What then is the meaning of this " unpublished census," authorised by no law? By whom and how was it taken, and what credit is due to it?

POPULATION.

To **THE** EDITOR of **THE** MORNING CHRONICLE.

SIR,

" *L'Ami des Hommes,*" in this day's *Morning Chronicle,* is referred to the Act. 55 Geo. III. c. 120, for the authority under which the late census of the population has been taken in Ireland. The *authentic returns* under which, will, it is believed, be laid before Parliament in the ensuing Session, and will be found, very probably, to justify the calculation of the increase of population in that country.

Jan. 11, 1822.   INDAGATOR.